THE PERSONAL NOTEBOOKS
OF
THOMAS HARDY

THE PERSONAL NOTEBOOKS OF THOMAS HARDY

with an appendix including the unpublished passages in the original typescripts of THE LIFE OF THOMAS HARDY

EDITED, WITH INTRODUCTIONS AND NOTES,

BY

Richard H. Taylor

Columbia University Press
New York   1979

Copyright © 1979 Richard H. Taylor
All rights reserved
Published in 1979 in the United States of America by
Columbia University Press
and in Great Britain by The Macmillan Press Ltd.
Printed in Great Britain

Library of Congress Cataloging in Publication Data

Hardy, Thomas, 1840-1928.
  The personal notebooks of Thomas Hardy.

  Includes index.
  I. Taylor, Richard Hyde, 1945–
PR4750.P4   1979   828'.8'03   78-15586
ISBN 0-231-04696-0

For
PAMELA
and
P.T. and J.H.T.

Contents

Acknowledgements

I wish to thank the Trustees of the Hardy Estate, the Executors of the late Miss Eva Dugdale and the Trustees of the Thomas Hardy Memorial Collection for kindly granting me permission to edit and publish the material in this volume, and Mr A. D. Martin of Lloyds Bank Trust Division for his ready assistance and co-operation. I am equally grateful to the Faculty of Arts, University of Edinburgh, who extended to me special research grants in support of visits to Dorchester. At the Dorset County Museum, where I have worked extensively in the Hardy Collections, the patience, helpfulness and good humour of the Curator have helped to make such visits a delight; I am greatly indebted to Roger Peers, and I should like to offer him and his excellent staff my warm appreciation and thanks.

My wife Pamela has been a splendidly lively support throughout the preparation of this book; her consistent interest and sense of humour have been great things and it is hard to thank her adequately. I also wish to record my great gratitude to Mr T. M. Farmiloe of the Macmillan Press for his enthusiastic encouragement and invariable courtesy, and to Mrs Judy Marshall for seeing a rather intricate text through the press so expertly. Special thanks are due to Professor Kenneth J. Fielding and Mr T. R. M. Creighton, of the Department of English Literature, University of Edinburgh. Tom Creighton's unrivalled knowledge of, and feeling for, Hardy has informed our many conversations to very stimulating effect. Similarly, Kenneth Fielding's scholarly expertise and advice have been invaluable; I am most grateful to him for the detailed and generous interest he has taken in my work on this book, and for his personal kindness.

Many of my friends, colleagues and students in Britain and Canada have been good enough to take an interest in this work and our friendly discussions, like those I have had with Hardyans met in Dorchester and elsewhere, have always been a happy stimulus towards its completion. For the same reason I am grateful to those who have written to me about the project, from both sides of the Atlantic, during the last few years.

Finally, I am extremely grateful to the following for their kindness and courtesy in assisting my work on this book in many and varied ways, and it gives me great pleasure to thank them here: Professor J. O. Bailey, University of North Carolina; Mrs D. Bartlett; Professor Lennart Björk, University of Stockholm; Mr D. W. Blake, Head Postmaster, Dorchester, and Mr F. C. Hamblin; Dr Ivan T. Borda; Professor Harold Brooks, University of London, and Mrs Jean Brooks; Professor Kenneth Cameron, University of Nottingham; Mr Kenneth Carter, County Librarian, Dorset, and the Reference Librarian; Professor Peter J. Casagrande, University of Kansas; Lord David Cecil, Professor Emeritus, University of Oxford; Messrs Christies, St James's, London; Messrs J. S. and G. S. Cox; Mr Peter G. Croft; Miss Brenda Davies, Head of Information, National Film Archive; Mr Bob Dixon; Mr John Elwell; Mr Michael Fardon; Miss Diane Greenwood; Professor Ian Gregor, University of Kent; Misses Marian, Olive and Dorothy Hudson; Major B. G. Kirby, Clerk to the Governors, Hardye's School, Dorchester; Mrs Winifred Lucas, English Place-Name Society; Professor Michael Millgate, University of Toronto; Mr Patrick Montague-Smith, Editor of *Debrett*; Professor Norman Page, University of Alberta; Mr F. B. Pinion, formerly of the University of Sheffield; Professor Richard L. Purdy, Yale University; Mr Stanley Reed, former Director, British Film Institute; Miss Sheila Strathdee; Miss Jill Strobridge; Mr John Taylor; Mrs Phyllis Taylor; Miss Joan Walmsley; Mrs Angela West; the Revd R. A. Wheeler, rector of Holy Trinity Church, Dorchester; Miss Ann Williams; Mr Reginald Williams, Department of Prints and Drawings, British Museum; and, by no means least, the Revd John Yates, Vicar of Haselbury Plucknett and the efficient, scholarly and convivial secretary of the Thomas Hardy Society, for his generous helpfulness on several occasions. All those of us who work on Hardy owe a special debt of gratitude to J. O. Bailey, F. B. Pinion and R. L. Purdy for their comprehensive published works, and I should like to add this to my personal thanks to them.

London   R.H.T.
June 1977

Introduction

GENERAL

In one of his commonplace books Hardy noted, with implicit affini-
tive feeling, Dickens's anticipation of a time after his death 'when
my personal dustiness shall be past the control of my love of order'.*
The ironic thought must have appealed to Hardy, whose own anticipation of that eventuality, tempered by discretion, led him in later
years to destroy many of his notebooks and diaries, and to leave
instructions (carried out by his widow) for the burning of others
after his death. But there was another stimulus to these activities
too. Hardy had been pained and offended by the intrusions of
speculative biographers and he was driven by their attentions to a
caution similar in spirit to that of Melbury in *The Woodlanders* (ch. 30):
'No man so furtive for the time as the ingenuous countryman who
finds that his ingenuousness has been abused.' If Hardy now
developed a new furtiveness regarding his papers, that quality had
much to build upon, for he had always essentially been the reticent
and elusive countryman, anxious to give no more away about himself than he needed to, before or after his death. The price of having
such holocausts in the garden is paid in the provocation of post-
humous speculation that dark secrets have gone up with the flames,
and Hardy has certainly not been immune from this. But to insist
upon such imaginings in the absence of any empirical evidence is to
chase shadows. The bonfires probably contained nothing so stirring
as we might wish to think, and are more likely to have been the
product of a naturally evasive temperament surprised into exag-
gerated caution by biographers who had touched upon some of
their subject's personal sensitivities. And after all Hardy was furtive
in an ingenuous way: he left a trail of clues behind him, from easily
decipherable shorthand symbols when making notes about his will
to the distinctive calligraphic hand of the architect with which he

---

*'Literary Notes, I' (Dorset County Museum). Hardy takes the observation from a
letter to John Forster, quoted in G. Hogarth and M. Dickens, eds *The Letters of Charles
Dickens* (London, 1880), Vol. I, p. 191.

rather naïvely sought to disguise his work on the *Life* typescripts. It seems fair to say that he was devious by rural intuition rather than by polished calculation. But whatever the motives for Hardy's perfectly legitimate sprinkling of a little sand in the eyes of his biographers, we are left with one certain fact: among his own papers we have no more than he wanted us to have.

Only eleven of Hardy's notebooks are extant, and of these six are commonplace books.* One notebook is in the private possession of Richard L. Purdy: it is dated 1865 and was used by Hardy to collect words and phrases from his reading to enlarge his literary vocabulary, and was entitled by him 'Studies, Specimens &c'. This is the only notebook not held in the Hardy Memorial Collection at the Dorset County Museum. The remaining four notebooks are personal notebooks in Hardy's own hand, and are transcribed in full in the present volume. Since they are varied in purpose and content I shall introduce each of them in turn.

THE 'MEMORANDA' NOTEBOOKS

Geoffrey Tillotson has said that 'scraps surviving from the pen of a great genius are saint's relics.'†He was referring to Dickens's letters but his persuasive evaluation might equally be applied to Hardy's 'Memoranda' books. This is not to exaggerate their importance: an author's private papers are emphatically less valuable than his art, and scholarly mills sometimes seem to grind exceeding small. But it recognises that these are unique fragments: a private record of some of the author's thoughts, observations, concerns and social activities over a period of six decades. Since so few of Hardy's papers, apart from letters, survive, we should value those which do — *valeat quantum valere potest!*, as Hardy writes beneath one of his own notes.

---

*'Literary Notes, I' (c. 1875–88) and 'Literary Notes, II' (1888–1900) contain extracts from books and articles copied out by Hardy or, often, by Emma Hardy. Another notebook, with 'IV' on the cover and the date '1867' inside it, is of the same kind and contains entries from the 1860s to the late 1880s. A fourth notebook is entitled 'Literary Notes, III' and contains cuttings from newspapers and weeklies and some typescript commonplace entries, from *c*. 1903. These notebooks are being edited by Lennart Björk in *The Literary Notes of Thomas Hardy*, the first of two volumes having appeared (Göteborg, 1974). A fifth notebook has 'III' on the cover and this heading above the text: 'Facts, from Newspapers, Histories, Biographies, & other chronicles – (mainly Local)', and a sixth follows the same pattern.
†'The English Scholars get their Teeth into Dickens', *Sewanee Review*, LXXV (Spring 1967), [325–37], 332.

In these notebooks Hardy is not addressing himself to his public or his friends or posterity, but to his own immediate purposes. The notes they contain are varied and there is much to delight the reader responsive to the nuances of Hardy's imagination. In one sense they are no more revealing than one would expect them to be: no startling confidences are reposed and no striking literary theories are enunciated. (In an extract from a musical review in 1921 ('Memoranda, II') Hardy underlines these words in red ink: 'Wagner has survived <u>not</u> <u>because he theorised well, but because he wrote first-rate music.</u>') They reflect the countryman's eye for passing detail, but also his reticence and restraint. They are valuable for more subtle revelations of the working of Hardy's mind, for showing him in his private workshop.

The entries, usually written in pencil, are neat and well-ordered and suggest the calligraphic care and precision of the architect. Hardy is revealed as a man interested in minutiae and as something of a pedant. He often seems as eager to conceal as to reveal: many notes are terse and shrewd and waste no words. Hardy's emotional engagement is found in his poems and is not generally to be sought here, though sometimes it is undisguised by laconic expression, as in the simple and poignant exclamation following a newspaper cutting recording the death of that 'one rare fair woman', his friend Florence Henniker – 'After a friendship of 30 years!' – or the remark after the death of his devoted dog Wessex at the end of 1926: 'Night. Wx. sleeps outside the house the first time for 13 years.' The rare flashes of passion (such as Hardy's characterisation of George Moore as 'that ludicrous blackguard') are the more telling for their rarity.

The range and variety of the entries show that Hardy was a compulsive note-maker, though we can never have a complete account of the extent of earlier notes. For 'Memoranda, I' has already been edited by Hardy himself: it is a compilation of extracts from earlier notebooks which were then destroyed, covering the years 1867–1920. Though it cannot be precisely established when Hardy disposed of these old notebooks, or how far his recopying continues into 'Memoranda, II', there are some clues. Two letters to Sir George Douglas in 1919 suggest that Hardy was making good progress in writing first the *Early Life* and then the *Later Years*,* in the

---

*'I have not been doing much — mainly destroying papers of the last 30 or 40 years, & they raise ghosts' (7 May 1919); 'I have been occupied in the dismal work of destroying all sorts of papers which were absolutely of no use for any purpose, God's or man's' (11 Sep 1919; National Library of Scotland, ms. file ref. 8121).

course of which he used old papers, notebooks and diaries which could then be discarded. As he copied those notes unused for this purpose, yet which he wished to keep, into 'Memoranda, I', he chose 1920 as the terminal date for the first notebook. This coincided with the end of ch. 36 in the *Life*, the last chapter that was Hardy's own work, and the original typescript at this point is concluded with a note in Hardy's hand: 'The rest is in small Notebooks of Memoranda beginning 1921'. Though 'Memoranda, II' commences with an entry dated January 1921, Hardy almost certainly wrote up the earlier entries from old notebooks in 1922 or 1923: a note in 'Memoranda, II' ⟨p. 74⟩ suggests that old notebook entries were being examined in 1922, and the inside cover bears the date 'Feb. 1923'. So 'Memoranda, II' is largely free from Hardy's own editorial attention, and is therefore less guarded, though at the same time some of its entries are trivial. 'Memoranda, I' is more reflective, more conspicuously the private notebook of an author; 'Memoranda, II', while initially following this pattern, increasingly takes the form of a personal diary, and is more extensively drawn upon for chs 37 and 38 of the *Life*, the concluding chapters written by Florence Hardy. Hardy continued to make new entries until 10 September 1927, just over three months before he died.

To gauge the original contents and measure of Hardy's personal notebooks we need to bear in mind not only these 'Memoranda' books but all the notebook entries that Hardy transposed into the *Life* and did not therefore recopy, and the old notes that he may have decided to leave out when he recopied his old notes in his early eighties. The editorial process itself altered the form of some notes, as some transitions between the typescript and the published version of the *Life* reveal. The note dated 20 October 1884 (*Life*, 168), for example, is presented as a *literatim* transcript from an old notebook:

> Query: Is not the present quasi-scientific system of writing history mere charlatanism? Events and tendencies are traced as if they were rivers of voluntary activity, and courses reasoned out from the circumstances in which natures, religions, or what-not, have found themselves. But are they not in the main the outcome of *passivity* – acted upon by unconscious propensity?

Yet the original typescript has a different form beneath the revisions which shaped its final version, and here the final sentence reads thus:

But are they not in the main the outcome of passivity – acted upon
by such and such a disposed person, or persons, who happened
to be born at such a time: – even he, not voluntarily but from a
simple propensity, taking it into his head to move himself and the
rest in such a way.

The revised version is neater and more urbane but it has been
shaped in a not quite straightforward way: what is presented as the
reflection of a man of 44 has actually been compressed and sharp-
ened by the accumulated wisdom and practice of a man almost forty
years older. We cannot be sure how many other notes transcribed
as 'originals' into the *Life*, or into 'Memoranda, I' and the earlier
part of 'Memoranda, II', have been similarly improved by their
author.

Hardy's principles of selection are equally elusive. If these notes
are in a sense the sweepings of his drawer, we may be sure that so
exacting a man as Hardy would not sweep indiscriminately. And if
some of them contain details he considered potentially useful for his
writing, it is not surprising that he should forget that he had already
used one or two of them (e.g., the note of August 1870, in
'Memoranda, I' ⟨p. 6⟩; cf. *Under the Greenwood Tree*, Pt II, ch.6). But
Hardy's title is oblique and reveals little of his intention:
'Memoranda / of Customs, Dates, &c – / (viz: Prose Matter).' The
cautionary note heading the first page of 'Memoranda, I' suggests
that the residual value of the notebook may be supposed to be in the
'facts' therein: 'This book is to be destroyed when my wife or
executors have done using it for extracting any information as to the
facts it records, it being left to their judgement if any should be made
public.' But whatever Hardy's reason for assembling these details,
they remain for us interesting illuminations of his reticent personality.

The notes fall broadly into three categories: literary and antiquarian, social, and personal. Possible lines for plots are stored
alongside literary notes from earlier notebooks, on poetry, poetic
form, the nature of art and the role of inspiration, and general
literary topics. Hardy is unsurprisingly shown as a careful reader of
the *TLS* and similar periodicals. Something of Hardy's other reading
is shown and in this respect these notebooks are valuably read in
conjunction with the commonplace books. Often he appreciatively
records someone else's articulation of sentiments and opinions
shared by himself, as when he emphatically underlines the words of

a correspondent to the *Sunday Times*: 'Art is good art only inasmuch as it *corroborates* something in our mental or emotional make-up, expresses for us some of the yearnings and aspirations that struggle for voice within us'; but sometimes Hardy's reading (as when he reads *The Letters of Henry James* and discovers pompously dismissive statements about himself) perceptibly touches a raw nerve. Some entries are merely working notes – poems to be placed in periodicals, the whereabouts of manuscripts, questions about royalties – but there are many examples of Hardy's individual and ironic view of minor events observed by, or reported to, him. Hardy's interest in his own genealogy, local tradition and folklore is confirmed in a number of notes of antiquarian interest. These can be personally revealing. We know that Hardy was fond of the macabre (indeed T.S. Eliot virtually accused him of diabolic morbidity) and that in 1877 he held a candle for a doctor cutting open a boy's body to examine the heart and stomach for an autopsy: it was not necessary to be a human candlestick in such circumstances. The same gloomy relish informs Hardy's 1919 note recording the details of the execution by burning of a Dorset woman in 1705 – how her body smelt of roast meat, and how milk from her bosoms squirted out in the faces of the constables and 'made 'em jump back'.

Deliberately personal entries, as one might expect, are more limited. But some insight may be palimpsestically glimpsed through Hardy's account of his social activities in later years. Before he abandoned novel-writing, Hardy tells us, he had kept up a record of his social life; it had been 'drudgery' to do it, but when he abandoned prose fiction he felt 'with a sense of great comfort . . . that he might leave off further chronicles of that sort' (*Life*, 291). Yet he can have had no real intention to do so since his 'Memoranda' books show, up to 1927, the continuation of such a record. It is less surprising to find visits from the vicar or Florence Hardy's sisters than to have a fuller account than the *Life* affords of the extent to which Hardy held court at Max Gate in his later years. Despite his celebration of local idiosyncrasies in his work, most of his recorded guests at least are from aristocratic or professional circles on the one hand, or the world of letters on the other. And the extent of Hardy's hospitality must at least partly dispel the notion that he was gloomily parsimonious in old age.

These private notes suggest too that the impression of Hardy as a much lauded great man who cared little for further appreciation, an

image wryly furbished by the author himself, is misleading. The
dismissive tone of Hardy's letter acknowledging his election as an
honorary fellow of the R.I.B.A. – 'age has naturally made me, like
Gallio, care for none of these things, at any rate very much' (which
can hardly have been encouraging to those responsible) – or of his
avowal in the introductory note to *Winter Words* that 'it would be idle
to pretend that the publication of these poems can have much
interest for me, the track having been adventured so many times
before today', does not wholly disguise the pleasure half-hidden
behind the disclaimers. Hardy's satisfaction is revealed in the notes
recording, with humility and freshness of appreciation, his visit to
The Queen's College, Oxford (where he had been elected an honorary fellow), in 1923, his receipt of gifts and other honours, and his
receipt of birthday tributes (especially those from younger writers).
And it is no misanthrope who is shown to have given generous and
friendly encouragement to, and commended the productions of, the
local Hardy Players; or who has received at Max Gate, with equally
clear interest and pleasure, the local carol singers, the Balliol Players
from Oxford and undergraduate musicians from Cambridge, and
the players from the Garrick Theatre who performed *Tess* in his
drawing-room.

Altogether it is very much the idiosyncratic mixture that one
would expect of Hardy, ranging from early notes showing his conception of *The Dynasts* crystallising in his mind to a wryly amused
note about a set of church furnishings being put up for sale, and
from a local epitaph that caught his fancy, scribbled at his request on
to a sheet of lavatory paper by Florence in 1925, to an early but
characteristic 1874 note interpreting snow on graves as 'a superfluous piece of cynicism in Nature'. And the second 'Memoranda' book
concludes with a pasted-in page containing some curiously secre-
tive notes in preparation for drawing up his will and revealing
further impulses of concealment: Emma's papers are to be gone
through again, manuscripts and notebooks are to be destroyed,
marks in printed books are to be erased, and 'M——ls' (meaning
'Materials', Hardy's word for the disguised autobiography that he
had been busy writing) is to be read through and deletions are to be
made if necessary. Hardy is again judiciously covering his tracks.
But he has at least left us these personal 'Memoranda' notebooks,
the saint's relics that have much to interest the reader alive to the
subtleties of Hardy's temperament.

An earlier selection of entries from these notebooks unfortunately contained many inaccuracies of transcription and annotation,* so a complete edition (containing also other notebooks and papers) has been thought advisable.

'SCHOOLS OF PAINTING' NOTEBOOK

This is Hardy's earliest extant notebook, written when he was almost 23 years old, and an example of his early autodidacticism. Dated 12 May 1863, it was written while Hardy was living in London (in lodgings at 16 Westbourne Park Villas, Bayswater) and working as an assistant architect for Arthur Blomfield at 8 Adelphi Terrace, near the Embankment. On 16 March 1863 Hardy had been awarded an R.I.B.A. prize medal for an essay on 'The Application of Coloured Bricks and Terra Cotta to Modern Architecture' but he had not yet published anything, and did not do so for a further two years ('How I Built Myself a House', a sketch, appeared in *Chambers's Journal* on 18 March 1865). Hardy worked in London from April 1862 until July 1867, and this furtherance of his professional career was not without incidents appealing to his imagination: he later recalled with ironic amusement the occasions when Blomfield deputed him to supervise the removal by night of many coffins and bones (including a coffin curiously containing one skeleton and two skulls) from the Old St Pancras Churchyard to make way for the railways. But it was also a period in which Hardy rounded his education and experience in other ways, regularly attending dances at Willis's Rooms, seeing new and classical plays, taking half-crown seats at Italian operas at Covent Garden, and going to performances of the English Opera Company. He also attended Dickens's readings at the Hanover Square Rooms.

Above all Hardy continued the self-help education that he had begun as an apprentice architect in Dorchester. In 1863 he began reading extensively again, immersing himself in the work of (among others) Horace, Byron, Ruskin, Thackeray, Newman and Trollope. He was a dedicated autodidact, voraciously reading in his lodgings, he tells us, from six to twelve most nights. That Hardy read yet more widely is shown by a leaf headed 'Diagrams shewing Human Pas-

---

*Evelyn Hardy, ed., *Thomas Hardy's Notebooks* (London, 1955). For comments on this edition see Richard H. Taylor, 'Thomas Hardy: A Reader's Guide', in *Thomas Hardy: Writers and their Background*, ed. Norman Page (London: Bell, 1977). Also Michael Millgate, *Thomas Hardy: His Career as a Novelist* (London, 1971), pp. 390, 406.

sion, Mind, & Character – designed by Thos. Hardy. 1863.', later pasted into his commonplace book (see Björk, I, pp. 2-3). This leaf, the only other note surviving from this period, shows that Hardy had been reading the work of the Utopian socialist François Fourier. As time went on he spent more and more time reading widely in English poetry, and by 1865 he had begun to write poetry himself. In that same year he enrolled for French classes at King's College; soon afterwards he contemplated writing plays in blank verse and went so far as to appear at Covent Garden as a nondescript in the pantomime, *The Forty Thieves*. His range of interests was Protean and his intellectual energies were stimulated by the city and his own intensely exploratory mind. He was a young man alive to the capital's offerings, tasting at first hand what the culture of Dorset had denied him, and gradually feeling his way to his own peculiar talents.

Hardy felt that his creative instincts were being stifled by the mechanism of his work as a draughtsman, and during 1863 he contemplated becoming an art critic. He could thus combine his love for both literature and architecture. But his rapidly developing enthusiasm for poetry pre-empted this scheme and, he wrote later, 'his preparations for such a course were . . . quickly abandoned' (*Life*, 47). It seems likely that the notes made in the 'Schools of Painting Notebook' were a part of these 'preparations'. If his listing of such schools is mechanical, by 1865 he had developed a much more sensible and intuitive method of apprehending the qualities of great art. Each day he went to the National Gallery and for twenty minutes concentrated upon the work of one master per visit: 'He went there from sheer liking, and not with any practical object; but he used to recommend the plan to young people, telling them that they would insensibly acquire a greater insight into schools and styles by this means than from any guide-books to the painters' works and manners' (*Life*, 52).

The wisdom of this approach implies by contrast the rigid pragmatism of Hardy's careful entries in the notebook two years earlier, and it is likely that his source was some 'guide-book' of the kind that he later deprecated. Several pieces of internal evidence encourage me to believe that Hardy's entries derive from some such source rather than a lecture. The entries are precise and neatly ordered and Hardy was able to take the time to head some of the groups in copperplate script. And such consistently correct spelling of often difficult European names would surely have eluded him at a lecture.

If Hardy's method of recording the Schools of Painting is rather pedestrian, it is no more so than his use of such references in the early novels. Hardy is a supremely pictorial artist and in his *mature* technique is, in every sense of Browning's term, a 'Maker-see'. Here, in citing the works and styles of painters in refinement of his own descriptions, he seeks both to stimulate in his readers a precise picture or image and to penetrate to its interior significance. On 3 January 1886, he noted: 'My art is to intensify the expression of things, as is done by Crivelli, Bellini, etc., so that the heart and inner meaning is made vividly visible' (*Life*, 177). In his later works his references to painters fulfil this criterion, as in his description of Angel Clare's approach to his father's parsonage after Tess's confession has rendered their marriage an instant failure: 'humanity stood before him no longer in the pensive sweetness of Italian art, but in the staring and ghastly attitudes of a Wiertz Museum, and with the leer of a study by Van Beers' (*Tess of the d'Urbervilles*, ch. 39). While the references here are used with evocative subtlety, in the early novels art references tend to be dropped in by the handful, like raisins into a bun. They seem obtrusive and pedantic, and in the thriller *Desperate Remedies*, for example, the roll-call of allusions to painters is incongruous. Hardy gradually learned to invoke painting associatively rather than referentially but inevitably his early and cumulative references to painters seem to be the self-conscious erudition of the self-educated man. The 'Schools of Painting Notebook' represents a stage in the process of acquisition of knowledge that had been begun in Hardy's youth, when he would read Cassell's *Popular Educator*, and which was so signally prominent throughout his five years in London.

THE 'TRUMPET-MAJOR' NOTEBOOK

Unlike George Eliot or Dickens, Hardy does not seem to have made preliminary notes for his novels, so the pocket book traditionally called the 'Trumpet-Major Notebook' is unique in containing extensive notes that were used in the writing of a specific novel. Hardy began to write *The Trumpet-Major*, a pastoral story set in the Napoleonic era, in the early months of 1879. It seems reasonable to assume that the subject was already in his mind when he was writing *The Return of the Native* in 1877-78 since that novel contains many references to Napoleon and the threatened invasion, notably in the reiterated recollections of Grandfer Cantle but also in relation to Eustacia. Napoleon is used as an ironic instrument in defining Eustacia, one of whose 'high gods' he is (along with the dictatorial Earl of Strafford, the powerful Canaanite prince Sisera and the warlike King Saul). The notebook shows that Hardy was busy gathering material about the period from the spring and summer of 1878 onwards: internal dating shows that he was in the British Museum on 30 and 31 May and 6 and 27 July 1878, and that he was there again in the spring and at least once in the autumn of 1879. It is not clear when the large amount of detailed contemporary material collected coalesced into a definite plan to write *The Trumpet-Major* as such: the first gathering is merely entitled '1803-5 Geo. III. notes — (I.) B.M. &c.', 'Geo. III.' being later stroked through, and the cover title – 'Notes / taken for "Trumpet Major" / and other books of time / of Geo III. / in /(1878 - 1879 -)' – was added later, after three separate gatherings had been bound together to form one notebook. But as early as May 1875 Hardy had made his first recorded note of intent to write an extended work, in some form, on the Napoleonic wars: 'Mem: A Ballad of the Hundred Days. Then another of Moscow. Others of earlier campaigns – forming altogether an Iliad of Europe from 1789 to 1815' (*Life*, 106). This was obviously realised in *The Dynasts* but Hardy's first venture into this era was in *The Trumpet-Major*.

Hardy's reading and research at the British Museum in 1878-79, sometimes aided by his wife Emma, exemplifies an admirable respect for historical precision, and he never took such pains over the preparation of any other novel. Its value in helping to create a pervasive historical flavour and *vraisemblance* is self-evident, but Hardy's motive for undertaking such careful study may have been as much personal as aesthetic. The Napoleonic wars had long held great fascination for him because of childhood reading and family associations. At the age of eight, he

> found in a closet *A History of the Wars* – a periodical dealing with the war with Napoleon, which his grandfather had subscribed to at the time, having been himself a volunteer. The torn pages of these contemporary numbers with their melodramatic prints of serried ranks, crossed bayonets, huge knapsacks, and dead bodies, were the first to set him on the train of ideas that led to *The Trumpet-Major* and *The Dynasts*. (*Life*, 16-17)

He also enjoyed in his youth 'extensive acquaintance' with old soldiers of the time (*Life*, 19), and thus impressions of the Napoleonic era were passed down to Hardy by word of mouth. The legends of 'Boney' were still alive to the countrymen of Dorset, and the 'Corsican Ogre' was still a villain of dumb-shows and puppet-shows, and was feared as an Antichrist.* In the preface to *The Dynasts* Hardy recalls that Wessex, within his own memory, was 'animated by memories and traditions of the desperate military preparations' for the contingency of a Napoleonic invasion. And Hardy was emotionally attracted too by the involvement of his collateral ancestor, Captain (later Vice-Admiral) Hardy of Trafalgar fame; whenever this famous forebear appears in the novel the author betrays a modest pride. But personal links, oral traditions and general historical awareness of the period were not enough for Hardy, and his extensive research evidences a deeper involvement and interest.†

The precision and range of Hardy's notes are impressive. He records many newspaper accounts of the time (notably from the *True Briton, Morning Chronicle, Naval Chronicle, St. James's Chronicle* and the *Morning Post*), details from local histories such as George Bankes's *Story of Corfe Castle* (1853) and James Dallaway's *History of the Western Division of the County of Sussex* (1815-30) and from personal biography as in George Landmann's *Adventures and Recollections of Colonel Landmann* (1852), and he copies details from caricatures by Gillray. He takes note of advertisements for modes of conveyance (curricles, chariots, gigs, chaises, Phaetons), as well as for ladies' and gentlemen's clothing. With respect to the latter Hardy also consults periodicals such as *The Gentleman's Magazine* and the *Lady's Monthly Museum*, from which he copies pictorial details as well as verbal accounts. He is equally painstaking regarding the dress of the military, making drawings after *The Soldier's Companion* of 1803 as well as the coat of Captain Absolute in a production of *The Rivals* at the Haymarket Theatre. The novel's descriptions cannot be faulted. Many of Hardy's notes are used or implied in the fiction, even when he finds only incidental use for some of them. He abstracts details from smuggling tales like *The*

---

*See Ruth Firor, *Folkways in Thomas Hardy* (Philadelphia, 1931), pp. 299–301.
†Hardy's preface to *The Dynasts* (Sep 1903) bears this out: 'When . . . *The Trumpet-Major* was printed, more than twenty years ago, I found myself in the tantalizing position of having touched the fringe of a vast international tragedy without being able, through limits of plan, knowledge, and opportunity, to enter further into its events; a restriction that prevailed for many years.'

Smugglers (1820) and Mary Kettle's *Smugglers and Foresters* (1851), and though he does not develop the theme Miller Loveday's liquor, in ch. 5, had 'crossed the Channel as privately as Buonaparte wished his army to do, and had been landed on a dark night over the cliff'. Hardy's vivid note on duels comes no nearer to being used than in the bantered threat of a duel between John Loveday and the *miles gloriosus* of the novel, Festus Derriman (ch. 28). Several accounts of hoarding of money and other riches, dating from 1805, seem to have generated the similar parsimony of old Squire Benjamin Derriman, and the late Mr Garland may have been born of the noted account of the landscape painter Smith, taken by Hardy from Dallaway's history of Sussex. Over thirty contemporary plays are listed in the notebook along with several notes on actors, actresses and attendances by the King and Royal Family at the Theatre Royal, Weymouth. The plays seen by the King in the novel, *The Heir-at-Law* (identified in manuscript though simply referred to as 'one of Colman's' in the final text) and *No Song No Supper* (ch. 30), and the actor Jack Bannister who played in the first, were seen by him in real life in July 1805. (A more oblique influence may be suggested, in so far as the theatrical terms in which the novel's lesser characters are conceived correspond to the conventions of many of these plays.) The descriptions of the Royal progress and the review on the downs are most signally fuelled by the details in Hardy's notebook.

The novel is informed throughout in general and in countless details by Hardy's research into the soldiers' historical movements and activities, and the regulations which they observed – such as the Army Regulations of 1788-93, the Army List, the Instructions and Regulation of the Cavalry (1799) and the Standing Orders of the Dragoon Guards (1795). From these orders are particularly excerpted the duties, dress and statutory definition of the rank of Trumpet-Major, and to all these of course John Loveday conforms. The notebook, therefore, comprises a comprehensive survey of the movements of George III, and his soldiers, in the years in which *The Trumpet-Major* is set, as well as recording details of military and local life, from vast international enterprises down to contemporary verbal expressions among the soldiery and the locals (Festus Derriman's hearty 'Damn my wig!' was discovered by Hardy, in the *Morning Chronicle* of 11 October 1805, to be an oath of the period). The notebook is fascinating in showing both the sort and range of material that Hardy considered to have potential, and in allowing us to trace by close reference to the novel the way that he used it.*

There is some overlap between *The Trumpet-Major* and *The Dynasts*, Part First (1904), so that the notebook informs the epic-drama too. Act First, Sc.I, is the first of several scenes set in Wessex, and in which therefore the author views the war from the same standpoint as the characters in *The Trumpet-Major*. King George and his court are again depicted proceeding to Budmouth, the soldiers ('We be the King's men, hale and hearty, / Marching to meet one Buonaparty') are of the same spirit and breed, and a stage-coach passenger employs the contemporary oath of 'Damn my wig!', ascribed in the novel to Festus. Scene IV describes the King's review (cf. the novel, ch. 12) and Scene V is set on Rainbarrows' Beacon, where the beacon-keepers and others discuss the rumours of invasion. In writing *The Dynasts* Hardy again had recourse to his old notebook.† Clearly he consulted it on other occasions too since the 'Trumpet-Major Notebook' yields the central incident in his story, 'The Melancholy Hussar of the German Legion'. Hardy found the details of the shooting of two soldiers for desertion, on Bincombe Down, in an 1801 *Morning Chronicle* report; he put a red cross in the notebook margin beside his paraphrase of this. He copied these details at the British Museum in May 1878, the story was written in 1889, and it was published in 1890.

Since the notebook is composed of three gatherings bound together, not all notes can be definitely ascribed to 1878-79 and miscellaneous notes at the beginning of the second gathering and at the end of the third bear no relation to *The Trumpet-Major* at all. Notebook pages 67-77 constitute the second and shortest gathering and must originally have been part of another notebook which Hardy then handed to Emma Hardy, who copied the list of eighteenth-century plays on pp. 76-77. A full page describes the relationship of Henriette d'Entragues to Henry IV of France in the sixteenth century, abstracted from Eyre Crowe's *History of France*; other pages are fragmentary and contain fugitive notes, most of

---

*Michael Edwards, in 'The Making of Hardy's *The Trumpet-Major*' (unpublished M.A. thesis, University of Birmingham, 1967), pp. 139–42, discusses Hardy's use of the notebook in writing the novel.

†See Emma Clifford, 'The "Trumpet-Major Notebook" and *The Dynasts*', *Review of English Studies*, n.s. viii (May 1957), 149–61; and Walter F. Wright, *The Shaping of 'The Dynasts'* (Lincoln, Nebraska, 1967), *passim*. Hardy uses the surname of the real beacon-keeper at Rainbarrows in *The Dynasts* — Whiting; cf. 'Memoranda, I', note of Feb 1871, notebook p.10.

which have been heavily deleted. Neither their source nor their purpose is clear, though they resemble the jottings of incidents in Hardy's 'Facts' notebooks, recording happenings that caught Hardy's imagination and which perhaps he regarded as material for potential transposition into his fiction.

Apart from some more brief notes at the end of the third gathering, including some comments by Victorian men of letters on the realism of the novelists Susan Ferrier, Maria Edgeworth and Jane Austen, towards the end of the notebook we find Hardy turning his attention to his next novel, the unduly maligned *A Laodicean*. In the course of that novel George Somerset argues with the Baptist minister Mr Woodwell over the merits of paedobaptism (chs 6-7). Hardy had been interested in this in his youth (see *Life*, 29-30) and had argued the case with the two sons of the Baptist minister in Dorchester, Mr Perkins, but in order to sharpen Somerset's arguments with philosophical precision Hardy fortified his own theological grasp through further reading in the British Museum in 1879. Notebook pages 111-18 abstract the detailed arguments and supportive references later advanced by Somerset in *A Laodicean* (ch.7). These notes, along with the principal contents of this pocket book so carefully sewn together and preserved by Hardy, help us to define the 'Trumpet-Major Notebook' as one of pragmatic application; pragmatic but not just utilitarian, since we are aware throughout of Hardy's emotional engagement with the issues, events and facts that are recorded therein.

Textual Introduction

1 PHYSICAL DESCRIPTION

'MEMORANDA, I'

Pocket notebook, 4" x 6½". Black stiff cloth cover. Narrow feint, no margin. 25pp. unused. Purchased at "F.G. Longman, Printer & Stationer, Dorchester" (rubber stamp on inside of back cover). The first part of the title, "<u>Memoranda</u> / of Customs, Dates, &c –", is written in black ink, the second part, "(<u>viz: Prose Matter</u>) / <u>I.</u>", in pencil, both on the first recto; they appear below the introductory note (in red ink) and rule, and above the commencement of the text (in pencil). The verso end cover is blank. There is no pagination by Hardy. The notes are written in pencil except where specified. Other variations, such as inserted leaves or gatherings, are indicated as they occur.

'MEMORANDA, II'

Description identical with that of 'Memoranda, I', even to the extent of 25 pp. remaining unused. Six pages at the beginning of the notebook have been clipped out, the stubs remaining. "<u>Feb. 1923.</u>" is written on the verso end cover. The title, "<u>Memoranda</u> – (<u>viz. Prose Matter</u>) / <u>II.</u>", is written (as the text) in pencil, on the first recto; it appears below the introductory note (in red ink) and half rule, and above the commencement of the text (in pencil). There is intermittent pagination by Hardy to page 70, after which 25 pp. are blank before the entries recommence.

'SCHOOLS OF PAINTING' NOTEBOOK

Pocket notebook, 4" x 6¼", from which half of the pages (those following the final entry) have been excised. The notes are written in black ink on seventeen consecutive pages, beginning on page 2. Black stiff cloth cover. The pages are unlined and there is no pagination by Hardy.

THE 'TRUMPET-MAJOR' NOTEBOOK

Octavo notebook, 6½" × 4¼", made up of three gatherings sewn together and enclosed within a card cover, presumably by Hardy himself, with the title inscribed thereon. The pages are unlined. Entries are in ink, except where otherwise shown. Several pages have been completely or partially excised as indicated in editorial notes, and where stubs or partial pages remain any contents are transcribed wherever legible. Hardy's pagination is erratic (see 'Calendar of Pagination' below) and editorial pagination is substituted here. Because of the method of binding some pages are upside down; where this occurs I have indicated it in footnotes, and have restored logical order in the transcription.

A NOTE ON HANDWRITING IN THE NOTEBOOKS

All notes are in Hardy's hand apart from (a) a note pasted into 'Memoranda, II' which is in Florence Hardy's hand, (b) a few notes in the 'Trumpet-Major' notebook which are in Emma Hardy's hand, and (c) a few typescript notes or brief newspaper extracts pasted into the 'Memoranda' notebooks. All these exceptions are indicated by editorial notes. Hardy's handwriting is almost always neat and legible throughout, and the notes are carefully spaced. Doubtful readings are acknowledged as such.

2 PRINCIPLES OF TRANSCRIPTION AND ANNOTATION

My aim has been to reproduce the original holographs, as faithfully as typeface allows, in a *literatim* text. Ampersands, contractions and interlineations are retained as they appear in the author's hand. The integrity of Hardy's text is preserved at the expense of retaining spelling errors, though these are indicated if the meaning of the note is otherwise impaired, and irregularities of punctuation have not been standardised except as indicated under 'Editorial Conventions' below. Ellipses are reproduced with the same number of periods as in the original. Editorial intrusions into the text are strictly limited and confined within pointed brackets. Other square or round brackets, or symbols other than footnote numbers, are Hardy's own. Hardy's indentation, spacing and full and half rules are preserved. Interleaved pages (or, sometimes, entire gatherings bound in) are indicated and the pages numbered consecutively as they appear.

There is pagination by Hardy only in 'Memoranda, II' and the 'Trumpet-Major' notebook but since Hardy's pagination is sometimes erratic I have thought it better to substitute continuous editorial pagination throughout each notebook. This makes clear where each notebook page begins and ends but avoids the confusion that might otherwise issue from Hardy's errors and inverted pages, etc.; and for purists details of his pagination are given below in the 'Calendar of Pagination'. In order to preserve fluency Hardy's separate pages are presented here as a continuous text where appropriate, though as elsewhere the beginning of a new page and its number are always shown in pointed brackets. Another minor alteration has been made for the convenience of the reader. Hardy (in 'Memoranda, I' especially) often heads the page with the year of the entry continuing from a previous page, or he does it if a new entry is made in or from the same year. Since the head of a printed page does not usually coincide with the head of a notebook page, such dating is silently deleted where it would otherwise break the continuity of the text to no essential purpose. Otherwise all dating is given exactly as it appears in the holographs.

The allusiveness of many of Hardy's notes is such that explanatory annotation is often necessary either simply to explain them or to refine our appreciation of their purpose or context. As far as possible persons and other references have been identified; where there is no note identification has either seemed unnecessary or has unfortunately been impossible. Some names (such as those of Florence Hardy's sisters, and of Hardy's brothers and sisters) recur in 'Memoranda, II'; though cross-references are given where it has seemed useful to do so, they are usually identified on their first appearance only. Similarly I have exercised editorial discretion in limiting the number of cross-references between Hardy's notes and his works. In both transcription and annotation I hope not to have strained at too many gnats; in both of these endeavours my principal concern has been for accuracy and the reader's convenience.

3 EDITORIAL CONVENTIONS

Word(s) or letter(s) enclosed within pointed brackets ⟨word(s)⟩=editorial insertion.

Word(s) enclosed within vertical lines |word(s)| = word(s), or sometimes letters, written and then deleted by Hardy.

word(s) # = word(s) illegible.

∧ word(s) ∧̇ = word(s) added above the line.

Hardy's sketches and symbols are reproduced and his rules and underlinings are approximated.

Hardy's contractions are inconsistent and have been standardised. Weymouth, for example, appears variously as Weyth Weyth, Weyth, etc., but is here represented as Weyth. Raised letters are lowered and succeeded by a period. Thus w^d becomes wd., M^{rs} becomes Mrs., etc.

Hardy's periods and dashes are often indistinguishable. Where there is any doubt they are standardised to periods.

Sometimes the date at the top of a notebook page interrupts the narrative: where this occurs it is silently deleted.

A number of abbreviations are used in notes:

Life = F.E. Hardy, The Life of Thomas Hardy (London: Macmillan, 1962).
DCM = Dorset County Museum.
Burney = Burney Collection of Newspapers (British Museum).
Colindale = British Museum Newspaper Library at Colindale.
S.P.R. = State Paper Room, now the Official Publications Collection (British Library).

4 CALENDAR OF PAGINATION

'*Memoranda, I*'
No pagination by Hardy.

'*Memoranda, II*'

Pagination by Hardy on the following pages only, located as shown.
    Top left of page: 6, 21, 24, 26, 31, 35, 39, 45, 47, 49, 51, 53, 56, 58, 66.
    Top right of page: 5, 7, 9, 11, 12, 13, 14, 15, 16, 17, 18, 19, 20, 22, 23, 25, 28, 30, 34, 36, 38, 40, 41, 42, 44, 46, 48, 50, 52, 54, 55, 57, 59, 60, 61, 62, 63, 64, 65, 67, 68, 69, 70.

'*Schools of Painting*' Notebook
No pagination by Hardy.

The 'Trumpet-Major' Notebook
FIRST GATHERING: All pagination in top right corner of page. Up to page 43 the pages are correctly numbered by Hardy as follows: 3, 5, 7, 9, 11, 13, 15, 17, 19, 21, 23, 25, 27, 29, 31, 33, 37, 39, 41, 43. But Hardy incorrectly numbers 45 as 44, and page numbers (in his pagination) 44, 46, 48, 50, 52 and 54 all appear one page behind the 'real' pagination. Hardy then makes a further error so that his page 55 appears *two* pages behind his page 54: numbered pages 55 and 57 are therefore two pages behind the 'real' pagination. Six pages are pasted upside down on to this gathering, but have no pagination.
SECOND GATHERING: No pagination by Hardy.
THIRD GATHERING: Since this was clearly originally a separate notebook it has a separate series of pagination in Hardy's hand, again always in the top right corner of each page specified. Hardy's pagination is given here, and enclosed within brackets are the corresponding page numbers assigned by me in this transcription: 1 (78), 3 (80), 5 (82), 7 (84), 9 (86), 11 (88), 13 (90), 15 (92), 17 (94), 19 (96), 21 (98), 23 (100), 25 (101), 27 (103), 29 (105), 31 (107), 33 (109), 35 (111), 37 (113), 39 (115), 41 (117). (Hardy erroneously numbers the page immediately following 23 as 25, hence the adjustments of corresponding pages in the transcription after this point.) There follow ten

pages on which Hardy's pagination continues from 43 to 61 but these pages are otherwise blank. One sheet is then excised. Hardy's final numbered pages, 65 and 67, are used upside down (and correspond to 120 and 121): see note 690.

'Memoranda, I'

⟨1⟩ This book is to be destroyed when my wife or executors have done using it for extracting any information as to the facts it records, it being left to their judgement if any should be made public.

T.H.

Memoranda

of Customs, Dates, &c —

(viz: Prose Matter)

I.

1867.

My father's description of the funeral of a singer or violinist at Stinsford formerly.[1]

"I am the resurrection," &c, was sung by the quire when the corpse was met, at the beginning of afternoon service (the funeral being on a Sunday). The body remained in the nave during the whole service. The 88th or 39th Psalm was sung instead of the ordinary ⟨2⟩ Psalm at commencement of service: I Cor. 15. read instead of the lesson for the day: The burial service psalms instead of the psalms for the day, & a funeral sermon delivered. At the end of service the congregation went out, & were followed by the funeral. The singers & players stood round at the foot of the grave & sang the

---

[1] Hardy's grandfather and father were successively the principal instrumentalists at Stinsford Church, 1801–42. Thomas Hardy the first (1778–1837) assembled the Stinsford musicians in 1801, himself playing bass-viol; later joined by his son Thomas (1811–92) on tenor violin. Hardy's grandfather also supervised the choir (see *Life*, 8–13). The funeral described here must have taken place before Thomas the first's death in 1837, on which occasion there was no such 'quiring' over the grave since the musicians were the principal mourners. The musicians are represented as the Mell-stock Quire in *Under the Greenwood Tree*, written four years later than this note, and in a number of poems (cf. 'Friends Beyond', 'The Rash Bride', 'The Dead Quire', 'To my Father's Violin', 'The Country Wedding', 'Winter Night in Woodland' and 'The Paphian Ball').

90th Psalm, v.3, 4, 5, 6, (Tate & Brady).[2] My grandfather with his 'cello used a "joint" stool (local name of a coffin stool) to sit on.

The widow – who went to bed every night with a thankful consciousness that the children were one day older.

⟨3⟩ 1869. March 8. At Moreton[3] some years ago a man called at a house & said that he wd. put in the bailiffs if he were not paid immediately what had been long owing to him. The people in the house were suffering from itch.[4] The money was handed out to him, with warning of the fact. After looking at it longingly he shook his head, & went on without taking it.

1869. Spring. . . . One of those evenings in the country which make the townsman feel: "I will stay here till I die – I would, that is, if it were not for that thousand pounds I want to make, & that friend I want to envy me."

⟨4⟩ 1870. April 25.

Nine-tenths of the letters in which people speak unreservedly of their inmost feelings are written after ten at night.[5]

30th. Thoughts seem to be epidemic. No sooner is a conviction come to than it appears in print.

May. A sweet face is a page of sadness to a man over 30 – the raw material of a corpse.[6]

---

[2] The choir adhered strictly to the metrical version of the Psalms by Nahum Tate (1652–1715) and Nicholas Brady (1659–1726), published 1696. In 1895 Hardy included Ps. 90 as one of three 'familiar and favourite hymns of mine as poetry' (*Life*, 275), and visiting his father's grave in 1919 he reflected on the superiority of this version over that of Isaac Watts, quoting both versions of vv. 4 and 5 for comparison (*Life*, 393).

[3] 6¼ miles east of Dorchester, in the area corresponding to the fictive Egdon Heath; mentioned as Moreford, the scene of Mop Ollamoor's courting in 'The Fiddler of the Reels'.

[4] Itch: a contagious disease, also known as scabies; a common result of insanitary conditions.

[5] When Hardy wrote this note he was living in lodgings at Weymouth, having returned there after his visit to St Juliot, Cornwall, on 7–11 March, when he had met Emma Lavinia Gifford for the first time. This may refer to their early correspondence, now no longer extant.

[6] Hardy himself was 30 on June 2. This early note is typical of his lifelong tendency

June 12. In growing older, the nearer we approach an age which once seemed to us hoar antiquity, the less old does its inherent nature seem to be.

⟨5⟩ 1870

July 30. When a young woman is eager to explain her meaning to a lover who has carelessly or purposely misunderstood her, there is something painful to an observer who notices it, although it is evidence of deep love. It somehow bespeaks that in spite of her orders to him to fetch & carry, of his devotion & her rule, he is in essence master.[7]

Aug. 9. E's[8] story of Miss R., the aristocratic old lady in Cornwall whom she knows. When she, Miss R., had fallen down in the street she was approached by some workmen to pick her up. "How dare you think of touching me!" she ⟨6⟩ exclaimed from the surface of the road. "I am the Honourable Miss ——" And she would not be helped to rise.[9]

August. In Cornwall. The smoke from a chimney droops over the roof like a feather in a girl's hat.[10] Clouds, dazzling white, retain

---

to 'see the skull beneath the skin', a particularly mournful trait in a young man. It is reflected in 'Her Father', a poem also written during his stay in Weymouth. Preoccupation with the decay of physical beauty is found in many poems (notably 'Amabel', 'The Well-Beloved', 'The Revisitation' and 'The Two Rosalinds'); in several novels, especially the tragic climax of *Two on a Tower* (ch. 41); and it furnishes the underlying theme of the story 'The Waiting Supper'.

[7] Cf. Elfride and Knight in *A Pair of Blue Eyes* (written 1871–2), where Elfride comes to prefer Knight over Stephen, finding it (in spite of her *hauteur*) 'infinitely more to be even the slave of the greater than the queen of the less' (ch. 22).

[8] Hardy's first wife Emma Lavinia Gifford (1840–1912), whom he married in 1874, lived in Plymouth until 1868. In that year the Giffords moved to Bodmin, Cornwall, and six months later Emma took a post as governess. She held it until her sister Helen married the Rev. Caddell Holder in 1869, when she went to live with them at the rectory in St Juliot, Cornwall.

[9] This anecdote of social division is ironically prelusive of Emma's own snobbery in later years, when she could record in her 'recollections' (1911): 'I have never liked the Cornish working-orders as I do Devonshire folk; their so-called admirable independence of character was most disagreeable to live with.' But at the time of their courtship Emma was clearly willing to relate this story, which Hardy no doubt appreciated as fuel for his radical ideas.

[10] Cf. *Under the Greenwood Tree*, written in the early summer of the following year: 'A curl of wood-smoke came from the chimney and drooped over the roof like a blue feather in a lady's hat' (Pt II, ch.6).

their shape by the half-hour, motionless, & so far below the blue that one can almost see round them.

We are continually associating our ideas of modern humanity with bustling movement, struggle, progress. But a more imposing feature of the human mass is its passivity. Poets write of "a motion toiling through the gloom." ⟨7⟩ You examine: it is not there.[11]

Oct. 15. It is, in a worldly sense, a matter for regret that a child who has to win a living should be born of a noble nature. Social greatness requires littleness to inflate & float it, & a high soul may bring a man to the workhouse.[12]

Oct. 25. Martha R——— (an old maid whose lover died) has his love letters to her bound, & keeps them on the parlour table.

E's letter of yesterday: "– – – this dream of my life – no, not dream, for what is actually going on around me seems a dream rather . . . . . ⟨8⟩ I take him (the reserved man)[13] as I do the Bible; find out what I can, compare one text with another, & believe the rest in a lump of simple faith."

Oct. 30. Mother's notion,[14] & also mine: That a figure stands in our

---

[11] A characteristic note on the impassive and involuntary nature of human progress. Cf. these notes (*Life*, 168 and 172): 'Query: Is not the present quasi-scientific system of writing history mere charlatanism? Events and tendencies are traced as if they were rivers of voluntary activity, and courses reasoned out from the circumstances in which natures, religions, or what-not, have found themselves. But are they not in the main the outcome of *passivity* – acted on by unconscious propensity?' (20 Oct 1884); 'History is rather a stream than a tree. There is nothing organic in its shape, nothing systematic in its development. It flows on like a thunderstorm-rill by a road side; now a straw turns it this way, now a tiny barrier of sand that' (spring, 1885).

[12] This note, suggestive of Hardy's own early attempts to win a living, begs the question of his own aspirations to 'social greatness'. At this time Hardy was writing, in a mood of some despondency, his first published novel, *Desperate Remedies*. In the novel the loosely autobiographical Springrove remarks (of the architectural profession) that 'worldly advantage from an art doesn't depend upon mastering it [but upon] a certain kind of energy which men with any fondness for art possess very seldom indeed – an earnestness in making acquaintances, and a love for using them. They give their whole attention to the art of dining out, after mastering a few rudimentary facts to serve up in conversation' (ch.3, pt 2).

[13] 'The reserved man' may refer to Hardy himself. This extract from Emma's letter suggests the reticence and initial impenetrability of her future husband.

[14] Jemima Hardy (1813–1904) was responsible for many of Hardy's early interests and attitudes. 'A woman with an extraordinary store of local memories' (*Life*, 321),

van with arm uplifted, to knock us back from any pleasant prospect we indulge in as probable.

A man named Sherwood, a boxer, or as we now say, a pugilist. He used his wife roughly, left her, & went to America. She pined for him. At last he sent for her to come with the children. She died of joy at the news.[15]

⟨9⟩ 1870. Dec. An experience, hard-won, by an inferior mind, often prompts a remark of profundity & originality not to be surpassed by one of her superior calibre.

1871. Jan. A mistake often made in foretelling young men's careers: that a given amount of brain power will result in a proportionate success; so many units, so much product.

Dawn. Lying just after waking. The sad possibilities of the future are more vivid then than at any other time. A man is no longer a hero in his own eyes: even the laughing child may have now a foretaste of his manhood's glooms; ⟨10⟩ the man, of the neglect and contumely which may wait upon his old age. It is the supremely safe time for deciding upon money ventures: no false high hope tempts one to run a dangerous risk. In fact, as the man who acts upon what he resolved before sleeping is the man of the most brilliant successes & disastrous failures, so the man who abides by what he thought at dawn is he who is found afterwards in the safe groove of respectable mediocrity.[16]

Hardy records that she directed with 'good taste' his childhood reading (she gave him Dryden's *Virgil,* Johnson's *Rasselas,* and *Paul and Virginia,* when he was eight), and she was ambitious for her son's education and success. In her own youth she had suffered 'very stressful experiences of which she could never speak in her maturer years without pain' (*Life,* 8).

[15] Cf. the ending of *Two on a Tower* (1882). Swithin returns from the Cape after an absence of three years and to Viviette's surprise renews his proposal of marriage, but with fatal effect: 'Sudden joy after despair had touched an overstrained heart too smartly. Viviette was dead' (ch. 41).

[16] Hardy had completed *Desperate Remedies* the previous month but at this time he was 'far from being in bright spirits about this book and his future', having on 15 Dec 1870 marked this passage in his copy of *Hamlet:* 'Thou wouldst not think how ill all's here about my heart: but it is no matter' (*Life,* 83). His immediate anxiety, which finds expression in this and the previous note, was largely due to 'money ventures': though his savings amounted only to £123, he had made an 'adventurous arrangement' with the publisher William Tinsley, to whom he paid £75 in this month (Jan 1871) towards the cost of the novel's publication. (It appeared in March.)

Feb. Whiting (son of the man who kept Rainbarrows Beacon) cutting furze on the heath in the rain.[17] He tells a woman he was so wet yesterday that he was obliged to ⟨11⟩ change his shirt every hour.

Woman. "I wonder you had shirts enough."

Whiting. "I hadn't. I had changed seven times, & then my wife brought me one of her shifts. I put it on, & went to bed. In the night I said, half-awake, half-dreaming: "Good God, if we bain't two women!"

Feb. 7. A pedlar came to Miss ——, an old maid, & in asking her to buy some of his wares addressed her as "Mother." She said, "How dare you cast such a scandal upon my character as to call me by that name!⟨"⟩

Feb. Some men waste their time in watching their own existence.

⟨12⟩ 1871.

Feb. Nothing is so interesting to a woman as herself.

Though a good deal is too strange to be believed, nothing is too strange to have happened.[18]

March 22. Smuggling, &c. While superintending the church music from 1801 onwards to about 1805, my grandfather[19] used to do a little in smuggling, his house being a lonely one, none of the others in Higher Bockhampton being then built, or only one other. He sometimes had as many as eighty "tubs" in a dark closet (afterwards

---

[17] Rainbarrows comprises three tumuli or prehistoric burial grounds situated on Puddletown Heath (a constituent part of 'Egdon Heath'), about half a mile south-east of Hardy's birthplace. The most prominent of the three had been a beacon-hill during the Napoleonic war, and features in *The Trumpet-Major*, *The Dynasts* and *The Return of the Native*, where Rainbarrow forms 'the pole and axis of this heathery world' (Bk I, ch.2). Furze-cutting is the occupation adopted by Clym Yeobright.

[18] A principle very evident in Hardy's prose fiction. Cf. *Life*, 150: 'The real, if unavowed, purpose of fiction is to give pleasure by gratifying the love of the uncommon in human experience, mental or corporeal' (July 1881).

[19] Thomas Hardy the first (see n.1) had married improvidently at 21 and had been set up in business as a builder by his father, who also built for him the house at Higher Bockhampton in which Thomas the first and his wife settled in 1801. From 1803 to 1805, when the south coast lay under threat of Napoleonic invasion, Hardy's grandfather served as a local Volunteer. His experience probably contributed to the similar smuggling episodes in the story 'The Distracted Preacher' (published 1879).

destroyed in altering staircase) each tub containing 4 gallons. The spirits often smelt all over the house, being ⟨13⟩ proof, & had to be lowered for drinking. The tubs, or little elongated barrels, were of thin staves with wooden hoops: I remember one of them which had been turned into a bucket by knocking out one head, & putting a handle. They were brought at night by men on horseback, "slung," or in carts. A whiplash across the window pane would awake my grandfather at 2 or 3 in the morning, & he would dress & go down. Not a soul was there, but a heap of tubs loomed up in front of the door. He would set to work & stow them away in the dark closet aforesaid, & nothing more would happen till dusk the following evening, when groups of dark long-bearded fellows would arrive, & carry off the tubs in two & fours slung over their shoulders – T.O. ⟨14⟩ The smugglers grew so bold at last that they would come by day, & my grandmother insisted to her husband that he should stop receiving the tubs, which he did about 1805, though not till at a christening of one of their children[20] they "had a washing pan of pale brandy" left them by the smugglers to make merry with. Moreover the smugglers could not be got to leave off depositing the tubs for some while, but they did so when a second house was built about 100 yards off.

Many years later, indeed, I think in my mother's time, a large woman used to call, & ask if any of "it" was wanted cheap. Her hugeness was caused by her having bullocks' ⟨15⟩ bladders slung round her hips, in which she carried the spirits. She was known as "Mother Rogers."

March, contd. Lonely places in the country have each their own peculiar silences.

Apl. 1871. In Church. The sibilants in the responses of the congregation, who bend their heads like pine-trees in a wind.[21]

---

[20] James Hardy (b. 1805), their second son and Hardy's uncle, who later played treble violin in the Stinsford Quire.

[21] The imagery recurs in the opening paragraph of the story 'An Indiscretion in the Life of an Heiress', first published 1878, where the congregation at Tollamore Church is described, 'the people swaying backwards and forwards like trees in a soft breeze'; and in the second stanza of the poem 'Afternoon Service at Mellstock', where the congregation is again shown 'swaying like the trees'.

May 7. My mother remarked today concerning an incident she had witnessed in which a man & woman were the characters, strangers to her: "They were mother & son I supposed, or perhaps man & wife, ⟨16⟩ for they marry in such queer ways nowadays that there's no telling which. Anyhow, there was a partnership of some kind between them."

May 29. The most prosaic man becomes a poem when you stand by his grave at his funeral & think of him.[22]

June. Old Midsummer custom: on old Midsr. eve, at going to bed:
"I put my shoes in the form of a T,
And trust my true love for to see."
Another:
On old Midsr. noon dig a hole in the grass plot, & place your ear thereon precisely at 12. The occupation of your future husband will ⟨17⟩ be revealed by the noises heard.[23]

Another old custom. Allhallows eve.[24] Kill a pigeon: stick its heart full of pins. Roast the heart in the candle flame. Faithless lover will twist & toss with nightmare in his sleep.

———————

1872. May 29.

"Well, mind what th'rt about. She can use the corners of her eyes as well as we can use the middle." (Heard in Dorset)

August. At Beeny.[25] The Cliff: green towards the land, blue-black

---

[22] This must have been written during a visit to St Juliot rectory. Its burden is echoed several times in Hardy's fiction, notably in Marty South's eulogy over Giles Winterborne in The Woodlanders (ch. 48).

[23] Midsummer's Eve is 23 June. Hardy had a lifelong interest in folklore and ancient customs, deriving accounts from local recollections as well as his reading. These primitive forms of divination were once widespread in country districts and his work contains several examples, including Mrs Penny's amusing experience in Under the Greenwood Tree (Pt I, ch. 8), on which Hardy was working at this time. See also the divination rites in The Woodlanders (ch. 20); and, for a comprehensive account of midsummer customs, Ruth Firor, Folkways in Thomas Hardy (Philadelphia, 1931), especially pp. 42-3, 45-8, 51.

[24] All Hallows' Eve, or Hallowe'en, is 31 October. In the old Celtic calendar this was the last night of the old year, the night of the witches, and many ancient superstitions attach to it. (See Firor, pp. 148-9.) For an example of pin-sticking, see The Return of the Native (Bk V, ch. 7).

[25] Beeny Cliff, on the north-eastern coast of Cornwall, rises 150-200 ft. above sea

towards the sea . . . Every ledge has a little starved green grass upon it; all vertical parts bare. Seaward, a dark grey ocean ⟨18⟩ beneath a pale green sky, upon which lie branches of red cloud. A lather of foam round the base of each rock. The sea is full of motion internally, but still as a whole. Quiet & silent in the distance, noisy & restless close at hand.

End of Aug. Brentor, nr. Tavistock. Church on the top.[26]
Like a volcano.

Sept 11, 1872. In London.

Saw a lady who when she smiled smiled too much – over all her face, chin, round to her ears, & up among her hair, so that you were surfeited of smiling, & felt you would never smile any more.

⟨19⟩ 1872

Oct 30. Returning from D.[27] Wet night. The town, looking back from S. Hill,[28] is circumscribed by a halo like an aurora: up the hill comes a broad band of turnpike road, glazed with moisture, which reflects the lustre of the mist.

Nov. 9. Went to Kingman's early.[29] A still morning: objects were as if at the bottom of a pool.

level and is almost one mile long, beginning a mile N.E. of Boscastle. Frequently visited by Hardy and Emma during their courtship, Beeny is recalled in Emma Hardy's *Some Recollections* [1911] (London, 1961), pp.50-1, 57-8, which also includes Hardy's own sketch of the scene, dated 22 Aug 1870 (p.82). Beeny assumes a dramatic role as 'the Cliff without a Name' in *A Pair of Blue Eyes* (chs. 21-2), in composition at this time; this note contributes to its description in the novel. Beeny features in many poems, notably 'Beeny Cliff' and 'The Going'.

[26] Five miles north of Tavistock in Devon, Brentor or Brent Tor (1100 ft.) is crowned with St Michael's, a thirteenth-century chapel.

[27] Dorchester. Hardy was returning to Higher Bockhampton, where he was completing *A Pair of Blue Eyes.*

[28] Stinsford Hill. Hardy would return home on the road to Puddletown, leaving Dorchester via Grey's Bridge and London Road.

[29] I have been unable to identify this reference.

Nov. 13. The first frost of autumn. Outdoor folk look reflective. The scarlet runners are dishevelled; geraniums wounded in the leaf; open-air cucumber leaves have collapsed like green umbrellas with all the stays broken.

———

⟨20⟩ 1872

Dec. "The Planet-ruler"
He used to come his rounds like a pedlar, passing through M———y[30] about every month. He carried a little bundle in his hand – a "fardlet" it was called – wore shoes, white stockings, old black coat and trousers. Had a room at Beaminster, into which some people had seen. His method of telling your fortune was to do it religiously, his first greeting being "The Lord hath sent us a fine morning: the Lord hath thought proper to send us rain." At the end, "The Lord will bless you," &c. People used to tell him the day & hour they were born; & the next time he came he would bring the ruling of the planets — a half-sheet of letter-paper written over. He told A. Sh———,[31] whose planet he ⟨21⟩ ruled, that she would have a large family, travel, &c. His charge was sixpence: some would get him to do it for fourpence.

Diana Chester was the opposite. She used to work her spells by the Devil.

The above planet-ruler or astrologer was said to have astrological diagrams in his room at Beaminster.

Another man of the sort was called a conjuror; he lived in Blackmoor Vale. He would cause your enemy to rise in a glass of water. He did not himself know your enemy's name, but the bewitched person did, of course, recognizing the form as the one he had expected.[32]

———

[30] Melbury Osmund (or Osmond), a village about 13 miles N.W. of Dorchester. The source of this account was probably Hardy's mother, who was born there on 21 Sep 1813.

[31] Aunt Sharpe: Hardy's mother's sister, née Martha Hand, born 24 Oct 1816. She married John Brereton Sharpe, a Norfolk land-steward, at Puddletown in 1841. The prophecy that she would travel was fulfilled: she and her husband emigrated to Ontario, where she died aged 43 in 1859.

[32] Hardy's work contains no rustic astrologer directly modelled on the 'Planet-ruler' (in the early nineteenth century a familiar connotation in country districts), though there are various forms of divination or prophecy practised or mentioned in *Under the Greenwood Tree* (Pt IV, chs. 3-4), *The Mayor of Casterbridge* (where Henchard consults Conjuror Fall in ch. 26), and *Tess of the d'Urbervilles* (ch. 21). The most prominent

⟨22⟩ 1873. Feb.

Shroving in Dorset.[33]
When going shroving they used to carry a bag for flour, & a basin for
fat. Their words were:

              "Ma'am, ma'am, ma'am
              I be come a shroving
              For a piece of pancake
              Or a piece of bacon
              Or a round ruggle-cheese
              Of your own making
              Ma'am, ma'am, ma'am.

Subjoined   ⎧ Hot, hot, the pan's hot,
at   ⎪ Buttery doors open,
Puddlehinton   ⎨ Pray mis'ess, good mis'ess
& other   ⎪ Is your heart open?
villages.   ⎪ I be come 'ithout my bag,
                 ⎩ Afeard I shall have nothing."

⟨23⟩ 1873 Feb.

At Melbury, on a certain day of the year, a family used to go round
to the houses saying:–
              Wassail, wassail,
              All round the town
              The cup is white
              And the ale is brown:
              The cup is made of an ashen tree
              And the ale is made of good bar–ley.
              We'll set the cup upon the bron' (brand)
              And hope we shall have good luck anon,
              Hope all the apple-trees 'ill bud, bear & bloo',
              This year, next year, the year after too,

---

conjuror is Trendle in the story 'The Withered Arm' (published 1888), who in Pt V
effects for Gertrude Lodge the phenomenon described in the final paragraph here.
An identical rite is recalled in Emma Hardy's *Some Recollections* (pp. 40-1), this time in
the form of a midsummer divination which took place at her Plymouth home in 1858,
when the glass revealed that Emma would marry a writer.

[33] Shrove-tide is the period just before Lent, and derives its name from the custom
of being shriven, or absolved of one's sins, before the fast. It was traditionally a time
for a final indulgence in eating and drinking.

For this our 'sail, our jolly wassail,
O joy go with our jolly wassail![34]

At Melbury Osmond there was a haunted barn. A man coming home drunk entered the barn & fell asleep in a cow's crib that stood within. He awoke at 12, & saw a lady riding ⟨24⟩ round & round on a buck, holding the horns as reins. She was in a white riding-habit, & the wind of her speed blew so strong upon him that he sneezed, when she vanished.

1873 Sept 17. One man is a genius in trifles, a fool in emergencies: another a fool in trifles, a genius in emergencies.[35]

Octr. Some rural person says of Cheapside that "it is a place he should like to retire to & spend his declining days in, being a romantic spot."

A good story or play might run as follows: A certain nobleman, a widower, has one son, a young man now lying at ⟨25⟩ the point of death. The nobleman his father is an old man, in great trouble that there will be no heir in the direct succession. Son dies. Among his papers are found a girl's letter – the letter of a girl whom the son had begged his father to keep from want, as he had seduced her. The father finds that she is going to have a child. He marries her, parting from her at the church door. He obtains an heir of his own blood.[36]

Nov. 3. A sunset. A brazen sun, bristling with a thousand spines, which struck into & tormented my eyes.

Nov. 4. It is raining in torrents. The light is greenish & unnatural, objects being ⟨26⟩ as if seen through water. A roar of rain in the

---

[34] This note appears on a separate sheet pasted in and is apparently written on the back of the copy of a letter.

[35] Cf. Hardy's note of May 1865: 'In architecture, men who are clever in details are bunglers in generalities. So it is in everything whatsoever' (*Life,* 48).

[36] This note contains the genesis of the plot of 'The Lady Icenway', written and published 1890 as one of the stories in *A Group of Noble Dames.* Although the germ of several of these stories may be found in John Hutchins, *History and Antiquities of the County of Dorset* (Hardy's library contained the 3rd edn., four vols, London, 1861–73), this note suggests that 'The Lady Icenway' was Hardy's own invention.

plantation, & a rush near at hand, yet not a breath of wind. A silver fringe hangs from the eaves of the house to the ground. A flash. Thunder.

Nov. 17. I knew a man who said he was once in great want. Passing by a grocery shop in a village he found that the occupants had run out of the house because of some accident at the back. He entered the shop, & found in a drawer the bag of money. He went off with it, feeling elated and provided for. When he got to a lonely place he opened the bag, & found it was full of farthings.

Dec. 23. Before day. A lavender curtain, with a pale crimson hem, covers the east & shuts out the dawn.

⟨27⟩ 1873

End of December. The originator of a depressing mental view, mood, or idea, is less permanently affected by its contemplation than are those who imbibe it from him at second hand. Jeremiah probably retired to rest & slept soundly long before the listeners to his fearful words closed their eyes, even though the miseries he spoke of would affect him no less than themselves.

1874. Feb 1. Sunday. To Trinity Ch. Dorchester.[37] The rector in his sermon delivers himself of mean images in a very sublime voice, & the effect is that of a glowing landscape in which clothes are hung out to dry.

March 13. Let Europe be the stage & have scenes continually shifting. (Can this refer to any conception of the Dynasts?)[38]

⟨28⟩ 1874

March. Kenfield, the mail-coach guard from London to Dorchester,

---

[37] Holy Trinity Church, High West Street. The incumbent rector was the Rev. Henry Everett.
[38] The parenthetical query was probably added by Hardy when he recopied this notebook in his eighties. This is the earliest indication of Hardy's design for *The Dynasts,* which he elaborated in further notes over two decades (see *Life,* 106, 114, 146, 148, 203, 284) before beginning the epic-drama in the early years of the new century. Part First was completed in Sep 1903.

lived at Higher Bockhampton in the eighteen thirties, the reason
probably being that the spot lay near the London Road, so that he
could take small packages to London on his own account, by collu-
sion with the coachman. He used to have butter brought to him by
old Hedditch the dairyman, also eggs. Also game, which he bought
of poachers – old Critchel for one. The provisions were packed into a
box, the box into a hamper, & the whole put into the boot of the
coach with the letter-bags, the boot being under the guard's seat, &
opening behind with a door on wh were "G.R.", a crown, & "Royal
Mail."

He carried 2 pistols, a cutlass, & a blunderbus in a long tin box
"like a ⟨29⟩ candle-box, in front of him; also a ball of tar-twine, & a
screw-hammer (in case of a break down) Also "a little time-piece
strapped on to him in a leather pouch," which when he got home he
placed on his mantel piece.

He kept a pony & gig to drive to Dorchester (2½ miles) to take his
seat on the mail coach, putting on his red uniform before starting, &
his dog's-hair hat with a gold band round it. He was on the coach
two nights out of three.

Meanwhile John Downton, a youth of the village whom he employed, would carry the packed hamper in the evening about 5
down through the plantation separating Higher Bockhampton from
the turnpike road, & knowing the exact time the coach would pass
wait at the plan= ⟨30⟩ tation gate for it, which pulled up for a
moment to receive the hamper, & rolled on again.

Although Kenfield went right through to London, there were two
or three coachmen to the journey. Whether they all knew of this
butter & game business cannot be said. Oliver of Dorchester, who
horsed the mailcoach, horsed it only as far as to Blandford, where
another contractor took on.

In bitter weather Kenfield drank mulled ale rather than spirits,
saying that spirits would not keep out the cold so long as the ale
would. When he retired from guarding the mail he took "The Coach
& Snow" Inn, Dorchester. He was very tall, with a high-bridged
nose that ran up into his forehead like a Greek's, ⟨31⟩ high cheek-
bones, rather thin face, & sunken eyes. When it had rained all the
way from London he, in common with the whole mail, looked much
weatherbeaten. In winter he wore a drab greatcoat over his red
uniform.

John Downton was always charged to be punctual in meeting the
coach. Kenfield used to jump off, catch up the hamper, & be in his

seat again in a moment. On the return journey he would fling the
empty hamper down without stopping.

It should have been mentioned that his uniform was a red frock-
coat, with blue flaps to the pockets, & a blue collar. In very cold
weather he was buskin-legged, i.e.: wrapped up round the legs like
a bantam hen; & wrapped round the neck. ⟨32⟩ There were three
guards employed between London and Dorchester in shifts, each
going the whole way when his turn came; & three below, from
Dorchester to Exeter. The other two guards in Kenfield's set drank
hard, & Kenfield sometimes had to do extra duty: e.g. return to
London again on the day of his arrival from the city. All the three,
Kenfield, Preedy, & Churchill, died in middle age, the exposure,
&c, trying them severely.

The guard used to blow his horn at every place where a mail-bag
was to be taken up; e.g. Puddletown.

When the mail arrived the first thing the guard did was to take out
the letter-bags & carry them into the Post Office (at that time the
house below the King's Arms, Dorchester.) He wd. then hand down
blunderbus & tools.

⟨33⟩ 1874

June. My Aunt Sharpe[39] died in Canada the Sunday before Aug. 30,
1859, at 4 p.m. At Paris, British North America.

July 1874. E.L.G's letter. "My work, unlike your work of writing,
does not occupy my true mind much . . . .
"Your novel seems sometimes like a child all your own & none of
me."[40]

July 25. After returning from the Olympic. Horace Wigan[41] as an

------

[39] Martha Sharpe, who had emigrated to Canada (see n. 31 above). Paris is a small
town in Ontario, 70 miles S.W. of Toronto.

[40] Hardy was at Higher Bockhampton writing *Far from the Madding Crowd*, which he
completed during this month. Emma Gifford encouraged Hardy and made fair
copies of his chapters but she also aspired to be a writer in her own right. The
following year she wrote a novel, *The Maid on the Shore* (typescript in DCM).

[41] Horace Wigan (1818?–1885), also noted for his dramatic adaptations and translations, was a stolid and undemonstrative actor best cast in roles calling for no display
of emotion. He managed the Olympic Theatre 1864–6 and appeared there regularly
1854–74, acting only occasionally at other theatres; this accounts for an error in
Hardy's note. On this date Wigan appeared at the Vaudeville Theatre, playing the
Earl of Pompion in Dion Boucicault's comedy *Old Heads and Young Hearts*.

actor is much underrated. His is the <u>still</u> manner: he hardly moves at all when speaking, & the effect is excellent, & more impressive than that of the gesticulating actors.

⟨34⟩ 1874

August. A scene in Celbridge Place.[42] Middle-aged gentleman talking to handsome buxom lady across the stone parapet of the house opposite, which is just as high as their breasts — she inside, he on pavement. It rains a little, a very mild moisture, which a duck would call nothing, a dog a pleasure, a cat possibly a good deal. He holds his plum-coloured silk umbrella across the parapet over her head, she being without a bonnet, & her black hair done up in a knot behind. She wears a rich brown dress, with a white "modesty piece" of lace (as old writers call it). He has nearly white whiskers, & wears a low felt hat. With the walking stick in his right hand he occasionally points at objects east & west. She gesticulates with her ⟨35⟩ right hand, which frequently touches the gentn's left on the parapet holding the umbrella.

Dec 19. 1874. Long Ditton.[43] Snow on graves. A superfluous piece of cynicism in Nature.

The Revd. Mr Wilkinson (Cornwall) married a handsome actress. She settled down to serve God as unceremoniously as she previously had done to Mammon.

1875. Jan 6. A curate or vicar, disgusted with the smallness of his stipend, or poverty of his living, goes into a remote county & turns cidermaker, dairyman, lime-burner, or what-not.

⟨36⟩ 1875

June 16. Reading Life of Goethe.[44] Schlegel says that "the deepest

---

[42] Hardy was lodging at 4 Celbridge Place, Westbourne Park, having returned to London in mid-July to correct the ms. of his novel. On 17 Sep he married Emma Gifford at St Peter's, Elgin Avenue, Paddington, about half a mile away.

[43] The Hardys had begun their married life in lodgings at St David's, Hook Road, Surbiton, within a mile of Long Ditton.

[44] G.H. Lewes, *The Life of Goethe* (London, 1873), p.310. Hardy's commonplace book 'Literary Notes, I' (DCM) shows that he was at this time reading this biography of Johann Wolfgang von Goethe (1749–1832), and he records several quotations from it on pp.9–10. Friedrich von Schlegel (1772–1829) was an eminent literary historian

want & deficiency of all modern art lies in the fact that the artists have no Mythology."

1876. Aug. Rain: like a banner of gauze waved in folds across the scene.

1877. Sept. Rapid riding by night, the moon & stars racing after, & the trees & fields slipping behind.

1878. Nov. The honest Earl. Earl is accidentally shut up in a tower — the Hardy monument, say — with a blacksmith's daughter. Goes to parson next day & says he feels it his duty to marry her. Does so. Finds her not so good as she seemed, & . . . . . .[45]

⟨37⟩ 1879

Feb. The old Dorchester Post Office.

Before my birth, & before it was at Frampton's, it was "up the steps," where the gin shop now is, or lately was — viz. the door above the King's Arms arch. In my childhood it was at the door below the King's Arms — Frampton's grocery shop. When the railway came it was moved into South Street, near the Alms House. Thence to opposite Greyhound Yard in the same street. Thence to where it now is.[46]

---

and proponent of ancient Hindu poetry. This criticism of the mythopoeic inadequacy of modern art occurs in his *Gespräche über Poesie* ['Dialogue on Poetry'] (1800), p. 274.

[45] An element of this plot is used in 'Andrey Satchel and the Parson and Clerk' in 'A Few Crusted Characters', written in late 1890, in which Andrey and his fiancée Jane Vallens are inadvertently locked in the church tower overnight. The Hardy monument was erected 1844 on Blackdown Hill, N.E. of Portesham, in memory of Hardy's famous collateral ancestor Vice-Admiral Sir Thomas Masterman Hardy (1769–1839), formerly of the *Victory*.

[46] The original site mentioned here was 29 High East Street; the former 'gin shop' is now the premises of Creech & Redfern Ltd. The P.O. then moved to 31 High East Street (now occupied by E. Parsons Ltd). The Southern Railway came to Dorchester on 1 June 1847. After Francis Lock was appointed Postmaster in 1846 the P.O. moved to 17 South Street (now Liptons' store); the almshouse is known as Napper's Mite. After the appointment of Charles Parsons as Postmaster in 1863, the P.O. moved to 53 South Street (now Timothy White's store) 'opposite Greyhound Yard'. The last sentence is presumably an addition made in the nineteen twenties, when Hardy recopied his 1879 note: the P.O. moved to its present site, 43 South Street, on 10 Dec 1906.

March 2: Sunset. Sun a vast bulb of crimson pulp.

July. Rainy sunset: the sun streaming his yellow rays through the wet atmosphere like straying hair. The wet ironwork & wet slates shine.[47]

⟨38⟩ 1879

July. Young man — fair, light chestnut moustache, straight Apollo nose, firm chin, red lips, handsome mouth, dark eyes — with a young lady. She wound up her umbrella & fastened it. He gently drew it from her hand, coolly unfastened it, shook it out, & rolled it up his way, twisting it round lightly in his hand, & making it smaller by half, as he gives it back to her. She smiles, just showing her teeth.

Aug. 10. J.Sp.[48] says that old Symonds, his mother's great-great-grandfather, & grandfather of the Betty Symonds whom great-grandfr. H. married, built their house wh. has on it the date 1675.

At Weymouth. Plaits visible on the comparatively smooth sea.

⟨39⟩ 1879. Aug.

At Weymouth, contd. Windy: chimney board necessary because of the high winds. Can hear the seven of them growling behind this chimney board at nights. You open the window; in comes the gale, down falls the chimney board, open bursts the door. The front door follows suit in bursting open. The carpet rises & falls in billows.[49]

---

[47] Hardy and his wife were now living at 1 Arundel Terrace, Trinity Road, Upper Tooting (now identified as 172 Trinity Road, Tooting).

[48] James Sparks (1805–74), joiner and cabinet-maker, married Hardy's maternal aunt Maria Hand in 1828. This note refers to Hardy's maternal ancestors the Hands (earlier known as the Hanns), who came from Blackmoor Vale. 'Great-grandfr. H.' is William Hann (1751–1828) who married Betty Symonds (1752–1828). They lived in Puddletown and among their four children was Hardy's grandfather George Hand (b.1773). 'Old Symonds' refers to J. Symonds, whose home was owned by the family for 200 years before being demolished in the eighteen seventies.

[49] In the latter half of August Hardy and Emma had taken lodgings in Weymouth, where his mother joined them for expeditions. Throughout their visit 'the port was mostly wet': Hardy made more extensive notes on the bad weather and its effects on visitors (transferred to *Life*, 129).

Dec. 4. Helen M—th..s's face.[50] A profile not too Greek for an English fireside, yet Greek enough for an artist's eye: arch, saucy style of countenance, dark eyes, brows, & hair, the last low on forehead.

1880.[51]

⟨40⟩
1881   Old Postilions[52]
July

23. Hired a wagonette at the George, & drove with E. & K. to Badbury Rings[53] – William Young, who drove us, had been a postilion since he was 16 till he got too old, & there was no posting to do. His work lay mostly in the saddle – not at the reins – suffers now from rheumatic gout, brought on by exposure & hard work. Has ridden along the Blandford Rd. on nights so dark that he had to feel his way by touching the hedge with his whip – the lights of the coach not showing far enough forward to light the postboy. (though he told how a lamp was sometimes fixed in the middle for that purpose) Had often gone with the coach, |tho| not as driver, but as postboy to the 2 extra horses which were hitched on when the coach was overladen, & ⟨41⟩ could not proceed.

Pointed out the cedar avenue at K. Lacy[54] – a cock pheasant on edge of the corn field – they are seen alone at this time of year, the hens being with the young ones. Told of young B.[55] & an old gentn's young wife. Property is in the hands of trustees, he says –

---

[50] Probably to read 'Helen Matthews', whom I have been unable to identify. The Hardys were frequently dining out in London at this time and the author recorded a number of descriptions of persons encountered.

[51] Though Hardy has written the date there are not in fact any entries from 1880 in the notebook.

[52] This page and notebook pp. 41–7 incl. are pasted in as an intact gathering from an earlier notebook. Both sides of the page have been used, unlike most of the present notebook. The writing is in ink, with the exception of '1881/July', which is in pencil.

[53] Hardy drove with Emma and his sister Kate (1856–1940). Since 25 June, the Hardys had occupied their new home 'Llanherne', The Avenue, Wimborne Minster (now 'Lanherne', 16 Avenue Road). Badbury Rings, five miles N.W. of Wimborne on the Blandford road, is an Iron Age hill-fort, believed also to have been a Roman posting station.

[54] Kingston Lacy, which Hardy visited on at least two other occasions (1878 and 1926) to see its collection of paintings, was the home of the Bankes family and is near Wimborne.

[55] Walter Ralph Bankes (1859-1904).

Showed an avenue of beeches planted by a previous Bankes – trees large in the hollows, small on the hills –

Pointed out Charborough[56] – The present owner $\left[\begin{array}{l}\text{Mrs.?} \\ \text{Miss Drax,}^{57}\end{array}\right.$ lives there alone – a quiet little lady – keeps no company. It is "heiress land" – old Drax lives at Holnest[58] – he carried off the armour from Charborough – though he had no right to it. He was only a lieut., named - - - - - Heard of Miss ⟨42⟩ Drax as an heiress – sent on a parson to smooth the way for him. Being of good address, & handsome, & she not in her first bloom, he won her. He & she, on one occasion rode a breakneck race against other relatives to get to the bedside of a rich aunt or uncle, & the will was made in their favour.

W.Y. drove the sheriff's carriage at Drax's assize.

Pointed out a house at the village by K. Lacy which was once an old-fashd. roadside inn.

Has driven Drax the 7 miles between his house & Wimborne station in 25, or 35, minutes. Has ridden 80 miles in a day. When on arriving at the end of a stage (?), there were no horses in to take on the carriage the same horses & postillion ⟨43⟩ were obliged to go on to the next, by act of Parliament.

In the stable in those old days were the head ostler, 2d. & 3d. ostlers, the horse keeper, & a postillion to every 4 horses. The head o. did little but receive orders & hand them on – the horse keeper attended to the littering &c. of the horses – one of the ostlers used to lie in the stables & others in the stable yard (where they had a bedroom, it seems). Were called up at all hours of the night to go on. On reaching the end of his journey he had to call up the next postillion; he received the money for the journey – 1/6 per mile for a

---

[56] Charborough Park, five miles W. of Wimborne Minster, is (by Hardy's account) the setting of *Two on a Tower*. The home of the Drax family, it has an imposing tower in the grounds. An amusing account of the difficulties experienced by Macbeth Raeburn, in 1895 sketching a frontispiece for *Two on a Tower* and who went to Charborough on Hardy's direction, in gaining admission to the grounds is given in *Life*, 267-8. Hardy himself entered Charborough House for the first time, for a meal, in the autumn of 1927, a couple of months before his death.

[57] Maria Caroline Sawbridge-Erle-Drax, who succeeded to the property on her mother's death in 1853 and who died unmarried.

[58] John S.W. Sawbridge (1800-87) assumed the surname and arms of Erle-Drax on marrying Jane Erle-Drax, 12 years his senior, in 1827. When she died in 1853 the property passed to their daughter (see n.57 above). Drax had bought the elegant stone mansion at Holnest in 1826; it is four miles S.E. of Sherborne. He occupied a fair amount of his time rehearsing his own funeral.

pair of horses – 3/- for 4. When the other postboy & horses had gone
on with the ⟨44⟩ carriage the first stabled his own horses, let them
stale &c, then received a glass of grog & . . . . . which were his pre-
requisites.

W.Ys right leg, outside, is discoloured – though not by bruising.
It was where the carriagepole used to rub for so many years – &
when the horses began to get weary they would lean in against the
pole.

W.Y. cannot get beer that he likes – which he prefers to grog –
home brewed – 12 bushels to the hogshead, such as used to be
made, the colour thereof being like port wine.

Assizes week – when he was at Blandf. they used to keep 20
horses in stable. The first judge arrived – 4 horses for him – this
carriage contained also his <u>personal</u> luggage – (but a previous carriage had ⟨45⟩ gone on with his books – a very heavy weight,
requiring sometimes 6 horses – Then 4 horses more were required
for the carriage of . . . . then the counsel on the circuit
required pairs – they usually rode in flys, & were driven in reins, not
by the regular postboys, but by the odd men of the stables.

The two judges never came together. The second judge came in
the same way some hours later but was not received by javelin men
too (I knew this before)

First judge – stopped at King's Arms Puddletown to robe himself
– then they drove on to Yellm. hill[59] – where he was met by sheriff &
javelin men & entered sheriff's carriage – the post-carriage following
behind, & going to the judges lodging where there was a meal
provided for the postboys.

⟨46⟩

W.Y. and Robt. Eyers began life together as fellow postboys. But
W.Y. was no scholar – & Eyers was.

In wet weather & at night the postillion wore a great coat – with a
strap to fasten it down in some way – boots hard to get off when wet.
W.Y. was out a great deal at night. Luggage carried in an "imperial"
at top of carriage. Carriages very heavy, what with luggage, servants &c. The postillion often did not know the rank or quality of the
people behind him. W.Y. had 2 suits of clothes – (i.e. blue jacket &c).

---

[59] Yellowham Hill, on the road between Puddletown and Dorchester, is less than
half a mile from Hardy's birthplace.

His whip he gave away 3 weeks ago "to a man who will know how to value it."

At Kingston Lacy there was beef & bread for all callers in a certain old Bankes's time.

Duty-ticket, stating the number of miles for ⟨47⟩ which the horses were hired, was given up at the first t.p. gate[60] through which the traveller passed – for this an exchange ticket was received, which had to be shown at every other turnpike g. (This is corroborated by Chambers's Rees Ency. which see for particulars.)

Before going a second stage gruel was given the horses, & they were allowed to stale – or they wd. have been dead horses: this is of the horses – not the mares.

⟨48⟩ 1882

Edith G. of Launceston[61] has lost her young man. She was engaged to him, when he told her that he had been intimate with another girl (a dressmaker) & that, as she was about to become a mother, ought he not marry her? She said yes, & that if he did not tell his father she would. He duly married the other.

May 25. Advt. in Western Gazette. "For sale, an octagonal pulpit 6 ft high by 2/11. Two tables of the Ten Commandments on wood, each 7 ft high, & 3/5 wide. Barrel organ in ornamental case 7/- high, 4/8 wide. The above in good order, & may be seen on applicn. to the C.W.s,[62] Haselbury, Crewkerne.[63]

Burial of suicides at cross roads abolished c 1830. (Stake driven through it: between 9 & 12.) Times

---

[60] Turnpike.

[61] Probably Edith Gifford: Hardy's wife's cousins lived in Launceston, Cornwall.

[62] Church Wardens.

[63] The parish of Haselbury Plucknett, 19 miles N.W. of Dorchester, is in Somerset. The chancel had been restored in 1878 in a period when 'the tables of the law' were swept away from churches all over the country, partly as a result of the Oxford Movement's impact on liturgy and partly of architects responsible in the name of Gothic for much wanton destruction of old and beautiful furniture. A new vicar presented a new organ to the church about this time and in May 1882 parishioners presented a new pulpit in memory of his predecessor (Somerset Record Office, Taunton, ref. 2/7/1 D/p/ha. pl. c/1664). The discarding of these church furnishings must have appealed to Hardy's sense of irony. He made similar observations in Feb 1879 (Life, 126), later including these with more serious appeals against 'abuse of ecclesiastical fabrics' in 'Memories of Church Restoration', a speech for the Society for the Preservation of Ancient Buildings (Cornhill Magazine (Aug 1906), 184–96).

(49) 1883.

The Autobiography of a Card Table.

1884. Dec. Poachers' iron swingels.

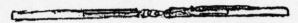

A strip of iron ran down 3 or 4 sides of the flail part, & the two flails were united by 3 or 4 links of chain, the keepers carrying cutlasses which would cut off the ordinary eel-skin hinge of a flail.

April, 1885. Friday. Wrote the last page of "The Mayor of Caster-bridge", begun at least a year ago.[64]

1885. Plot for play or novel.
A goodlooking woman, with a thirst for fame, tries literature, & fails. Is quite heartbroken. Marries a ⟨50⟩ commonplace man. Then she meets a philosopher, who tells her that notoriety is as good as fame.

   She determines to be renowned for her gallantries. In carrying this out she conceives such a dislike to it that she continues chaste in deed. When all England is ringing with her name (as the cause of a divorce, say) she meets a pure young man, & loves him passion-ately. Then she sees her punishment ahead. How can she persuade him of her, comparative innocence? -----

1885.

U. Sh.[65] was either in the 9th Lancers (Queen's Royals), or more probably the 5th (Royal Irish) Lancers, 4 years. Riding master I believe. Date cd. be found out by referring to old Army L.

⟨51⟩ 1885

Great U. John of P.T.[66] [W.H.'s father] used to wear a blue coat,

---

[64] In *Life*, 171, Hardy gives the exact date, 17 April, and adds the phrase 'and frequently interrupted in the writing of each part'.
[65] Probably Uncle [John Brereton] Sharpe, who later emigrated to Canada (see n. 31 above).
[66] Great Uncle John of Puddletown, brother of Hardy's maternal grandfather George Hand (1773–1822). 'W.H.' was his son William.

brass buttons, cord breeches, & leather gaiters; & an apron twisted round him. Died aged 63.

Oct. 1888. A game that used to be played at Bockhn. All kinds of materials are put down in a circle (wood, iron, brick, etc.): girls blindfolded, turned round, & made to crawl from centre. Whichever material they crawl to will bear upon their future husbands vocation.[67]

Melbury Osmund. The Swetmans are buried near the yew tree at the South-west of the churchyard.[68]

Sept 12. 1890. The Legend of the Cerne ⟨52⟩ Giant.[69] Threatened to descend upon Cerne and ravish all the young women on a particular night, & to kill the (young?) men next day. They were goaded to a desperate courage, & waylaid him & killed him, afterwards cutting his effigy on the hill. He lived somewhere up in the hills, was waited on by wild animals, used to steal the farmers' sheep, eating one a day. The "Giant's Head" Inn, near, evidently related to the tradition.

Xmas Day. F. was one of the singers in Lady Susan's time.[70] On

---

[67] Another traditional divination ritual (see nn.23 and 32 above).

[68] Identification of their precise location is no longer possible since the gravestones are now illegible. The Swetmans are among Hardy's maternal ancestors, Elizabeth (Betty) Swetman (1778–1847) having married George Hand in 1804.

[69] The Cerne Giant is carved on a chalky hillside by the village of Cerne Abbas, five miles N. of Dorchester. The 180 ft. high figure is of a naked man, with explicit phallic properties, bearing a huge club (which alone measures 90 ft.). Generally considered to be of Romano-British origin, the Giant was long associated with local fertility rites, though it was also believed to represent an ithyphallic divinity dating from the Bronze Age. Reference to the Giant is made in 'A Few Crusted Characters'; Tess of the d'Urbervilles (ch.48); The Dynasts, Part First (II.v).

[70] Lady Susan O'Brien (1743–1827), daughter of the 1st Earl of Ilchester, always held a romantic interest in Hardy's mind. In 1764, against her father's wishes, she secretly married a young Drury Lane actor, William O'Brien (1738–1815): it was a noted aristocratic scandal, recorded by Walpole among others. The Earl insisted that O'Brien abandon his theatrical career and the O'Briens spent some years in Canada, but after the Earl's death Lady Susan's brother (the new Earl) had O'Brien appointed Receiver-General for Dorset and gave them Stinsford House, the scene of this recollection. Here the Stinsford choir, with Hardy's father and grandfather, would practise among the 'singers' referred to here. The O'Briens were buried in Stinsford Church in a vault built by Hardy's grandfather; a commemorative tablet remains there. Lady Susan is affectionately recalled in the Life (9, 163–4, 250).

Xmas Eve they were let in on the terrace as afterwards by the Williams's. He sang more than once to her before she died. On the evening of Xmas Day they used to go in & sing ⟨53⟩ in the hall at the bottom of the staircase by the terrace door. The old lady would speak to them from the top of the stairs. [1820–1827]

1893. April. A wrinkled worn-out ballet dancer (Lydia Thompson,[71] say) might be discovered living in a remote cottage in a wood or by the sea.

P.T.[72] G.Gfr. H. & G.G.Mr. buried
close to west face of ch. tower.
M.O.[73] G.Gfr. & G.G.Mr. Swetman
overb. by Swaffields.
G.Gfr. & G.Grm. Childs,[74] near
others of the Childs family.
Valeat quantum valere potest![75]

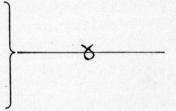

1899. Jan 25. A principle of conduct: acquiescence, but recognition.[76]

1899 later. Pessimism. Was there ever any great poetry which was not pessimistic? . . .

---

[71] Lydia Thompson (1836–1908), English actress who was originally a ballet dancer and who became famous in burlesque, which she introduced into America with a troupe of golden-haired English girls in 1868. She remained there until 1874 and subsequently alternated between New York and London, managing the Strand Theatre (1886–8) and appearing for the last time in 1904. The note was apparently written in London.

[72] This entry appears on the opposite otherwise blank page; all seven lines are bracketed together and the line from the point of the bracket extends across the entire width of the right-hand page. The reference in the first two lines is to St Mary's Church, Puddletown. Great Grandfather [William] Hann (1751–1828) and Great Grandmother are indicated.

[73] St Osmund's Church, Melbury Osmund. Great Grandfather and Great Grandmother Swetman: John Swetman (1733–1822) and Maria Childs Swetman (?–1802). The Swaffields are not identified.

[74] Hardy has accidentally foreshortened the relationship by a generation. These are in fact his great-great-grandparents, Joseph Childs (1703–?) and Mary Hurlstone Childs (?–1746), parents of Maria Childs Swetman.

[75] 'May this be valued as much as it is worth!'

[76] A suggestion of stoicism: perhaps the artist's necessary 'recognition' in submitting to the demands (and criticism) of his public while recognising that it is the nature of his position which requires this. In the week of 11 Dec 1898, Hardy's first volume of poetry, *Wessex Poems*, had been published. At the time of this note Hardy was preoccupied with the mixed reviews that were appearing (see *Life*, 299–302).

"All creation groaneth," &c.

"Man that is born of woman," &c.

"Man dieth & wasteth away," &c. T.O.

⟨54⟩ "I go hence like the shadow that departeth" &c. (& other Psalms)[77]

Is that pessimism, & if not, why not? The answer would probably be because a remedy is offered. Well, the remedy tarries long.

1900. July. They were playing puff & dart at Buckland Newton,[78] when a man had his eye accidlly. shot out.

Dec 6. Helen Catherine Holder died.[79] Buried in Ch. yard, Crofton Old Ch. near Lee on the Solent.

Nov. 1901. Short Story – that has been told me as true in essentials.

Mima Pawle. In the garden-house at Upper Mellstock. Dressed as a bride. Meditates. Old Drayne, who has kept her, has gone out to hunt up Tom C. to go to church with her ⟨55⟩ & marry her that morning, as he has agreed to do, the bribe being that he shall acquire with her the house, garden, orchard, &c. for life, where old D. & Mima have been living, D. having arranged to go to another part of England.

She is thinking, will T.C. enter to fetch her to church, or will he break his word at the last minute, & old D. come back saying he cannot find T. She has agreed to wed this man, if he is willing, for

---

[77] 'We know that the whole creation groaneth, and travaileth in pain together until now' (Romans 8:22); 'Man that is born of a woman is of few days, and full of trouble' (Job 14:1); 'Man dieth, and wasteth away: yea, man giveth up the ghost, and where is he?' (Job 14:10); 'I go hence like the shadow that departeth' (Ps. 109, v.22). Hardy's reflections may have been prompted by Emma's gift to him of a new Bible on his 59th birthday, while they were renting a London flat, inscribed: 'T. Hardy, from E.L.H., June 2, 1899. At Wynnstay Gardens, Kensington.' (The Bible is in the DCM.)

[78] Nine miles N. of Dorchester.

[79] Emma's only sister, formerly Helen Gifford, worked first as a governess and then as companion to an eccentric old lady of county stock before marrying, in 1869, the Rev. Caddell Holder (1803–82). They lived at St Juliot. Helen was the rector's second wife and he was many years older. Hardy records several outings with Emma and her sister during his courtship. Lee-on-the-Solent, Hampshire, is by Gosport on the south coast.

the sake of the child, & T.C. has agreed because he wants the house for his parents.

As a matter of fact he did come, & married her.[80]

Aug. 1902. A squire in a remote part of Wessex brings home his bride.
T.O.
⟨56⟩ She finds in the manor house a woman who has had children by him.
(Cf. The Andromache of Euripides.)[81]

Tinsley paid £30 for the copyright of Under the Greenwood Tree, sending £10 afterwards for the Tauchnitz edn.

The same publisher paid £200 for the right to print "A Pair of Blue Eyes" in Tinsley's Magazine & to issue it afterwards in 3 vols. (only). From an old note.[82]

1908. Dec.20. Sunday.
C.M.H.[83] brought from Puddletown "An account of the Inhabitants of Piddletown Parish (compiled by the vicar) 1724.

"Second house in Back St. John Hardy,

T.O.

---

[80] Hardy never used this plot, though the name Pawle (used in 'A Few Crusted Characters' a decade earlier) recurs in Grammer Pawle in The Dynasts, Part Third (written 1906–7).

[81] It is odd that Hardy should note this plot since he had in effect used it in 'The Withered Arm', written five years earlier. Andromache, the story of the wife of the Trojan hero Hector, is one of the earlier plays of the Greek tragedian Euripides (480–406 B.C.).

[82] A recapitulation of Hardy's success in dealing with publisher William Tinsley, who offered £30 (which Hardy regarded as 'a trifle') for the copyright of Under the Greenwood Tree on 22 Apr 1872, forwarding the sum on 20 July, and promising the further sum of £10 for the continental Tauchnitz edn. on 4 Oct. Meanwhile in July, because of the encouraging reviews of this novel, Tinsley had intimated his interest in having another story to run for twelve months in his magazine and encouraged Hardy to sign an agreement immediately. But Hardy, growing wary, bought and read Copinger on Copyright overnight and the next day insisted on and achieved better terms. The sum of £200 was detailed in a letter sent by Hardy on 27 July. The episode is recalled good-humouredly in the Life, 88–90, and a calendar of Hardy-Tinsley letters is included in Richard L. Purdy, Thomas Hardy: A Bibliographical Study (London, 1954), pp. 329–35.

[83] Charles Meech Hardy, a Puddletown builder; Hardy's second cousin.

⟨57⟩ widower; born in 1658. alone."[84]

— — — — — ~ — — — — — —

"In 8th & last house on ye. side of ye. water, & near ye. Great Bridge, & betwixt both. Thomas & Mary Symonds,[85] two ancient people & anabaptists. 2 daus., Joan abt. 29, & Jane abt. 22. They have 2 sons & 2 daus. more out at service or married."

———

1909. June 20. Sunday. To Bockhn.
From Affpuddle Church register:-
"Roger Hann was buried Aug 23. 1759.
"William, son of Roger & Sarah Hann.
bap. Jan.5. 1751."
This William was the fr. of George H. by his wife Betty, née Symonds. George H. married Betty Swetman.[86]

———

⟨58⟩ 1909

Mem. The words used (Jan 1909) in respect of the Dorchester Grammar School Governors are . . . . "to act in the Trusts of the Scheme for the Admn. of the Foundation & Endowments thereof" &c. The same words are used to the "Napier's Prize Endowment" conjoined.[87]

———

---

[84] The position of this Hardy in the author's genealogy is not clear. Hardy's great-grandfather was named John (1755–1821), also of Puddletown, but the John recorded here (b. 1658) must have preceded him by two if not three generations.

[85] Probably among Hardy's maternal ancestors, possibly the grandparents or great-grandparents of Betty Symonds, later Hardy's own gt.-grandmother. The Anabaptists formed a sect of the nonconformist Baptist Church, believing in baptismal immersion not of children but of adults. (See *A Laodicean*.)

[86] George and Betty Hann were Hardy's grandparents, William and Betty his great-grandparents. Affpuddle is three miles E. of Puddletown and seven miles N.E. of Dorchester.

[87] In this month Hardy was appointed a governor of Dorchester Grammar School, which had been endowed by one of his Elizabethan ancestors, and he retained the position until Jan 1926, when he resigned because of his age (85). The Napier's Prize Endowment is a small charity originally established to support the very poor of Dorchester: 'A yearly sum of 10l. shall be applied for prizes to the value of 1l. each, five for boys and five for girls, such boys and girls being the children of poor parents' (from para. 10 of the scheme, approved 15 Oct 1889). The fund is now used to provide Religious Education prizes.

"Swinburne's[88] way consisted in throwing over whatever subject the poet treated an atmosphere of poetic glamour . . . . The subject does not exactly disappear, but it ceases to be more than a sort of accompaniment to the treatment. Even then, & when the accompaniment itself is most prominent, it is <u>universalized</u> to an extent wh. wd. delight the most Aristotelian of critics . . . The heroine of Dolores is every woman of the enchantress kind . . . Individuality shd. not be looked for first in Mr. S.

[1909] G. Saintsbury.[89] Bookman.

1910. Dates. King Ed died in May. O.M. conferred in July by King G.[90] Col. the Hon. H.C. Legge[91] writes just after to say that "the Order of Merit ranks after the G.C.B. (Kt. Grand Cross of the Bath) & before the G.C.M.G. (Kt. Grand Cross of St Michael & St. George.) but gives no precedence." [what does this mean?][92]

27 Nov. 1911. Sent £20 to the Pension Fund Soc. of Authors, making £25 in all.[93]

---

[88] Algernon Charles Swinburne (1837–10 Apr 1909): two days after his death Hardy wrote an appreciation of his work (Life, 344–5). They had been friends for two decades though Hardy had admired Swinburne's poetry for much longer, having been thrilled as a young man by the unconventional Poems and Ballads, a volume ill-received by critics, in 1866. (In 1905 they laughed together over having been 'the two most abused of living writers'.) In turn Swinburne praised Hardy's novels and poems. A visit to Swinburne's grave by Hardy in 1910 occasioned 'A Singer Asleep', an elegiac poem rendering Hardy's admiration for Swinburne and his poetic style.

[89] George Saintsbury (1845–1933), at this time Professor of English Literature at Edinburgh University, a prolific literary critic and historian, often quoted with implicit approval in Hardy's literary notebooks.

[90] Edward VII died 6 May 1910, and Hardy watched his funeral procession from the Athenaeum. The Order of Merit was founded 1902 as a special distinction for eminent men and women, limited in number to 24. Hardy records that 'this sign of official approval of his work brought him pleasure' but adds of the ceremony on 19 July: 'afterwards I felt that I had failed in the accustomed formalities' (Life, 350). But the O.M. was not the only honour offered Hardy: on 2 Nov 1908, the Liberal Prime Minister Herbert Asquith had asked Hardy to accept a knighthood; extant letters make it clear that Hardy promptly declined.

[91] Col. (later Sir) Harry C. Legge (1852–1924), Secretary and Registrar of the Order of Merit, 1907–24.

[92] This means that the O.M. carries with it no special title or personal precedence. The letters O.M. after the names of members of the Order follow after G.C.B. and precede G.C.M.G. The order of precedence and the order of precedence of letters are not necessarily identical. For instance V.C. comes before K.G. in order of precedence of letters but not in the order of precedence.

[93] See 'Memoranda, II', note of July 1921, and n.

⟨59⟩

1913. March 8. Holder's tablet in St. Juliot Church, Cornwall.[94]

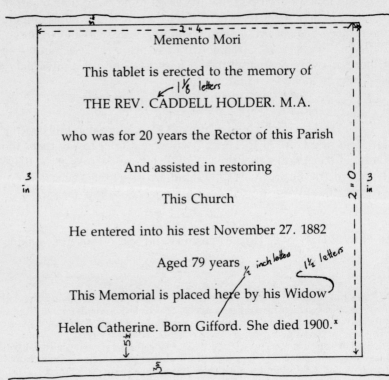

All Rom. Caps except name, wh. is Egyptian. 1st Mrs.
Holder died, June 1867 aged 60. – Mr. Gard, Builder
& Mason, Boscastle. (for any small job)

(x It was on December 6th)

---

[94] After Emma's sudden death on 27 Nov 1912, Hardy returned (on 6 Mar following) to the scenes of their courtship 43 years earlier. The Rev. C. Holder, born the son of a judge serving in the W. Indies, was recalled by his sister-in-law Emma as 'a very Boanerges in his preaching' (*Some Recollections*, pp. 45–6; *Life*, 67–8). His genial personality and his stories were affectionately remembered by Hardy (*Life*, 155–7). Hardy presumably recorded the exact measurements of the memorial tablet since he was preparing to erect one of his own design in the same church, in memory of Emma. It was commissioned in Plymouth on his return journey.

⟨60⟩

1914. Jan 27. £39, added to Lilian's[95] annuity, making £52 total: towards the cost of which £220 was her aunt's money, being the amount her aunt had in Plymouth stock that came to me. The rest was mine.

1915.

The Sculptor Alfred Stevens.[96]

"Stevens's father was a painter, & the commandments in our church [Blandford St Mary] were painted by him, & his name is in the corner – 'G. Stevens, Blandford, 1825'"

(Letter from Miss Penny, daughter of old incumbent, to Mrs. Egerton.)

There was a Stevens lecture by someone – printed in Western Gazette. Feb.28. 1912.

⟨61⟩

"A war conducted with energy cannot be directed merely against the combatants of the enemy State and the positions they occupy, but it will and must in like manner seek to destroy the total intellectual and material resources of the latter. Humanitarian claims, such as the protection of men and their goods, can only be taken into consideration in so far as the nature and object of the war permit.

"International Law is in no way opposed to the exploitation of the crimes of third parties (assassination, incendiarism, robbery and the

---

[95] Ethel Lilian Attersoll Gifford was Emma's niece. When Emma's younger brother Walter, who worked at the P.O. Savings Bank in London, died in 1898, the Hardys took his children Gordon and Lilian into Max Gate, where they lived for several years. Lilian, who helped with Hardy's domestic affairs after Emma's death, remained intermittently until his second marriage. In a letter she called him '"Daddy-Uncle" . . . that is what you are to me, and God bless you' (27 Nov 1913; DCM). In his will (24 Aug 1922) Hardy bequeathed £250 to purchase a further annuity for Lilian.

[96] The distinguished sculptor Alfred Stevens (1818–75), son of a house-painter, was born in Blandford. After copying old masters and studying (for a period working under Bertel Thorvaldsen) in Italy 1833–42, he became well known for decorative designing. From 1856 he laboured at his best-known work, the Wellington Monument in St Paul's, one of the finest pieces of modelling in England. Hardy, searching with a prospective biographer for facts and scenes associated with Stevens, had discovered the house of the sculptor's birth in Aug 1913.

like) to the prejudice of the enemy . . . . The necessary aim of war gives the belligerent the right and imposes on him the duty, according to circumstances, the duty not to let slip the important, it may be the decisive, advantages to be gained by such means."

"The German War Book," issued by the
Great General Staff.[97]

June 1915.
An Agreement with the Turner Film Co. for "Far from the Madding Crowd"[98] – the right having been transferred to them from Herkomer.[99]

⟨62⟩ 1915

Note on Sir T.M. Hardy:[100]

"Weymouth. Capt. Hardy, Lord Nelson's captain, was waiting the return of His Majesty, & had a long conversation with him." Morning Chronicle. Sept. 3. 1805.

For inscription, Gloucester Hotel:-[101]

---

[97] Newspaper cutting pasted in.

[98] The film had been planned since at least 1913. Hardy wrote to Mrs Henniker on 21 Dec of that year: 'Sir H. Herkomer is doing films of *Far from the Madding Crowd*, for the picture palaces: young Herkomer came here a few days ago to get local colour, and has photographed the *real* jug used in the malt-house.' The film was made in 1915 at Walton-on-Thames studios by Turner Films, adapted, produced and directed by the American Larry Trimble. Florence Turner (1888–1946), in 1907 the first film actress to become a star by name, played Bathsheba with Henry Edwards (1882–1952) as Oak. The cast also included Campbell Gullan (Troy), Malcolm Cherry (Boldwood), Marion Grey (Fanny) and Dorothy Rowan (Lyddie). A trade show, for which Hardy wrote a 450-word synopsis (DCM), took place at the West End Cinema on 16 Nov 1915, and the 4580 ft. film was generally released on 28 Feb 1916. No print is known to have survived.

[99] Sir Hubert von Herkomer (1849–1914), British portrait painter who became Slade Professor at Oxford in 1889, was also a playwright, composer, singer and actor.

[100] Sir Thomas Masterman Hardy (1769–1839), born in Portesham, Dorset, was descended (like Hardy himself) from the Hardys of Jersey. Associated with Nelson from 1796, his flag-captain from 1799, he survived the Battle of Trafalgar (1805) and was made a baronet in 1806. In 1830 he became First Sea Lord and was promoted Vice-Admiral in 1837. Of lifelong interest to the author, his ancestor appears (as Captain Hardy) in *The Trumpet-Major* and *The Dynasts*.

[101] In 1916 Hardy wrote an inscription for a plaque to commemorate the association of the building with George III but it was shortened to this simple statement (today on the front pillar of the hotel's portico): 'THIS HOTEL/ FORMERLY/ GLOUCESTER LODGE/ WAS/ THE SUMMER RESIDENCE/ OF/ KING GEORGE III/ 1798–1805.'

1805. Present at Weymouth:

July 13 to Oct 4. – K. George III, Queen Charlotte, & the Princesses Amelia, Augusta, Mary.

Sept 2. Prince of Wales; Duke of Sussex

" 3. Capt Hardy calls on King

" 20. Dk. of Cumberland, the Ld. Chancellor (Ld. Eldon), Ld. Mulgrave, Count Munster, Mr Pitt, Mr Villiers, Dk of Cambridge, Dk of York.

Oct 4. Their Majesties leave Weymouth.

⟨63⟩ Sept. 1916.

St. Juliot. In the Churchyard.[102]

"In memory of Anne wife of the Revd. C. Holder, rector of this parish, who died June 4, 1867. aged 60 years." (coped slate tomb.) It seems that Mr Holder must have been buried in the same grave, as there is no other sign of his grave near. The granite coped tomb next the first Mrs. Holder's is that of a Mr Freeman.

Inside the church the tablet to Caddell Holder the rector is fixed in the wall-space between the 2 windows to the West of Emma's tablet. The latter looks very well.

Charles Church, Plymouth.[103] North enclosure. 2 stones to the Giffords (which seem to have been removed from their ⟨64⟩ original place by the vault near east end of Church at the "restoration," to give room for steps to the vestry, & the vault mutilated or destroyed.)[104]

Left-hand Stone:

---

[102] Hardy had gone to see if his design and inscription for Emma's memorial tablet, ordered from Plymouth in 1913 (see n.94), had been properly carried out. Florence Hardy, whom he had married on 10 Feb 1914, accompanied him.

[103] Emma Hardy was born in Plymouth in 1840 and spent her first 18 years there. This church, dedicated to King Charles the Martyr, was attended by her family when they lived at the north end of the town. Hardy visited the church with Florence on the return journey from St Juliot.

[104] Emma had lamented these alterations five years earlier: 'it is sad to see the stones removed which grand and great grandparents had put up in years gone by over their vaults, and wept and reflected upon' (*Some Recollections*, p.12).

"In memory of Helen,[105] daughter of William Davie, late of Stonehouse, and relict of Richard Ireland Gifford of Bristol, who died on the 23rd of February A.D. 1860, aged 79 years"

"Charles Augustus Yolland, Lieut. R.N.[106] (who married Catherine Eliza Gifford, daughter of the above-named) died on the 25th of March, 1848, aged 42 years."

Right-hand stone:

"In memory of Philip Henry Gifford,[107] son of Richard Ireland Gifford, who departed this life May 7, 1830, aged 20."

"Sarah Flower, died 16th March 1831 ⟨65⟩ aged 64. A faithful servant in the family for 40 years."

"Helena Charlotte, wife of Robert Watson Esq. Surgeon of Devonport, and eldest daughter of the above Richard Ireland Gifford and Helen his wife, who departed this life the 18th day of July, 1832 (?), aged 30 (?)"

[Here follow some illegible verses]

"Nathaniel Richard Gifford"[108] [rest of inscription illegible]

In the churchyard, <u>south</u> of the Chancel, is a grave with a stone coping, & a horizontal marble cross within the coping, where are buried John Attersoll Gifford (son of the beforementioned Helen) & his wife Emma.[109]

---

[105] Helen Gifford (1780–1860), Emma's grandmother, 'a remarkably beautiful person', who lived with Emma's family since Emma's father was Helen's favourite son (see *Some Recollections*, pp.15–16).

[106] There was a double marriage between Emma's father's family and the Yollands, who lived at Stoke-Damerel. Lt Charles Yolland (1806–48) married Emma's Aunt Catherine, and his sister married Emma's uncle, Dr Edwin Hamilton Gifford (later Archdeacon of London), who officiated at the wedding of Emma and Hardy at Paddington in 1874.

[107] He would have been Emma's uncle but died ten years before she was born.

[108] Emma's father's youngest brother, who died of typhus at 16.

[109] Emma's parents. John Attersoll Gifford (1808–90), a solicitor, had (it is claimed) first been engaged to Emma's mother's sister, who died of scarlet fever at 18, and from this time on he drank heavily. But he kept a pledge of temperance for many years before and after Emma's birth. He married Emma Farman in Monmouthshire on 24 Apr 1832. In politics a Tory, fond of playing the violin, he enjoyed his social life. Though he had a sharp intellect, increasing outbursts of drinking forced him to retire early, whereupon he and his family were supported by his mother's income. It was on her death in 1860 and the division of her money that the Giffords were forced to move to Bodmin and live more modestly.

⟨66⟩ 1917.

HAMLYN: HARDY – On the 20th Nov., 1917, at Suffield Church, Norfolk, by Bishop Hamlyn (uncle of the bride and bridegroom), assisted by the Revd. W. Hamlyn, ANDREW DOUGLAS, of the Nigerian Civil Service, second son of the Revd. W. and Mrs. HAMLYN, The Vicarage, Claybrooke, to RUTH, second daughter of the REVD. and Mrs. HENRY HARDY, The Rectory, Suffield.[110]

Jan 11. 1918.

Mr. Noel Buxton, in the Hibbert Journal condemns any attempt to liberate a people not suffering from cruelty, merely for the sake of political independence.[111]

17 March 1918. For diarrhoea (Dr. Gowring)[112] No vegetables, no meat, no eggs, no soup; only milk & rice, & brandy, & dry biscuits (on which I tried a little salt.

"One remembers how von Wilamowitz declared that he wd. go on reading Thomas Hardy & Anatole France"[113] . . . . . Times Lit. Sup. Jan. 16. 1919.

---

[110] The Rev. Henry Hardy, rector of Suffield since 1915, was a distant relative of Hardy. The groom's father, the Rev. William Hamlyn, had been vicar of Claybrooke since 1913. His brother, the Rt Rev. N. Temple Hamlyn (1864–1929), formerly Bishop of Accra, was vicar of Eaton, Norfolk, 1908–21. This wedding announcement is in a newspaper cutting pasted in.

[111] Noel Edward Noel-Buxton (1869–1948), later Baron Noel-Buxton, was at this time Liberal M.P. for N. Norfolk; he was later a Labour M.P., 1922–30. After much political experience overseas earlier, he was the author of several books on the Empire and oppressed peoples. The Hibbert Journal (1902–68) was a quarterly review of religion, theology and philosophy.

[112] Dr Benjamin Gowring, then practising at 49 High Street, Dorchester.

[113] Sentence taken from the leading article, 'The Scholar in Politics', written in the aftermath of the Great War: 'How many French and English scholars have had to deplore that submergence of all fairness in the passions of the moment which has cut them off from the German scholars whom they knew! Sometimes the bitterness has been mitigated; one remembers how Von Wilamowitz declared that he would go on reading Thomas Hardy and Anatole France' (TLS, No. 887 (16 Jan 1919), 26). Ulrich von Wilamowitz-Moellendorff (1848–1931), eminent German classical philologer, was a specialist in Greek tragedy.

⟨67⟩ 1919

Jan 25. Mr Prideaux[114] tells me more details of the death of Mary Channing (burnt for the poisoning of her husband, [not proven]) in 1705, in Maumbury Ring, Dorchester. They were told him by old Mr. ——, a direct descendant of one who was a witness of the execution. He said that after she had been strangled & the burning had commenced, she recovered consciousness [owing to the pain from the flames probably] & writhed and shrieked. One of the constables thrust a swab into her mouth to stop her cries, & the milk from her bosoms (she had lately given birth to a child) squirted out in their faces "and made 'em jump back."[115]

The above account, with other details handed down from my respected ancestor who was present (such as the smell of roa⟨s⟩t meat, &c.) gives sufficiently horrible picture.[116]

⟨68⟩[117]

1920. (Letters of H.J. reviewed in Times Lit. Sup. 8 April 1920)[118]
H. James on Swinburne:
"I should have liked to see you formulate & resume a little more of the creature's character & genius."
To Gosse II.258.

---

[114] Charles Prideaux, then secretary of the Dorset Field Club, was Curator of the Dorset County Museum from 1932 till his death in 1934.

[115] The first para. on this page (from '1919' to 'jump back') is pasted in from an earlier notebook. The square brackets are Hardy's.

[116] Hardy records with relish these additional details of an execution which had long held his imagination. In Ch. XI of *The Mayor of Casterbridge* (1886) Hardy had told 'that in 1705 a woman who had murdered her husband was half-strangled and then burnt there in the presence of ten thousand spectators. Tradition reports that at a certain stage of the burning her heart burst and leapt out of her body, to the terror of them all, and that not one of those ten thousand people ever cared particularly for hot roast after that.' The poem 'The Mock Wife' (*Complete Poems*, pp.762–3) is based on the incident. Hardy referred to it again, in more detail, in an article on 'Maumbury Ring' in *The Times* (9 Oct 1908, 11), and explained his reasons for believing that Mary Channing was innocent, a caution reflected in the 'not proven' of this note.

[117] Notebook p. 68 is pasted in from an earlier notebook.

[118] *The Letters of Henry James*, selected and edited by Percy Lubbock, Vols. I and II (London: Macmillan, 1920). The leading review article (*TLS*, No.951 (8 Apr 1920), 217–18) remarks the malignity of some of James's pronouncements, including the one on Hardy. This selection of extracts taken by Hardy from the book itself reflects his indignation on behalf of his good friends A.C. Swinburne (see n.88), George Meredith and Rudyard Kipling.

id. on Meredith:
- - - - - -The unspeakable Lord Ormont . . . insufferable &
unprofitable pages . . . I doubt if any equal quantity of extravagant
verbiage, of airs & graces, of phrases & attitudes, of obscurities &
alembications, ever started less their subject" &c. – I.225.

id. on Kipling:
"the great little Rudyard" I.349

id. on T.H.
"The good little Ts. Hy."[119]

⟨69⟩ 1920.

7 June. "At a Special Meeting [of the Royal Institute of British
Architects] at 8 p.m. . . . . the following candidates were elected by
show of hands . . . . .
As Hon. Fellow: Hardy, Thomas, O.M."[120]
[R.I.B.A. Essay Medallist. 1862].[121]

---

[119] James's references to Hardy occur in letters to R.L. Stevenson. 19 Mar 1892: 'The
good little Thomas Hardy has scored a great success with *Tess of the d'Urbervilles*,
which is chock-full of faults and falsity and yet has a singular beauty and charm' (Vol.
I, p.194); 17 Feb 1893: 'Most refreshing . . . was the cool trade-wind . . . of your
criticism of *ces messieurs*. I grant you Hardy with all my heart . . . I am meek and
ashamed where the public clatter is so deafening – so I bowed my head and let 'Tess of
the D. 's' pass. But oh yes, dear Louis, she is vile. The pretence of sexuality is only
equalled by the absence of it, and the abomination of the language by the author's
reputation for style. There are indeed some pretty smells and sights and sounds. But
you have better ones in Polynesia' (Vol. I, pp.204–5). Hardy was inevitably hurt by
these harsh and condescending remarks by a friend (whom he later called 'the
Polonius of novelists'). But to Hardy James had 'a ponderously warm manner of
saying nothing in infinite sentences' and his subjects were 'those one could be
interested in when there was nothing larger to think of'. Hardy's comments on James
can be found in the *Life*, 132, 181, 211, 246, 370; most were written *after* Hardy had
read James's opinions about him, and the revelation that in 1879 James was rejected
by the Rabelais Club for the lack of virility in his writing is added in Hardy's
calligraphic hand as a late insertion to the original typescript of his disguised autobiography. James's comments are cruelly dismissive but Hardy had the last word.
[120] Regarding this fellowship Hardy wrote on 7 Mar 1920 to the R.I.B.A. Vice-
President, John Slater: 'Age has naturally made me, like Gallio, care for none of these
things, at any rate very much . . . But at the same time I am very conscious of the
honour of such a proposition, and like to be reminded in such a way that I once knew
what a T-square was' (*Life*, 404).
[121] Having begun his architectural apprenticeship in Dorchester in 1856, Hardy
went to London as an assistant to Arthur Blomfield in 1862. That year he won a prize
medal from the R.I.B.A. for his essay 'The Application of Coloured Bricks and Terra
Cotta to Modern Architecture', and received the award in 1863 at the Institute's
offices in Conduit Street, London, from Sir Gilbert Scott.

W. de la Mare's long syllable:

Note. The only previous instances I know of the redundant long syllable at the end of a line, used by Walter de la Mare, occur in Beaumont & Fletcher, & Leigh Hunt. (v. works of those writers)

1920

————————————————————————

These notes are continued in next Memorandum book (similar to this) beginning 1921.)[122]

---

[122] 25 pages of this memorandum book remain unused.

'Memoranda, II'

⟨Inside cover⟩

Feb.1923.[123]

⟨1⟩

This book is to be destroyed when my executors have done with it for any necessary reference.

T.H.[124]

Memoranda — (viz: Prose Matter)

II.

1921.

Jan 1. Sat up, & heard the New Year rung in, Connie[125] being here.

— Jan. To tea at Stinsford Vicarage.
— Mr. Cowley[126] lent me copy of the Stinsford Register. Among the

---

[123] This seems to indicate the time when Hardy either began or finished recopying old notes into this second 'Memoranda' book. An entry in the *Life* (418) 'from an old note' and dated 26 Feb 1923, suggests that Hardy was still much occupied in extracting details from old notebooks for his disguised autobiography: the 'old note' in question no longer survives outside the *Life* itself. Since 25 pp. of the first notebook are unused Hardy must have chosen 1920 (when he was 80) as an appropriate terminal date for its recopied notes. In this second notebook, with entries commencing on New Year's Day 1921 but presumably written up again in 1923, there is a perceptible change in the tone and content of what Hardy records. While some notes are similar in form to those in 'Memoranda, I', others are distinctly more personal and domestic, so that in part this book becomes a diary of Hardy's activities and its contents are drawn upon for the later chapters of the *Life*. This date is inscribed on the inside cover.

[124] The instruction is written in red ink.

[125] Constance Taylor Dugdale, a sister of Florence Hardy.

[126] The Rev. H.G.B. Cowley, vicar of Stinsford, 1911–36.

entries were the following connections[127] of the Hardys (see heads-
tones):

"1723. 15 Apl. John Knight of Norris Mill buried.

"1737. 29 Dec. Judith, d. of John & Ann Knight. [burd]

"1739. 14 June. James Knight [burd.]

"1744. 1 Mar. Thomas s. of John Knight [bur]

"1755. 25 May. The Widow Knight[128]

⟨2⟩

"1757. 19 Nov. Jane. d. of John & Ann Knight [burd.]

1764. 2 Apl. Jane. d. of James & Ann Knight [burd.]
                          S.P.

1765. 28 May. Jane wife of James Knight [buried]

1771. 1 Feb. John Knight [buried]

"   2 July. Farmer Knight [buried]

1773. 18 Apl. The Widow Knight of St. Peter's, Dorchester [buried]

1776. 28 Jan. Jane d. of James & Molly Knight (?) [buried]

1783. 4 Feb. Molly wife of James Knight [buried]

1792. 22 Jan. Widow Knight [buried]

1809. 13 May. Jane[129] d. of Th. & Mary Hardy [bur.]

1810. 1 Feb. Priscilla dau. of John & Eleanor Knight [bur.]

" . 12 Feb. James Knight [buried]

1668. 2 Feb. Willm. Davis & Jane Knight [mard.]

1716. 14 June. Jethro Dober & Sarah Knight [md.]

1717. 21 Dec. John Strode & Mary Hardy [md.]

1717. 4 Jan. Wm. Knight & Mary Syms [md.]

1735. 26 May. Thomas Brown & Mary Hardy [md]

1743. 30 Jan. Wm. Runyard & Dorothy Knight [m]

⟨3⟩   Baptisms.

1720. 10 Nov. Mary d. of Richd & Mary Knight.

1731. 17 Dec. John s. of John & Ann Knight.

---

[127] The Knight family was related to the Hardys through the marriage of the
author's great-grandfather John Hardy (1756–1822) to Jane Knight (1758–1825).

[128] Jane Knight (1675–1755), widow of John Knight of Norris Mill (1676–1723)
above.

[129] Jane Hardy, the 4th child of Hardy's grandparents, died in infancy.

1733. 9 May. James s. of John & Ann Knight.

1735. 2 Apl. Jenny d. of John & Ann Knight [died Decr]

1737. 3 Apl. Judith d. of John & Ann Knight

1742. 13 March. Thomas s. of John & Ann Knight.

1749. 21 July. Ann d. of John & Ann Knight

1757. 16 May Elizth. d. of James & Jane Knight

1771. 1 Mar. Jane d. of James & Molly Knight

1775. 6 Dec. Jane d. of James & Molly Knight

1777. 10 Feb. James s. of John & Jane Keats

1779. 7 July. Jonathan s. of James & Molly Knight

1784. 28 Mar. George, s. of Eve Trevillian[130]

1791. 17 July. Jonathan s. of Eve Trevelyan

1795. 20 Sept. Hannah, base d. of Eve Trevelyan

1803. 21 Aug. John, s. of Thos. & Mary Hardy

1803. 8. Oct. Sarah d. of Wm. & Susa. Dart

1805. 10 May James s. of Th. & My. Hardy

1807. 26 July Mary Anne d. of Th. & My. Hardy

In 1809, Jane, d. of Th. & M. Hardy born & buried. not in register

1811. 28 Apl. Priscilla d. of John & Eleanor Knight

1812. 31 Jan. Ths.[131] son of Ths. & My. Hardy.

⟨4⟩ 1921.

Margery[132] here before leaving April for Canada – & little boy.
April F & I paid a visit to the Granville Barker's[133] at Netherton Hall.

---

[130] Eve Trevelyan is celebrated as Eve Greensleeves in the poem 'Voices from Things Growing in a Churchyard' (*Complete Poems*, pp.623–5), written about six months later: 'I, who as innocent withwind climb,/ Sir or Madam,/ Am one Eve Greensleeves, in olden time/ Kissed by men from many a clime,/ Beneath sun, stars, in blaze, in breeze,/ As now by glow-worms and by bees,/ All day cheerily,/ All night eerily!' (stanza 5). A footnote identifies her as Eve Trevillian or Trevelyan, 'the handsome mother of two or three illegitimate children, *circa* 1784–95'. Hardy records that Walter de la Mare went with him to Stinsford, and read the poem, on 17 June 1921 (*Life*, 413). In an unpublished passage Hardy says that he 'had discovered the story of Eve Greensleeves, of the poem, during his researches in the copy of Stinsford Register in January of this year. She was Eve Trevelyan' (typescript, DCM).

[131] Hardy's father (b. 28 Nov 1811), son of Thomas (see n.1) and Mary (1772–1857) Hardy. John, James and Mary Anne were Hardy's uncles and aunt.

[132] Florence's sister Margaret Alicia, who married Lt Soundy of the Royal Flying Corps in 1917, and her son Thomas Henry Soundy (b. 1918).

[133] Harley Granville-Barker (1877–1946), dramatist, actor-manager, Shakespearean critic, and his second wife Helen. A Fabian and champion of repertory theatre, Granville-Barker's best-known play was *The Voysey Inheritance* (1905). He produced an abridged version of *The Dynasts*, prepared by Hardy, at the Kingsway Theatre, London (25 Nov 1914–30 Jan 1915). Netherton Hall is in Sidmouth, Devon.

April 29. Margery left
Sunday May 1. F & I lunched
Apr at Herringston[134]
Wed. May 4. F. went to Enfield.[135]
Friday May 6. Margaret sailed for Canada

Times. May 3. 1921. Deaths
GIFFORD. – On the 28th April, at St. Mary's Abbey, Mill Hill,
ELLEN PRISCILLA GIFFORD (SISTER PRISCA, O.S.F.), third
daughter of the late Ven. E.H. Gifford, D.D.[136]
May 11. J M Barrie & Lady Cynthia Asquith came.[137]
12. F. took them to Bockhampton[138] – Left

⟨5⟩ 1921

May 11. Charles Moule died – He is the last of "the seven brethren."[139]

May 27. Was going to London this week but did not, on account of
death of Barrie's adopted son.[140]

---

[134] Home of Hardy's friends Capt. and Mrs Berkeley Williams; 1½ miles S. of
Dorchester.

[135] Florence Hardy had spent all her life before marriage at 5 River Front, Enfield,
home of her parents Edward Dugdale (for 40 years headmaster of St Andrew's
National School, Enfield) and his wife Emma.

[136] One of Emma Hardy's cousins, daughter of Dr Edwin Gifford, former Archdeacon of London; she had become a Sister of the Order of St Francis. (This is a
newspaper cutting pasted in.)

[137] Sir James Barrie (1860–1937), Scottish novelist and dramatist, author of *The
Admirable Crichton* (1902) and *Dear Brutus* (1917) but best known for the dramatic
fantasy *Peter Pan* (1904). A friend for many years, he was at Max Gate when Hardy
died in 1928 and he arranged for Hardy's burial in Poet's Corner, Westminster
Abbey.

Lady Cynthia Asquith (1887–1960), novelist and biographer, was Barrie's secretary
1918–37. This visit is recalled in her *Portrait of J.M. Barrie* (London, 1954), pp. 104–11;
and in 'Thomas Hardy at Max Gate', a 1956 BBC Home Service talk reprinted in
Monographs of the Life, Times and Works of Thomas Hardy, No.63 (St Peter Port, Guernsey, 1969).

[138] Lady Cynthia says that it was Hardy who accompanied them.

[139] Charles Walker Moule (b.1836), Senior Fellow and President of Corpus, Cambridge. In their youth he and Hardy had 'visited mediaeval buildings together, and
dived from a boat on summer mornings into the green water of Weymouth Bay' (*Life*,
387). 'The seven brethren' were the outstanding sons of the Rev. Henry Moule, vicar
of Fordington 1829–80: Henry (1825–1904), George (1828–1912), Frederick
(1830–1900), Hardy's close friend Horace (1832–73), Arthur (1834–?), Charles
(1836–1921) and Handley (1841–1920).

[140] Michael Llewelyn Davies had been drowned with another undergraduate when

May 26 or 27. Middleton Murry[141] came & stayed a night.

29. (Sunday) Lord Coleridge[142] came to tea, also Walter Mills his marshal.

June 2. Birthday remembered by newspapers, & an address from younger writers.[143]

June 5. To Netherton Hall – met Putnam.

June 9. To Kingston House with F. & on to Sturminster Newton with Mr. Hanbury.[144]

Performance in castle ruins – tea at Archdn. Wards. To Riverside.[145]

⟨6⟩

Lit. Supt. article on Coventry Patmore's criticisms.
(May 26. 1921)[146]

". . . Much of Wordsworth (here Mr Patmore would not agree) is oppressive because the poet has not seen nature with intensity either in relation to his poem, to himself, or to other human beings; but has accepted her as something in herself so desirable that description can be used in flat stretches without concentration. Tennyson is, of course, the master of these Victorian poets who carried descriptive writing to such a pitch that if their words had

bathing outside Oxford on 19 May. His barrister father had died in 1907 and his mother in 1910, on which occasion Barrie adopted their five sons.

[141] John Middleton Murry (1889–1957), literary critic and later biographer of his wife, short story writer Katherine Mansfield (1888–1923).

[142] Bernard, 2nd Baron Coleridge (1851–1927), High Court Judge 1907–23.

[143] The address, signed by 106 writers & presented by a deputation at Max Gate on Hardy's 81st birthday, was conceived by St John Ervine & is reproduced in the *Life*, 412–13. Hardy was also given a first edition of Keats's *Lamia*.

[144] Kingston Maurward House, which Hardy had known since childhood, was owned from 1916 by Mr (later Sir) and Mrs Cecil Hanbury. As a result of their close friendship Hardy became godfather to their daughter Caroline in Sep 1921, when his gift to her was the manuscript of the poem 'To C.F.H.' in a silver box. The house is the original of Knapwater House in *Desperate Remedies*.

[145] *The Mellstock Quire*, adapted from *Under the Greenwood Tree* by Alfred H. Evans (1862–1946) in 1910, was performed by the Hardy Players. Riverside Villa, Sturminster Newton, was the home of Hardy and Emma from 3 July 1876 to 18 Mar 1878, and in it Hardy wrote *The Return of the Native*. It was the first home Hardy owned. The Ven. Algernon Ward was the present incumbent of Sturminster Newton vicarage.

[146] *TLS*, No. 1010 (26 May 1921), 331: a review of Patmore's *Courage in Politics, and Other Essays* (London: Humphrey Milford, 1921). The poet Patmore (1823–96), friend of Tennyson and Ruskin and a contributor to the Pre-Raphaelite journal *The Germ*, was greatly impressed by the 'unequalled beauty and power' of Hardy's *A Pair of Blue Eyes*, which he continually had read aloud to him from 1875 to 1896 (cf. *Life*, 104–5, 302).

been visible the black birds would certainly have descended upon
their garden plots to feed upon the apples and plums. Yet we do not
feel that this is poetry so much as something fabricated by an
ingenious craftsman for our delight. Of the moderns Mr Hardy is
without rival in his power to make Nature do his will, so that she
neither satiates nor serves as a curious toy, but appears at the right
moment to heighten, charm, or terrify, because the necessary fusion
has already taken place. The first step towards this absorption is to
see things with your own eyes."[147]

⟨7⟩

June 12. Sunday. To Stinsford etc.
√ " 16. Walter de la Mare came.[148]
" 17. To Stinsford with W. de la M.
" 18. de la M. left. F & I went to Bincleaves, Weymouth, being
fetched by the Reynolds's in their car, & brought back.

√ 20. Mr Spicer-Simson came to make a medallion.[149]
25. Mr & Mrs Masefield called – also Mr & Miss Dampier
Whetham.[150] Rain at last after long drought.

28. To High Stoy[151] with Col. & Mrs. Inglis.
29. The Inglises. Dean of Salisbury & Mr Niven.[152]

---

[147] The editorial principle adopted in this transcription is to present Hardy's
abbreviations and contractions as they appear but this has been waived for this entry
since this short passage contains almost 50 contractions, the faithful reproduction of
which would serve no sensible purpose.
[148] The poet Walter de la Mare (1873–1956), a frequent visitor at Max Gate during
Hardy's last decade. 'I am getting to know quite a lot of the young Georgians,' Hardy
told Florence Henniker, 'and have quite a paternal feeling, or grandpaternal, towards
them' (letter, 2 July 1921). In the middle of one night shortly before he died, Hardy
asked for de la Mare's 'The Listeners' (in a first edition given him by the author during
this 1921 visit) to be read to him.
[149] Theodore Spicer-Simson depicted Hardy's head on a bronze medallion in an
edition of 25 copies. Hardy's cast, No.3, is now in the DCM.
[150] John Masefield (1878–1967), another 'Georgian' poet, became Poet Laureate in
1930. Cecil Dampier Whetham, formerly Fellow and Tutor of Trinity College, Cambridge, who owned a dairy farm in the country of The Woodlanders, had three years
earlier received Hardy's permission to name a breed of pedigree cattle he was
establishing the Hintock herd. His sister Catherine published a volume of war
verses.
[151] High Stoy (846 ft.) is a wooded hill ½ a mile N.W. of Minterne Magna and 9 miles
N. of Dorchester.

30. Mr & Mrs Nicholson. Mr. N. sketched me.[153]

√ July 1. Nicholson finished.

2. Company of actors preparing film of Mayor of Casterbridge.[154]

⟨8⟩

FAMOUS HARDY PLAYER TO WED. – Widespread interest has been aroused by the announcement that Miss Gertrude Bugler,[155] the popular leading lady of the Hardy players, is shortly to be married to her cousin, Mr. Ernest F. Bugler, farmer, of Woodbury House, Beaminster. The prospective bridegroom was during the war captain in the 35th Sikhs, and won the Military Cross. The ceremony will take place at Stinsford Church – the "Mellstock" church of Mr. Thomas Hardy's novels – on |Monday,| Sunday September |19th,| 11th and it will probably be attended by the Hardy players, with whom Miss Bugler has been so long associated in her dramatic triumphs.

---

[152] The Dean, Dr Andrew Burn; the rector of St Peter's, Dorchester, Dr George Niven.

[153] (Sir) William Nicholson (1872–1949), founder member of the National Portrait Gallery, 1911. This sketch was for *Selected Poems of Thomas Hardy* (London: Riccardi Press Books, 1921), with portrait and title-page design by Nicholson.

[154] This 5500 ft. film was made by the Progress Film Co., produced by Frank Spring and directed by Sidney Morgan. The cast included Fred Groves (Henchard), Pauline Peters (Susan), Warwick Ward (Farfrae), Nell Emerald (Furmity Woman) and Mavis Clare (Elizabeth-Jane). Hardy was invited by the film-makers to watch some of their location filming and he drove with the actors through Dorchester to Maiden Castle. He had already approved the scenario and promised to 'see to the dialect of the titles' (letter to Morgan, 22 Mar 1921).

[155] This entry is a newspaper cutting pasted in; the emendations as indicated are in Hardy's hand. Gertrude Bugler (1896–), the beautiful daughter of a Dorchester baker, first met Hardy in 1913 when she was rehearsing the role of Marty South, but it was after the war that she had her most notable success as Eustacia (1920) and Tess (1924). In early 1925, after the latter performance, Frederick Harrison (manager of the Haymarket Theatre, London) invited Mrs Bugler to play Tess in London, with Hardy's encouragement. But Florence Hardy intervened and, pleading that the project was overexciting her husband, persuaded Mrs Bugler to abandon this chance of a lifetime. Sydney Cockerell's diary records Florence's anxiety because Hardy had ignored her 45th birthday, been offhand and 'spoke roughly to her', and her distress over 'his infatuation for the local Tess, Mrs Bugler, which had been the subject of much gossip in Dorchester' (Wilfrid Blunt, *Cockerell* (London, 1964), pp. 214–16). Hardy was undoubtedly charmed by Gertrude Bugler, who later recalled his laughter and personal kindness. After her last visit to Max Gate during his lifetime, Hardy insisted on accompanying Mrs Bugler down the drive, and suddenly told her: 'If anyone asks you if you knew Thomas Hardy, say "Yes, he was my friend."' (Cf. Gertrude Bugler, *Personal Recollections of Thomas Hardy* (Dorchester: Dorset Natural History and Archaeological Society, 1962), reproducing a talk given on 7 Apr 1959.)

⟨9⟩

July 3. Sunday. To St. Peter's. Bockhampton.[156]

July 5. Bicycled with F. to Kingston to inquire for Mrs. Hanbury & Mr. Jeune,[157] & thence to Talbothays.[158] Tea in summr. house. Bicycled home.

6. Mr Jeune called.

12. F. went to London to see Lady Barrett.[159]

13. Returned.

20. Bazaar in aid of County Hospital. Supported Ld. Ellenborough[160] at the opening ceremony. F. also on platform, & the mayor of Dorchester. F. presented with a nosegay.

In evening driven in by Dr. Cosens to see the dancing in B. Gardens.[161] Saw "The Lancers"

———————

[July. Agreed to pay annual subscriptn. to Society of Authors of £2. 2. 0 till further notice][162]

———————

[156] Hardy attended matins to hear the morning hymn, 'Awake, my soul' by Bishop Thomas Ken (1637–1711), sung by the choir to the setting of François Barthélémon (1741–1808). This had been arranged for him by the rector and inspired the sonnet 'Barthélémon at Vauxhall'.

[157] Mrs 'Dodo' Hanbury (see n.144), who was pregnant, and her father, Symonds Jeune, both of whom had been unwell. Jeune was Clerk of the House of Lords. He and his late brother, whom Hardy had known very well, were related to the author by marriage: the second wife of Emma Hardy's uncle Dr Edwin Gifford (see n.106) was their sister. Francis Jeune, a divorce court judge, became Baron St Helier and died in 1905.

[158] A house built near West Stafford (two miles outside Dorchester) by Hardy's brother Henry on farm land previously owned by their father. Henry lived there with their sisters Mary and Katherine.

[159] Lady Florence Barrett (d.1945), surgeon and gynaecologist, specialist in sexual function and conception control.

[160] Col Cecil Law, 6th Baron Ellenborough (1849–1931) of Prince of Wales Road, Dorchester; formerly a professional soldier and at this time chairman of the Dorset Territorial Association.

[161] Dr William Burrough Cosens, then practising in Dorchester, drove Hardy to the Borough Gardens. This note continues on notebook p.11.

[162] Hardy had succeeded George Meredith as President of the Society of Authors in 1909. In June 1920 he received a deputation to mark his 80th birthday and in August was sent an illuminated address by members (now in DCM). The last thing that Hardy ever wrote, on 10 Jan 1928, the day before he died, was a cheque for his subscription to the society's pension fund.

⟨10⟩

<u>Stravinsky:-</u>[163]

Mr. Simmonds of Putney has, at any rate, assimilated one of the static principles and fixed ideas of all ages, for he says "<u>Art is good art only inasmuch as it *corroborates* something in our mental or emotional make-up, expresses for us some of the yearnings and aspirations that struggle for voice within us.</u>" So evidently there is hope for him if he takes the trouble to educate himself. But if Stravinsky expresses his yearnings and aspirations he must be atavistic as well as merely very young, for one can only imagine that he must throw back to one or other of those priests of Baal who leaped upon the altar and cut themselves with knives while the more sophisticated Elijah (*vide* Mark Twain) was putting into effect his discovery of the uses of petroleum.

Piccadilly, July 25.   C.G. GREY[164]

Sunday Times. July 31, 1921.
also –

But all this is interesting only as doctrine, or as analysis. It really does not matter a farthing's worth in the long run; <u>all that matters is the quality of the music.</u> All Europe, a generation or two ago, was full of similar expositions of the ideals of Wagner and of Liszt. Wagner has survived <u>not because he theorised well, but because he</u> wrote first-rate music. Liszt's theories of instrumental music were, as far as they went, quite as good as Wagner's theories of musical drama; but no one troubles about Liszt's theories now, because the best music he could write in illustration of them was only second-rate.

Ernest Newman.[165] ib.

---

[163] Both of these entries are newspaper cuttings pasted in; the underlining in each passage is by Hardy and in red ink. 'Sunday' to 'also—'and 'Ernest Newman. ib.' are also in Hardy's hand. *'Vide'* is the newspaper's italic.

[164] C.G. Grey (1875–1953), celebrated writer on aviation.

[165] Ernest Newman (1868–1959), author of studies of Strauss and Elgar; his *magnum opus* was *The Life of Richard Wagner* (4 vols., 1933–47). He was music critic of *Sunday Times*, 1920–58.

⟨11⟩[166]

danced (for probably the last time) at my request. Home at 10.
Outside our gate – full moon over cottage – Band still heard playing.
21.
23. "Barthélémon at Vauxhall" – (my sonnet) appeared in "The
Times."[167]
24. Sunday. People came.

26. With F. called on Mr. and Mrs. Cochrane at Athelhampton.[168]
28. Letter in Times about "Hardy" players.[169]
29. Leader in Times about the same.[170]
31. Sunday. Mr Odell Shepard (Prof. of Eng. Litre. Trinity College,
Hartford, Connecticut, U.S.A.).[171]

August

⟨12⟩ 1921.

Sept. 1. At christening of Mrs. Hanbury's little girl "Caroline Fox"[172]
– 12.30 afterwards lunched

---

[166] This continues from the penultimate entry on notebook p.9 ('Saw "The Lancers"').

[167] See n.156.

[168] Athelhampton is a small village near Puddletown; George Cochrane, J.P., was
at this time lord of the manor. Athelhampton Hall, a fifteenth-century mansion with
sixteenth-century additions, is the setting for the poem 'The Dame of Athelhall'.

[169] From R.L. Bosworth Smith, Broadstone, 23 July: 'The Hardy Players/Coun-
tryside Drama' (The Times, 28 July 1921, p.13). He praises the players who 'do
something to encourage the people to read and take a pride in the writings of their
own famous authors . . . [and] help to make one class understand another better.'
Recent performances of Far from the Madding Crowd and Under the Greenwood Tree at
the manor house at Bingham's Melcombe, with an audience of nearly 800, had raised
over £100 for charity. The correspondent hopes that other owners of beautiful houses
will throw them open so that 'all sorts and conditions of people are brought together
for a few hours and share a common joy in the beauties of nature.'

[170] 'Drama and Village Life', p.11. Following the theme of the previous day's letter
the editorial observes that 'rarely are the means of raising money for charity as
beneficial to the community as the money raised; yet we cannot doubt that Dorset
and its visitors get as much good out of the plays as the charities get out of them. . . .
Local drama . . . gives at least a glimpse of what art is and of the place that art can hold
in ordinary life.' The sentiments of letter and editorial would appeal to Hardy.

[171] Odell Shepard (1884–1967), American author and critic.

[172] Hardy was godfather (see n.144).

4. To Stinsford evens service with F. A beautiful evening. Evening Hymn W Tallis.[173]

14. Mr. Schuster, & his nephew Mr Wild, came to lunch, bringing Siegried Sassoon[174] with them in their car.

Sept 16. Up to this date the following poems not yet collected in a volume have appeared in periodicals:-

–"Barthélémon at Vauxhall." Times July 23.21[175]
–"Jezreel." Times. Sept 27. 1918. ('no copyrt.')[176]
"According to the Mighty Working." Athenaeum
April 4. 1919.[177]
T.O.

⟨13⟩

"The Master & the Leaves." The Owl. Apl.1919.
   (also privately printed by F.)[178]
"Faintheart in a Ry. Train." London Mercury about Nov.1919.[179]
"The Whitewashed Wall." Reveille Magazine Autumn 1918.[180]
"The Peace Peal." Graphic. About Aug.'19.[181]

---

[173] 'Glory to thee, my God, this night' by Bishop Ken, set to a tune by Thomas Tallis (c.1515–85) which first appeared in Day's Psalter (1560).

[174] Siegried Sassoon (1896–1967), author of satirical war poetry, also well-known for Memoirs of a Fox-Hunting Man (1928) and Memoirs of an Infantry Officer (1930), both semi-autobiographical fiction. In 1919 he arranged for Hardy to be presented with a bound volume of original poems from 43 poets in honour of his 79th birthday.

[175] Page 11. Hardy was collecting poems for his forthcoming Late Lyrics and Earlier volume, the ms. of which was despatched to Macmillan on 23 Jan 1922, and which was published on 23 May following. All the poems listed here, with the exception of 'The Peace Peal', are included.

[176] Page 7. No copyright was reserved since it was a wartime poem, inspired by the capture of the ancient Palestinian city by the British in Sep 1918.

[177] Page 129.

[178] The Owl (May 1919), p.5. Also privately printed by Florence Hardy in Sep 1919, in an edition of 25 copies.

[179] 'Faintheart in a Railway Train', published as 'A Glimpse from the Train', London Mercury (Jan 1920), p.265.

[180] Nov 1918, p.175.

[181] Collected in Human Shows, Far Phantasies, Songs, and Trifles, published 20 Nov 1925.

"By $\left\{ \begin{array}{l} \text{Mellstock} \\ \text{Henstridge} \end{array} \right\}$ Cross[182] at the Year's End" – <u>Fortnightly.</u>
Dec.1919.[183]
"Going & Staying." London Mercy. Nov.1919[184]
"The Country Wedding." Newman Flower. Cassell.[185]
"At the entering of the New Year." <u>Athenaeum</u> 1920–1?[186]
"And There was a Great Calm." <u>Times</u> Nov.11.20.[187]
"The Woman I met." London Mercury. Apl. 1921[188]
"The maid of K. Mandeville." Athenaeum. Ap.30.20[189]
"The two houses." N.Y. Dial. Aug.1921.[190]
"The Sailor's Mother." Anglo-Italian Revw. 1918[191]

(contd. next leaf)

⟨14⟩ 1921

Sept. latter half. Sitting to Mr. Ouless.[192]
Oct. 14. John Masefield & Mrs M came on their way to Galsworthy[193]
at Manaton. Brought a full-rigger ship as a present for me – made by
himself.[194] Sitting to Ouless still.[195]

---

[182] 'Mellstock' in the original title was replaced by 'Henstridge'.
[183] Pages 801–2.
[184] Page 7 (minus the third stanza).
[185] Originally entitled 'The Fiddler's Story' (in a privately printed edition of 25 copies for Florence Hardy), the poem appeared in *Cassell's Winter Annual, 1921—22*, pp.67–8, in response to a request from Newman Flower. The annual appeared two months later than this note.
[186] 31 Dec 1920, p.881.
[187] Page iii of a special Armistice Day supplement.
[188] Pages 584–6.
[189] 'The Maid of Keinton Mandeville'; page 565.
[190] Pages 127–9.
[191] Sep 1918, p.1.
[192] Walter William Ouless (1848–1933). Originally a subject painter, from 1880 he concentrated on portraiture and built a reputation as one of its most reliable exponents; elected R.A. in 1881 and a Senior Academician in 1924.
[193] John Galsworthy (1867–1933), playwright and author of the series of novels collectively entitled 'The Forsyte Saga', of which the main theme is the acquisitive instinct, from *The Man of Property* (1906) to *Swan Song* (1928). When the former appeared, Hardy told Mrs Henniker that he 'began it, but found the people too materialistic and sordid to be interesting' (letter, 12 Sep 1906). Galsworthy became a good friend and was a pall-bearer at Hardy's funeral. His home was at Wingstone, nr. Manaton, Moretonhampstead, Devon.
[194] 'This ship had been named by its maker *The Triumph*, and was much valued by Hardy, who showed it with pride to callers at Max Gate, with the story of how it arrived' (*Life*, 154).
[195] Hardy bequeathed this portrait in oil to the National Portrait Gallery.

18. In afternoon to Stinsford with F. A matchless Oct. sunshine, mist, & turning leaves.

Nov. 7. The Stanleys came as cook & odd man.[196]

Dec 31. New Years' Eve. Heard the muffled peal in bed.

Nov. 4. "Voices from things growing" sent to London Mercury.[197]

Nov 4. "An autumn rain-scene" sent to Fortnightly."[198]

Nov 7. "The Haunting Fingers" . . . to New Republic[199]

[See later]

⟨15⟩   1922.

January. In bed with a chill (the old bladder complaint)[200] the last fortnight or so of the month. Added a Preface to the Poems.[201]
23. Sent MS. of Poems entitled "Late Lyrics & Earlier, with many other verses" to Macmillans'.[202]

Feb. chill getting better slowly.
11. Katy called.[203]
Feb.12 Florence seized with influenza
" 13, 14: trying days.
" 18. Whibley & Ernest Debenham called.[204]
19. F. seems better.

---

[196] Mrs Adolphine Stanley, formerly housemaid to Florence Hardy's parents in London, recalled her and her husband's service with Hardy, whom she found 'a difficult and a quaint man', in *Hardyana* (*Monographs*, No.14 (Beaminster, Dorset, 1967), pp.14–17), though her recollected dates do not correspond to Hardy's.

[197] Published Dec 1921, pp.119–20.

[198] Published as 'A December Rain-Scene' in *Fortnightly Review* (Dec 1921), p.881.

[199] Published 21 Dec 1921, p.103; later entitled 'Haunting Fingers'.

[200] An unpublished typescript passage in the *Early Life* (DCM) says that Hardy had been troubled intermittently with this since his illness in 1880.

[201] This 'energetic' preface, Hardy's longest and most explicit essay on poetry and the state of criticism, was regretted by some friends who thought that 'it betrayed an oversensitiveness to criticism which it were better the world should not know' (*Life*, 415). See the Appendix for more of Hardy's reactions to critics.

[202] Hardy's sixth volume of poetry, containing 151 poems.

[203] Hardy's younger sister Katherine (1856–1940), a former schoolteacher.

[204] Charles Whibley (1859–1930), scholar, critic and journalist; (Sir) Ernest Debenham (d.1950), of Blackdown House, Briantspuddle, Dorset.

Wedny. Feb. 15. Caddy came as gardener at 30/- a week[205]

⟨16⟩

Feb 21. See in The Times an announcement of the death of Charles Edwin Gifford, C.B. (on the 18th), at Margery Grove, Lower Kingswood, Surrey, aged 78 – Paymaster-in-Chief, Royal Navy, "who for 47 years served in the accountant branch of the R.N. & held many important posts on the staffs of Admirals & also at the Admiralty."[206]

Feb 23. Poems sent to Macmillan to arrange for periodicals, before the volume comes out:[207]
    Weathers[208]
    Summer Schemes
    The Garden Seat
    I was not he
    The selfsame song
    The Children & Sir Nameless.[209]

⟨17⟩

1922. April 6. Sent to printers the corrected revise of Late |Poems| Lyrics & Earlier.

---

[205] Mr Caddy remained until 1926 when he was succeeded by Bertie Norman Stephens, whom Hardy engaged at 32/– a week.

[206] Charles Gifford, son of one of Emma Hardy's brothers, was recalled by Emma as one of 'two bright boy-cousins' (*Some Recollections*, p.28). After his death Hardy wrote to Mrs Henniker: 'So friends and acquaintances thin out, and we who remain have to "close up"' (1 Mar 1922).

[207] Hardy had written to Sir Frederick Macmillan on 21 Feb offering to forward some of the many poems in the forthcoming volume which had not been published in magazines, after receiving requests for such from American periodicals 'as if they were suddenly waking up after long indifference.' Macmillan replied that Hardy could expect 'a considerable sum' for the poems so that it might be worth while to postpone the volume for a few weeks. Hardy replied on 23 Feb enclosing these poems and agreeing to the proposal, and remarking that 'if . . . we should inadvertently anticipate the magazine, well, I could return the payment or a part of it as I imagine the chief advantage of letting the poems be published serially over there is the publicity they will obtain.' In fact this was rather short notice and Macmillans only succeeded in placing two of the poems before the volume was published on 23 May. The others have had no separate publication. Hardy took a detailed interest in business transactions relating to his works.

[208] *Good Housekeeping* (May 1922), p.5.

[209] *Nash's and Pall Mall Magazine* (May 1922), p.198.

April 12. Mem: William Kethe, who versified the 100th Psalm (old vn. "All people that on earth do dwell") was rector of Child Okeford, Dorset, 1561–1608. [v. Dic.Nat.Biog.][210]

April 5 (about) Barrie came for one night.
14. Good Friday. Cockerell[211] came for one night. Barkers came to tea.

24. Twenty books given to the Grammar School Boys' Library. 5 by self (Madding Crowd, Greenwood Tree, Mayor of C, Blue Eyes & Laodicean) & 15 by other writers, with a request that the librarian or head master will ⟨18⟩ examine if they are fit, & change any that may not be so; as I don't know the ages of the boys, & only send my own because asked to.
 The other books were.

Stories by English Authors (Houghton, Mifflin)	10
War Poetry (American Anthologists)	– 2
Eudocia (E. Philpotts)[212]	– 1
Dewar's Glamour of Earth[213]	– 1
Windmill Lane – Allen Clarke[214]	– 1

<u>Prose & Poetry</u> – "It is certain that the poetic form, by music as well as brevity, has conveyed you out of yourself & made its whole effect

---

[210] William Kethe (d.1608?), Protestant divine, from 1554 exiled with others at Frankfurt during the Marian prosecutions. Mary died 1558 and Kethe returned to England 1561, becoming rector of Okeford Superior in the parish of Child Okeford. He accompanied the Earl of Warwick to Le Havre 1563 as minister to the English army. Kethe is now remembered chiefly for his 25 metrical psalms, first printed in the English Psalter issued at Geneva, 1561. Child Okeford is 3 miles E. of Sturminster Newton.
[211] Sydney Carlyle Cockerell (1867–1962), friend of several literary figures including in his youth Ruskin and William Morris, was Director of the Fitzwilliam Museum, Cambridge, 1908–37. In 1911 Hardy invited him to distribute his mss. among various libraries and upon Hardy's death Cockerell was appointed, with Mrs Hardy, his literary co-executor.
[212] Eden Philpotts, *Eudocia* (London: Heinemann, 1921). Philpotts (1862–1960), a literary disciple influenced markedly by Hardy in several novels, became a friend around 1915.
[213] George Dewar, *The Glamour of the Earth* (London: G. Allen, 1904).
[214] Allen Clarke, *Windmill Land* ['Rambles in a rural, old-fashioned country, with chat about its history and romance': concerning Lancashire] (London: J.M. Dent, 1916).

more swiftly: & this may be a sign that poetry is made out of feelings not necessarily deeper than the feelings in prose, but more intensely concentrated"

Times Lit. Sup. 27 Apl. 22[215]

⟨19⟩

Thursday Ap. 27. F. has gone to London to attend Private View to-morrow, &c.

May 22. With F. in Mr. Wm. Watkins's car to Bournemouth & back.[216]

May 23. "Late Lyrics & Earlier" published

24. In Mr. W. Watkins's car to Sturminster Newton by Slyres & P'hinton. Back by Bishops Caundell & the Sherborne Road. Took F. & K.[217]

26. To Talbothays (car) by way of Stinsford Ch. & Higher Bockn. House at the latter shabby, & garden. Just went through into heath, & up plantation to top of garden.[218]

⟨20⟩

May 29. From old notes written before "The Dynasts":-[219]

---

[215] *TLS*, No. 1058 (27 Apr 1922), 266: leading review article (265–6) on J. Middleton Murry, *The Problem of Style* (London: Humphrey Milford, 1922). The preceding sentence is: 'Read, for instance, a fine lyric or two of Mr Hardy's, and then the scene after Tess's revelation or the first chapter of "The Return of the Native". It is hard to say that there is more emotion in the poetry than in the prose; you cannot be sure, even, that the lyrics are more "personal". But it is certain . . .'

[216] William Watkins was the hon. sec. of the Society of Dorset Men in London. Hardy relates that Watkins's death in Apr 1925 was apparently sensed in advance by the dog Wessex, who greeted his friend at Max Gate on 18 Apr with a 'piteous whine' and behaved uneasily throughout the visit. Next morning Watkins's son telephoned the news that his father had died suddenly about an hour after returning to his hotel (*Life*, 427–8).

[217] Slyres Lane (the present B3143) is a direct route to Piddlehinton, which is 4 miles N. and slightly E. of Dorchester. Hardy was visiting his former home at Sturminster Newton on this occasion. Bishop's Caundle (present spelling) is 14 miles N. of Dorchester and the Sherborne Road is now the A352. Hardy and Watkins were accompanied by Florence and Hardy's sister Kate. Motoring was one of Hardy's favourite relaxations in later years and this was a popular drive.

[218] The *Life* adds: 'It was becoming increasingly painful to Hardy to visit this old home of his, and often when he left he said that he would go there no more' (415).

[219] Cf. 'Memoranda, I', notebook p. 27, note of 13 Mar 1874.

We – the people = Humanity – a collective personality – (Thus "we" could be engaged in the battle of Hohenlinden, say, & in the battle of Waterloo)
– Dwell with genial human on "our" getting into a rage for "we" knew not what.
The intelligence of this collective personality Humanity is pervasive, ubiquitous, like that of God. Hence, e.g., on the one hand we could hear the roar of the cannon, discern the rush of the battalions, on the other hear the voice of a man protesting, &c.
Tit: "Self-slaughter": divided agst. ourselves"
   Now these three (or 3,000) whirling through space at the rate of 40 miles a second – (God's view).

T.O.

⟨21⟩

"Some of our family who" (the We of one nation speaking of the "we" of another)
– A battle. army as somnambulists – not knowing what it is for –
– "We were called Artillery" &c "We were so under the spell of habit that" (drill)

It is now necessary to call the readers attention to those of us who were harnessed & collared in blue & brass . . . .
Poem – the difference between what things are & what they ought to be (stated as by a god to the gods – i.e. as god's story.)
Poem – I = First Cause. omniscient, not omnipotent – limitations, difficulties &c from being only able to work by Law. (His only failing is lack of foresight.)
We will now ask the reader to look ⟨22⟩ eastward with us . . . at what the contingent of us out that way were doing.
Poem. A spectral force seen acting in a man (e.g. Nap.)[220] & he acting under it – a pathetic sight, this compulsion.

Patriotism, if ∧ aggressive & ∧ at the expense of other countries, is a vice: if in sympathy with them, a virtue.⟨o⟩

---

[220] Napoleon.

July (during)
- F. Henniker[221] came – drove in Blackmoor Vale
- Siegried Sassoon came
- Edmund Blunden   ''   [222]
- E.M. Forster[223]
20th. With the latter to performance of Mids. Night's Dream on lawn of Trinity Rectory.
- July – garden party at Athelhampton (Mrs. Cochrane)[224]
Eva Dugdale here.[225]
Aug 2. Cycled with F. to Talbothays.[226]

⟨23⟩

√ Aug. I am convinced that it is better for a writer to know a little bit of the world remarkably well than to know a great part of the world remarkably little.

Aug 4. Squire, Belloc, & Gregory came.[227]
    12. Sir Clifford Allbutt[228] & Lady A came.

---

[221] Florence Henniker (1855–1923). Born the Hon. Florence Mil·······, married Lt (later Major-Gen.) Arthur Henniker, 1882. Hardy met her in 1893 and found her a 'charming, *intuitive* woman'. Fifteen years his junior, she was also a writer (six novels, three volumes of stories) and Hardy collaborated with her on the story 'The Spectre of the Real' (1893, his only collaboration). They enjoyed a close friendship and a fairly large correspondence survives (*One Rare Fair Woman*, ed. E. Hardy & F.B. Pinion). Hardy's emotional attraction to her is clear and a telling statement in the typescript of the *Later Years* is omitted from the published version: 'Some of his best short poems were inspired by her.'
[222] Edmund Blunden (1896–1974), poet and scholar, later author of a critical biography of Hardy (1942). Blunden recalls this two-day visit in *Guest of Thomas Hardy* (*Monographs*, No.10 (Beaminster, Dorset, 1964)).
[223] Edward Morgan Forster (1879–1970), novelist, whose works include *Where Angels Fear to Tread* (1905), the semi-autobiographical *The Longest Journey* (1907), *Howards End* (1910) and *A Passage to India* (1924).
[224] See n.168.
[225] Florence Hardy's sister.
[226] Hardy was fit enough to cycle well into his eighties; he was now 82.
[227] (Sir) John C. Squire (1884–1958), essayist and short story writer, successively literary editor, then editor of the *New Statesman* (1913–18) and editor of the *London Mercury* (1919–34); Hilaire Belloc (1870–1953), poet, novelist, essayist, biographer and critic; I have been unable to identify Gregory.
[228] Sir T. Clifford Allbutt (1836–1925), Regius Prof. of Medicine at Cambridge since 1892. Hardy gives a vivid account of being taken to a private lunatic asylum by Dr Allbutt, then a Commissioner in Lunacy, in 1891 (cf. *Life*, 236). There is good evidence that George Eliot drew the character of Lydgate in *Middlemarch* (1872) at least in part from Allbutt.

Times
Sat. Aug 12
1922
         LOCK. – On Friday, the 11th Aug., at "The Toft,"
         Bridlington, BENJAMIN FOSSETT LOCK, Judge of
         the County Court, East Riding Circuit, aged 74.
         Funeral at Priory Church, Bridlington, on Tuesday,
         15th Aug.[229]

Sunday 13. Lady Crewe, Ld. Aldington & | Miss (?) | Mrs Baring | (?) |
came to tea. Also Mr Jeune & Lady Brackenbury.[230]

22. Sir Maurice de Bunsen & Lady De B. & girls called.[231] Also Mr.
Jeune & Mr Arnold Forster.

Sept 4. F's sister Ethel[232] came
     5. F. went to London & Enfield

⟨24⟩

The Sánkhyas use them[233] to prove that the whole world,[234] every
constituent part is for an end, has for its author that which possesses
no sentience – nature.
     F. Hall. Hindu Philos. Syst. (1862)[235]
               from Ox. Dic., "Sentience"[236]
[See Hall, Fitzedward.[237] Dic. Nat. Biog. 22d Supplt.]

---

[229] Judge Lock, born in Dorchester, former vice-president of the Society of Dorset
Men in London, of which Hardy had been president. An early friend, his death
occasioned the poem 'Nothing Matters Much' (*Complete Poems*, p.819). This is a
newspaper cutting pasted in; Hardy has written the reference beside it.
[230] Lady Crewe (d.1967), daughter of Lord Rosebery, who married Mrs Henniker's
younger brother Robert, Lord Crewe, as his second wife in 1899; Symonds Jeune (see
n.157); Lady Brackenbury, wife of Sir Cecil Brackenbury of the Indian Civil Service.
[231] Sir Maurice de Bunsen (1852–1932), retired diplomat, and his wife Berta; they
had four daughters.
[232] Mrs Ethel Manwell Richardson
[233] I.e. God's works.
[234] Insert 'of which'.
[235] Fitzedward Hall, *The Hindu Philosophical System* (London, 1862), p.77.
[236] Defined in the OED (whence Hardy takes the quotation from Hall) as 'the
condition or quality of being sentient, consciousness, susceptibility to sensation'. The
Hindu notion appeals to Hardy's ideas of an insentient Will.
[237] Fitzedward Hall (1825–1901), philologist who spent many years in India and
later became Prof. of Sanskrit at Cambridge. He edited the *Sankhyapravachana* (1856)
and the *Sankhyasâna* (1862), fourteenth and fifteenth-century works on the Sankhya
materialist system of philosophy.

⟨25⟩

returning 7th. [238]
Sept 8. Cockerell came.
9.
10. Sunday. To lunch at the Hornby's Chantmarle, [239] taking Cockerell to stay.
11. In Newman Flower's [240] car, with him & his wife & boy, & F. to Sturminr. Newton, & back by Bishop's Caundell, Glanville's Woolton, Middlemarsh, & Dogbury Gate, where we lunched. Walked to top of High Stoy with Flower (probably for the last time), thence back home. [241] A beautiful drive.
12. F, Ethel, & I to Puddletown.
13. Ethel left.

19. F.W. Slater came (for signature) [242]
Oct 12. Walked across Boucher's Close to Eweleaze Stile. [243]
Oct 13. F. went to London & Enfield for Madeline Allhusen's [244] wedding tomorrow.

⟨26⟩

R. Bridges [245] on Free Verse.
"The main effectual difference between the rhythms of the old metrical verse & of fine prose is that in the verse you have a greater

---

[238] The entries on this page continue in sense from those on notebook p.23.

[239] Charles Harry St John Hornby (1867–1946), barrister and founder of the Ashendene Press, Hardy's third choice as literary executor.

[240] Newman Flower (1879–1964) of Blandford, author, later chairman and owner of the publishers Cassell & Co., and his first wife, Evelyne. Flower was knighted in 1938.

[241] The recollective poem 'Under High-Stoy Hill' (*Complete Poems*, p. 787) probably derives from this 'last time' walk.

[242] Hardy had written to F.W. Slater (of Harper & Bros., New York) on 11 July asking why their 1921 sales report showed no returns for the 21-volume Anniversary edition. Sales had been poor and Slater persuaded Hardy to sign sheets for insertion into the edition.

[243] The *Life* adds: 'Boucher's Close is a green-wooded meadow next to Stinsford Vicarage, and the Ewelease Stile is the one whereon, more than fifty years before this date, he had sat and read the review of *Desperate Remedies* in the *Spectator*' (417). This April 1871 review was so harsh that at the time Hardy wished that he were dead.

[244] Daughter of Mrs Henry Allhusen; see also note of 2 Nov, notebook p.27.

[245] Robert Bridges (1844–1930), Poet Laureate 1913–30, was an outstanding metrist, best known for his philosophical poem on the artistic spirit, *The Testament of Beauty* (1929). Hardy met Bridges, who was one of the contributors to his 79th birthday tribute, several times after 1908. But in 1895 he had written to Mrs Henniker: 'I seem to see nothing in many modern writers but *form* – good form, certainly. I am led to say

expectancy of the rhythm . . . . . & the poet's art was to vary the expected rhythm as much as he could without disagreeably baulking the expectation.

London Mercury Nov. 22[246]

⟨27⟩

Oct or Nov. H.M.M's Ave Caesar in London Mercy.[247]

Oct 14. "Wilton" (old Stinsford tune) played in St James's, Piccadilly at M.A's wedding.[248]

29. Mr Lapworth of the film co. called.[249]

Nov 2. Dorothy Allhusen & her daughtr. Elizabeth came.[250]

---

this by having tried to discover a great poet in Robert Bridges. But he hands the torch on no further than the rest of them do' (12 Aug 1895).

[246] 'Humdrum and Harum-Scarum: A Paper on Free Verse', *London Mercury*, VII (Nov 1922) [54–63], 55.

[247] Horace Mosley Moule (1832–73), fourth son of the Rev. Henry Moule (see n.139), Hardy's closest friend in early years. Distinguished in scholarship at both Oxford and Cambridge, gifted musician and teacher, Moule guided young Hardy through his classical studies, enlarged the scope of his reading and encouraged his writing. Hardy regarded him as 'a scholar and critic of perfect taste'. For several years Moule was a literary reviewer, in which capacity he praised Hardy's work. In 1873 Hardy visited Moule in Cambridge. Before parting, on the morning of 20 June, they went to King's College Chapel: 'A never-to-be-forgotten meeting. H.M.M. saw me off to London. His last smile' (*Life*, 93). The recollection was poignant because they never met again before Hardy received the shocking news on 24 Sep that his friend had committed suicide three days earlier. Moule had cut his own throat, murmured 'love to my mother – easy to die', and the coroner had ruled temporary insanity. Moule is the subject of several of Hardy's poems (notably 'A Confession to a Friend in Trouble', 'Standing by the Mantelpiece' and, on Moule's death, 'Before my Friend Arrived'), and is probably the prototype for Henry Knight in *A Pair of Blue Eyes*.

Hardy published Moule's six stanza poem 'Ave Caesar' in the *London Mercury*, VI (Oct 1922), 631–2, with a biographical sketch recording that Moule 'had early showed every promise of becoming a distinguished English poet. But the fates said otherwise.'

[248] Madeline Allhusen's wedding. Of the Stinsford instrumentalists Hardy recalled that 'in their psalmody they adhered strictly to Tate and Brady . . . such tunes as the "Old Hundredth", "New Sabbath", "Devizes", "Wilton", "Lydia", and "Cambridge New" being their staple ones' (*Life*, 10).

[249] Charles Lapworth. A film of *Tess* was being made by the Metro-Goldwyn Pictures Corp., New York, and Hardy obtained permission for their filming inside the Bindon Abbey enclosure, near Wool, the site of the stone coffin into which Angel placed Tess. The eight-reel film, with scenario by Dorothy Farnum, was released in 1924.

[250] Dorothy Stanley, daughter of Lady Jeune by her first marriage, married Henry Allhusen (1867–1928) of Stoke Poges in 1896. Hardy attended the wedding. Her daugher Elizabeth, 'a charming girl, died soon after [1926], to Hardy's grief' (*Life*, 418).

3. Motored with them & F to Dogbury Gate & round by Holywell home.

Nov. 13. Letter from Pro-Provost of Queens, Oxford, (Rev. E.M. Walker LL.D.) to say it was decided to elect me to a Hon. Fellowship.
14. Accepted

15. Election Day: & Tilley's[251] play from Desperate Remedies. Dorchester Dramatic Society.
17. Mrs Inglis came. Went with her & F. to Tilley's play.

⟨28⟩

Nov 18. Brewery fire.
" 19. Sunday. Admiral & Mrs Fisher called.[252]
" 20. Announcement in Times that I had been elected Hon. Fellow of Queen's Oxford. Mrs Inglis left. To Stinsford (& Talbothays) with F. (M. died 24th)[253]

27. E's death-day, 10 years ago. Went with F. & tidied her tomb, & carried flowers for hers & the other two tombs.[254]

– Dec. Asked to be the first Hon. Fellow of Wessex Society of Architects – Accepd.[255]

---

[251] T. Harry Tilley, retired monumental mason who lived in Dorchester all his life, leading actor in the Dorchester Debating and Dramatic Society and later the society's producer. He adapted, with Hardy's assistance, several novels for the stage. *A Desperate Remedy* was presented at Dorchester on 15–17 Nov 1922, and in London on 21 Nov.

[252] Adml. (Sir) William Wordsworth Fisher (1875–1937), Chief of Staff of the Atlantic Fleet, and his wife Cecilia. Two days later he invited the Hardys to lunch on board H.M.S. *Queen Elizabeth* and the visit took place on 23 June following. 'More than once, upon the invitation of Admiral Fisher, [Hardy] had had a pleasant time on board a battleship off Portland' (*Life*, 419). These included H.M.S. *Dreadnought* and the U.S. flagship *Louisiana* in 1910, and H.M.S. *St. Vincent* in 1913.

[253] Hardy's sister Mary (b.1841) had died on 24 Nov 1915. Formerly headmistress of Dorchester Elementary Girls' School, she is buried in Stinsford churchyard.

[254] Emma Hardy's unforeseen death on 27 Nov 1912 surprised in Hardy a reserve of emotion and yearning regret unsuspected after their virtual estrangement in his wife's later years. He wrote to Edward Clodd on 13 Dec: 'One forgets all the recent years and differences, and the mind goes back to the early times when each was much to the other – in her case & mine intensely much' (British Museum). This inspired the elegiac 'Poems of 1912–13', undoubtedly among his finest.

[255] At the invitation of (Sir) Ian MacAlister (1878–1957), sec. of the R.I.B.A. 1908–43,

– Dec. 27. Connie came.
– New Year's Eve. H. & K.[256] came to 1 o'clock dinner – stayed to tea
– left 5.30.
   Did not sit up.

⟨29⟩

Mem.
MSS. not in existence – (among others)
– Architectural Prize Essay (1862)[257]
– Poor Man & Lady[258]
– Rejected scene or two of Dynasts (Saragossa, St Petersburg)[259]
– Alicia's Diary.[260]
– A Mere Interlude.[261]
– The Waiting Supper.[262]
– Ethelberta.[263]
– Desperate Remedies[264]

---

in a letter on 29 Nov; Hardy accepted on 2 Dec. But he declined an invitation from MacAlister earlier in the month to serve on a committee for the commemoration of the bicentenary of the death of Sir Christopher Wren.

[256] Henry and Kate, his brother and sister.

[257] 'The Application of Coloured Bricks and Terra Cotta to Modern Architecture', awarded an R.I.B.A. prize medal. (See n.121.)

[258] 'The Poor Man and the Lady', Hardy's first novel, written in 1867 but never published. The vicissitudes of its submission first to Macmillan, then to Chapman & Hall (where it was read by George Meredith), are recorded in the *Life* (58–63). Though the novel was abandoned Hardy incorporated parts of it in *Desperate Remedies* (1871), *Under the Greenwood Tree* (1872) and *A Pair of Blue Eyes* (1873), and adapted the rest into 'An Indiscretion in the Life of an Heiress', published in *New Quarterly Magazine* (July 1878), 315–78.

[259] Hardy's provisional list of scenes in Part Second of *The Dynasts*, published at the end of Part First (1903), includes St Petersburg in III.2, though the scene was later abandoned. There is no indication where Saragossa might have appeared.

[260] Published in the *Manchester Weekly Times*, 15 and 22 Oct 1887; subsequently (with the two following stories and others) in *A Changed Man* (1913).

[261] Published in the *Bolton Weekly Journal*, 17 and 24 Oct 1885.

[262] Published in *Murray's Magazine*, Jan and Feb 1888.

[263] *The Hand of Ethelberta*, written 1875 and published the following year, after serialisation in *Cornhill Magazine* (July 1875–May 1876).

[264] Hardy's first novel to be published. Written mainly between autumn 1869 and spring 1870 and completed in Nov or Dec, *Desperate Remedies* appeared in 1871. The original manuscript was discarded even before submission to a publisher in favour of a fair copy made by Emma Gifford, 'having been interlined and altered, so that it may have suffered, he thought, in the eyes of a publisher's reader by being difficult to read' (*Life*, 83).

⟨30⟩

1923.

Jan 1. Learn that J.B. Braithwaite (senior partner) has retired from the firm.[265]

2. F. went to London to see specialist, &c[266] – & on to Mrs Henniker at Epsom.

3. Re-appointed Governor of Grammar School for 3 years.

8. F. returned.
13, 14, 15 &c. F. ill with bad cold. Latter part of month. Ill with bad cold & on into February –
Feb. Poem on "Woman," &c. in "L. Mercury"[267]
" . 10. C.M.H. died.[268]

⟨31⟩

Depositories of T.H's MSS.
[Partly copied from a list sent by Mr. John Lane,[269] who made further inquiries]

Title	Whereabouts
"P. of Blue Eyes" =	4 instalments in possession of Mr John Lane.[270]
"F. Madding Crowd" =	Mr A.E. Newton, Philadelphia.[271]

---

[265] Foster & Braithwaite (lawyers) of London EC2.

[266] Florence Hardy was suffering from cancer of the throat and underwent a successful operation for removal of the growth on 30 Sep 1924 (see Hardy's notes, 29 Sep, 30 Sep and 9 Oct 1924). But she continued to suffer intermittently and it was of cancer that she died aged 58 on 17 Oct 1937.

[267] 'On the Portrait of a Woman about to be Hanged', London Mercury (Feb 1923), 344. Inspired by the case of Mrs Edith Thompson who, with her lover, had murdered her husband in Ilford in 1922. She was hanged on 9 Jan 1923. Hardy's poem, dated 6 Jan, blames the 'Causer', and asks the woman 'why, since It made you/ Sound in the germ,/ It sent a worm/ To madden its handiwork' (Complete Poems, p.780).

[268] Hardy's second cousin, Charles Meech Hardy of Puddletown.

[269] John Lane (1854–1925), publisher, founder of the Bodley Head (1889), famous as a literary club as well as a place of business; published The Yellow Book (1894–7). Lane was also an ardent antiquarian.

[270] In fact only three instalments survive, now in the Berg Collection, New York Public Library.

[271] Now in the possession of Mr Edwin Thorne.

"Return of Native" =	Mr Clement Shorter[272]
"Trumpet Major" =	Windsor Castle Library[273]
"Mayor of Casterbge." =	Dorset County Museum, Dorchester.[274]
"Group of Noble Dames" =	Library of Congress, Washington (a large portion).[275]
"Tess of the D'Us." =	British Museum[276]
"Jude the Obscure" =	Fitzwilliam Museum Cambridge (some pages missing)[277]
"Wessex Poems" =	Birmingham Art Gallery[278]
"Poems of the Past & the Present" } =	Bodleian Library, Oxford.[279]

[continued next page]

(32)

"The Dynasts" = British Museum.
Time's Laughingstocks = Fitzwilliam Musm.[280]

(Additional to the above)
"Under the Greenwood Tree" = Mrs Hardy[281]
A superseded chapter of "Far from Madding Crowd" } = Mrs Hardy[282]
"The Woodlanders" = Mr Howard Bliss[283]

---

[272] A gift from Hardy in 1908, the ms. was bequeathed by Shorter, on his death in 1926, to the Royal University of Dublin (now the National University of Ireland), where it remains in University College library.

[273] Presented to King George V in Oct 1911, the ms. is in the Royal Library. Sydney Cockerell was, at Hardy's request, distributing the manuscripts.

[274] Presented by Hardy in Nov 1911.

[275] Presented in Oct 1911. Includes the stories 'Barbara of the House of Grebe', 'The Marchioness of Stonehenge', 'Lady Mottisfont', 'The Lady Icenway', 'Squire Petrick's Lady', 'Anna, Lady Baxby', and 'The Lady Penelope'.

[276] Presented (with *The Dynasts*, below) in 1911.

[277] Presented in Oct 1911: this was Cockerell's choice for the Fitzwilliam, of which he was then Director.

[278] Birmingham City Museum and Art Gallery; presented in 1911.

[279] Presented in Oct 1911.

[280] Presented in Oct 1911, with *Jude*. Cockerell chose Hardy's most recently published collection of poems.

[281] Bequeathed on her death in 1937 to the DCM.

[282] Chap. 23, now in the DCM.

[283] This ms. was never owned by Bliss. It remained at Max Gate until Mrs Hardy's death and was then bequeathed to the DCM.

"The Duke's Reappearance" =Mr. Edwd. Clodd[284]
(this is printed in the vol. "A Changed Man")
A Short Story (name forgotten) = Mr Gosse[285]
"The 3 Strangers" (in Wessex Tales) = Mr. Sydney Cockerell[286]
"Satires of Circumstance" = Mrs Hardy[287]
"Moments of Vision" = Mr Hardy[288]
"Late Lyrics" = Mr. Hardy[289]
"The Well Beloved" = unknown
"A Changed Man" = unknown[290]
"The Waiting Supper"
"Alicias Diary"   } not in existence
"A Mere Interlude"

[T.O.]

⟨33⟩

[Continued from previous page]

"A Laodicean" = not in existence[291]
"Hand of Ethelberta" = not in existence
"Desperate Remedies" = not in existence
"Poor Man & the Lady" = not in existence
"Architectural Prize Essay, 1862 = not in existence
"Human Shows" – Mr. Hardy.[292]

---

[284] Given to Clodd in Mar 1912, this story is now in the Hardy collection, University of Texas. Edward Clodd (1840–1930) was sec. of the London Joint-Stock Bank, 1872–1915. Author of many books on myth, folklore, the occult, and religion and evolution, he was a convinced rationalist.

[285] Hardy gave 'A Few Crusted Characters' to Gosse in July 1913; it is now in the Berg Collection. (Sir) Edmund Gosse (1849–1928), a close friend for many years, was translator to the Board of Trade (1875–1914) and librarian of the House of Lords (1904–14). But he was best known as a man of letters: biographer, linguist, critic, and friend of most of his literary contemporaries.

[286] Given on 29 Sep 1911, in gratitude for Cockerell's help in distributing manuscripts; now in the Berg Collection.

[287] Given on her 44th birthday, 12 Jan 1923; now in DCM.

[288] Presented to Magdalene College, Cambridge, on 7 Feb 1928, in fulfilment of a direction in Hardy's will that an ms. should be given to the college of which he had been elected an Hon. Fellow in 1913.

[289] Bequeathed on Mrs Hardy's death to the DCM.

[290] Berg Collection.

[291] Hardy burned the ms. Most of the novel had been dictated by him during a severe illness in 1880–1.

[292] Presented to Yale University Library in Apr 1939, by Florence Hardy's sister, Eva Dugdale.

⟨34⟩

Feb. 1923.
From the Western Morng. News. 17. Feb 23

WATSON. – February 15th, at 8, Portland-villas.
Elizabeth Ellen, widow of the late R.W.G. Watson,
solicitor, of Devonport, and Chief Magistrate of Lagos,
W. Africa. No flowers, by request.[293]

Feb. 26.
A story (rather than a poem) might be written in the first person, in
which "I" am supposed to live through the centuries, in my ancestors, as one person, the particular line of descent chosen being that
in which qualities are most continuous. (from an old note)

March 14. F. went to London & Enfield.
April 1. Easter Sunday.
" 4. Motored with F. & Connie, (who is at Weymouth) to Abbotsbury.[294]
" 5. In to-day's Times:

   HENNIKER. – On the 4th April, 1923, of heart failure,
   the HONOURABLE MRS. ARTHUR HENNIKER. R.I.P.

After a friendship of 30 years![295]

⟨35⟩

Tennyson – wrote in the third person to Elkin Mathews: "The best
editions of the best books he would fain have, not mere literary
curiosities."
(From Heffer & Sons[296] Catalogue, Cambridge)

---

[293] The widow of Emma Hardy's 'cousin bred to the law, a barrister who went to
Lagos as Governor – the first one – and died there of the climate, and drink' (*Some
Recollections,* p.24). This is a newspaper cutting pasted in.
[294] Six miles N.W. of Weymouth.
[295] In view of Hardy's affection for Mrs Henniker, an exclamation poignant in its
simplicity. See n.221. The announcement is on a newspaper cutting pasted in.
[296] Long-established booksellers. '*The . . . books*' is underlined in red ink.

⟨36⟩ 1923

April 7. Cockerell came. Met the St John Ervines here.[297]

9. Motored with Cockerell to Sturr. Newton
10. Cockerell left
F. Henniker buried today at 1 o'clock at Thornham Magna, Eye, Suffolk – (Station, Mellis).[298]
Portrait of F. Henniker in Sphere. Apl. 14.

April (1st. week) signed petition for Poel.[299]

12th. Prof. Read of Sydney, & Dr. Lock, came[300]
13. Signed appeal to University & citizens at Oxford to support a movement for the Oxford Playhouse, in view of raising the standard of acted drama in England.[301]
21 Signed petition for abridging sentence of Walter Crotch (4 yrs.) on the ground that he has already suffered 2 years of it nearly, & ⟨37⟩ that he raised £25,000 to establish a home for Blinded Soldiers, & is in ill health.[302]

During April. Finished rough draft of The Queen of Cornwall.[303]

---

[297] St John Ervine (1883–1971), novelist, dramatist and drama critic, and his wife Leonora. See also n.143.

[298] Hardy did not attend. Thornham Hall, seat of the Henniker family, was in this parish.

[299] In response to a request (31 Mar) from Harley Granville-Barker to help obtain a Civil List Pension for Poel. William Poel (1852–1934), actor, stage director and author, revolutionised stage production by presenting Hamlet without scenery in 1881. From that year he managed the Royal Victoria Hall (Old Vic) and in 1895 founded the Elizabethan Stage Society, presenting plays without textual alterations for scenic purposes. Poel declined a knighthood shortly before his death.

[300] John Read (1884–1963), Prof. of Chemistry, Universities of Sydney (1916–23) & St Andrews (1923–63), and author of several plays in West Country dialect. The Rev. Walter Lock, D.D. (1846–1933) of Keble Coll., Oxford; Canon of Christ Church and Lady Margaret Prof. of Divinity, 1919–27. He was the brother of Hardy's friend Judge Lock (see n.229), and both were sons of the solicitor H. Lock of Dorchester.

[301] In response to a request (9 Apr) from James B. Fagan (1873–1933), actor–manager, producer and playwright, who in Oct 1923 opened the Oxford Playhouse, where he gathered a company of young and distinguished players.

[302] Hardy's support was solicited by A.E. (Mrs Cecil) Chesterton. Crotch, formerly director of a bank, had been jailed for fraud.

[303] The finished ms. was sent to Macmillan on 30 Aug and The Famous Tragedy of the Queen of Cornwall was published on 15 Nov. It was performed by the Hardy Players at Dorchester on 28–30 Nov. See also Hardy's note of 15 Nov 1923.

May – made imaginary view of Tintagel Castle.[304]

May 24. To Shaftesby[305] Arts & Crafts Exhn. with F. & Mr. & Mrs W. Watkins.

√ 26. W. & Mrs de la Mare came.

27. To Weyth. & Herringston with the de la Ms.

28. Gave the play (Q. of Corn.) to Tilley. During this week sat to Mrs Mitchell for model of head.

[1923]

June 2. Birthday. letters & telegrams. Mr Newman Flower called.

3. Sunday. The Granville Barkers & Max Beerbohm[306] came to tea.

⟨38⟩

1923

June 10. To Netherton to the G. Barkers. (Sun)

Relativity. That things & events always were, are, & will be (e.g. E.M.F.[307] &c. are still living in the past)

June 21. Went with F. on board the Queen Elizabeth, on a visit to Sir John de Robeck, Lady de R. & Adml Fisher.[308]

22 Col. & Mrs Inglis came.

25. Monday. To Oxford by road in Mr. Watkins's car. Went by way of Salisbury,[309] Hungerford & Wantage. Called at Fawley.[310]

---

[304] 'Imaginary View of Tintagel Castle at the Time of the Tragedy', a fine and delicate drawing remarkable for a man almost 83 years old, appeared as the frontispiece of *The Queen of Cornwall*. It was Hardy's last drawing and is now in the DCM.

[305] Shaftesbury.

[306] Hardy's friend for many years, (Sir) Max Beerbohm (1872–1956), essayist, short story writer, caricaturist and critic, notable for his wit and incisive irony. Hardy is entertainingly satirised in 'A Sequelula to "The Dynasts"' in *A Christmas Garland* (1912).

[307] Emma, Mother, Father.

[308] Cf. n.252. Adml. Sir John de Robeck (1862–1928) was at this time Commander-in-Chief of the Atlantic Fleet.

[309] Here 'they stopped for a little while to look at the Cathedral, as Hardy always loved doing, and at various old buildings, including the Training College which he had visited more than fifty years before when his two sisters were students there, and which is faithfully described in *Jude the Obscure*' (*Life*, 420).

[310] The Berkshire village (translated into Marygreen in *Jude the Obscure*) where Hardy's paternal grandmother, Mary Head, spent the first 13 years of her life. Jude's surname is taken from the village.

Arrived at the Provost's Lodgings, Queen's, betwn. 4 & 5: received by Miss Lefroy & the Provost. Dined in Hall, meeting Revd. E.M. Walker[311] the Pro-Provost, Mr Elton[312] the Dean, &c. Had to[313]

⟨39⟩

Latin Graces.

Before. Benedictus Benedicat[314]   Best
After. Benedicto Benedicatur[315]

Before. Agimus Tibi gratias, Omnipotens Deus, pro his et omnibus
       donistuis, quae de largitate tuâ fruimur. Per Iesum
       Christum Dominum Nostrum.[316]
Before. Benedictus.[317] Benedicat. Per Iesum Christum Dominum
       Nostrum.

"To extract a magic out of the familiar." Lit. Sup. 28.6.'23.[318]

⟨40⟩

1923

borrow a gown, not having brought mine. Went up after dinner to take wine in the Common Room. Looked at views in High St. with Mr. Elton.

---

[311] Walker had informed Hardy of his election to an Hon. Fellowship at Queen's the previous November and invited him on 18 June for this visit.

[312] Godfrey Elton (1892–1977), later Baron Elton, scholar and author. His account of Hardy's visit is in the *Life*, 420–2.

[313] Continues on notebook p. 40.

[314] 'May the blessed [Lord] bless.'

[315] 'May blessing be given to the blessed [Lord].'

[316] 'We give to you thanks, almighty God, for these and all your gifts, which from your bounty we enjoy. Through Jesus Christ our Lord.'

[317] There should be no punctuation here.

[318] *TLS*, No. 1119 (28 Jun 1923), 437: review of Katharine Mansfield, *The Dove's Nest, and Other Stories* (London: Constable, 1923). 'She [K.M.] looks at a flower or a person's dress or a lesser trifle, and it is suddenly alive and distinct, yet refracted by meaning, vibrating with little currents of emotion. To extract an intimacy from casual things and a queer magic out of the familiar is, of course, a modern passion . . . Like a writer very different from her in other ways, Mr. Lawrence, she was able to realize not only the glancing impression, but the tone and quality of a whole story through an image somehow made true.'

June 26. Lunch in Convn. Rm. Fellows & Wives, afterwards photographed in garden in a group. In aft. Mr Watkins drove us & Mr
Elton to call on Dr Lock[319] at Christ Church, & afterwards to Boars
Hill to call on Masefield. Tea with them. Back into Oxford to Martyrs
Meml. & round to New College. Service at 5. Dined in Hall.
27. Daisy Gifford[320] called just before we left. Met Mary Lock in
street. Back home by way of Newbury, Winchester & Ringwd.[321] Mr
Watkins slept at Max Gate & left next morning early.
28. To lunch with the Popes[322] at Wrackleford, & on to Bridport, tea
with Udals:[323] thence to presentn. of portrait to Sir R. W^ms Talked to
several including Lady Ilchester.[324] Drove to Symondsbury – &
home.
29. Mr. Peacock called.[325]

⟨41⟩

1923
July . . . F. went London; Eva here.

July 20. Went to opening of Drill Hall Dorchester by the P. of Wales.
Very hot. Took Mr Winwood[326] in my car. Talked to a good many.
Tune of the Dorset Regt. as the companies marched up into the
yard. Introd. to Prince on the platform by Ld. Ellenborough.[327]
Drove to Max Gate with him. Lunch, there being also present Ld.

---

[319] See n. 300.
[320] Emma Hardy's cousin, daughter of Archdeacon Gifford.
[321] Ringwood, Hampshire.
[322] Alfred Pope (1842–1934), former solicitor, and his wife Elizabeth. A local J.P.
and lord of the manor, Pope was chairman of the governors of Dorchester Grammar
School, 1908–29, and author of local antiquarian pamphlets. Wrackleford House is
two miles N.W. of Dorchester.
[323] John Symonds Udal, former Chief Justice of the Leeward Islands, first met
Hardy nearly 40 years earlier. He wrote *Devonshire Folk-Lore* (privately printed,
Hertford, 1922).
[324] Lady Ilchester (d. 1956), formerly Lady Helen Stewart, only daughter of Hardy's
friend Lady Londonderry (whom he met in 1893 and 'who remained his friend
throughout the ensuing years' (*Life*, 257) until her death in 1919). Hardy attended her
wedding to Lord Stavordale, who succeeded as Earl of Ilchester in 1905, in 1902.
[325] (Sir) Walter Peacock (1871–1956), Keeper of the Records of the Duchy of Cornwall, 1908–30. This call was probably in connection with the visit of the Prince of
Wales the following month.
[326] Thomas Winwood, M.A., J.P., of Syward Lodge, on the road just behind Max
Gate.
[327] Col. Cecil Henry Law, 6th Baron Ellenborough (1849–1931), formerly a professional soldier and at this time chairman of the Dorset Territorial Association, lived at
Montrose, Prince of Wales Road, Dorchester.

Shaftesbury, Adml. Sir Lionel Halsey, Sir Godfrey Thomas, Mr Walter Peacock, Mr Proudfoot & Mr Wilson. Photographed on lawn.[328]

25. Sassoon & Blunden took lodgings at Came Rectory[329] – leaving Aug. 1.
Aug. 11. Young Ralph Bankes & his sister Daphne[330] came to tea. Cockerell & Christopher[331] came for week-end.
26. Hamlin Garland[332] & Mrs. came.

⟨42⟩

1923
Aug.21. Lunched with F. at the Cochranes, Athelhampton.
22. Drinkwater and Daisy Kennedy[333] came to lunch. She played violin. When they were gone H.G. Wells & Rebecca West called.[334]
– Aug. 30 (about) Mr Eves began portrait.[335]
– Sept 9. Lunched with the Ilchesters at Summer Lodge, Evershot, called at Chantmarle on the Hornbys on our way back, & had tea.
– Sept 16. With Colonel Lawrence[336] to lunch with the Granville Barkers.

---

[328] Lord Shaftesbury (1869–1961), Lord Lieutenant of Dorset 1916–52; Adml. Sir Lionel Halsey (1872–1949), Comptroller and Treasurer to the Prince of Wales, 1920–36; Sir Godfrey Thomas (1889–1968), Private Sec. to the Prince of Wales, 1919–36; Walter Peacock (see n. 326); Messrs Proudfoot & Wilson were stewards of the Duchy of Cornwall. (Cf. *Life*, 422.)

[329] One mile S. of Dorchester, former home of the poet William Barnes (1801–86).

[330] Of Kingston Lacy (cf. 'Memoranda, I', notebook p. 41). Henry John Ralph Bankes (1902–   ), who had succeeded to the property on the death of his father in 1904, and his sister Daphne Maude Adelaide.

[331] Sydney Cockerell's son Christopher (1910–), who later invented the Hovercraft.

[332] Garland (1860–1940), an American author best known for his realistic studies of the Middle West, recalled visiting Hardy in *Afternoon Neighbours* (New York, 1934).

[333] John Drinkwater (1882–1937), poet and dramatist, and his fiancée; they were married in 1924. Drinkwater later dramatised *The Mayor of Casterbridge*, presented at the Barnes Theatre, 8 Sep 1926, and (with Hardy's attendance) at Weymouth on 20 Sep.

[334] Novelists Herbert George Wells (1866–1946) and Rebecca West (1892–). Rebecca West was at this time Wells's mistress, and their son (the novelist Anthony West) had been born at the beginning of the war.

[335] This portrait by Reginald Grenville Eves (1876–1941) is in the National Portrait Gallery. Eves painted another portrait of Hardy in 1924, which was auctioned at Christie's on 12 July 1974.

[336] Thomas Edward Lawrence (1888–1935), famous as Lawrence of Arabia, headed

– Sept. 20. H.A.L. Fisher,[337] & Adml F. to tea.
– 21. Lunched at Kingston & met Augustus John.[338]
 24. News of death of John Morley[339] yesterday.
– Sept 26. Lord & Lady Stuart of Wortley called on their way from
Tintagel home. Also Lady Cynthia Colville & Mrs Cavendish Ben-
tinck of Corfe Castle. Also E.M. Forster.
– 27. Signed codified Agrt. with Macmillans

⟨43⟩

✖ 340

Nov.15. "The Famous Tragedy of the Queen of Cornwall" published. Hardy's aim in writing this is clearly given in a letter to a
friend.[341]

Arab forces with conspicuous bravery in guerrilla warfare against Turkey during the
Great War, gaining immense influence with his troops. But after the war he enrolled
as a private soldier and was now serving with the Royal Tank Corps at Bovington
Camp, nr. Dorchester, visiting Max Gate by motorcycle. Hardy called Lawrence 'one
of his most valued friends' and obviously admired the man of action, while Lawrence
found a remarkable repose in the old author: 'Hardy is so pale, so quiet, so refined
into an essence: and camp is such a hurly-burly . . . If I were in his place I would never
wish to die: or even to wish other men dead. The peace which passeth all understanding; – but it can be felt, and is nearly unbearable. How envious such an old age is'
(1923 letter to Robert Graves, in David Garnett, ed., *The Letters of T.E. Lawrence*
(London, 1938), p. 429). Lawrence himself was killed in a motorcycle accident in 1935.
His account of his war experiences was published in *Seven Pillars of Wisdom* (privately
printed, 1926; London, 1935).
    [337] Herbert Albert Laurens Fisher (1865–1940), historian, elder brother of Adml.
Fisher.
    [338] John (1878–1961) painted Hardy's portrait in the autumn and Hardy said of it
later: 'I don't know whether that is how I look or not – but that is how I *feel'* (*Life*, 436).
It is now in the Fitzwilliam Museum, Cambridge.
    [339] Morley (1838–1923) [Viscount Morley, cr.1908], critic, biographer and Liberal
politician, who, as reader for Macmillans, had commended the 'stuff and purpose' in
Hardy's first unpublished novel, *The Poor Man and the Lady*, in 1868. (See Charles
Morgan, *The House of Macmillan* (London, 1943), pp.87–94.)
    [340] This entry is a typescript carbon copy pasted in on the verso, opposite Hardy's
entry of 15 Nov on the recto, where there is a corresponding symbol (see notebook
p.44 *infra*).
    [341] The friend was Harold Child, who had written on 9 Nov saying that he would
be reviewing *The Queen of Cornwall* for *The Times*. This copy of the letter, presumably
typed and pasted in for later inclusion in Hardy's disguised autobiography, is reproduced (with slight changes in punctuation and one or two words) in the *Life*, 422–3.
The rather emotive assertion that Hardy's 'temerity . . . will doubtless be punished by
reviewers' is discreetly altered to 'be criticized'.
    Harold Child (1869–1945), author and critic who helped to found the *TLS* in 1902,
was for many years a drama critic for *The Times*.

"The unities are strictly preserved, whatever virtue there may be in that. I, myself, am old-fashioned enough to think there is a virtue, in it, if it can be done without artificiality. The only other case I remember attempting it in was "The Return of the Native." The original events could have been enacted in the time taken by the performance, and they continue unbroken throughout. The change of persons on the stage is called a change of scene, there being no change of background.

"My temerity in pulling together into the space of an hour events that in the traditional stories covered a long time will doubtless be punished by reviewers, if they notice it. But there are so many versions of the famous purpose in any way - - as, in fact, the Greek dramatists did in their plays, notably Euripides.

"Wishing it to be thoroughly English I have dropped the name of Chorus for the conventional onlookers, and called them Chanters, though they play the part of a Greek chorus to some extent. I have also called them Ghosts. (I don't for the moment recall an instance of this in a Greek play). Whether the lady ghosts in our performance here will submit to have their faces whitened I don't know!

I have tried to avoid turning the rude personages of, say, the fifth century into respectable Victorians, as was done by Tennyson, Swinburne, Arnold, etc. On the other hand it would have been impossible to present them as they really were, with their barbaric manners and surroundings.

(44)

1923
Oct 3. Lady St Helier came to lunch from Newbury – left by 4.37 train.
     Also the Granville Barkers & McDougalls.

Nov. 15. "The Famous Tragedy of the Q. of Cornwall" published.
⋇ [opposite]
24. Annivy of E's birth, M's death.[342]
Mon. 26. To a rehearsal of Q. of C. with Mr Child, & F.
27. Annivy. of E's death 1912.[343]

---

[342] Emma Hardy, b.1840; Mary Hardy, d.1915.
[343] See n.254.

28. Mr Cockerell came – also Col. Lawrence. They dined, & took F. to the play. (Q. of C.)[344]
29. Matinée. 30 – Went with F. & Mrs Inglis to the performance. Drinkwater & Daisy Kennedy there.
Dec 4. F. to London & Enfield.
" 10. Death of Sir F. Treves[345] announced – Died at Lausanne 7th. Dec.
25 Xmas Day. Wet. A. Pope called. To Winwood's to tea.

⟨45⟩

Dec. 28. To Stinsfd. & Talbothays.
Dec. 30. Sunday. Bernard & Mrs Shaw[346] & Col Lawrence to lunch. Mr Niven called about leaflet of hymns for F. Treves's funeral.
31. New Years Eve. To Weymouth to lunch with St J. Irvines at Royal H.[347] Did not sit up. Heard the bells in the evening.

"Either through the interactions of Ether & Matter, or otherwise . . .
And a demonstration has been thus given us that memory & affection, & personality generally, are not functions of Matter, but only utilize Matter for communicn. with those in material surroundings."

Sir Oliver Lodge   19th. cent   Jan 1924[348]

---

[344] 'The great difficulties which the play presented to amateur actors, unaccustomed to reciting blank verse, who were at their best in rustic comedy, were more or less overcome, but naturally a poetic drama did not make a wide appeal. However, the performance, and particularly the rehearsals, gave Hardy considerable pleasure' (*Life*, 423).

[345] Sir Frederick Treves (1853–1923), eminent surgeon who was also surgeon to the King, had attended school with Hardy's sister Mary, and from his father's shop Hardy bought his first writing desk. 'Because of the early association and the love which they both bore to the county, there was a strong link between these two Dorset men' (*Life*, 423).

[346] George Bernard Shaw (1856–1950), Fabian and prolific dramatist, later a pallbearer at Hardy's funeral.

[347] Royal Hotel.

[348] Sir Oliver Lodge, 'Outlook on the Universe', *Nineteenth Century*, XCV (Jan 1924) [137–146], 144. Lodge (1851–1940), by academic profession a physicist and first Principal of Birmingham University, devoted much time to psychic research.

⟨46⟩

1924.

Jan 2. Frederick Treves's funeral – St Peters[349] – Very wet – Sad procession through the rain to the cemetery. Casket in a little white grave.

Lord Dawson[350] & Mr Newman Flower came out to tea.

5. My poem "In Memoriam F.T." appears in The Times.[351]

Feb 17. Mr Middleton Murry came. 18. left.

Feb 21. F. went to London. Q. of C. performance[352]

March 7. To Stinsford with F. (E. first met 54 years ago)[353]

F. sworn as J.P. about now.

11. F. read a paper to the Dorchester Debating Society.

⟨47⟩

[Various passages recalled by the Byron centenary.][354]

"Nature, in her most dazzling aspects or stupendous parts, is but the background & theatre of the tragedy of man."

(Morley. Critical Miscellanies.) "Byron"[355]

Morley also says that Byron was the enemy of a society "which only remembered that man had property, & forgot that he had a

---

[349] Dorchester.

[350] Lord Dawson of Penn (d.1945), Physician-in-Ordinary to Edward VII, George V, Edward VIII and George VI.

[351] 5 Jan 1924, p.11. After considerable revision, included as 'In the Evening' in *Human Shows* (1925); *Complete Poems*, p.820. With Hardy's permission Lady Treves used three lines from the first version on her husband's grave in Dorchester Cemetery.

[352] This performance 'was not altogether a success, partly owing to the only building having no stage suitable for the performance, a rather small concert platform having to be used' (*Life*, 424).

[353] At St Juliot (cf. n.5).

[354] See also note of 14 July, notebook p.50. In June Hardy was invited by Sir Rennell Rodd to sign a petition to admit Lord Byron (1778–1824) to Poet's Corner, Westminster Abbey. Hardy replied 27 June: 'I give my name and support to the proposed letter to the Times with pleasure. Whatever Byron's bad qualities he was a poet, & a hater of cant, & I have often thought some memorial of him should be at Westminster' (DCM). The letter was published on 14 July, but the Dean of Westminster refused the petition because of Byron's 'openly dissolute life' and 'licentious verse' (letter to *The Times*, 19 July 1924, p.13). Hardy mocked the Dean's letter in 'A Refusal' (*Complete Poems*, pp.801–3).

[355] John Morley, *Critical Miscellanies* (London: Chapman & Hall, 1871), p.262.

spirit."[356] He was penetrated "with the distinctively modern scorn & aversion for the military spirit, & the distinctively modern conviction of its being the most deadly of anachronisms."[357]

"Byron . . fills men with thoughts that shake down the . . . Temple of Comfort." Morley[358]

". . . our world of an aristocracy materialized & null, a middle-class purblind & hideous, a lower class crude & brutal." M. Arnold.[359]

T.O.

⟨48⟩

1924

April 1. The Times in its notices of the monthly reviews agrees with Mr Middleton Murry in "The Adelphi" in the latter's smashing criticism of that ludicrous blackguard George Moore; book called "Conversations in Ebury Street," in which I believe I am libelled wholesale, though I have not seen the book.[360] (N.B. Mr G.M's disciples to whom these things are related are E. Gosse, John Free-

---

[356] Ibid., p.268.

[357] Ibid., p.273.

[358] Ibid., p.283.

[359] Matthew Arnold, 'Byron', *Macmillan's Magazine*, XLIII (Mar 1881), 377; *Essays in Criticism*, Second Series (London, 1888), p.202. Cf. Hardy's note, 26 Apr 1888: 'Thought in bed last night that Byron's *Childe Harold* will live in the history of English poetry not so much because of the beauty of parts of it, but because of its good fortune in being an accretion of descriptive poems by the most fascinating personality in the world – for the English – not a common plebeian, but a romantically wicked noble lord. It affects even Arnold's judgement' (*Life*, 207).

[360] Moore (1852–1933), Anglo-Irish novelist, dramatist and short story writer, had angered Hardy since 1886 when, in *Confessions of a Young Man*, he had attacked Hardy's style and disparaged *Far from the Madding Crowd* as 'but one of George Eliot's miscarriages' (ch.10). Moore's vicious and spiteful attacks reached a climax in *Conversations in Ebury Street* (1924), where Hardy is accused of 'lack of invention, brain paralysis', subjected to *ad hominem* mockery, and dismissed as the author of 'ill-constructed melodramas, feebly written in bad grammar' to which Moore adds that 'bad grammar flourishes in weak minds' (chs. 5 and 6). Hardy thanked Murry for his defence in *The Adelphi*, Vol. I, No.11 (Apr 1924), 951–8, which is vigorously contemptuous of Moore, properly accusing him of 'senile indecency': 'Mr. Moore cannot tell the truth. The lie festers in his soul, and a smell of corruption comes out of all his works.' *The Times* (1 Apr 1924, p.9) confesses 'a worldly joy' on reading Murry's well-justified rebuke. Hardy's uncommonly explicit condemnation of Moore in this note is prelusive of his final retort in a short poem dictated on his death bed in 1928, apparently the last thing he ever wrote. It is now in the DCM. The ironical poem, entitled 'Epitaph' (labelled 'Last lines dictated by T.H., referring to George Moore'), concludes: 'Heap dustbins on him:/ They'll not meet/ The apex of his self-conceit.'

man – Tonks, Granville Barker, W. de la Mare, & Cunningham Graham, &c.)[361]

April 3. Mother died 20 years ago to-day.

May . . [1924]
June 2. Birthday. Letter, among others from Willm. Perkins the Baptist.[362]

⟨49⟩

"We do not want carefully constructed pieces of [verse] mosaic. Force is what we need." Mark Rutherford.[363]
"His [Byron's] mind was never to him a kingdom" A. Symons.[364]
"He added [more] history to Waterloo because his tread was on an empire's dust' –
[& more height to the Alps because he strode them"]

———— ib.

"The novel in the hands of Dickens & Thackeray . . . . was timid beside Don Juan." Oliver Elton. Survey of Eng. Lit.[365]

"It is always the lover who writes poetry, whether the object be the absolute or his mistress: its subject is always that expansion towards some external thing."
————Lit. Supt.

---

[361] John Freeman (1880–1929), poet and reviewer; Henry Tonks (1862–1937), painter and Slade Prof. of Fine Art, London University, 1917–30; R.B. Cunninghame Graham (1852–1936), author of vivid tales and travel books. Others, see notes *supra*.

[362] William Perkins, 'a son of the Baptist minister, Mr. Perkins, whom, in his youth, Hardy had so respected. This correspondent was one of the young men who had met him at the Baptist Chapel at the eastern end of the town for a prayer-meeting which was hindered by the arrival of a circus./ More than sixty years had elapsed since Hardy had had any contact with this friend of his youth' (*Life*, 424).

[363] Pseudonym of William Hale White (1831–1913), novelist of spiritual self-revelation.

[364] Arthur Symons (1865–1945), prolific poet and critic.

[365] Oliver Elton (1861–1945), literary historian; in Vol.II, *Survey of English Literature* (London, 1912), p.180.

"He [Rimbaud] divorced his thought as far as he could from all other thought & expressed it as directly & as tersely as he cd." [Squire[366] in Obsr.]

⟨50⟩

1924
June 11. Rutland Boughton came about the Queen of Cornwall.[367]
12. Drove with R.B. & F. to P.Town[368] via Tincleton Rd. & Coomb.
13. R.B. left.
June 16. Monday – "Compassion appeared in The Times.[369]
June 30. Cockerell came.
July 1. The Balliol Players performed The Oresteia[370] as "The Curse of the House of Atreus," on Max Gate Lawn. Mr A.L. Cliffe = Clytaemnestra: Anty. Asquith = Cassandra: Walter Oakeshott = Orestes H.T. Wade-Gery = Agamemnon: Electra = A.M. Farrer.[371]
Afterwards tea. Mr & Mrs Granville Barker.
– The B.P. had come on bicycles, sending on their theatrical properties on a lorry that sometimes broke down.

8 July. Sent MS. of Queen of Cornwall to Macmillan for lending to Toronto Exhibition.
14 July. Joint letter to Times on propriety of a memorial to Byron in Abbey x – Balfour. Asqth. Ll.G. Crawford. Gosse. Kenyon. Lucas.

---

[366] J.C. Squire (see n.227) writing in *The Observer*.
[367] Rutland Boughton (1878–1960), composer, set *The Queen of Cornwall* to music. His operatic version was performed at Glastonbury and elsewhere in 1924. Hardy 'found Mr Boughton a stimulating companion, and was interested in his [left wing] political views, though he could not share them' (*Life*, 425).
[368] Puddletown.
[369] Page 15. The poem written 22 Jan is an ode in celebration of the centenary of the Royal Society for the Prevention of Cruelty to Animals, and was published without copyright.
[370] A trilogy of plays by Aeschylus, first performed in 485 B.C. The Balliol Players were undergraduates from Oxford, welcomed by Hardy: 'always sympathetic to youth, and a lifelong admirer of Greek tragedy, he fully appreciated this mark of affection and respect.' (Cf. *Life*, 425–6.)
[371] Several of the players later attained a wider distinction: Anthony Asquith (1902–68), film director; Henry Theodore Wade-Gery (1888–1972), Wykeham Prof. of Ancient History at Oxford, 1939–53; Walter Oakeshott (1903–), Rector of Lincoln College, Oxford, 1954–72, and Vice-Chancellor, 1962–4.

G.M. Trevelyan. T.H. R.K.: Newbolt: Mackail: Bingm. R. Rodd[372]
23 July. To Stinsfd. Chyd. (Fr. died 20th. G.F. Aug 1st.)[373] with F..
Aftds. to Bockhn. & Rushy P.[374] (Eva[375] here – gone motoring with
H.)

⟨51⟩

"The foolish man wonders at the unusual, but the wise man at the
usual." Emerson.[376]

⟨52⟩

Aug 4. Bank holiday. (War declared 10 yrs ago.)
Went to Netherton Hall.[377]
6. Siegfried Sassoon came with friend; also Col. Lawrence (Private
Shaw).

9. At tea: S.S. & friend, Mr Jeune & Lady Brackenbury.
Mr & Mrs Tomlinson & Col Lawrence

Aug 28. With F. by car to Glastonbury to see & hear Rutland
Boughton's music verson of Queen of Cornwall.
25–30. Sat to Mr S. Youriévitch the Russian sculptor for bust.[378] (His
London address is Crown Chambers, 9 Regent St. S.W.1)

---

[372] Former Prime Ministers (Earl) A.J. Balfour, H.H. Asquith, David Lloyd George;
Lord Crawford and Balcarres (1871–1940), Trustee of National Portrait Gallery and
British Museum; (Sir) Edmund Gosse; Sir Frederick Kenyon (1863–1952), Director of
the British Museum, 1909–30; E.V. Lucas (1868–1938), essayist; G.M. Trevelyan
(1876–1962), historian; Hardy; Rudyard Kipling (1865–1936); Sir Henry Newbolt
(1862–1938), barrister, author and poet; J.W. Mackail (1859–1945), classical scholar,
critic, biographer and poet; Laurence Binyon (1869–1943), poet; Sir Rennell Rodd
(1858–1941), diplomat. *The Times* (14 July 1924), p. 15. See also n. 354.
[373] Hardy's father died on 20 July 1892, and his grandfather on 1 Aug 1837.
[374] Rushy Pond, about half a mile from Hardy's birthplace.
[375] Eva Anne Dugdale, Florence Hardy's sister, motoring with Hardy's brother
Henry.
[376] Ralph Waldo Emerson (1803–82), American philosopher and poet.
[377] In Sidmouth, Devon; home of Harley and Helen Granville-Barker (see n.133).
[378] Serge Youriévitch had asked permission on 21 July and sent photographs of the
completed bust on 11 Nov. It was exhibited at the Royal Academy exhibition in 1925.
The bust 'was made in Hardy's study at Max Gate, and though he enjoyed conversation with the sculptor he was tired by the sittings, probably on account of his age,
and definitely announced that he would not sit again for anything of the kind'
(*Life*, 426).

Sept 2. H. & K. came in morning. In aft. Mrs Mitchell &c. & brought bust.[379]

3. F. went to London & Brighton.

16. F. went to London to Dr. & Mrs Head's.[380]

17. Gr. W. Went to cinder path – cloudy: windy.[381]

⟨53⟩

☼ [382] In the autumn of 1924 Hardy was asked by the Dorchester amateur players for something they might do that winter. To save himself trouble he exhumed an old dramatization of Tess of the d'Urbervilles – done at the request of several stage ladies[383] – which he had cast aside many years earlier, having come to the conclusion that to dramatize a novel was a mistake in art: moreover that the play ruined the novel, and the novel the play.[384] However he handed over the play to the company, and they produced it with such unexpected success at Dorchester and Weymouth that it was asked for in London and in the following year produced there by professional actors.[385] [Hardy was therefore charged with an ambition for practical stagery, when in fact the whole proceeding had been against his own judgement and mainly an act of good nature.][386]

---

[379] For the modelling of which Hardy had sat during the week of 28 May.

[380] Dr (later Sir) Henry Head (1861–1940), eminent neurologist, a friend who attended at Hardy's last illness. With his wife, Ruth, he published in 1927 an anthology, *Pages from the Works of Thomas Hardy*.

[381] Great Western: Hardy often walked along the cinder path by the railway, to the rear of Max Gate.

[382] This entry is a typescript carbon copy pasted in on the verso, opposite Hardy's entry of 17 Oct on the recto, where there is a corresponding symbol (see notebook p.54, *infra*).

[383] In 1894–5 several prominent actresses (including Mrs Patrick Campbell, Ellen Terry, Eleanora Duse and Sarah Bernhardt) had asked Hardy for the opportunity to play Tess. He prepared a five-act dramatisation but because of the 'notorious timidity' of London managers the play was abandoned as unsuitable, though it was produced in New York in 1897. Their decision still rankled in 1924 (see Hardy's note of 29 Nov, notebook pp.55–6), when Hardy took great interest in the Hardy Players production and in the performance of Gertrude Bugler as Tess (see n.155). It was produced on 26–9 Nov at Dorchester & on 11 Dec at Weymouth.

[384] In a letter dated 29 Nov 1924 (Purdy, p.78) Hardy advised Macmillan against publication of the dramatisation since 'its publication might injure the novel by being read as a short cut.'

[385] With Gwen Ffrangcon-Davies in the title role (see notes of 9 and 21 Aug, 7 Sep, Oct, 2 Nov and 6 Dec 1925).

[386] This apparently disingenuous claim is omitted from the account of the play in the *Life*, 426.

⟨54⟩

29 Sept. Monday. F. went to London G.W.R.[387] 12 noon, to Fitzroy House Nursing Home. Miserable morning. I accompanied her to station with Wess.[388]

30. Telegrams saying operation had been "quite satisfactory" & "growth completely removed: patient doing well."[389]

Oct 9. F. returned from London after opn.
17. Rehearsal of Tess play in drawing room by Dorchester players.[390]
☼ [see opposite][391]

22. In car with F. to the barn at the back of Kingston Maurward old manor house, where as a child I heard the village young women sing the ballads.[392]

End of Oct. Sunday. To Woolbridge Manor House with F.
Dr & Mrs Smerdon, Gertrude B.

⟨55⟩

& young Atkins – rehearsal of scene from Tess in parlour.[393]
Nov. 21. To rehearsal of Tess in Corn Ex.

---

[387] Great Western Railway.

[388] Hardy's dog Wessex.

[389] See also note of 2 Jan 1923, and n.266. May O'Rourke, then Hardy's secretary, recalls: 'As we had arranged, I was at Max Gate early on that morning: when Hardy greeted me I was shocked to see the change in his appearance. Suspense was taking a heavy toll on him; and it was a relief when at last news came that the operation was over, and had been successful. Hardy was still acutely aware, and indeed appeared dazed' ('Thomas Hardy: His Secretary Remembers', *Monographs*, No.8 (Beaminster, Dorset, 1964), p.32). The operation was performed by the eminent surgeon Mr James Sherren.

[390] Recalled by Norman J. Atkins, who played Alec: 'Mr. Hardy helped us rearrange the furniture to give us space in which to act and was in one of his best moods, but it was to Tess that he directed most of his animated conversation.' But Hardy was 'scratchy' to Atkins for 'being too nice to Tess' in his performance ('Hardy, Tess and Myself', *Monographs*, No.2 (Beaminster, Dorset, 1962), p.14).

[391] Refers to typescript carbon copy pasted in on the verso (see n.382).

[392] Hardy 'looked around at the dusty rafters and the debris, considering possibly the difference that seventy years had made, and his manner as he left the barn was that of one who wished he had not endeavoured to revive a scene from a distant past. Almost certainly he was the only human being left of that once gay party' (*Life*, 426–7). Cf. also *Life*, 19–20.

[393] The idea of a rehearsal at Wool Manor, as the original setting of the honeymoon

24. J.M. Barrie, & Harold Child came to attend rehearsal. Col Lawrence came & met them at dinner, & all went.

25. Barrie & Child left.

26. Wedy. 1st perfce. of Tess play. Sassoon & E.M. Forster came. Col. L. met them in theatre. I sat in wings.

27. Cockerell came. Sassoon stayed on & went with us to matinée. Tea with the players in Town Hall. Met G.B's husband. [394] Cockerell went also to eveng. p. F. Harrison there. [395]

29. Mr Casson & Basil Dean's [396] sec. at the play. The last performce. Supper afterwds. in Council Chamber –

Thus a play produced in a merely accidental manner by amateurs in ☼· [397]

T.O.

⟨56⟩

from back

☼· 1924, showed by its success at this late date that it could probably have made a fortune to a theatre-manager if it had been brought out by a professional company in the eighteen-nineties when it was written. [398]

⟨57⟩

Dec 11. Motored with F. to Weymouth for performance of Tess.
        Dined with the Mayor between the two performances. Obliged to attend 2nd performance. Auction of programme. Motored home by moonlight.

---

scene (Wellbridge manor-house in the novel), was conceived by Dr E.W. Smerdon, who played Angel Clare. The setting inspired a notable performance by Gertrude Bugler: 'undoubtedly she was the very incarnation of Tess Durbeyfield, and as [Hardy] sat and watched he appeared to be deeply moved' (N.J. Atkins, op. cit., pp.15–16). The party then returned to Max Gate.

[394] Gertrude Bugler's husband Ernest, a farmer at Beaminster.

[395] Frederick Harrison, manager of the Haymarket Theatre, who offered Mrs Bugler the chance to play Tess in London (see n.155).

[396] Lewis Casson, actor and manager; husband of Sybil Thorndike, who had been in correspondence with Hardy about the Tess play but who eventually decided not to accept it for publication. Basil Dean, theatrical producer, was then managing director of the Drury Lane and St Martin's Theatres.

[397] The symbol signifies that the note continues on the following verso.

[398] See n.383.

12. Mrs Doyle Jones called about illustrns.
Mr Bliss[399] lunched.
24. Xmas Eve. Sent play to Mr Harrison.

25. Christmas Day. K.[400] came to (early) dinner.

31. New Years eve – sat up, & heard Big Ben & London church bells by wireless ring in the new year.

End of 1924.

––––––––––––

⟨58⟩

"In every representative of Nature which is a work of art there is to be found, as Prof. Courthope has said, something wh. is not to be found in the aspect of Nature wh. it represents; & what that something is has been a matter of dispute from the earliest days of criticism."
(L. Pearsall Smith. "Four Words." S.P.E.)[401]
    The same writer adds, better use the word "inspiration" than "genius" for inborn daemonic genius, as distinct from conscious artistry.[402] [It seems to me it might be called "temperamental impulse" wh. of course, must be inborn]
Dans la création d'un bonheur sans mélange
Être plus artiste que Dieu."
Quoted by Théoph. Gautier, meaning Art.[403]
                                    ib.

––

[399] Howard Bliss, friend of Hardy from 1920 until the author's death, now owner of a collection of Hardy mss.
[400] Hardy's sister Kate.
[401] Logan Pearsall Smith, *Four Words: Romance, Originality, Creative, Genius*, S.P.E. Tract No.XVII (Oxford: Clarendon Press, 1924). Hardy was a member of the Society for Pure English, founded 1913, and Pearsall Smith (1865–1946) was the hon. sec. This quotation is taken from p.38 of the tract.
[402] Ibid., p.41.
[403] Ibid., p.44, from Gautier, *Histoire du Romantisme* (1872), p.65. Théophile Gautier (1811–72), French poet and novelist, was an extreme Romantic in youth and later an exponent of 'art for art's sake'.

⟨59⟩

1925.

Jan – sent "The Absolute Explains" to the Nineteenth Century. [404]

10. Cockerell came.
11. Sunday. Lawrence dined.
12. F.s birthday. Mrs Gertrude Bugler lunched. Cockerell left. [405]
Feb. 2. To Stinsford & Talbothays.

Feb 7. M. Frèdèric Lefèvre, Editor of "Les Nouvelles Litteraires,"
& Mlle. Yvonne Salmon (or Sahnon) called. [406]
– Connie came.
March 20. Ld. Curzon died. [407]
March (latter part) Cockerell came.
   30th (about) Middleton Murrys came to lodings ⟨lodgings⟩ in
Dorchester.

⟨60⟩

April 10. Good Friday.
" 11. People came to tea.
" 12. Easter Sunday – people at tea. Miss Howe recited some of my
poems.
April 17. To Kingston Russell to see Mrs Doyle Jones's sketches for
Tess.
" 18. Mr Watkins called in evening – left at 10. Heard next day that he
had died during the night at the King's Arms. [408]

---

[404] Published Feb 1925, pp.157–60.
[405] Florence Hardy complained to Sydney Cockerell that Hardy had overlooked her birthday because of his 'infatuation' for Gertrude Bugler (see n.155), but this note shows that Hardy not forgotten it. Cockerell noted in his diary: '12th January. Walked into Dorchester with F.H. in the morning. She told me that she had been in such a fret in the night that she would go mad. It was her birthday (45) but he had not alluded to it in any way. . . . Mrs. Bugler came to lunch . . . On the face of it there does not seem to be much harm in her . . . T.H. went through the new scenes of Tess with her. F.H. begged me to stay to make things easier, or I should have left in the morning' (Blunt, op.cit., p.215).
[406] Yvonne Salmon translated *The Dynasts* into French.
[407] George, Marquis Curzon (1859–1925), Hardy's friend in the 1890s, an eminent politician, former Viceroy of India, Lord Privy Seal, Leader of the House of Lords and Foreign Secretary.
[408] William Watkins, sec. of the Society of Dorset Men in London: see n.216, and *Life*, 427–8.

20. Cockerell and his daughter came to lunch on their way from Cambridge to Chantmarle.[409]
22. Attended funeral of Mr Watkins with F. at Dorchester Cemetery.
28. Death of Harry Pouncy.[410]
30. F. went to London & Enfield.
May 1. F. at R. Academy Private View – returned in evening.
23. To Netherton Hall.
May 26. Letter & Leader in Times on a Thomas Hardy Chair of Literature & a Wessex University.[411] Letter signed by (T.O.) –

⟨61⟩

E.K. Chambers (C.B., D.Litt.): Prof. Sir A.T. Quiller Couch: Prof. Sir Israel Gollancz, Litt.D. Sir Fredk. G. Kenyon, K.C.B.: Sir H. Newbolt Litt.D. Horace Annesley Vachell, & Duke of Wellington.[412] President. University College Appeal.

May 31. Whitsunday.

June 2. Birthday. Many telegrams & letters.
H. & K. came in morning.
  Capt & Mrs Berkeley Williams called[413]

---

[409] Home of C.H. St John Hornby (see n.239).

[410] County organising and general sec. of the Dorset Farmers' Union; the Pouncys were a long-established Dorchester family.

[411] The letter to the editor (p.17) promotes the creation of a Thomas Hardy Chair of English Literature at the University College of Southampton: 'the professorship may and should be brought into being at the college without delay.' The editorial (also p.17), 'A Thomas Hardy Chair', encourages the establishment from the existing university college of a University of Wessex, so called because Hardy 'has opened our eyes to Wessex, and has spread a loving pride in Wessex far and wide among English-speaking peoples.' Commending Hardy as 'one of the great figures in English literature', the leader urges contributions to the appeal fund for the Chair in his name. But no University of Wessex has been formed, and no such Chair has ever been endowed.

[412] The signatories: E.K. Chambers (1866–1954), literary critic and civil servant in the Education Department; Sir Arthur Quiller-Couch (1863–1944), literary critic and Prof. of English Literature at Cambridge; Sir Israel Gollancz (1863–1930), philologist and scholar, Prof. of English, London University; Sir Frederick Kenyon (1863–1952), Director, British Museum, 1909–30; Sir Henry Newbolt (1862–1938), barrister, author and poet; H.A. Vachell (1861–1955), prolific author; the 4th Duke of Wellington (1849–1934).

[413] Capt. Berkeley Williams (1865–1938), landowner, J.P. and former professional soldier, and his wife Winifred.

June 15. Margery S.[414] came. 18. left.

18 – Undergraduate musicians from Cambridge came & played. S. Cockerell with them. Pieces by Gibbons, Purcell, Arne, Mozart, Haydn. &c. Part songs. &c[415]

July 15. Deputation from Bristol Univy. with Hon. degree of Litt.D.[416]

⟨62⟩

1925.

About 3rd week in July. Mr Philip Ridgeway[417] requested "Tess" play for Barnes Theatre – sent him copy of play

July 29. Sent off Poems. "Human Shows" to Macmillan.[418] Also signed Agreement for Tess play & posted it.

9 Aug. Sunday: Barnes Theatre people came.

Mr Ridgeway, Miss Gwen Ffrangçon-Davies, Mr Filmer, Mr Hammond Mr Holt Sec

12. Philpotts came

13. Lady Ottoline Morrell[419] & Mr U. came

21. Aug. Sat. Barnes Theatre people came

"Truth is what will work" said Wm. James.[420] (Harpers.) A worse corruption of language was never perpetrated.

---

[414] Florence's sister, Margaret Alicia Soundy.

[415] The visit was arranged by Sydney Cockerell.

[416] Hardy's fifth honorary degree, the others being LL.D. (Aberdeen), Litt.D. (Cambridge), D.Litt. (Oxford), LL.D. (St Andrews).

[417] Ridgeway (1892–1954) was an actor and producer, whose 'Philip Ridgeway Company' presented *Tess* at the Barnes Theatre.

[418] *Human Shows, Far Phantasies, Songs and Trifles* was published on 20 Nov. Hardy's seventh volume of poetry, and the last to be published during his lifetime, it contains 152 poems.

[419] Lady Ottoline Morrell (1873–1938), patroness in London of an intellectual and aesthetic circle containing some of the leading artists and writers of the day, including Bertrand Russell, D.H. Lawrence, Augustus John, Lytton Strachey, Virginia and Leonard Woolf, W.B. Yeats and T.S. Eliot.

[420] William James (1842–1910), American empirical philosopher and elder brother of Henry James. He believed abstract ideas to be truth if 'they work', i.e. do not challenge our other experience or accepted ideas.

⟨62(a)⟩

Sacred
to the memory of
Robert Reason
Who departed this life
December 26th 1819
Aged 56 years
Dear friend why should you
mourn for me
I am but where you
soon must be.[421]

⟨63⟩

1925
Sept 7. First performance of Tess at Barnes.[422]

Oct 9. Walked to Stinsford in morning. F. copied Robert Reason's headstone, made legible by the Sun. (see opposite)[423]
Oct . . . Miss Gwen F.D. & Mr Lewis came
Oct 24. "Tess of the d'U" began as a serial in John o' London's weekly.[424]
Nov 2. "Tess" removed to Garrick Theatre
" 6. Margie & boy left for Canada.[425]F. & K. went with them to Southn. in car.

---

[421] This is written in a large hand by Florence Hardy on one sheet and a fraction of a second sheet of lavatory paper, and pasted on to the page (see also note of 9 Oct and n.423). 'Although Robert Reason had died twenty-one years before the birth of the author of *Under the Greenwood Tree,* he was faithfully described in that novel as Mr. Penny, the shoemaker, Hardy having heard so much of him from old inhabitants of Bockhampton. He used to regret that he had not used the real name, that being much better for the purpose than the one he had invented' (*Life*, 429). (The inscription is reproduced, with minor errors, in the *Life*, 'why' and 'but' being omitted from the last two sentences.)

[422] With Gwen Ffrangcon-Davies (1896–   ) in the title role, the play opened at the Barnes Theatre on 7 Sep transferring to the Garrick on 2 Nov and ran for a total of 131 performances. There was a revival at the Duke of York's from 23 July 1929, running for several weeks, this time with Gertrude Bugler (see n.155) eventually making her only London appearance.

[423] Hardy had long intended to decipher the lettering in order to recarve the letters with his penknife. But he usually visited Stinsford in the afternoon or evening and only on this uncustomary morning walk did the sunlight reveal the inscription, which Mrs Hardy promptly copied onto lavatory paper (see p.62(a) and n.421).

[424] 24 Oct 1925–10 July 1926; the first serial publication of the unbowdlerised text.

[425] Margaret and Thomas Soundy.

End of Nov. "Human Shows" published.
Nov 30. Sir Regd. & Lady Pinnie[426] came, with Mrs Watts

Dec 6. Sunday. Company of players from the Garrick Theatre came, & performed Tess in our drawing room – about 25 players, also photographers, &c.[427]

Oct. Copy of The Three Wayfarers sent to Oxford:[428] returned later.
Dec 1. Copy of ditto sent to Mr Philip Ridgeway.

(64)

18 Dec (about) Little Caroline Hanbury came[429]
19 Dec. Hamo Thornycroft died.[430]
20. Siegfried Sassoon & Byam (?) Shaw[431] came to tea. Staying at Weymth.
21. ditto – 22. They called on their way to Oxford.
23 Mary's birthday –[432]

---

[426] Sir Reginald and Lady Hester Pinney of Racedown, Dorset, a house in which Wordsworth, his sister and Coleridge had stayed. Hardy visited the house in 1925 and asked Lady Pinney to find out about Martha Brown, whom he had seen hanged nearby when he was 16. She did so and in his letter of thanks (20 Jan 1926) Hardy recalls: 'I remember what a fine figure she showed against the sky as she hung in the misty rain, and how the tight black silk gown set off her shape as she wheeled half-round and back.' (See Lady Hester Pinney, 'Thomas Hardy and the Birdsmoorgate Murder 1856', Monographs, No.25 (Beaminster, Dorset, 1966), an essay written in 1956.)

[427] A detailed account of the occasion, written by a member of the company, is in the Life, 429–30.

[428] Hardy's dramatisation from the story 'The Three Strangers' (1883); a one-act play first performed in 1893 at Terry's Theatre, London, and by the Hardy Players in 1911. He revised the dramatisation for a performance at Keble College Oxford, on 21–22 June 1926.

[429] Hardy's god-daughter (see notes of 9 June (& n.144) and 1 Sep 1921), now four years old.

[430] Sir Hamo Thornycroft (1850–1925), prominent sculptor, whose bronze head of Hardy was later presented to the National Portrait Gallery. 'Hardy had a warm regard for the sculptor, whose fine upstanding mien spoke truly of his nobility of character. The hours Hardy had spent in Sir Hamo's London studio and at his home were pleasant ones, and they had cycled together in Dorset while Sir Hamo was staying at Max Gate' (Life, 430). Siegfried Sassoon, his nephew, left Max Gate for the funeral in Oxford with a laurel wreath from Hardy (see note of 22 Dec).

[431] Glen Byam Shaw (1904–   ), actor and director, later Director of the Shakespeare Memorial Theatre. In 1926 he was in repertory under J.B. Fagan at the Oxford Playhouse.

[432] Hardy's sister Mary, b.1841, d. 1915.

She came into the world . . . And went out . . . And the world is just the same . . . not a ripple on the surface left.
25. Christmas day.

31. New Year's Eve.
F & I sat up – Heard on the wireless various features of N.Y. Eve in London – dancing at Albert Hall, Big Ben striking twelve, singing Auld Lang Syne, G.S. the King, the Marseillaise, hurrahing.

End of 1925.

☼ July 1926. Note. – It appears that The Theory exhibited in "The Well-Beloved" in 1892[433] – has been since developed by Proust still further:- "Peu de personnes comprennent le caractère purement subjective du phénomène qu'est l'amour, et la sorte de création que c'est d'une personne supplémentaire, distincte de celle qui porte le même nom dans le monde, et dont la plupart des éléments son tirés de nous-même"
(Ombre. I. 40.)[434]
"Le désir s'élève, se satisfait, disparait – et c'est tout. Ainsi, la jeune fille qu'on épouse n'est pas celle dont on est tombé amoureux"[435] (Ombre. II, 158, 159.) &c. see "Marsyas."[436] Juillet 1926.

⟨65⟩

1926

Jan 1. Connie came.

Jan. 6. Resigned Governorship of Dorchester Grammar School.
Feb. 1. Signed sheets (338) retd. to Macmillans.[437]

---

[433] The 'Platonic Idea' of idealistic philosophy that a man loves not the reality of a woman but the vision or image of her that exists in his own mind, exemplified in The Well-Beloved by the constant migration of Jocelyn Pierston's love from woman to woman.

[434] 'Few people understand the purely subjective nature of the phenomenon of love, and the way it is the creation of a supplementary person distinct from the one who bears the same name in the world, and most of whose elements are drawn from ourselves.' Marcel Proust, A l'ombre des jeunes filles en fleurs, in A la recherche du temps perdu.

[435] 'Desire arises, satisfies itself, disappears – and that's all. Thus, the girl whom one marries is not the person with whom one fell in love.'

[436] 'Revue de littérature et d'art', founded 1908.

[437] In 1926 Macmillan published a special edition of Tess of the d'Urbervilles, 325 copies on large paper, and Hardy agreed to sign the sheets (Purdy, p.77).

? June. F. Macmillan came with Whibley.[438]

June. 525 sheets in course of signing for "Dynasts"[439]

– June 29. Balliol players performed the Hipollytus of Euripides on the lawn.

– June. Message sent to Weymouth, Massachussetts.[440]

✼ [opposite][441]

? July. D. Macmillan came.[442] Took back the 525 sheets signed for edn. of "The Dynasts."

Aug. 3. Subscribed to Curzon Memorial Fund.[443]

Aug. W. Macmillan came.

. . . Sept. Mayor of Weymouth & deputation called with message from Weymouth, Mass. in answer to mine.

8 Sept. Mr Drinkwater's dramatization of "The Mayor of Caster-bridge" produced at the Barnes Theatre.[444] 14th. F. went with Mrs. B.

⟨66⟩

✼ [445]She told me an amusing story when showing me a letter to Sir John Bankes from Charles the First, acknowledging that he had borrowed £500 from Sir J. Many years ago when she was showing the same letter to King Edward, who was much interested in it, she said "Perhaps, Sir, that's a little matter which could now be set right." He replied quickly "Statute of Limitations, Statute of Limitations."

⟨67⟩

End of Sept. With F. on a visit to Mrs Bankes at Kingston Lacy.[446] ✼

---

[438] Charles Whibley (see n.204).

[439] In Apr 1927, Macmillan published a special edition, 525 copies on large paper, and, as in n.437, Hardy agreed to sign the sheets (Purdy, pp.134–5), a task which he completed in July.

[440] A message of friendship carried by a deputation from Weymouth, England.

[441] The symbol refers to the note of July 1926, above, pasted in on the verso.

[442] Daniel Macmillan (1886–1965), Director (1911–65) and Chairman (1936–63) of Macmillan & Co.

[443] See n.407.

[444] See n.333.

[445] This note is written on the verso; the symbol refers to the note 'End of Sept.' on the recto (see below).

[446] Mrs Henrietta Bankes, widow of Walter Ralph Bankes (1853–1904). The note is on the verso, p. 66.

20 Sept. Performance of Mayor of C. at Weymouth by London company, a "flying matinée." Motored down with F., Mr Ridgeway, & Drinkwater, who called before we started. Beautiful afternn. Scene outside the theatre finer than within. Snapshotters for newspaper illustrations very pestering.[447]

Oct 14. Critics: they fix the rank of their author by his value as an artificer, not as an inventor, a shaper, not as a creator. Critics of plays likewise.

Sabotage and the policy of ca' canny[448] are after all fraud and perfidy, just as much as the exploits of the swindling grocer, the political concessionaire or the profiteer.[449]

"False Dawn" by A. Carthill. (Blackwood)[450]

⟨68⟩

1926
22 Oct. Special illustrated edition of Tess published.[451]

29 Oct. "Time & Chance" by Mary Stella Edwards. Prefce. by Gilbt. Murray. Hogarth Press 5/-[452]

---

[447] Cf. Life, 432–3: '[Hardy] received a great ovation in the theatre, and also, on his return to Max Gate, from an enthusiastic crowd that collected round the Pavilion Theatre on the pier. From balconies and windows people were seen waving handkerchiefs as he drove past.'

[448] Scottish expression for trade union policy of limiting output by 'working to rule' or calling a strike.

[449] This is a newspaper cutting pasted in.

[450] A. Carthill (pseudonym of Bennet Calcraft Kennedy), False Dawn [on the causes of revolutions] (Edinburgh and London: W. Blackwood, 1926). Cf. Hardy's note, 24 Jan 1888: '[I am] equally opposed to aristocratic privilege and democratic privilege. (By the latter I mean the arrogant assumption that the only labour is hand-labour – a worse arrogance than that of the aristocrat, – the taxing of the worthy to help those masses of the population who will not help themselves when they might, etc.) Opportunity should be equal for all, but those who will not avail themselves of it should be cared for merely – not be a burden to, nor the rulers over, those who do avail themselves thereof' (Life, 204). Under the heading 'Trade Unionism', Hardy was asked in Shop Assistant (21 June 1919), p.405, to define his concept of progress, to which he replied: 'I favour social re-adjustments rather than social subversions – remembering that the opposite of error is error still.'

[451] Signed by Hardy (see n.437) and with wood engravings by Vivien Gribble.

[452] A volume of poems, published by Leonard and Virginia Woolf at the Hogarth Press, 1926. Virginia Woolf had visited Hardy on July 25.

1 Nov. Went with Mr Hanbury to Bockn & looked at fencing, trees, &c, with a view to tidying and secluding the Hardy house.[453]

_____

Nov. Col Lawrence called to bid goodbye (India)[454]

_____

24 Nov. Mr W.L. Courtney asked for poem for Fortnightly Revw.[455]

_____

Beging. of Dec "The Lady in the Furs" (a poem) appeared in Saturday Review:[456]

_____

Dec (1st week) – walking with F. by railway. Saw bullocks & cows going to Islington (?) for slaughter –[457]

_____

– Dec. 10. Returned corrected proof of "A Philosophical Fantasy" to Mr Courtney for F.R.

⟨69⟩

1926

17 Dec. In Times, Morning Post, &c. to-day is an account of the sales yesterday at Hodgson's Rooms, Chancery Lane – in which details

---

[453] 'That was his last visit to the place of his birth. It was always a matter of regret to him if he saw this abode in a state of neglect, or the garden uncherished' (_Life_, 433).

[454] 'Hardy was much affected' by this parting from T.E. Lawrence; see n.336 and cf. _Life_, 434.

[455] W.L. Courtney (1850–1928), editor of the _Fortnightly Review_, 1894–1928. Hardy sent 'A Philosophical Fantasy', published in Jan 1927, pp.1–4.

[456] 4 Dec 1926, p.669.

[457] 'Hardy thought of this sight for long after.' The pencil sketch represents the rows of trucks 'with animals' heads at every opening, looking out at the green countryside they were leaving for scenes of horror in a far-off city' (_Life_, 434). In his will, dated 1922, Hardy had bequeathed some money to encourage the discovery of means of alleviating the sufferings of animals in transit to the slaughterhouses.

are given of the prices fetched by some of my books – first edns. autogd. &c –[458]

23 Dec. St Peter's Carol Singers came & sang "While Shepherds watch'd" to my grandfather's & father's tune[459]

25. Christmas day.

27 Our famous dog "Wessex" died at $\frac{1}{2}$ past 6 in the evening. 13 years of age.[460]

28. Wx. buried.[461] K. & P.A. came to tea.

" Night. Wx. sleeps outside the house the first time for 13 years.

30. "Wessex Programme" on wireless.[462]

31. New Year's Eve. Did not sit up.

End of 1926.

⟨70⟩

1927

"A Philosophical Fantasy" appears in Fortnightly January number.[463]

Jan. 3 – onwards. Men putting in pipes for town water.

---

[458] 'Sale Room', *The Times*, p.11 Three items with autograph inscriptions to Florence Henniker (*Desperate Remedies*, 1892 edition; *A Laodicean*, 1882 edition; and *The Dynasts*, 1903–8, first editions of the three parts) brought, respectively, £49, £43 and £445. An 1877 edition of *Far from the Madding Crowd* brought £25 10s. A group of letters to and from Hardy about *The Woodlanders* and *Wessex Tales* copyrights and production costs was sold for £53, and a 1903 letter from Hardy about the world serial rights of a story in *Pall Mall Magazine* for £20 10s. Hardy was always interested in the financial details attaching to both present and former editions of his works.

[459] The tune which they used to play at Stinsford, a copy of which he had given to the rector.

[460] Wessex, the Hardys' notorious wire-haired terrier, was feared by domestic staff and guests alike, several victims having been bitten by him. Lady Cynthia Asquith, surely without literal truth, recalled of her 1922 visit that 'Wessex was specially uninhibited at dinner-time, most of which he spent not under but on the table, walking about unchecked, and contesting every single forkful of food on its way from my plate to my mouth' (op. cit., p.383). But Hardy, to whom Wessex had been a faithful and valued companion, was much saddened by his death: cf. 'Dead "Wessex" the Dog to the Household' (*Complete Poems*, pp.915–6).

[461] In the shrubbery on the west side of Max Gate, with a headstone inscribed: 'THE/ FAMOUS DOG/ WESSEX/ August 1913–27 Dec. 1926/ Faithful. Unflinching.'

[462] On the BBC's penultimate day as the British Broadcasting Company (from 1 Jan it became the British Broadcasting Corporation), the 'Wessex Programme' was broadcast from 8.0 to 9.30 p.m. from London, Bournemouth and several stations around the country. Introduced by Florence Hardy, it included Hardy's one-act play, *The Three Wayfarers*, some readings from his works, and music.

[463] 'Hardy liked the year to open with a poem of this type from him in some leading review or newspaper' (*Life*, 436).

6 July. The Balliol Players (Oxford) performed "Iphigenia in Aulis" on the lawn. Mr Philip Mason[464] slept here.
7 Cockerell came to lunch.
21. Laid the commemoration stone of the Dorchester Grammar School, & delivered short address on T.H. the founder.[465]

Aug. To Bath & back by car.[466]

Sept 18. Sent copy for new edition of Selected poems to Macmillan.[467]
19. Mr Weld of Lulworth Castle & Sir F & Lady Keeble (Lillah McCarthy) called.[468]

⟨The entry of 19 Sep 1927 is the final entry in Hardy's notebook. There follow 25 unused pages before random earlier entries (following) are found at the end of the notebook. Hardy's pagination ends here but is continued editorially for the last 5 pages.

Hardy continued to be active through the autumn and early winter but began to be ill on 11 Dec, and came downstairs for the last time on Christmas Day. On the evening of 11 Jan 1928 he had a sharp heart attack and shortly after 9 o'clock, in his 88th year, he died.⟩

⟨71⟩

Addresses &c
H.'s[469] Brickyard – particulars

At Broadmayne – Brickyard containing 4 acres, with 3 cottages – best

---

[464] Philip Mason (1906–   ), later a writer and diplomat.
[465] An account of this occasion, and a transcription of the address delivered by Hardy 'in a clear resonant voice', are in the *Life*, 437–9.
[466] 'On the way they had lunch sitting on a grassy bank, as they had done in former years, to Hardy's pleasure. But now a curious sadness brooded over them; lunching in the open air had lost its charm, and they did not attempt another picnic of this kind' (*Life*, 439–40).
[467] In the Golden Treasury series. The volume was published as *Chosen Poems* in Aug 1929.
[468] Herbert Weld, explorer and archaeologist; Sir Frederick Keeble (1870–1952), Prof. of Botany at Oxford; Lady Keeble (1875–1960), the actress Lillah McCarthy, formerly married to Harley Granville-Barker (whom she divorced in 1918).
[469] Hardy's brother Henry, who had carried on the family building business since the death of their father. Broadmayne is three miles S.E. of Dorchester.

Broadmayne clay in large quantity. Inspected by Government – which estimated the clay as being of the best quality.

A Kiln on the ground, capable of burning 25,000 bricks at a burning.

Howard J. Sachs.[470] 30 Pine St. New York (a dealer who buys MSS.etc)

"The English Place-name Society" c/o The Philological Society.
Prof. A. Mawer. University Coll.[471] [apropos of names left out of Ordnance Map, &c]

Freeman   De la M.
Tonks   Gosse.
Gran. B
Cunn. Gr.[472]

⟨72⟩

Addresses &c. –

Green pencils ⎫
              ⎬   E. Wolff & Son. London.
also yellow, &c. ⎭

"Split inf."
"The mind seems more to feel after than to definitely apprehend them"
Walter Bagehot (quot. Times Lit. Supt. 28 Jan 1926)[473]

---

[470] Sachs owned, and sold, several of Hardy's manuscripts.
[471] The English Place-Name Society was founded 9 Jan 1923. Prof. (Sir) Allen Mawr (1879–1942) was the first Director of the society and at this time Prof. of English Language, Liverpool University. He was also a member (and later president) of the Philological Society. There are no records of correspondence between Hardy & Mawr.
[472] It is not clear why Hardy lists again those he associated, in his pained and angry note of 1 Apr 1924, as disciples of George Moore (see nn.360 and 361).
[473] It is unclear whether Hardy is quoting Bagehot's example approvingly or, as a member of the Society for Pure English, disdaining the use of the split infinitive. The

⟨73⟩

Books.[474]

English & Scottish Popular Ballads.
from F.J. Child, by Helen Child Sargent & G.L. Kittredge.
Houghton Mifflin & co. Boston & New York. Cambridge Edn. 1
vol.[475]

——————

English Metrists. by T.S. Omond – 10/6 net (Humphrey Milford.
Oxford Univy. Press)[476]

——————

Decadence & other Essays, by de Gourmont transl. by Bradley.
Grant Richards 7/6 net[477]
Einstein & the Universe, by C. Nordmann. Fisher Unwin. 10/6[478]
Rousseau's Nouvelle Héloïse. 1 vol. Charpentier. Hachette,
Adelaide St. Strand.[479]
– Euripides: |Aesch. | Soph: Xenoph.[480]
– Worsley's Concepts of Monism.[481]
– Mrs. Siddons. by Mrs A Kennard.[482] 1887. Eminent Womn. series
– Thomas Hardy. Poèmes. Traduction Française de J. Fournier –
Pargoire – Paris. Librarie de France. F. Sant' Andrea et L. Marcerou.
110 Boulevard Saint-Germain. 1925.[483]

———————————————————————————

form may fall within the scope of Hardy's appeal in 1912 against 'the appalling
increase every day in slipshod writing that would not have been tolerated for one
moment a hundred years ago' (speech to the Royal Society of Literature, *The Times* (4
June 1912), p.7). On the other hand Hardy is himself, as Lionel Johnson noticed, 'an
inveterate patron of the split infinitive'. Bagehot is quoted in a leading article on the
centenary of his birth: *TLS*, No.1,254 (28 Jan 1926), 49–50.

[474] Apparently a list of books that Hardy intended to read or, since prices are often
included, to buy.

[475] London, 1904; edited from the collection of Francis J. Child.

[476] 'Being a sketch of English prosodical criticism from Elizabethan times to the
present day.' Oxford: Clarendon Press, 1921.

[477] William Aspenwall Bradley, trans. R. de Gourmont, *Decadence, and Other Essays
on the Culture of Ideas* (London, 1922).

[478] Joseph McCabe, trans. Charles Nordmann, *Einstein and the Universe* ['A popular
exposition of the famous theory'] (London, 1922).

[479] Jean-Jacques Rousseau, *La Nouvelle Héloïse* [1761].

[480] The three great Attic tragedians, Euripides (480–406 B.C.), Aeschylus (525–456
B.C.), Sophocles (496–406 B.C.); and Xenophon (430?–355? B.C.), Greek historian.

[481] Arthington Worsley, *Concepts of Monism* (London: T. Fisher Unwin, 1907).

[482] Mrs Arthur [Nina H.] Kennard.

[483] This French translation of Hardy's poems is noted in ink.

B.B. Rogers's translation of Aristophanes – a wonderful transln.
(F. Harrison.)[484]
Wm. Sandys' Christmas Carols, 1833.[485]
Pilgrim's Progress. Several Edns. Oxfd. Univy. Press[486]
Heine's Poet. Works 4 vols. Heinemann 5/- each.[487]
Thelyphthora, or Female Ruin, by Martin Madan, Chaplain to the
Lock Hospital 1780 (in favour of polygamy)

⟨74⟩

Things ⚮ Done[488]

Examine ♂[489] and get a clear idea, & then arrange accordingly,
of trustees, executors, & literary executors ⚶ [see back][490] in my
case. Have ▾ both the latter kind of ex^ors – & which wd. arrange
about burial?[491]

See same as to H—y & K. & F.[492]

What is |posted up| meant at St. Church on burial in old Chyd.?
Is the exprss'n. no new grave – if not, it is not clear about opening
old[493]

---

[484] Benjamin Bickley Rogers, trans. *The Comedies of Aristophanes* (London, 1902); *Aristophanes, the Poet* (London, 1920). Recommended, either personally or in print, by Hardy's friend, Positivist & author Frederic Harrison (1831–1923).

[485] *Christmas Carols* ['ancient and modern, including the most popular in the West of England, and the airs to which they are sung'].

[486] Ed. Edmund Venables (Oxford: Clarendon Press, 1925).

[487] *The Poetical Works of Heinrich Heine* (London: W. Heinemann, 1917).

[488] The remaining entries appear on a separate sheet of unlined white paper pasted on to the back cover of the notebook and folded over. The entries after 'T.O.' are on the reverse side of the folded sheet. Several entries are stroked through as indicated. The symbols constitute a form of shorthand, apparently for concealment, but it is a rather half-hearted attempt at secrecy since Hardy's meaning is quite clear. This first symbol means 'which have to be' (though Hardy's shorthand, here and below, is not quite standard).

[489] 'My will.' The symbol in the following line means 'I'. These preparatory notes were made before Hardy's will was signed on 24 Aug 1922.

[490] Refers to the final fold of the sheet (see below, final entry).

[491] Hardy appointed Lloyds Bank Ltd to be Trustees and Executors of his will, and his wife and Sydney Cockerell as Literary Executors.

[492] His brother Henry, sister Katharine, and Florence Hardy. The gross value of Hardy's estate was £91,707.14.3. Henry (d.1928) left £40,628.4.6; Florence Hardy (d.1937) left £48,010.8.8; Kate (d.1940) left £74,165.5.10.

[493] 'It is my wish that I may be buried in Stinsford Churchyard Dorset near to the Grave of my parents and if possible in my wife Emma's Grave or close at the foot thereof' (Hardy's will, para.2). In the event successful demands that Hardy should be buried in Poet's Corner, Westminster Abbey, were met by a curious compromise: Hardy's heart was cut out and buried in a casket, on 16 Jan 1928, in Emma's grave.

— Bequest to Animal Soc. (say Dumb Friends league) – to be called
E.H. Bequest – or 2 beds Hospital – "Emma H." & "Florence H"[494]
— Go through E's papers again.[495]
— Consolidate directions to Lit. Exors & place them in a prominent
place of first access.
— Continue to examine & destroy useless old MSS, entries in note
books, & marks in printed books.[496]
— Divds. to be paid to Bank not Self.[497]
— Sell Bank Shares.

? Put on G.G.F.s headstone.[498] "She was of the Knight family, many
of whom lie here adjoining."
    Get Mr. Lamb,[499] or other, to make sketch from photo. of Emma,
to match Strang's of F. (for N.P.G.)

                                                          T.O.

⟨75⟩

Put in 𝟼𝟼 [500] that ⏀ [501] have written no autobiogy. but that ⏝ [502]
wife has notes sufficient for a memoir.[503]

---

[494] 'To the Society for the Prevention of Cruelty to Animals Fifty Pounds. To the
Council of Justice to Animals Fifty Pounds. It is my wish that the two last-mentioned
legacies shall be applied as far as practicable to the investigation of the means by
which Animals are conveyed from their Homes to the Slaughter houses with a view
to the lessening of their sufferings in such transit and to condemnatory action against
the caging of wild birds and the captivity of rabbits and other animals' (Hardy's will,
para.7). Hardy did not call this the Emma Hardy bequest, nor were the hospital beds
endowed.
[495] A search through Emma's papers after her death had proved a harrowing
experience for Hardy. He discovered a highly critical manuscript headed 'What I
think of my husband', which he promptly destroyed. No doubt he wished nothing
similar to survive.
[496] Another instance of Hardy's extreme caution lest his papers should after his
death be misinterpreted or misused.
[497] Lloyds Bank is given charge of Hardy's financial affairs in para.22 of his will.
[498] 'G.G.F.' is obviously an error since Hardy means his great-grandmother, Jane
Hardy [née Knight] (1758–1825).
[499] Presumably the artist Henry Lamb (1883–1960).
[500] 'My will'.
[501] 'I'.
[502] 'My'.
[503] This is not mentioned in Hardy's will but in a Private Memorandum (so headed)
entitled 'Information for Mrs. Hardy in the preparation of a biography'; it is clearly
designed to conceal Hardy's own authorship of the Early Life and Later Years. Page 1

— |Destroy framed profiles.|
— Get & frame photos. of Fr. |& M.|[504]
— |Enquire if one-vol. Dynasts is on sale in United States (of Macmn. & Lemperley)| Yes[505]
— Investigate if Harpers pay a royalty on the "Anniversary" Edn. (Eng. Wessex Edn)[506]
— Arrange & weed out study – 1: books useless – for sale. 2: books possibly useful – for another room.
— Ansr. letters.
— F. A list of my works arranged chronologically.[507]
— See how corrections stand in respect of each edition: get a set properly corrected: & destroy useless proofs in cupboard.
— Desty. schemes of dramatization for the different stories: & experiments in Tess dramatizⁿ – except the final one, which mark "an experiment."[508]
— Read M——ls,[509] & dele. if necess.

✗ [510]According to Mr Meade (F. & B.)[511] it is best not to limit the functions of each by special definition, but to mention their functions collectively.

---

begins, in Hardy's hand: 'As there seems to be no doubt that so-called biographies of myself will be published which are unauthorized & erroneous, one having already appeared, it becomes necessary that an authentic volume should at any rate be contemplated by her, & materials gathered by her while there is time.' Mrs Hardy is not enjoined to include all facts to which she has access, 'if any should seem to be indiscreet, belittling, monotonous, trivial, provocative, or in other ways unadvisable.'

[504] Father and mother.

[505] The one-volume edition of The Dynasts had been published in Nov 1910. Paul Lemperly was an American book collector in Cleveland, Ohio.

[506] Another clue suggesting that these notes were made in the early summer of 1922. On 11 July Hardy wrote to F.W. Slater of Harpers asking why their sales report to Dec 1921 did not contain returns for the 21-volume Anniversary edition of 1920.

[507] This was never done by Florence Hardy.

[508] See Hardy's note of Sep 1924 (notebook p.53) and n.383. Ingeniously intent on covering his tracks, Hardy characteristically depreciates the status of his dramatisation.

[509] 'Materials' – Hardy's evasive term to describe the Early Life and Later Years, then in process of secret composition. A number of deletions were made, by Hardy and others, at different stages (see appendix).

[510] The sheet pasted in is folded over at the edge and this final entry appears on the fold. It refers to the arrangements which Hardy was contemplating with regard to his executors (see notebook p.74).

[511] Foster & Braithwaite, investment brokers, 27 Austin Friars, London EC2.

'Schools of Painting Notebook'

⟨1⟩

———————— //

School of Florence – Cimabue –
1240–1302. founder – Bold sublimity –
Giotti – Raphael of his age. 1300–36. – more harmony and softness –
less of the harshness of the Christian Greeks – painted the portrait of
Dante –
Buffalmacco – excelled in crucifixions and Ascensions – want of taste
– skilful in draperies.
Andrea Oreagna.
Stefano Florentino, grandson of Giotti. works all perished – Tom-
maso, his son called Giottino from his genius – Taddeo.
Gaddi – died 1352.
Paolo Uccello – corrected perspective errors.
Masolino da Panicale – "errors in light & shade.

⟨2⟩

|his| P. Uccello's scholar Masaccio or Maso di Giovanni truth – died
1443 – best of the succeeding Florentine painters studied in his
school – e.g. two monks –
1. B. Giovanni Angelico, a monk – remarkable beauty in his angels –
2. |Phillipo| Filippo Lippi – gentler order of genius, sweetness &
gracefulness – died 1469.
   Bonozzi Gozzoli – studied under Angelico died 1478.
   Raffaellino del Garbo, school of Lippi –
   Domenico Corradi –
   Antonio Pollainolo – skill in compos^n and anatomy – first Italian
painter who dissected bodies.
   Luca Signorelli
   Leonardo da Vinci – supplied all that the Flo. Sch. seemed to
want, exc: colour – two styles – 1 - shadow and contrast. – 2. more
quiet. b.1452 no scholars – characteristics – calm, solemn, majestic –
variety & invention

⟨3⟩

Michel Angelo – rival of Da Vinci – gt. wk. Battle of Pisa, perished
– Ceiling of the Pope's chapel. – Ceiling & walls of Sistine Chapel,
"Last Judgement" – force grandeur, sublimity, awe – his defects are
extravagance of expression.

Sebastiano del piombo ⎫
Ricciarelli   ⎬ followers ⎰ colour
Baccio della Porta   ⎭   ⎨ spirit
                                    ⎱ sweetness

Andrea del Sarto – natural

Iacopo Carrucci ⎫ pupils
Rosso   ⎭

Swarms of followers of Michel Angelo – (design the leading
characteristic of this school –)

i.e. Lodovico Gigoli — Gregorio Pagani
Francesco Furini
Carlo Dolci — last of the Fl: school.

Siena School. Eve to the Florentine Adam

Guido. ⎫ contempy. with Cimabue
Mino   ⎭
Pietro Lorenzetti

⟨4⟩

Taddeo
Domenico Bartolo – old dryness gone.
Matteo di Giovanni

Genga   ⎫. foreign
Signorella ⎭

Iacopo Pacchiarotto – (native)
Kazzi - - -   "
Mecherino – imitated Perugino.
Per|r|uzzi – modesty & fineness
Francesco Vanni b.1663. last & best artist. ths. sch.

Roman School

Luco – Cavallani – instd. by Giotti.
Pietro Borghese. |c.146| c.1458 – memorable –

Pietro Perrugino – b.1446. hard & dry, but graceful & charm of colour.

Raphael – b.1483. ideal beauty, loftiness, & volupts. . the rival of M. Angelo. – chief glory, his Transfiguration – in emulation of Michel Angelo's cold. by Sebastiano, in the chapel of St Peter.

⟨5⟩

This great work just finished when the painter died 1520. handsome, mild, not a scholar.

Julio Romano. – pupil of Raphael – imitd. M Angelo.
Pellegrino da Modena " "   "   . resembled R. most. – decline of Roman Sch. – partly restored by –
Frederigo Baroccio – style of Corregio – great harmony.
Morigi da Caravaggio – darkness & clouds
Andrea Sacchi b.1600 – repose.
Pietro da Cortona
Carlo Maratti d.1713.

~~~~~~

Neapolitan School.
Tommaso de Stefani – conty. with Cimabue
Simone   "   " Giotti
Antonio Solario – blacksmith – heads beautiful.
Andrea Sabbatini – emulated Raphael.
Corenzio ⎫
Ribera   ⎬
Caraciolo ⎭
Massimo Stanzioni – style of the Car|r|aci

⟨6⟩

Bernardo Cavallino – genius & debauchery d.1656.
Salvator Rosa. b 1614 – savage beauty.
Aniello Falcone – battle pictures.
Luca Giordano. b.1629 – extraordinary talents for imitating any master. he pleased by a certain deceptive grace – not natural in tone or colour.

Venetian School.
Andrea da Murano lived in 1400 – first noted artist

Bartolommeo – 1st. who painted in oil of this sch:
Gentile da Fabriano – founder of the Gt. Vn: Sch.
Giovanni Bellini this sch: owes eminence
Giorgione Barbarelli. b.1478 – under the last – excelled his master –
 grandeur – despised minuteness – rich colour –
Sebastiano del Piombo his scholar – associate of M. Angelo – added
 rich colr. to M.A's outline with rare skill.
Titian – b.1480 – studied under Bellini at first imitd. Giorgione –
afterds. style of his own, less bold, but true.
 the first picture in his own

⟨7⟩

 manner is Archangel Michael & Tobias 1507. – deep & lustrous
 colouring in his wks. more than design – lucid clearness –
 Tintoret, his follower, stern & terrible.
 Tintoretto, his son – more hesitation.
 Bassano. lofty & varied.
 Paul Veronese b.1532 – neglected the antique for the study of
 nature.

School of Mantua. –
 oldest of the schools of Upper Italy
Andrea Mantegna – first of note.
Julio Romano – scholar of Raphael. – design – ardour – softness.
 after him this sch. died out.

School of Modena.
Pellegrino – disciple of Raphael.
Alberto Fontana.
Nicolo dell Abate
 The painters of this school distinguished themselves in architecte.

⟨8⟩

School of Parma.
 Lodovico da Parma – manufd. Madonnas.
Antonio Allegri – ⎱ b.1494. very original – poor – rose up, no one
da Correggio ⎰ knows how – assumption of the Virgin, in the
 cathl. of Parma his great work in wh. he
 equalled M.A. & R. Mengs, in his estimate

of Italian genius gives the 1st. place to Raphael, 2nd. Corregio 3rd.
Titian – "An ideal beauty, with not so much of heaven as in Raphl.
yet surpassing that of nature, but not too lofty for our love." great
knowlge. of lights & shades.

Francesco Mazzuoli, called ⎱ another great light
Parmegianimo ⎰
  grace, almost to excess.
Girolamo Mazzuoli, his cousin & pupil – excelled in perspective –
fine light & shade – figures rather careless, grace inclines to affec-
tation action to violence.

⟨9⟩

School of Cremona
  Melone and Boccacci|a|no
Giulio Campi. dignity. variety of styles.
Camillo, son of Boccacci|a|no – style strong and beautiful.
Battista Trotti – loveliness in the heads

School of Milan
Vincenzio Foppa
Donato Montorfano. clearness
  Da Vinci gave great impulse to this school.
Bernardo da Luino. – heads seem to live.
Gaudenzio Milanese.

Bolognese School
Francesco Francia b.1450. choiceness of colour –
  fulness of outline
  Lodovico Caracci – went to nature.
  Annibale"⎱ his cousins –
  Agostino"⎰ [instructed by him]

⟨10⟩

  The Caracci triumphed over the old artists and founded a style of
their own. Lodovico had less fire than his cousins, but he excelled
them in grace and grandeur – died 1619. Annibale d.1609 Agostino
d.1602.

Domenico Lampieri   }
                          noblest pupil of the Caracci,
otherwise Domenichino }
   his style of painting almost theatrical – lays the scene amidst arche. – beauty of his angels. –
Francesco Albani.
Guido. b.1574 – gt. genius of this School. sweetness his charm – the upward look of his countenances. d.1642.
Giovanni Francesco Barbieri, or Guercino.

School of Ferrara
Galasso Galassi 1400–50.
The Two Dossi – immortalized by Ariosto in his national poem.
Benvenuto da Garofalo. b 1481.
Girolano de Carpi.

⟨11⟩

Bastiano Filippi – After M. Angelo – aspired after the bold & terrible

School of Genoa.
Perino del Vaga. style of Raphael.
Luca Cambiaso . . Rape of the Sabines. has been extolled as worthy of Raphael
Giovanni Battisti Paggi
Valerio Castello. b 1625.

German School.
   All Germany in early days seems to have been one vast studio for Saints, Angels, and Madonnas.
Albert Durer – b 1471 – his skill in engraving equalled his talent in painting. d.1528.
Lucas Kranach b 1473. painter & engraver, old men & women –
Giulio Giorgio Clovio – a different order, a little of Raphael's spirit –
Hans Holbein – b.1498. Dance of Death.

⟨12⟩

came to England [temp. Hy VIII] – also archt. – d 1554.
John Rothenhamer.
Schwarts (Christopher). b 1550 – fine colouring.
Felix Mayer.

School of Spain.
Pedro Campana. Luis Morales.
Pablo Cespedes.
Guiseppe Ribera known as Spagnoletto. b.1589 – gloomy & horr-
ible.
Don Diego Velasquez. b 1594. natural. & expressive rather gloomy
Alonso Cano.
Bartolomeo Roman
Francisco Collantes – broh. landspe. into repute.
Murillo – the chief boast of Spain b 1613 his holy family in N.G.
equals Da Vinci, Raphl. & Correggio in sweetness of col: & freedom
of touch. often coarse, never mean. often incorrect, never weak in
character. d 1682.
Antonio Castrejon.

⟨13⟩

   Mem – The "colouring of Venice the design of Florence and the
outline of Rome"

French School.
Cousin & Blanchard – early –
Simon Vouet – 1582. gt. facility
Nicholas Poussin, his rival & enemy. b.1594.
   "Taking of Jerusalem" "Last Supper" inventors of the Grand
   Historical Landspe.
Gaspar Poussin – also landscape.
Peter Valentine – painted humble life
Claude Lorraine 1600. went to nature – nothing at figures – 1682
Le Seur ⎱ 1617   poetic – simple
Le Brun ⎰ 1619   genius extensive sameness in heads
Iacopo Corteso

Watteau – grotesque. d 1721
Vernet – Caylus – Greuze
James Louis David b.1750

⟨14⟩

Flemish School
Hubert Van Eyck 1366.
John Van Eyck 1370 – brother – discovd. art of painting in oil.
Henry Stenwyck – 1550.
Peter Paul Rubens 1577 –
    majesty & pomp – warmth of colour – deficient in soft and sublime
    inspiration consps: in Italian painters. Living life. voluptuousness
    – beauty of expression rather than form. d 1640.
Snyders 1571 dogs and hunting.
Mompert – Crayer. James Jordaens
    1594, natural & free. Janseens
Rombouts
David Teniers. humour, drollery, vulgarity – truthful. d.1694

⟨15⟩

Anthony Vandyke – b 1598 – dignity grace – great in portraits.
"Christ crucified between theives" – 1641.

Dutch School.
    owes none of its fame to dignity of subject. This sch. arose with
Luke of Leyden b.1490
Van Ryn Rembrandt – b.1604 – stands at the hd. all his pictures seen
by an uncommon light. – gt. finish at first,* aftds. rough vigour. No
sense of beauty or grandeur – exhibited man just as he found him.
⟨Correspondent asterisk and reference in left margin, as follows:⟩

* St. John in the Wilderness
Albert Cuyp. 1606. Followed nature, with. the strange light of R.

Terbourg. Adrian Brouwer,
Adrian Ostade 1613 – boorish drollery. The Teniers of the Dutch
Sch:
Gerard Douw – gentle & humorous.
Nicholas Berchem. 1624 – landscape, grace

P. Wouwerman – horses introduced –
Paul Potter – cows & calves –

⟨16⟩

Jacob Ruysdael – 1636. landscape
Vandervelde – chiefly sea views –

British School
William, Monk of Windsor ⎫ Mid.   abt.
Walter, of Westminster   ⎭ Ages   1292
Reformn. separated art & the Church.
After the Restorn. Verrio & La Guerre painted pagan gods by the
yard.
Sir P. Lely   ⎫ likeness painters of a
"Godfrey Kneller ⎭ better order –
turned their subjects into gods and goddesses.
Hogarth. 1697 Painted life as he saw it – he saw it as a satirist – cared
not for the beau ideal of art. painted the folly he observed.
Wilson. 1713. Creator of B. Landscape
poor . . Librarian to the Academy. his talent not appreciated
Sir Joshua Reynolds 1723. gt. power in portraits, correct taste – little
imagination
Gainsborough. 1727. people landscapes – joyousness & vigour.
("Wilson" to "vigour." bracketed in left margin, with the following
note:)
Members of the R.A. Sir J. first prest. ⟨president⟩
Romney. 1746. Lady Hamilton his chief model.

⟨17⟩

Benjamin West. 1738. historical and epic. soul & poetry wanting in
his pictures, exc. Death of Genl. Wolfe.
James Barry. 1741 at Cork. his notions more lofty than his productions –
Allegorical.
Henry Fuseli. 1741. b. at Zurich, came to London
rejoiced in the vast, & wonderful – of serenity & tranquillity he was
ignorant.
David Allan – b. in Scotland.

James Northcote – historical
Allan Ramsay. & Henry Raeburn. Sch:
Blake. Opie. Cornishman .
Morland. a profligate. printed boors &c.
Sir T. Lawrence. 1769 called the 2nd. Reynolds. but had little of his breadth & vigour, tho' his powers of expression – more of the polite & graceful than the vigo|u|rous.
Constable – truth
Bonington – elegance
Stothard – beauty & sweetness
Hilton – beauty – colour & accuracy.
Newton – care – truth & elegance.

———————— // ————————

'Trumpet-Major Notebook'

Bsh. Museum

Notes
taken for "Trumpet Major"
& other books of time
of Geo III.
in
(1878 – 1879 –)

King George at Weymouth:
1789, 1791, 1792, 1794, 1795
1796, 1797, 1798, 1801, 1802,
1804, 1805 –

⟨1⟩
1803–5 |Geo. III.| notes – (I.) B.M.&c.

The magistrates acting under the alien act would do well to direct a very scrutinizing eye to the academies in the metropolis & its vicinity, in all of which Fch.[512] tutors are employed, many of whom are known to be inveterate enemies to the country which affords them an asylum.

True Briton[513] Oct 18, 1803

Dover. Oct.31.[514] A Prussian vessel came into the Harbour last night, which left Calais yesterday morning. She sailed from Flushing a few days before & by the accounts the master collected there it appears that the troops in the Island of Walcheren amount to 20,000;

---

[512] French.
[513] *The True Briton*; fol. (Burney).
[514] The whole section from 'Dover. Oct 31.' through to 'member for Corfe Castle.' on p. 6 is not in Hardy's hand but apparently that of Emma Hardy.

12,000 French & and the rest Dutch. There is a Frigate & eight schooners at Flushing, & eight or ten Schuyts, fitted out as gun vessels, each carrying two four pounders; four more Schuyts are building but are quite at a stand for want of shipwrights. The inhabitants & more particularly the fishermen[515] (2) complain heavily of the distress brought on them by the war. An uncommon degree of strictness is observed at Calais, to prevent anything being known of the nature of the preparations |being| carrying on there. This vessel was not suffered to remain more than one tide in Calais. & the master having been taken out of his vessel by a military guard & undergone an examination at the Commissary's Office was reconducted on board in the same manner without being allowed to call at any house, or to speak to any person in the streets & if he attempted to look about he was checked by the guard & told he must look straight forward. He learnt afterwards from a Calais man who came on board that Mengaud, so notorious for his incivility, bordering in some instances on brutality to the English had been lately dismissed in disgrace. There are no gun-boats at Calais, but at Boulogne, he understood there are about a hundred. All the houses at the left of the entrance into Calais harbour to the Town Wall, are removed – whether distroyed by our bombardment or purposely (3) taken down could not be learnt.

Deal –
The signal post |s| on the heights about 4 miles from hence on the road to Dover is daily visited by a great number of persons. Mr Pitt has ∧ paid ∧ the Lieutenant a visit every day. Nothing new has been observed from thence lately, except a review of troops on the French coast, which occupied the whole of Thursday & Friday last. The Officer states that both those days the horizon was so very clear, that he could distinctly see with glasses an immense body of troops.
True Briton. Nov.2. 1803

From Bankes story of Corfe Castle.[516]
Milton Abbey. Blandford
Oct. 12th. 1803.

My dear Bankes
    The spring tides take place next Saturday, and the informa-

---

[515] The word is obscured by an ink blot and therefore repeated on p. 2 but is only transcribed once here.
[516] George Bankes, *The Story of Corfe Castle* (London, 1853) [10351.f.41].

tion to Government is so precise that the Isle of Wight is the enemy's object that it is not improbable they may avail themselves of this ensuing spring-tide; if they do not, their attempt must be ⟨4⟩ postponed another month. Under these circumstances I would not fail of giving you this notice, in confidence that you will keep it to yourself, & only so far prepare Mrs. Bankes & your family as to be able to remove them upon the first intelligence of the enemy's being off the coast. I have to beg of you that you will give directions for an assemblage of fagots, furze & other fuel, also straw to be stacked & piled on the summit of Badbury Rings, so as the whole may take fire instantly & the fire be maintained for two hours. The general direction if you will take the trouble of ordering the execution is that this beacon may be fired whenever the beacon off St. Catherine's (Christ Church) is fired to the eastward, or whenever the beacons on Lytchet Heath or Woodbury Hill, are fired to the westward, but not from the demonstration of any coast signal.

I am, my dear Bankes
Yours most sincerely
Dorchester.[517]

⟨5⟩

Milton Abbey. Blandford
Oct.18.1803

My dear Bankes.

Many thanks for your care of the beacon on Badbury & generally for the contents of your letter on the 16th. instant. As to the first I have thought a watch & guard necessary for the two I have erected – one above Chizlebourne Common, in my grounds & the other upon Bullbarrow; but the guard to say the truth, is more against the wanton than against any other description of persons ⟨.⟩ The expense of them, no great object indeed will be defrayed by Government; & I am authorized to send in my charges to the Commissary General. As to the other part of your letter it is very handsome, & I shall be glad to avail myself of your services. at the present it only occurs to me that, if upon the alarm of an enemy's being off the coast, you should be |tr| disposed to transport yourself to this house, I should receive you with great satisfaction; & something might occur to one of us, in which you might find employment

---

[517] Transcribed from Bankes, pp. 278–9.

⟨6⟩   I am ever my dear Bankes most sincerely yours
                          Dorchester.[518]
The writer of these was the Earl of Dorchester then Lord Lieutenant
of the county of Dorset⟨.⟩ This nobleman was honoured with the
intimate confidence of King George III & was in habits of private
correspondence with the members of his Cabinet. These letters are
addressed to Henry Bankes. Esq. then member for Corfe Castle.[519]

B.M. May 30.78[520]
King at Weymouth – Aug 1805[521]
   ı ı ı — ——— – after Aug 27, Weymouth was dull, & King did
not go out for some days, in consequence of death of Dk of Gloucester.
Aug 27. One of H.M.'s Brigs brought into Weymouth 2 smugglers
boats laden with liquor, supposed to be Hollands, wh. was safely
lodged in the custom house. The crews, amounting to 14, were sent
on board the King's ships.
                          Morning Chronicle[522] Aug 29/05

⟨7⟩   1805

Morning Chronicle. Sept 5. 1805.

      "Weymouth, Sept 3. . . . Capt. Hardy, Ld. Nelson's Cap-
tain, was waiting the return of his majesty [from riding on horseback, early, accompd. by Dukes of York, Cumberland, & Cambridge, from which ride he returned soon after 9 o'clock] & had a
long conversn. with him . . "The weather proving fine, a little after
12 o'clock his majesty, the Prince, Dukes of York & Cambridge,
Pcesss.[523] Augusta, Sophia, & Amelia, rode to Dorchester."
Weymouth, Sept.5.
A grand field-day on Bincombe Downs.[524]   ib Sep.7
The Prince [of Wales?] at Weyth. at this time.

---

[518] Bankes, pp. 279–80.
[519] Bankes, p. 278.
[520] These notations indicate the dates of Hardy's research in the British Museum.
[521] From here to 'Aug 29/05' in pencil.
[522] *The Morning Chronicle; and London Advertiser*; fol. (1801– at Colindale).
[523] Princesses.
[524] Underlined in red pencil. The reference in the left margin is also in pencil.

. . . Attracts much company. numbers come in for miles round," &c
. . . Sept 9. "The grandest esplanade this season."

(The King | seems to | rides early almost every morning) ib. Sept 11.
A pleasure boat from Deptford sailed within a mile of Boulogne,
received no interruption from enemy.   ib.
Weymouth Sept 15. King goes to theatre. The Unity privateer of this
port brings in a rich prize

(margin, rotated) Cf. Part III.21

⟨8⟩   <u>1805</u>

Sept |16| 14. Saturday. Nelson arrived at Portsmouth on Saturday
morning at 6 o'clock & instantly went on board the Victory. It was
expected that she would proceed to sea forthwith."   ib. Sept
16.

    More particulars of his arrival at Portsmouth &c are given in
ib. Sept 17. & that "he went on board the Victory, which had
dropped down to St Helens." He embarked from the South-sea
beach. accompd. by . . . . "who dined with him on board the Victory, after wh. those gentn. went to Southampton in the Commissioners yacht. A number of people followed his Lordship & cheered
him when he embarked. The Victory with the Euryalus frigate, got
under weigh on Sunday. The Royal Sovereign [& others] will follow."

    On this Sept 14. the King was still at Weymouth, & went to
theatre.

    In the number of M.C. for Sept 18. is an account of a lady
swindler in west of England who obtains goods from shops, &
delivers them into the hands of her servant in livery who attends
her.

⟨9⟩   <u>1805</u>

Sept |29| 20. Grand field day of the regiments in camp, before his
Majesty, under the command of the Dk. of Cumberland. The line
extended from Ridgway Hills to Upwey, & on to the Bridport Road.
It reached upwards of three miles. The hills were covered with
carriages and spectators. The artillery made a very grand appear-
ance. The Lord Chancellor, Ld. Mulgrene, Count Munster, Mr Pitt
& Mr Villers, accompd. his M.
Sept 25. H. Majesty visits "The Promenade Rooms" at Weymouth

(where?) "Old Rooms?" The North York Militia march from here today. &c ib. Sept 27.

Sept 27. Weymouth. Royal family at Theatre – King walked as far as the T.P. gate. The German legion passed him on their way to Southampton – Soon after 11. the R. Family set off for Earl of Dorchester's seat at Milton Abbey. Their Majesties went in their travelling carriages – the Pcesses in their coaches. They were followed by the Countess of Ilchester &c – A great concourse of people assembled at the Noble Earls Mansion from neighbg. villages to see them.

⟨10⟩   1805

Splendid preparations were made – Cooks from London &c.

Sept 29. Weyth. The whole of the German legion marched from here yesterday, with their artillery. Combats |by| at single-stick for several prizes on a stage in front of Mrs Buxton's house to-morrow. Much sport expected – £4 for him who breaks most heads.

Milton Abbey. The Messenger arrives with despatches for H.M. to sign.

30th. King returns to Weyth. sees sports.

Oct 1. Details of the single stick &c. in Mrs B's field
                    ib. Oct 3.

Portsmouth Oct 1. Two ships laden with cabbage, potatoes & carrots, for the use of Ld. Nelson's fleet will sail under convoy.   ib.

Oct 4. Their Majesties leave Weyth.   ib. Oct 4.

A young man hires a boat at Dover. to go out pleasing, for which he agreed to pay the 2 men a guinea. They accordingly stretched across Channel 8 or 10 miles, in full view of the Fch. coast, but when about to put about he earnestly entreated them to land him on the Fch. coast, as near to Calais as they cd. as he had particular business there, & wished to see a friend. They refused,

⟨11⟩   1805

&c. He spoke in broken English &c. Brought back before magistrates – after a long examination he was sent on to London.   ib. Oct 4.

Duel at Cheltenham ——————————————   ib.

Oath of the period "Damn my wig" –   ib. Oct 11

Portsmouth Oct 16. The "Ld. Eldon" will sail in a few days with
bullocks for Ld. Nelson's fleet.

Ship news. ib. Oct 18.

Particulars of Lottery Tickets – ib. Oct 21.

Oct 23. The nimble ∧ cutter ∧ [525] arrives from Gibraltar with
despatches. Lord Nelson arrived off Cadiz Sept 28th. & immediately
took command of the fleet. &c. ib. Oct 23.

Ships are to convey bullocks from Barbary to Ld. Nelson's fleet –
Ship.news ib. 'An indecent policy was opened at Lloyds on Thursday – in wh. 10 guineas were offered to receive 100 in case Bonaparte
shall be killed in 3 months. ib. Nov 2.

Nov.7. First news of Victory of Trafalgar – ib.

---

back
July 13. King arrives in Weymouth. (July 15 ib.)
1805. (details of arrival given.
14th. he inspects the camp at Weymouth. ib 16

⟨12⟩ 1805

The encampment consists of 9000 men – ib July 17

July |19|20. The King rides to the camp at ½ past 6, & returns a little
before 9. (to see artillery). & on 19th. he "took a short ride to the
cavalry camp" before breakfast – [so that the camp must have been
nearer than Bincombe?]

July 22. The Boulogne camp appears making up again for the season. ℮

July 28. Divine Service at the camp, "performed at the drum head of
each regiment." ib. July 30 Drum-head court marshall. A C.M.
called suddenly, or in the field. Dic.

Weymouth Aug.12. Last night 3 soldiers belonging to the 31st. regt.
were detected breaking open the Royal Oak public house at
|Upwey| Ridgway. They were examined before the mayor this
morning, & committed to Dorchester gaol. ib. Aug 14.

Sudden apprehension of invasion at Dover, Deal, &c, a tremendous
firing having begun. ib. Aug 14.

Duel with swords at Wurtzbourg – horrid – they send for a cutter to
renew the edge of the sabres, wh. were blunted – while he was

---

[525] Insertion, indicating that Nimble is a ship's name.

doing it the enemies continued to assail each other with bitter invectives. It occurred in an apartment, the owner encouraging one of the combatants

⟨13⟩   <u>1801</u>

with his voice. One run through the lungs. The owner of the house, by urging them to fight, seems to have been the incentive. ib. Aug 23. 1805

June 30.1801, was on a Tuesday.[526]

1801. The King &c. arrive in Weymouth July |4| 3rd.
|July 4. Saturday.| (Friday) – Walk on esplanade, in evening fireworks – & a brilliant illumination –
July 4. After breakfast the King & his attendants rode to the camp on the Dorchester road, to inspect the North Devon Militia, & proceeded to
{ Radipole
{ Bincombe (?)[527]
where the Regiments of Hussars & Artillery are stationed . . . ." Morning Chron. July 4. 1801.
[Tuesday? Tu. was chief market day. W. Guide[528]]
X[529] – "On Wedny. morning | two privates | of the York
                                | private and corporal[530] |
Hussars were shot on Bincombe Down, nr. W. pursuant to the sentence of a court martial, for desertion, & cutting a boat out of the harbour, with intent to go to France, but by mistake they landed at Guernsey, & were secured. All the regts. both in camp & barracks, were drawn up, viz the Scotch Greys, the Rifle Corps, the Stafford, Berks, & N. Devon Militia. They came on the ground in a mourning coach, at- ⟨14⟩ tended by 2 priests; after marching along the front of the line they returned to the centre, where they spent about 20 minutes in prayer, & were shot at by a guard of 24 men; they

---

[526] This entry, and the lines above and below, in pencil.
[527] Bracket and 'Bincombe (?)' in pencil.
[528] Weymouth Guide.
[529] Large cross in red pencil.
[530] In pencil; the vertical lines enclosing this alternative reading are Hardy's.

dropped instantly, & expired without a groan. The men wheeled in sections, & marched by the bodies in slow time.   – ib.[531]

1804[532]

May 31. B.M.

"There has been a very heavy press all down the river these 2 or 3 days past, & a very numerous supply of seamen has been obtained from our late homeward bound fleets. It is a great pity that the necessities of the state require that such measures shd. be resorted to, as preventing these very useful persons from an opporty. of coming home to their families after the long absence which a voyage to either the East or West occasions." Morning Chron. Aug 18th. 04

1804. The Royal Family arrived at Weyth. Aug 25. (for route see further on.)

Received at Dorchester by a party of the German Legion &c. During this month they go to theatre, reviews &c. No lodgings can be had – balls &c – great gaiety

                ib.

⟨15⟩   1804

1804 – End of Aug. Invasion hourly expected - ib.

        Several families quit Margate.

Sept.3. Weymouth – Yesterday afternoon the Dorchester Volunteers arrived here in their new carriages, which have been lately constructed for carrying 30 of them at a time with great expedition. ... &c. --

                Sept 5. ib.

---

[531] This is Hardy's source for the central incidents of his story 'The Melancholy Hussar of the German Legion', sent to Tillotson's Newspaper Fiction Bureau in Oct 1889, and first published in the *Bristol Times and Mirror* (4 and 11 Jan 1890); subsequently collected in *Life's Little Ironies* (1894) and transferred to *Wessex Tales* in 1912. On 27 July of the year before this note made in the B. M. Hardy noted: 'James Bushrod of Broadmayne saw the two German soldiers [of the York Hussars] shot [for desertion] on Bincombe Down in 1801. It was in the path across the Down, or near it. James Selby of the same village thinks there is a mark' (*Life*, 116); the square brackets are Hardy's, indicating the addition of details to his original notebook entry.

[532] Date in pencil, as on pp. 15–17 following.

Sept 8. Weyth. Cavalcade to Bincombe Down – grand review before H. majesty, & sham fight – roads blocked with carriages – King, D. of Cumberland &c, being present. Review over by 12 noon. Fete at Weyth. after review. Theatre in evening. – ib. Sept 10

Sept 12. At Weyth. the most strict military vigilance is exerted to guard the Royal residents. Not only the frigates & other armed vessels are every night posted in a line across the mouth of the harbour [bay][533], but two lines of centinels, one at the water's edge & another behind the Esplande. occupy the whole harbour [bay] after 8 every night. The Kings guard mounts every night round Gloucester Lodge, & outlying pickets are so stationed on the hills around the town as to command the harbour. There is besides a battery of 6 24 pounders on the point of the

⟨16⟩   1804

{ Nothe?[534]
{ Mole which commands the entrance, & a camp of flying artillery on the opposite shore, consisting of twelve 6 pounders & several howitzers. Added to this a camp of four thousand men horse & foot within a few minutes march.

ib. Sept 14.

Sept 23. Weyth. yesterday forenoon, a review on Bincombe downs of all the troops in the neighbourd.

Sept.30. Weyth. Grand Naval Fête yesterday –

ib. Oct 2

Oct 10. Royal Family go to Milton Abbey.   ib. Oct 12

17. Troops march to Bincomb downs, to be brigaded with the Flying Artillery.   ib. 19

18. Ball at Royal Hotel – –

21. H.M. was so well pleased with the Dorset. Yeom. Cavalry in their difft. evolutions yesterday at their review that he has been pleased to signify his royal will that in future they shall be called R.D.Y.C.   ib. 23

Oct 29. R. Family leave Weyth.

---

[533] Insertion and square brackets in pencil, as identical bracketed entry below.
[534] Alternative reading in pencil.

1803 Morning Chronicle

July 19. Speech of the Sec. at War for arming the population – ib. July 19

⟨17⟩   1803

Oct 17 An american gentleman lands at Dover from Dieppe in |private| hired boat – 18 gs.

Oct 10, & some weeks following. Enemy expected every moment – Margate people one day believed the expedition had sailed – seeing a large fleet.

Nov. 9. Confidently affirmed that a large body of the enemy was landed on our coasts – & other rumours.

Nov 14. Ship news. Plymouth – an invasion of the Western ports from Brest is deemed probable.

15. Brest fleet supposed to have put to sea. The Diamond frigate has fallen in with 2 Fch. ships &c.

A smuggling lugger (The Hazard) – the joint property of T, S T,[535] & M'G. & all of them had acquired considerable property by her successful voyages. (T. is the captain)

... A freight of madder, flax, cheese, or apples, two thirds of which kinds of merchandize generally covered another third of tea brandy &c.[536]

⟨18⟩

... Before the end of the month an express informed the partners that she (The Hazard) was in sight on her return. Fairy Cove had been agreed upon, & as the cargo was intended chiefly for the interior a number of carts were got ready – disguised as carriers carts .... With the assistance of the sailors they were soon loaded with ankers & half ankers of brandy, boxes & tea chests. ... met 6 men ... . on their approach they turned out to be no others than a neighbg. supervisor of Excise & his myrmidons ... who had received information that a smuggler was on the coast making signals, in consequence of which he had procured assistance [the Lieut at home] &

---

[535] The latter originally an M now superimposed by T.
[536] This para., from 'A smuggling lugger', in pencil.

was going around direct for the Fairys Cove. . . . The supervisor sent forward a guager to reconnoitre.

The <u>Smugglers</u>, tale of Scotland 1820.[537]

(Time of story 17 – when "the war breaking out & the successful invasion of Holland by the French had rendered the Dutch our enemies.")

⟨19⟩

"Smugglers & Foresters"[538] a novel – time, since coast guard & preventive stations have been established.

The smuggling vessel is a lugger, manned by F'chmen. & commanded by an Englishman. A boat puts off from the revenue cruiser (after she has fired a gun) & was rowed towards the French-man – the boat reached the lugger, & the men sprang on deck. . . The boat seemed to have been cast loose. - - they had cut the painter away - the boat drifted empty - The next moment its late crew were thrown overboard – one after another, overpowered by numbers, from the deck of the smuggling vessel – & were left to perish or regain their boat as chance directed.

A boat was just being launched lower down the beach. It was fully manned &c.[539]

⟨20⟩

Portsmouth. Sept 26. 1804. The Poulette of 24 guns, Capt. Dunbar, on her returning from off Havre, chased the Lion cutter, of Hastings, a most notorious smuggler = & although the Poulette flies like a witch & every advantage was taken by Capt. D. that an expert seaman cd. devise, in battening down, &c, the P., she escaped, after a very hard & singularly circuitous chase

Naval Chron[540] 1804

A Lieut & 6 men board a ship.[541]

A Bill for the more effectual prevention of smuggling.   ib. 1805.

---

[537] *The Smugglers* ('a tale descriptive of the sea-coast manners of Scotland'), 3 vols. (Edinburgh, 1820) [12612.cc.27].

[538] Mary Kettle, *Smugglers and Foresters* (London, 1851) [12625.a.5].

[539] This and previous para. in pencil.

[540] *The Naval Chronicle* ('containing a general and biographical history of the Royal Navy of the United Kingdom') (London, 1799–1818) [293.i.1–25 and k.1–15].

[541] In pencil.

"Excise & custom house officers to examine vessels. ... Officers of excise, &c.

B.M. July 6. 78
Morning Chronicle for 1803.
The Atalanta, of 18 guns, Capt. Maesfield was paid of in Hamoaze last Sat 7. & her crew ⟨21⟩ discharged. Capt M. immediately re-commissioned her, & seamen already enter fast into her: she has been the most fortunte. ship since the war of any of the cruizers against the smugglers, having captured 8 sail, with nearly 2000 ankers of spirits, besides bale goods; each seaman has shared more prize money in the last 6 months than his wages have amounted to.
Jan 13. – A small smuggling vessel, the Hope of Lymn, was yester-day from stress of weather obliged to come into Yarmouth harbour. She was immedy seized by the Custom House Officers, with her cargo, consisting of 112 tubs of spirits. The crew report that the master was washed overboard the preceding night. ib.

—

Parisian fashions. It is still the prevailing fashn. to throw over the forehead a thick tuft of hair dressed out in ringlets &c.   ib.

—

. . . . stealing a 7 shilling piece . . . . a half-crown.   ib.

—

Dresses at Her Majesty's card party   ib. Jan 19
Coaches – A new handsome coach, painted a ⟨22⟩ fine drab – red morocco leather sleeping cushions &c – – (Duke) / A new genteel chariot, painted a fine dark green. (Esq)
A landau, the body painted Devonshire brown.
                    ib.

—

Post chaise. –   ib.

—

48 out of 50 young men are crops. Powder is scarcely worn in full dress. Round hats are disappearing & cocked hats with black feathers are coming into fashion. The more dashing bucks wear them with an edging. Ruffles & frills plaited – ib – Paris fashions, Jan 29.

—

Real India Long Shawls being now the most fashionable articles of dress for ladies of distinction – price 6 to 50 guineas. White orange, crimson, brown, blue, yellow, green &c.

Advt. ib.

—

Sailed on a cruize against the smugglers. The Eagle 14 guns, Capt W. . . . Ranger, 14 guns, . . . 10 guns, &c all revenue cutters, & prime sailers. ib. Jan 31.

⟨23⟩

. . He was in his own carriage . . It was a thick day, & the glasses were all up . . He took down the left glass – &c. "Trial for highway robbery   ib.

—

Col. Despard at his execution . . - "dressed in boots, a dark brown great coat, his hair unpowdered."

ib. Feb 22.

—

Order from the Admiralty Board came down to the admiral of this port (Plymouth) . . . . . no young gentn., having served 6 years according to the usual routine of the service, shall be confirmed as lieut. until he has been in England, & examined by the Commissioners of his Majesty's navy at Somerset House. . . . Great exertions are making here to procure volunteer seamen for the following ships . . . . Posting bills, with various offers of encouragement are stuck up at all the places where seamen resort.

ib. Feb 23.

⟨24⟩

Picked up – a book belonging to H.M.S. – with a lieut. & 13 men aboard – they had been engaged in making soundings, &c

ib.

—

Breach of Promise & Elopement – interesting.

ib. March 2.

—

Portsmouth. Last night, about ½ past 10, in a most sudden manner, the severest impress for seamen took place in this port, & every person having a seafaring appearance was secured. In a very short time upwards of 500 were in the difft. guard houses & ships in the harbour. The Merchant Vessels were entirely stripped, the Masters not even left on board. ib. March 11.

Mansion House. Yesterday above 120 seamen & others, who were impressed in the city . . . were examined before the Ld. Mayor & Capt Roch –, the regulating captain. A surgeon attended in an adjoining room, who examined the state of ⟨25⟩ their health & body, when some were discharged, & those approved of were sent on board a frigate off the Tower. A very great concourse of persons crowded round the M.H. all day, many of them the friends of the sailors.

ib. Mar. 11.

—

Plymouth. Mar 10. | Yesterday | Last night one of the hottest presses for the navy took place at this port that was ever remembered. The mariners from Stonehouse Bks. were stationed in parties in the towns of P. Dock & Stonse. & seized almost every one they met, whether seaman or otherwise. The boats from the men of war & frigates were employed in sacking the merchant vessels dispersed over the harbours of . . . . & some hundreds of hands were picked up & conveyed on board the guard ships in Hamoaze. Parties of marines were yesterdy ⟨26⟩ dispatched to the villages situated near the ⅄ [542] roads leading from hence, for the purpose of picking up stragglers.

ib. May 14. 1803

Annual Register,[543] Oct.2. <u>1804.</u> Dorchester Barracks were nearly destroyed by fire, in consequence of some of the German Legion falling asleep while smoking their pipes.

Route of R. Family to Weyth. in Aug <u>1804</u> Woodyates Inn, Blandfd. & Dorchr. . . . . Supper at Andover – 2 young princesses sleeping there – on, during the night, to Salisbury &c. & arriving in W. at 4 or 5 in <u>morning.</u>

  Morning Chronicle.

[542] Hardy's symbol is not clear, somewhat resembling an H, though X for 'cross' is also a possibility and seems to yield more sense.

[543] *The Annual Register* [New series, 1801 (–12; 1820–26)], 18 vols (London, 1802–27) [299.f.17 to h. 1].

The manner & appearance assumed by our fashionable women are
formed from the different costumes of ancient Greece & Rome, &
modern France & India: producing a compound style totally
unadapted to the climate of this country.

. . . Nothwithsg. the occasional severity & peculiar variability of our
atmosphere the drapery (as cloathing is now called) of our ladies is
such as wd. suit the soft air of Italy.

— Letter in Gent.'s Mag.[544] Nov 1804

⟨27⟩

Ladies in patterns excluded from St James's Park
St James's Chronicle[545] Dec 31 1804
Letter expostulating with ladies & recommending them to resume a
habit suited to our climate – & not to wear muslins in January.

ib.
—

Summer dress, 1804. muslin frocks – shawls of crimson muslin.
Caps à la Paysanne again appear.   ib.
—

October fashions – a round dress of white muslin, long sleeves. A
Barcelona handkf. crossed over the bosom & tied behind.
(Promenade.) ib.
Morning bonnet of blue silk . . . straw bonnet.
ib.
—

The modern beau in the Dog-days [1804]
a lady's letter on gents. fashions:- (in answer to an old gent's
ridiculing the ladies' wearing muslin to such an unlimited degree,
no petticoats, & no pockets):-
Fatigued by the heat at Weymouth, &c . . .
I observe the males parading about in pantaloons & boots, whilst I
can scarcely bear my muslin gown & coat . . . . two fancy ⟨28⟩
waistcoats . . . small-clothes, large enough to admit 2 persons –
shoulders stuffed . . . neck surrounded with yards of muslin, which
forms an asylum for the lower part of the face – whilst the collar of
the shirt protects the ears, & keeps them from observation . . . .

---

[544] *The Gentleman's Magazine; or, Monthly Intelligencer*, 103 vols (London, 1731–1833)
[2120.f.–2121.h].
[545] *St. James's Chronicle; or the British Evening Post* (London, 1761–1866), fol. (S.P.R.).

Half-boots made to cover the knee, whilst the whole ones will scarcely reach over the calf of the leg.
ib. Oct 1804

Morning post.[546] 1805
Weymouth July 13. In a great bustle for several days past with the preparns. for receptn. of R. family. Numbers sat up all night to be gratified with the sight of the arrival of the R.F. & this morning by 4 o'clock the entrance to the town from the London Rd. was crowded. A few minutes before 5 o'clock their Majesties, & the Pcsses Amelia, Augusta & Mary arrived . . . . The windows & streets were filled, & they were received with huzzas & every demonstrn. of joy. Soon (29) after 9 o'c, his M. rose, & after breakfst. came out of the Lodge, accompanied by the Dk. of Cumb. H.M. appeared in excellt. health & spirits, & none the worse for the fatigues of the journey. Sir B.W. Sir H.N. Capts (3), Officers of the Staff. Gen —— & several Hanoverian Officers paid their respects to his M. & congratulated him upon safe arrival. H.M. in a short time mounted his horse, & rode to the camps, accompanied by the above officers, with Ld. Dundas, & Mr Browne. After H.M. had reviewed the camps, he rode to the pier head & viewed the improvemts.

H.R.H. D. of Cumbd. is appointed C. in Chief of the Weyth. Camp." July 15.

Weyth. July 14. H.M. inspected Camp . . . Her M. & 3 of the Pcsses. went in a coach drawn by 6 cream cold. horses, & the other 2 Pcsses in another drawn by 4 . . . . . Diamond frigate in the bay . . In evening the town brilliantly illuminated – the grand hotel, libraries & several (30) houses exhibiting very tasteful transparencies. The band belonging to the German legion returned from the camp soon after their M's . . . . .
H.M. when he went to the camp wore a round hat turned up on left side, with a cockade & military feather in it . . . . Rooms added, for use of H.M.'s servants. Sharpshooters encamped on the fort . . .

This morning another frigate hove in sight of this port, & fired a royal salute."

---

546 The *Morning Post*; fol. (1801– at Colindale).

ib July 16.
(such news at length every day following.)

—

Female fashions July 29. 1805.

    White India muslin cloaks, or patent net ditto, much the rage. The former lined with azure blue sarsenet. Lace veils, blk & white, & purple & grey parasols universal. White Chip bonnets greatly in vogue. ib.

—

In an account of a girl living with a man in boy's clothes, as his son, her ⟨31⟩ dress is described – she wore nankeen trousers, a yellow Marseilles waistcoat, & brown jacket. appeared as a youth of 14.
ib. Nov.7

1805 Feb. The Abergavenny. East Indiaman, went down off Portland Bill.

1805. Morning Post

Jan. new Edn. of Bruces's travels.

''   Household Bread 1.2¾ per quartern loaf. best 1–4¼

''   Mail Coach overturned on Marlbh. Down, owing to the extreme darkness of the night. Coachman's back broken – no passengers injured.

1805. Lady's Magazine.[547]

    April London fashions – Black crepe turban with jet ornaments . . . drawn crepe tucker – for Afternoon dress.

Hair almost down to the eyebrows

[Hue's mother][548]
"black velvet turban" – "a turban cap" (elsewhere)
Walking dress March.

---

[547] *The Lady's Magazine* ('or entertaining companion for the fair sex') (London, 1770–1818) [P.P.5141].

[548] 'Hue's mother' replaces another entry, deleted and now illegible.

Caravan hat. brown velvet pelisse.
huge white muff. petticoat, worked.
white muslin. showing
about a foot.

Waist under armpits in all cases.

⟨32⟩

June – Yellow straw hats very prevalent.

—

"I bowed with the most tender & respectful air, almost touching the
ground with my hat."

—

In the summer – full dress is a cap of worked muslin with lace
border.

—

Lady's Monthly Museum[549] 1805
March. Morning dress. A biggin of plain muslin, lace border, &
trimmed with pale blue . . . . . A muslin shawl tied round the neck, &
carried over the bosom to tie behind.

White Mlin.
Blue
Lace

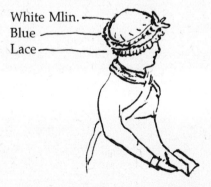

---

[549] *The Lady's Monthly Museum* ('or Polite Repository of Amusement and Instruction . . . By a Society of Ladies'), 16 vols (London, 1798–1806) [P.P.5153.i].

Nov. 1805 – Walking dress – . . . . Muslin habit shirt [covering the part of neck that wd. otherwise be naked

⟨33⟩

To be sold – a handsome curricle . . . to go as a one-horse chaise occasionally, the head made to take off. – Advt. 1805.
"One horse gigs" – ib. "Landaulet." ib.
"Town chariots." ib.
"Chaise & harness – . . . An excellent curricle hung chaise & harness." ib.
"Phaetons" — ib.
"A modern phaeton, for 4 horses – ib.
"An excellent curricle, for town or travelling." ib
Wanted, an out-door apprentice to a respectable dancing-master. A young man of good figure . . . . who can play the violin.
"two wheeled chaises, with & without heads." ib[550]

B.M. 27 July.78.
Regulns for H.M.'s Forces. 1788–93.[551]
A sum not exceeding 22 guineas may be given for each recruit horse, for remounting the Regts. of Dragoon Guards & Dragoons. 171

⟨34⟩

Ammunn. to be carried by each soldier 56 rounds. 32 in a pouch on his right side, 24 in a cartridge box, by way of magazine, to be worn occasionally upon the left side.

[550] All of p. 33 to 'ib' in pencil.
[551] A Collection of Regulations, Orders, and Instructions formed and issued for the use of the Army in consequence of the Pay-Office-Act and other occasions subsequent to 24th of December, 1783, etc. (London: War Office, 1 Jan 1788), fol. [534.m.15.(3)]; Rules and Articles for the better government of all his Majesty's Forces, From the 24th day of March, 1789 [517.c.22.(2)], . . . March, 1790 [517.c.22.(4)], . . . March, 1791 [517.c.22.(6)].

The cartridge box . . . to be fixed to the bayonet belt.
The cross belts for pouch & magazine to be made of buff leather . . .
The Gayters to be made of black woollen cloth (instead of linen) with white metal buttons.
The light infantry to have a small priming horn (?)

_____

Clothing.
Cloth coat, looped with worsted lace
Waistcoat – pr. of good cloth breeches.
Shoes . . . neck cloth . . Hat, bound with white tape.
For fusiliers, grenadier companies, & drummers, black bear-skin caps.

⟨35⟩

Rules . . . Embodied Militia 1794.[552]

	s	d
Black cloth gaiters . . .	4.	0
One Hair leather		2½

Foraging Cap.
Shoes, stockings, socks, shirts . . . Knapsack . .
Pipe clay & whiting – clothes brush – 3 shoe brushes (per year) black ball . . worsted mits
A powdering bag & puff 2 combs . . Grease & powder for the hair – per year 3/- . . Washing.

_____

Manual & platoon. 1804.[553]
        Part of drill.
Prime │ Bring the firelock down . . to the priming position . . . . .
  &   │ Open the pan . . . draw the cartridge from the pouch . . . bite
Load │ off top of c. . . Shake some powder into pan . . Shut the
        pan . . – Shake the powder into the barrel, putting in after it
        the paper & ball.

---

[552] *Certain Rules and Orders to be observed by the embodied Militia* ('Additional Rules and Orders, etc.') (London, 1793) [288.a.10.(2)].
[553] *The Manual and Platoon Exercises* [1 Nov 1804] (London, 1804) [289.a.34].

⟨36⟩

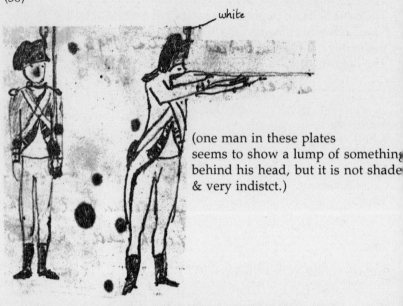

white

(one man in these plates
seems to show a lump of something
behind his head, but it is not shade
& very indistct.)

From Soldiers Companion – |1804| 1803[554]

From Regulations &c. 1786.[555]

    Bound up with several others & called "Military Tracts."
"..... shape of Hats."
        (—)
— Officers & men in general, when under arms, or on duty, (the
Fuzileer-Corps, & the Grenadier & Lt. Infantry Comps., when they
shall wear their caps, excepted) shall, for the future, wear their hair
<u>clubbed</u>: The non-comd. officers ⟨37⟩ & men, to have a small piece of
black polished leather, by way of ornament, upon the club.
    The whole to wear black stocks .... & black cloth gayters.

---

[554] *The Soldier's Companion* ('containing instructions for the drill, manual and platoon exercise ... Intended for the use of the Volunteers of this country') (London
[1803?]) [1140.a.29].
[555] *General Regulations and Orders for his Majesty's Forces* 12th April, 1786 (London,
1786) [288.b.20].

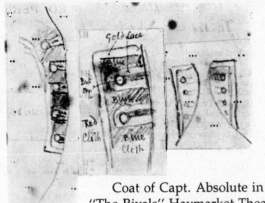

Coat of Capt. Absolute in
"The Rivals" Haymarket Theatre.

(38)

B.M. Morning Post. 1803
Detailed account of a ball, giving descripn. of the room, dances —
&c —
June 29.
[556] // – This M. Post for 1803 June–Nov. contains more details
about the invasion than any other paper I have seen.

Army list for 1815 – March.[557]
Divided into parts – 1 part being called "Foreign Corps" – & sub
headed – "The Kings German legion" – This consists of 2 regts. of
Light dragoons, & 3 regts. of Hussars – 8 battalions of infantry, some
artillery &c.

Morning Chronicle. Monday July 5. 180|3|2.
Weymouth July 3. Her royal Highness Pcss Amelia arrived here
yesterday afternoon at 4 o'clock, attended by Lady Cathcart, Gen.
Garth, & Col. Fitzroy. The Guards on her R. Highness arrival
presented arms as a salute, but did not fire on account (39) of the
Pcesses being rather fatigued by the journey.

---

[556] Two lines marking the passage, in green pencil.
[557] *The Monthly Army List (The Army List)*, (London, 1798–1940) [B.S. 45/140].

Their Majesties & the Pcess Augusta, Eliz. & Mary arrived at ½ past 7 this evening – in perfect health, being escorted by a party of the Guards & the Scots Greys. . . . The people greeted the R. Family with loud acclamations, repeatedly exclaiming "Long live the King."

ib. July 6.

We.yth. July 4. Marchsses Ladies . . . . are arrived. Sirs . . . . . also arrived. The King attended divine Service this morning. The 1st. regt. of foot guards & the Scotch Greys marched in here on Friday evening to do King's Duty.

A genl. illumination took place last night. – ib. July 8. Weyth. July 7. His maj. & Pcess Aug^sta & Eliz., attended by Lady Cathcart, in a landau, took an excursion round the pleasant village of Upwey &c. Weather very wet.

⟨40⟩

Morning Post. July 6. 1801. (Monday)

Weyth. July 4. On Friday morning their maj. arrived . . by yacht . . . about 4 in aftern. "The shore was lined with spectators who greeted the R. fam . . . . The troops were drawn out on the sands & fired a feu de joye, wh. was answered from Portland Castle & the ships in the road.

Band played while the R.F. were at dinner . . . . This morning after breakfst. H.M. & attendants rode to Camp on D. Road to inspect the N. Devon Militia, & proceeded to Radipole where the Hussars & artillery are stationed

returned to W. inspected Berks. Militia & afterds. Col. M's Corps.

⟨41⟩

1804. Morning Post. Tuesday Aug 21.

The 1st. batt. of Staffordsh. Militia marched from Windsor yesterday on their way to Weyth. to attend the R. Family.   ib. Aug 23.

They will change horses at . . . Salisbury, Woodyates Inn, Blandford & Dorchester.

ib. Sat. Aug 25.

The R. Fam. set out from Windsor to Weyth. yesty. morng. at ½ p. 9. in the follg. order.

Their Majs. in a post chariot & 4

The Psses. Auga. Eliz., & Mary, attended by the Countess of Aylesbury, in a coach & four.
The Pcses. Sophia & Amelia, attended by Lady Matilda Winyard & Isabel Thynne, in a Coach & 4.
The Duke of Cambridge, attended by Genls. Cartwright & Fitzroy.
<u>Aug.27.</u>
W. arrived Aug 25. Inhabitants waiting for them in great crowds – went to bed – got up at 7 (or 9) Went to the Horse Barracks & inspected the Hanovn. Legion, which are a fine body of men.

⟨42⟩

Weyth. ib. Aug 25. (1804)
        This afternn. H.M. inspected the German Legion of Light & heavy horse, in Gloucr. Row. The word of Command was given by the Dk of Cumberland, as General of the District, who appeared in his full uniform as Col. of 15th. Dragoons. The Dk accompd. the King in his uniform as a Gen. officer. His Maj. was on a beautiful charger. The Legion having gone through some evolutions the Light Horse filed off at the bottom of the town, the Heavy over the sand opposite the Esplanade, to make room for the Somerset Militia, who with the Weyth. volunteers formed a line in Gloucester Row & the word was given by Gen. Munro; the bands of music playing. The Queen & Pcsses. were at the window of G. Lodge the whole time: the King's band of music also played opposite the house. King highly pleased – talked with the officers of the difft. regts. & the officers belonging to the Royal Yacht which lay ⟨43⟩ in the bay – after wh. the family came out on the Esplanade & stood while a royal salute was fired by ships in the bay. The King on going spoke to those who surrounded him telling them to depend on the wooden walls of old England. In the eveng. the whole town was illuminated. Harveys library was the grandest. There were fireworks on board the ships & on the Esplanade. All beauty & fashion were present. The town is full – there are no lodgings or houses to be got.
Weyth. Aug 27.
. . . The Germn. Legion & the Somerset Militia will be upon the parade this & every evening during the stay of the royal family.
. . . . Last night the whole of the officers belonging to the Hanovn. legions were presented to the R. Family at the Kings lodge.

ib. Aug 31.

Nothing can equal the shameless dissimulation & flattery wh.
characterize the minions of the Corsican Tyrant.

⟨44⟩

– A great deal at this time is written about the "Machines for the
conveyance of troops."

– 4 boards placed across as seats that the soldrs. may sit with faces to
horses instead of sideways, as in the late invention.

Weyth. Aug 31.

          Grand ball last night, given by the Master of the Ceremonies
at the Royal Hotel, for his benefit – received a greater honour than
any M. of C. ever received in this country, by the R. Fam. honouring
his benefit with their company The attraction of their presence was
sufficient to ensure a very full attendance.

("Promenade Rooms" ante)[558]

Later –

The Dorchr. Volunt. come in the new carriages (conveying 30 at a
time) to be inspected by H.M.

⟨45⟩

Sept 8. Review on B. Downs closed at 12 o'c. Afterds. a grand fete
given by their Majs. – being their wedding day – danced from 3 till 8.
The R.F. then went to the theatre.

                    (look at this again   )
                    (as there is much more.)

N.B. The autumn of 1804 was one of alarm at the expected invasion,
equally with 1803, though perhaps not to such an intense degree. So
that the beacon-firing &c, may be in either year.

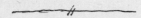

Adventures of Col. Landmann.[559]

1790 – The cocked hat was worn by men of every rank & station in
the army, & also by a vast number of civilians; and was properly a 3
cornered hat, with all the sides turned up nearly alike, & all nearly

---

[558] This line in pencil.

[559] George Thomas Landmann, *Adventures and Recollections of Colonel Landmann*
('late of the Corps of Royal Engineers'), 2 vols (London, 1852) [10815.c.31].

equal in extent – the three cocks equally projecting. This hat Ld. H.[560] wore quite square to the front . . .[561]

⟨46⟩

ib. 1804 – Menaces of invasion had in no degree subsided, & it was thought necessy. to protect the R. Fam. from being carried off by a coup de main, for W.[562] was not fortified. In order to remedy this . . . 5 or 6 frigates constantly in roadstead, & a large military force was quartered in the town & neighbd., from wh. force a whole regt., gen⟨era⟩lly in these times 600 to 1000 men strong, mounted piquet every night[563]
– Dk of Cumberland, noon – in dressing gown & slippers extended on a sofa, & engaged in reading a pamphlet.
– Capt. S. of 15th. Lt. Dragoons – H.R.H's equerry.[564]
– R. Fam. were out by 6. in morng. Such early hrs. at Gl. Lodge produced equally early movemts. throught. the popn. – shops opened at ½ past 5. by 6 the streets were as thronged by all the fashionables at court, & also by those who were anxious to be thought so, as Regt. St. at 3. p.m. The Great Attraction was to be the Queen & Pcsses walking from Glo. L. to their bathing machines – or to cheer them on their embarkn. with the King on bd. the R. yacht. These water excursions occurred 3 or 4 days in every week – all day at sea[565]

⟨47⟩

– 6 a.m. The Queen in the street – a little old woman, small black silk bonnet, & the remainder of her person covered by a short plain scarlet cloth cloak . . . . [preceded by] a tall stout fellow in a scarlet livery, with a long gold headed cane – the running footman.[566]

The King invariably dined at 3. In order that he might be on the esp. at 6, in readiness to receive the salutes of the officers as they

560 Heathfield.
561 Landmann, p. 29.
562 Weymouth.
563 Landmann, p. 298.
564 Ibid., p. 299; 'Capt. S.' = Captain Stephens.
565 Ibid., pp. 300–1.
566 Ibid., p. 302

marched past when mounting picquet – the D. of Cumbd. & all the military & civil officers immedy. connected with the court, also dined at same hour.

After dinner on Espl. I took up my post as usual with the Dk's staff, three paces in rear of the Dks of Cumb & Camb.[567]

—

Ld. Haukesbury on esplanade – light blue coat, black velvet collar & cuffs, raised gilt buttons, stamped with a crown & a cipher: his drab coloured hat . . . breeches of faded nankeen, & his white cotton stockings in wrinkles – high shoes, & silver buckles.[568]

– Landing from yacht, King condescendingly returns the salutations with his hat in his hand, which he did not replace until he had proceeded many yds. on the shore – people & company forming an avenue.

⟨48⟩

– all met on the wharf by a large assemblage of well dressed persons, cheering, waving handkfs. &c. It was 6 o'clock. King left the royal ladies to return to G. Lodge – he proceeds to Espl. to receive the salutes of the piquet.

—

The 1st. Somerset Militia, whose tour of duty it was to mount the piquet, advanced in ordinary time, formed in open column as usual, & as soon as the drum major (who marched at the head of the band) came up, & began to flourish his dazzling silver balloon headed cane with the large tassels, & had transferred the same to his left hand, & placed his right hand over the front of his hat, the King immedy. seized his own hat by the forecock & swinging it out with his right arm to the fullest extent he cd. reach, dropped his arm close down to his side, & preserved that posture till the drum major had gone past & commenced to return the cane to its former position, upon which H.M. replaced his hat on his head . . . The King took more notice of the d. majors salutes than of any other person.[569] The band having wheeled to the left, so as to form ⟨49⟩ immedy. in front of the King, leaving the necessary space for the regt. to march between them & the king. Lieut Col. Leigh, commanding the regt.,

---

[567] Ibid., pp. 304–5.
[568] Ibid., p. 305.
[569] This sentence is encircled and the enclosure is attached to an arrow up the left margin as far as the break line above 'The 1st. Somerset Militia'.

next came up, well mounted, & saluted, but the King merely raised his hat, & instantly replaced it. The king noticed the salutes of the other officers by a slight & hasty touch of his hat, & even the Major & Adjutant, who brought up the rear, although mounted on prancing horses & saluting H.M. in the best style, were allowed to proceed almost totally unnoticed. The king now turned towards his staff – among them Lieut. Gen. Garth – remarked that the sash H.M. wore was a very handsome one . . . of crimson nettled silk – a very full sized one . . . King took off one of his military white gloves – the kings cane slipped from his hold . . The Kings hat fell off
—

– Soon after 8 I presented myself at G.L. was ushered into a magnifict apartt., where I joined a large party of 30 officers on the staff, & members of the household – the whole of them engaged in discussing a splendid royal breakfast.

⟨50⟩

1797. The reguln. with regard to hair was that it shd. be allowed to grow a foot or 15 in long at back of head. This was tied with black ribbon so as to form a queue, commencing close to the head: side hung down over the ears, & cut off level with their tips. The top was cut very short, & rubbed up with hand pomatum.
(Read this book again – contains much about dress of persons – naval officers – customs of same &c.–]

Instructions & regulations . . . Cavalry. 1799[570]
Inspection or review.
Marches 6 ground in open column of such front as circums allow. – Forms on the alignment in close order . . . . The trumpets assemble on the right of the regt. in two ranks; & the staff, &c, of chaplain, surgeon, mate, adjutant, are on the right of the trumpets in the line of front rank, one horse's length from it . . . . In this disposn. the genl. is awaited.
    When the reviewing gen. presents himself the ⟨51⟩ whole Draw Swords . . . during this operation the whole of the trumpets

sound . . . . The gen then goes to the right (& comes round to his place)

The March past – The trumpets move forward & place themss. in 2 ranks before the comg. off. & sound a march – The farriers are a horses length behind the centre of their troops, & the quartermasters behind the farriers . . . When they arrive about 10 yds short of the genl. The officers salute with the commanding officer, & at the last motion of dropping their swords dress to the right.

In this manner the column proceeds & makes 3 more wheels at the angles of the ground till the leading ½ squadn. has arrived on the line of passing the genl. it there halts about 30 yds. from him & the other ½ squads. continue to close up. – The trumpets join their sevl. troops in order to file past with them.

To the front, file! As soon as the leading ½ sq. halts it is ordered to file past & immedy. commences.

– Trumpet, Captain, lieutenant, cornet, serjts. corpls. privates, from which every flank brings the ⟨52⟩ tallest men in front; first the front rank, then the rear rank, closed by the farrier & q.master.

—

[The book to get for details of dress & everything is "Standing Orders" for any particular regt.]

———————— *//* ————————

Standing Orders of Queen's Dragoons <u>Gds</u> 1795[571]

Trumpeters.

Watering order – trumpets   slung at their backs. In common going about his quarters he must not wear his trumpet

Trumpet Major

as he Does not ride out in watering order, he has nothing to do with the stable dress . . . .

On Sundays must wear his laced hat . . . .

He must wear his uniform coat, waistcoat & breeches, black leggins, sword with the belt over the coat, blk. stock & turn over, plain hat & feather, hair clubbed, regimental rosette, & powdered, gloves & cane. When for a parade or any duty whatever, he must be dressed as above, with his trumpet slung. His trumpet sling is of red & silver

---

[571] *Standing Orders, Forms of Returns, Reports, Entries, &c., of the Queen's Dragoon Guards* (London, 1795) [288.e.22].

⟨53⟩

Cannon. 1808. This year the men's hair wh. had been worn long, powdered, & tied in a queue, was ordered to be cut short.

(2nd. Dragoon Guards)

The 13th. Lt. Dragoons were at Dorchester Weyth. Radipole &c in 1807 –

Dallaways Hist of Sussex[572] –

Smith. landsc. p. – During many years was frequently under the necessity of applying to portrait for a maintenance. His leisure was dedicated to rural excursions – in wh. he transferred innumerable scenes to his portfos. wh. he afterwds. composed into pictures. He was in the habit, to facilitate this plan, of using a camera obscura; to which circce. may be attributed a certain stiffness of manner wh. pervades his best works . . . . By means of this they contracted the surrounding scenery into a landscape, the strength, sweetness & finishing of which no pencil cd. equal. It ⟨54⟩ was their object to approach as nearly as poss. to the perfect represn. of nature; & to this method of study may pps. be justly described, not only the eminent & characc. perfns. but also the slight defects of their style of painting.

288.e.22. Standing Orders 1795 Queens Dragoon Gds.

Recruiting –The parties to beat up at one Guinea & a Crown, unless an increased bounty is given: the Crown to drink His M's health – the Guinea to be laid out in necessaries for the recruit . . . .

The parties to beat up at all places of amusement, & market towns within 20 miles of their stations.

Dress of the Trumpet Major.

As he does not ride out in watering order he has nothing to do with the stable dress, though he must have one in his possession because he may be called upon to ride out. He must wear his uniform coat, waistcoat ⟨55⟩ & breeches, black leggins, sword with the belt over the coat, black stock & turn over, plain hat & feather, with his hair clubbed in the exact regimental form, with the regimental rosette, & powdered, gloves & cane.

When for a parade, or any duty whatever, he must be dressed as above, with his trumpet slung. His trumpet sling is of red and silver.

On Sundays . . . . laced hat.

He must have a blk. regimental cap to wear at the riding-school & horse drills

Dress of Sergeants.

The regiml. coat, waistc. & breeches, blk. leggins; the cap, with a blk & white uniform feather in it; hair clubbed in the regl. form, . . & neatly powdered; the small sword . . . gloves . . & the regimental cane.

The S.M. always to wear his hat & feather, but in other respects his dress is like that of another sergts. exceptg. that his hat is laced like an officer's, & his coat of finer cloth – besides ⟨56⟩ a distinction in the epaulette.

Dress of the officers –

All officers in quarters must wear their uniforms with lappels buttoned back, regiml. small swords, with the belt under the coat, & regiml boots. Nothing is so unmilitary as to see them walking about in plain cloaths, & it is therefore absolutely forbid. Nor must they on any account wear any waistct. & breeches with their uniform but white cloth kerseymere, leather, or plush . . . . . The breeches to buckle at the knee. They must wear the plain regiml. hat & feather.

No boots must be worn but the exact regiml.; but in the aftern. when officers are off duty, they may be worn pushed down.

Trumpeters.

They inflict the corpl. punishmt. of the regt.

They must pay implicit obedce. to the T. Major.

They must repair to the practice room at the hour fixed by the T. Major.

T. Major.

He is to rank in the regt. as a Sergt. & he has an extra allowance of 6 guineas a year ⟨57⟩ in conseqce. of his appointmt.

He must exert over the trrs. a full authority & if any one behaves towds. him with the least impropriety or neglects his orders, he must confine . . report to adjutant &c –

He is answerable to the Officer commanding the regt. for the instruction of the Trs. in the T. & the instruments on wh. they play. This in his principal duty, & he must pay the utmost attentn. to it . . .

He must attend to the S.M. for orders at orderly time, & warn his trumprs. for sounding.

He must never be made to punish.

He must form on foot parades at the head of the Trs. & act towds. them as a Serjt.

On no account to drink with a Tr. but to associate with the Sergts.

He is to take care that the trs. come regly. to the soundings, & that they are properly dressed on all occasions.

He is never to take out the band to play ⟨58⟩ anywhere witht. the permission of the Commg. Officer.

Dress of Trumpeters.
At riding out in watering order – stable dresses, trumpets slung at their backs, & foraging caps on; hair clubbed, witht. powder.

"Commanding officer of a quarter, not being the Head Quarter of a regt."

Serj. Major.
1st. Non C.O. in regt. after Q.M. Extra 6 gs. yr. in conseq. & he has the advantage of taking letters from the post . . . .

Dress of rank & file.
When riding out in watering order they must be in stable dresses, foraging caps, hair clubbed witht. powder & regl. switches.
"the pieces flinted"
No man is ever to appear in the streets without trousers, leggins, or boots, according to the duty he is upon; in short no man is to be seen with stockings.

⟨59⟩

Adventures of Col. Landmann.
1792 – Dr. M. rather good looking, between 40 & 50, square built, of middle stature; his hair frizzed & queued, & abundantly powdered; white satin waistcoat, white breeches, & white silk stockings; his chocolate cold. ct. lined with white silk, & the buttons very

large. A beautiful little painting on each, covered with a glass set in a
gold rim. Such b's were worn by persons of fashion.

Standing Orders Q. Dragoon Gds.
> Horse drill – pistol.

Right glove to be taken off, & the goat skin thrown back.
Draw yr. rt. pistol.
Ld. yr. p. . . . . Open the pan, prime, cast about, & load; as soon as
loaded seize the p. by the butt. . . . In loading, the barrel to be kept to
the front, & the ramrod to the body.

⟨60⟩

Draw. yr. left p. . . .
Draw yr. rt. p. . . .
Cock yr. p.
To the rt. present! The man comes smartly to a present, looking well
along the barrel to the object.
Fire! . . . . as soon as fired, go on with the loading motions.

. . . .

Draw left p.   Same as right.

⟨61⟩

Naval Chron 1803–5[573]
The Young Officers Compann. by Lord de Ros[574]
Monday.

|Smuggling captures in newspapers 1803–5|
|"Preventive service." "Smuggling."|
|Levers novels.| [575]

---

[573] In pp. 61–6 the material is upside down in the notebook. Hence in consecutive
pagination that which is transcribed here as p. 61 appears on the 66th, p. 62 on the
65th, etc. *The Navy Chronicle* ('containing a general and biographical history of the
Royal Navy in the United Kingdom'), ed. J. S. Clarke, 40 vols (London, 1799–1818)
[293.i.1–25 & k.1–15].

[574] Baron William De Ros, *The Young Officer's Companion* ('or, Essays on military
duties and qualities, with examples and illustrations from history: a new edition, i.e.
an adaptation of the anonymous work *The Military Mentor*') (London, 1851)
[1398.b.4].

[575] Charles Lever (1806–72), popular novelist best known for his rollicking pictures
of military life and Irish fox-hunting society.

√ The Smuggler – James – Routledge.[576]
Ditto – by Banim[577]
      navy & volunteers.
Costume – Uniform. (look in Catge for Naval, Navy)
Divine service at the Drum Head of each regt. ("Camp")
See "Magazines" for date, & "Periodicals"[578]
Weymouth guides for the date.
Costume of country people.
Father & daughter by Mrs Opie – 1801 – & others[579]
Belinda ———— Edgworth – 1801 – & others[580]
See in Biog. Dic. if there is any Elizabeth Ann Hayes.[581]

    |(The air)   Th care|
             air
   |(Tha Th ever (there)|
  |Scotch – Theh said: Tek the tickets: terrains (trns)|
 |Greenhill – 23. The Common: Woolwich|

1129. 12. 0 – £16. 2/-[582]

(62)[583]

The Parliamentary evidence of some notorious smugglers.[584] Watts catalogue.[585] B.M.
The Ladys Magazine[586] begun in 1772

---

[576] G. P. R. James, *The Smuggler: a tale* (London, 1845) [N. 2470].

[577] John Banim, *The Smuggler: a tale* (London, 1831) [N.813].

[578] Refers to British Museum Catalogue.

[579] Mrs Amelia Opie, *The Father and Daughter* (London, 1801) [12614.aaa.26].

[580] Maria Edgeworth, *Belinda* (London, 1801) [012611.e.31]. Entries from 'The Smuggler' to here in pencil.

[581] Apparently not.

[582] This entry and the four deleted lines above in pencil.

[583] This page and pp. 63–6 in pencil.

[584] Sir Stephen Janssen, *Smuggling Laid Open* ('comprehending, among other particulars, the Parliamentary Evidence of some notorious Smugglers') (London, 1763) [1102.h.4.(11)].

[585] Robert Watt, *Bibliotheca Britannica* [or *A General Index to British and Foreign Literature*], 4 vols (Edinburgh, 1824) [2036.b]. Hardy's entries below show that he made good use of Watt's index in his search for contemporary materials.

[586] *The Lady's Magazine* ('or entertaining companion for the fair sex') (London, 1770–1818) [P.P.5141].

The European Mag. & Monthly Review.[587] (illus)
The Monthly Magazine –[588]
The Universal Magazine[589]
The Naval Magazine 3 vols. 1798–1801[590]
   (All these from Watts.)

      Gen. Cata.
Tab 1292a.   Caricatures. 12 vol. Lond.
                  1734–1844 fol[591]
533.d.24 Observations for the use of Officer of Royal Navy. London
1804 8vo[592]
1239 – The Royal Navy. Portsmouth 1872 etc. 4to[593]

Bath Characters, or sketches from life 1802.[594]
               (Watts.)
Glig-gamena Angel-Leod – or the sports & Pastimes of the People of
England – from earliest period to present time – 1801 – Watts.
                           Vol 3. | [595]
                           3 M. |

---

[587] *The European Magazine and London Review* ('By the Philological Society of London'), 87 vols (London, 1782–1825) [P.P.5459.z].
[588] *The Monthly Magazine and British Register*, 60 vols (London, 1796–1825) [257.c.1–19. 258.c.1–21. 259.c.1–20].
[589] *The Universal Magazine of Knowledge and Pleasure* (London, 1747–1803) [P.P.5439.a.].
[590] *The Naval Magazine, or Maritime Miscellany* (Dec 1798–June 1801); not in B.M. but, as Hardy's note makes clear, his source for these titles was Watt's *Bibliotheca Britannica*.
[591] Twelve made up volumes of caricatures, including individual volumes containing the work of Bowles and Carver, Bowles, Gillray (2 vols), Cruikshank, Woodward, Rowlandson, and several miscellaneous volumes.
[592] *Observations and Instructions for the use of the . . . Officers of the Royal Navy . . . By a Captain in the Royal Navy* (London, 1804) [533.d.24].
[593] *The Royal Navy* ('in a series of illustrations lithographed in colour from original drawings by W. F. Mitchell'), 2 vols (Portsmouth, 1872–81) [8805.ff.12].
[594] Peter Paul Pallet [pseud. for Richard Warner], *Bath Characters; or, Sketches from Life* (2nd ed., London, 1808) [12330.cc.22].
[595] Joseph Strutt, *Glig-Gamena Angel-Leod* ('or, the Sports and Pastimes of the People of England; including the Rural and Domestic Recreations, May-games, Mummeries, Pageants, Processions, and Pompous Spectacles, from the earliest period to the present time') (London, 1801) [7915.k.9].

"English." "people"
Edward, or Various Views of Human Nature.[596] ib.

⟨63⟩

Gen Cata.
– Fashionable Court Guide[597] – see how far back
– see Ephemerides.[598] Gentleman's register. &c
  Court & City Kalendar[599]
  Gents. Compte Annual Calendar[600]
See "periodical pubs. London.
  |Gent. & Lady's Palladium| [601]
  Gents Annual[602]
  Gents Budget[603]
  —— Diary[604]
  Gazette.[605] &c &c

---

[596] John Moore, *Edward* ('òr, Various Views of Human Nature, taken from Life and Manners, chiefly in England'), 2 vols (London, 1796) [635.f.22,23].
[597] P. Boyle, *The Fashionable Court Guide, or the Town Visit Directory for the year 1792* [and *1794*] (London, 1792, 1794); continued as *Boyle's New Fashionable Court and Country Guide and Town Visiting Directory (Boyle's Court Guide) for the year 1796 (–Jan., 1925)* (London, 1796–1924) [P.P.2506.sdc].
[598] Category in B.M. Catalogue.
[599] *The Court and City Kalendar; or Gentleman's Register* (London, 1745–69) [P.P.2506.gab].
[600] *The Court and City Register* [after 1770 the title is *The Court and City Register, or Gentleman's complete annual Kalendar*] ('Containing I. An Almanack . . . II. New and correct lists of both Houses of Parliament. III. The Court Register. IV. Lists of the Army and Navy'), 67 vols (London, 1742–1808) [P.P.2506.a].
[601] *The Gentleman and Lady's Palladium* ('by the Author of the Ladies' Diary' [John Tipper]) (London, 1752–55) [P.P.2477.pb]; presumably deleted by Hardy since these years do not fall within the scope of his research.
[602] *The Gentleman's Annual* ('being the New Year's Supplement to the Gentleman's Magazine') (London, 1871–1901) [P.P.6704.e]; as n.601, Hardy would have found this too inappropriate.
[603] *The Gentleman's Budget* ('a monthly journal of amusing, instructive, and enter-taining literature') (London, 1872) [1866.a.10(2)]; as n.602.
[604] *The Gentleman's Diary, or Mathematical Repository* [1741–1800], 3 vols (London, 1814) [P.P.1534.b].
[605] *The Gentleman's Gazette; or, London Magazine of Fashion for January, 1832* (London, 1832) [P.P.5225]; as n.602. From *The Gentleman and Lady's Palladium* to here Hardy has been reading down the B.M. General Catalogue under 'Periodical Publica-tions.–London.'; for the next entry he returns to search under the heading 'Ephemerides'.

Ephemerides
P.P. 2517.4 The Gents & Lady's diary for 1800, 03, 04[606]
8vo

✗ Recollections of Col. Landmann.[607] (GIII at Weyth.)

["Watering-call. Stocqueler.[608]]
 Brande's Military Dic.[609]
James's Military Dic[610] (about 1809)
✗ Rose's Instruction for Hussars – s.d.[611]
✗ Neville (Capt. L. on the Discipline of Lt. Cavalry. plates s.d.[612]
Cooper's Practical Guide for the Lt. Infantry officer – plates – s.d.[613]
Skeene. Capt. Ridg. Master of the cavalry Depôt
         Military Instructions . . . Cavalry Service 1808. 8vo[614]
Herries, John C. Instructions for the use of Yeomanry & Volunteer
Corps of   Cavalry – 1804–5 2 vols 8vo[615]

---

[606] *The Gentlemen's and Ladies' Diary and Almanac* (London, 1799–1808) [P.P.2517.q].
[607] See n.559. Extensive extracts are copied on notebook pp. 45–50, 59.
[608] Joachim Stocqueler, *The Military Encyclopaedia* (London, 1853) [1397.h.9].
[609] Perhaps Hardy means W. T. Brande, *A Dictionary of Science, Literature, and Art* ('with the derivation and definition of all the terms in general use') (London, 1842) [740.g.12]; since this does not answer Hardy's description, Brande may have edited a military dictionary which I have been unable to identify.
[610] Charles James, *A New and Enlarged Military Dictionary* ('or, alphabetical explanation of technical terms, etc.') (London, 1802) [534.f.9].
[611] Unidentified, but perhaps H. M. Rose, *A Pocket Dictionary for Military Officers* ('containing a definition of all the tactical terms now in use, with other matter belonging to the art of war') (London, 1816) [not in B.M. Catalogue].
[612] Crosses in red pencil.
[613] T. H. Cooper, *Practical Guide for the Light Infantry Officer* ('comprising valuable extracts from the most popular works on the subject, with farther original information, and illustrated by a set of plates on an entire, new, and intelligible plan') (London, 1806) [8838.b.64].
[614] Robert Skeene, *Progressive Military Instructions for forming Men and Horses in the Rudiments of Military Service* (London, 1807) [8830.bb.19]. There are minor variants in the title and publication date in *Bibliotheca Britannica*, from which Hardy has copied this entry, the previous four and the next one: *Military Instructions for forming young Men and Horses in the Rudiments of the Cavalry Service* (1808).
[615] John Charles Herries, *Instructions for the use of Yeomanry and Volunteer Corps of Cavalry*, 2 vols (London, 1804–05) [not in B.M. Catalogue].

⟨64⟩

Hackett Capt. Explann. of the Manoeuvres of a Regt. of Cavalry – 20 engravings 1811 – 8vo[616]

James (Charles) Charges, opinions & sentences of courts martial.
"James II 152" catge[617]
– – – – Mil. Dicy. – – – – 153[618]
✗Voyle's Military Dictionary (New)[619]
✗Cannon's History of (The Different regiments)[620]

—

✗Egerton's List – 1809. By His M.'s Command[621]
✗General regulations & orders.[622]
✗Annual Army List.[623] (see Periodical Pubs. – Europe – G.B. & Ire-
✗ land)
✗Manual & Platoon Exercise[624]
✗A manual for volunteer infantry[625]
✗Military library, with charts & plates. 2 vols. 4to[626]
✗James's Regimental Companion.[627]
✗Treatise on Military Equitation, with plates. by Lieut Col. W. Tyn-
dale.[628]
✗Instructions for young Dragoon officers, plates.[629]
[631]
✗Rules & Regns. for the sword exercise of the Cavalry. 30 plates.[630]

---

[616] William Hackett, *Explanation of the various Manoeuvres of a Regiment of Cavalry* ('elucidated by 20 engravings') (London, 1811) [not in B.M. Catalogue].

[617] Charles James, *A Collection of the Charges, Opinions and Sentences of General Courts Martial* ('as published by authority; from the year 1795 to the present time; intended to serve as an appendix to Tytler's treatise on military law') (London, 1820) [513.e.14].

[618] See n.610.

[619] George Elliot Voyle, *A Military Dictionary*, 3rd ed. (London, 1876) [2248.a.1].

[620] Richard Cannon, *Historical Records of the British Army* ('comprising the history of every Regiment in his Majesty's Service'), 70 vols (London, 1835 [1837]–53) [8829.c.1–70].

[621] Perhaps the list of 'military' publications of T. Egerton.

[622] *General Regulations and Orders for the Conduct of His Majesty's Forces in Great Britain* [20 Aug 1799] (London: War Office, 1799) [G.19828].

[623] *The Monthly Army List (The Army List)* (London, 1798–1940) [B.S.45/140].

[624] *The Manual and Platoon Exercises* [1 Nov 1804] (London, 1804) [289.a.34].

[625] *A Manual for Volunteer Corps of Infantry* (London, 1803) [G.19829].

[626] Unidentified; perhaps Andrew Boehm and F. R. Schleicher, *New Military Library*, 4 vols (Marbourg, 1789–90) [not in B.M. Catalogue but listed in *Bibliotheca Britannica*].

Planchés Cyclopaedia of Costume. published as far as part 21.[632]
19

⟨65⟩

See entry of Geo into Weyth. 1801 (July 3) by water.

        7½ in evening   1802
        Did not come.   1803
        4 in morning ⎰ - 1804 (Aug 25. left Oct 29)
                ⎱   1805

Any descripn. of York Hussars.
Are they same as German Legion.
Precise uniform of the S. Major.

    Printed for T. Egerton –
Remarks on Cavalry, by Gen. Warnery.
    Many plates – 1809[633]
Hints to the gentn of the Corps of Mounted Yeomanry – plates –[634]
The drill sergt. with plates.[635]

8828bbb   Regulations to be observed in the supplying the troops
. . . in the home encampments
                    London 1803. 80[636]

---

[627] Charles James, *The Regimental Companion* ('containing the relative duties of every Officer in the British Army'), 4th ed., 2 vols (London, 1803) [1397.a.3].

[628] William Tyndale, *A Treatise on Military Equitation* (London: The Author, 1797) [8824.ccc.33].

[629] *Instructions to Young Dragoon Officers* (London, 1794) [not in B.M. Catalogue].

[630] *Rules and Regulations for the Sword Exercise of the Cavalry* (London: War Office, 1796) [8831.bbb.6].

[631] Crosses and symbols in red pencil.

[632] James Robinson Planché, *A Cyclopaedia of Costume* ('or, Dictionary of Dress: including notices of contemporaneous fashions on the Continent, and a general chronological history of the costumes of the principal countries of Europe'), 2 vols (London, 1876–79) [2020.g].

[633] Charles De Warnery, *Remarks on Cavalry* ('translated from the original by G. F. Koehler') (London, 1798) [62.e.6].

[634] Unidentified.

[635] *The Complete Drill-Sergeant* ('containing . . . instructions for the drill, manual and platoon exercise. By a late Lieutenant in His Majesty's Marine Forces'), 2nd ed. (London, 1798) [1140.i.1].

[636] *Regulations to be observed in the supplying of the Troops* ('with the several articles (Bread, Wood, Straw, etc.) to be furnished to them, under the direction of the Commissary General, in the home encampments') [25 June 1803] (London, 1803) [8828.bbb.29.(1)].

288.d.24   Anno Regni Georgii III . . . rules for the better governmt.
of such of our forces as shall consist of natives of foreign states.
Eng. & Germ. F P. Lond 1804 8o[637]

———————— *H* ————————

– Instructions & regulations for the movements of Cavalry.[638] (see
for review on down) copy review – chap.
– Particulars of Bandmasters & drum-majors.
– Trumpet & Bugle Sounds for Mounted Services 1/6[639]
– May B. Master wear plain dress?

⟨66⟩

See if any book of standing orders for other regt. than dragoon gds.

—

Wrights caricature history of the Georges.[640]
Gilrays caricatures.[641]
"Hector M'Intyre" – & "Harry Lorrequer."[642]
        old soldiering stories – particularly the former.
Dress regulations for officers of the army.[643]
Rowlandson's plates.[644] Also Ackermanns. (of soldiers)[645]

---

[637] *Anno regni Georgii III. . . . quadragesimo quarto [c.75] . . . an Act (passed 14th July, 1804) for enabling Subjects of Foreign States to enlist as soldiers in his Majesty's service* ('Rules and articles for the better government of such of our forces as shall consist of natives of Foreign States') (London, 1804) [288.d.24].

[638] *Instructions and Regulations for the Formations and Movements of the Cavalry* [17 June, 1796. Drawn by Sir D. Dundas], 3rd ed. (London: War Office, 1799) [186.a.9].

[639] *Trumpet and Bugle Sounds* is in B.M. only from 1886, i.e. later than Hardy's note-taking.

[640] Thomas Wright, *Caricature History of the Georges* ('or, Annals of the House of Hanover, compiled from the squibs, broadsides, window pictures, lampoons, and pictorial caricatures of the time') (London, 1868) [9525.ff.4].

[641] The satirical cartoons of James Gillray (1757–1815), whose subjects included contemporary social follies, leading politicians, the French, Napoleon and George III. See notebook pp. 78–84. Hardy probably consulted James Gillray, *The Caricatures of Gillray* ('with historical and political illustrations, biographical anecdotes and notices') (London, 1818) [745.a.6].

[642] Charles Lever's story 'Harry Lorrequer' first appeared in the *Dublin University Magazine* in 1837.

[643] These were entitled *Dress Regulations for the Officers of the Army* from 1874 but the edition current in the period of Hardy's research would be *General Orders* [Relative to the Dress of the Officers of the Line. 4 May 1796.] (London, 1796) [288.a.10.(5)].

[644] Thomas Rowlandson, *Loyal Volunteers of London and environs* ('in their respective uniforms . . . designed and etch'd by T. Rowlandson') (London, 1798) [189.d.1].

[645] Rudolph Ackermann, *Illuminated School of Mars* ('or, Review of the loyal volunteer corps of London and its vicinity') (London, 1799).

⟨67⟩[646]

inn – never goes out except at night – Innkeeper notices this – communicates with Ld. K. Ld. K & the innkeeper arrive too late – F. is gone – catch him at another inn – Col. K. struggles with him – Ld. K. shoots him dead.

Lord Kingsborough was tried for the act in Irish House of Lords. 18th. May 1798. He is acquitted –

Mary was placed, under a feigned name, in the family of a Welsh clergyman – her host himself being ignorant of her quality & condition. She is a splendid talker. Tells her own adventures as if they were an old tale she had heard. Tears in the young clergymns. eyes. She tells that she is the woman – He marries her –

⟨68⟩

Hist of France – by Eyre Evans Crowe –
          5 vols. Longmans 1863.[647]

Vol III.:- p.352

Margaret of Valois consented to a divorce with King Hy IV. that he might marry Marie de Medicis – But ere Henry cd. behold his new bride he became enamoured of the charms of Henriette d'Entragues – (She was the dau. of the Count d'Ent. & Marie Touchet, who previous to her marriage with the count had borne to Chas IX a son, known as the Count d'Auvergne). 100,000 crowns and a written promise of marriage was the price which Henriette demanded. Sully on being consulted gave the money but tore the promise however the king patiently rewrote & handed to the lady. The monarch unfortunately laid little stress upon promise or oath written or unwritten. Accustomed to make light of them in politics he deemed those ⟨69⟩ wrung from his gallantry of little worth. The promise to Mademoiselle Henriette was to marry her if she should give birth to a son within a certain period. This she failed to do a terrific storm having caused her to give birth to a dead-born child &

---

[646] The pagination now continues consecutively since the 'upside down' pages 61–6 (see n.573) are succeeded by a new gathering. But the first two pages of this new gathering have been cut out along with one inch of the top of p. 67, on which the entry now begins in mid-sentence. This is the shortest gathering, transcribed as pp. 67–77.

Page 66 marks the end of the first gathering, to which pp. 61–6 did not originally belong, though they are pasted on to the last page of the gathering in such a manner that they become a constituent part of it.

[647] Eyre Evans Crowe, *The History of France*, 5 vols (London, 1858–68) [09210.ee.3].

this relieved the king from a promise shamefully made upon the eve of his marriage with Marie de Medicis which took place at Lyons. But Henry's connection with Henriette d'Entragues did not cease. He created her Marquise de Verneuil brought her to his home to inhabit the same palace as the Queen to whose plaints & resentment he showed small consideration. Marie de Medicis was indeed neither of a person nor of a character calculated to command so volatile a prince & so confirmed a voluptuary. Her figure as represented by Rubens and as described by Henry himself was "terribly robust." nor did she seem to know how to win his affections or command his respect. Sully did his utmost to appease the quarrels of the royal spouses & often partially succeeded. Yet he might not have been able to prevent Henry from sending Marie back to Florence had she not given birth in September 1601 to the Dauphin the future Louis the Thirteenth.[648]

⟨70⟩[649]

Maltese Knight – Kills a man in a duel – dying request of his opponent that his sword be taken to Têtefoulques, his ancestral home. Every Friday a spectre appears, requesting it. At last the Knight goes – ruinous place – hall with pictures & trophies. he sits up in the hall – gusty – the pictures sway & the trophies of swords &c. rattle.

⟨71⟩[650]

| #   #   #   #   #   #   #   #

received a letter through the 3d. post anonymously sent: contains codicil to will . . . reward offered for sender . . never appeared.   #

————————————//————————————

---

[648] The following page has been excised. There follow a succession of four stubs of pages: of these, three small fragments–one small fragment each of three separate pages–have been allowed to remain, all surrounding matter having been carefully cut out. (Though it seems unlikely, it is at least possible that one passage Hardy excised from the notebook contained the 275 or so words that he copied from C. H. Gifford's *History of the Wars* (1817) and later transposed virtually unchanged into Ch. 23 of *The Trumpet-Major*. For this Hardy was later excoriated by critics on the grounds of plagiarism: for a full description of the episode, see C. J. Weber, *Hardy of Wessex* (1940; rev. ed. 1965), pp. 116, 118–22.)

[649] A half-page fragment.

[650] These entries appear on the verso on the previous page; they are heavily deleted and partially illegible.

|Clavell – old man died – will adventured for – house keeper's daughter produces one – which she said he had dictated to her . . . gave all the property to her intended lover. Forgery.|

|Roberts – Not quite 100 yrs. ago Mr. Roberts was posting from Holyhead to London – man of small fortune – was dining out at a small roadside|

———————— *#* ————————

⟨72⟩[651]

The fate of Seaforth. Husband away – Lady uneasy – Warlock (man with second sight) is brought to her – tells her that her husband is on his knees before a beautiful lady in Paris – Countess is enraged at the scandal, for it was uttered in public – has the Warlock hung. Husband returns, &c – ib.

———————— *#* ————————

⟨73⟩[652]

J. never turned his face from a poor relation. On that occasion Sir F. O'Neill showed to his ldp. the last remnant of his family plate, a silver cream ewer . . . . . . engraven with crest . . . also the Patent of Baronetcy, with its large old fashioned wax seal, & his parchment pedigree . . . In a little outhouse a broken carriage . . . emblazoned . . the red hand almost effaced.

⟨74⟩[653]

|& it became necessary to look at the powers of his lease. Redmond goes to ⟨Alligoe?⟩ park – gets bundle of leases – takes them to his chambers in Dublin. Sitting in his study that evening, &|

⟨75⟩[654]

The Shakespeares . . A Thunderstorm drives Lord Moira under a tree – a boy keeping cows takes shelter with him – they talk. &c. ib.

---

[651] A quarter-page fragment.
[652] A quarter-page frament, on verso of p. 72.
[653] A quarter-page fragment, entries heavily deleted and one word almost illegible.
[654] A quarter-page fragment, verso of p. 74.

⟨76⟩[655]

|Woman – Carrier pigeon at C.   #   #   –|

|— |

|Men with 3 toads.—| [656]   Crocker –

Boro. Surveyor

Sale.

Holland.

"The Provoked Husband" – & "The Sultan."[657]

The Clandestine Marriage

Fortune's Frolic

The Rivals & Lock & Key

{ She stoops to conquer

{ The Agreeable Surprise

{ The Soldiers Daughter

{ No song no supper

{ The West Indian

{ All the World's a Stage

---

[655] Upside down therefore list of plays commences on consecutive pagination p. 77, here given as 76, and ends on p. 76, here given as 77.

[656] Deleted passages in pencil.

[657] Pp. 76–7 apparently in Emma Hardy's hand. These plays and comic operas are identified as follows (dates given are those of first production): Sir John Vanbrugh (1664–1726), who left it unfinished, and Colley Cibber (1671–1757), who finished it, *The Provok'd Husband* (comedy, 1728); Isaac Bickerstaffe (d. 1812?), *The Sultan; or a Peep into the Seraglio* (farce, 1775); George Colman the elder (1732–94) and David Garrick (1717–79), *The Clandestine Marriage* (comedy, 1766); John Till Allingham (fl. 1798–1810), *Fortune's Frolic* (farce, 1798); Richard Brinsley Sheridan (1751–1816), *The Rivals* (comedy, 1775); Prince Hoare (1755–1834), *Lock and Key: or Bamboozell* (a musical entertainment, 1796); Oliver Goldsmith (1730–1774), *She Stoops to Conquer* (comedy, 1773); John O'Keefe (1747–1833), *The Agreeable Surprise* (comic opera, 1781); Andrew Cherry (1762–1812), *The Soldier's Daughter* (comedy, 1804); Prince Hoare, *No Song, No Supper* (opera, 1790); Richard Cumberland (1732–96), *The West Indian* (comedy, 1771); Isaac Jackman (fl. 1795), *All the World's a Stage* (farce, 1777); John Tobin (1770–1804), *The Honeymoon* (comedy, 1805); Mrs Frances Brooke (1724–89), *Rosina* (comic opera, 1782); John O'Keefe, *The Young Quaker* (comedy, 1783); Elizabeth Inchbald (1753–1821), *Animal Magnetism* (farce, 1788); John O'Keefe, *The Poor Soldier* (comic opera, 1783); John O'Keefe, *Peeping Tom* (comic opera, 1792); Susannah Centlivre (1667?–1723), *The Busybody* (comedy, 1709); Thomas John Dibdin (1771–1841), *Of Age Tomorrow* (musical farce, 1800); George Colman the younger (1762–1836), *The Heir-at-Law* (comedy, 1797); same author, *Ways and Means* (comedy, 1788); Susannah Centlivre, *A Bold Stroke for a Wife* (comedy, 1718); Prince Hoare, *The Prize* (musical farce, 1793); Thomas King (1730–1805), *Lovers' Quarrels, or Like Master Like Man: an interlude in one act altered from the Mistake of Sir J. Vanbrugh* (n.d.); Mrs Hannah Cowley (1743–1809), *The Belle's Stratagem* (comedy, 1780); David Garrick, *The Irish Widow* (farce, 1772); Thomas Morton (1764?–1838), *A Cure for the Heart-Ache* (comedy, 1797); John O'Keefe, *Modern Antiques: or the Merry Mourners* (farce, 1791).

The Honey Moon & Rosina
The Young Quaker & Animal Magnetism
The Poor Soldier & Peeping Tom
The Busy Body, & of Age tomorrow
The Heir at Law & Ways & Means
A bold stroke for a Wife & The Prize
Lovers Quarrels
The Belle's Stratagem & The Irish Widow
A cure for the Heartache & Modern Antiques

⟨77⟩

The Chapter of Accidents & Bon Ton[658]
The School for Scandal

⟨78⟩[659]

Gillrays Caricatures[660] –   B.M.III.

Grates, about 1800

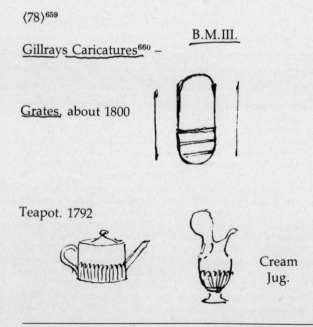

Teapot. 1792

Cream
Jug.

---

[658] Sophia Lee (1750–1824), *The Chapter of Accidents* (comedy, 1780); David Garrick, *Bon Ton, or High Life Above Stairs* (farce, 1775); R. B. Sheridan, *The School for Scandal* (comedy, 1777).

[659] Page 78 marks the beginning of the third and final gathering; Hardy begins a new series of pagination in what was originally a separate notebook.

[660] See n. 641.

Coal Heaver 1783. the knee-buttons
of his breeches unfastened – his
stocking down – iron buckle on shoe

1799 – Man suffering from gout – his foot swathed in flannel, & the
knee of his breeches unbuttoned. Chairs with oval backs – red
padded – frame with gilt facings. &c.

At Vauxhall – 1783 – Ladies in red & green shoes – white buckles.

1800. Old men playing fiddle, with lady. O. men in white stockings
– shoes & buckles – muslin neckcloths – blue coat with |gilt| yellow
buttons one – green the other – cut square ⟨79⟩ at hips – & buttoned
up in both cases – one old man bald headed – other white haired no
wig on either.

N.B. the square cornered ∧ swallow ∧ tail coat seems to have
come in about 1800

A tea party – same date – All the gents. coats as above – with the
addition of a |brown sun| burnt umber one – All buttoned up –
white waistcoat showing below
The remainder of dress as above. buff & pale sepia breeches – blk.
shoes & buckles – white stockgs. Clergymans coat black. Old

woman in a red gown & white muslin neckerchf. & blue slippers peeping out. All the women with ∧ a ∧ large feather in each head dress – standing up (probably intended to curve backwards but shown as accidentally twisted round.) Ball headed man with wig. Candles on tables – tall fluted c. sticks.

1800 – Cockney
     sportsman's
     hat

⟨80⟩

Vulgar Cockney sportsman – ∧ red ∧ plaid ∧ pocket ∧ handkf. bottle of porter – low crowned hat – red waistcoat, unbuttoned the three lower buttons – coat like   fustian.

1805 – A card party – gilt candlesticks like Ionic pillars – old man ∧ (parson.) ∧ with wig – younger man without – the old man has ruffles – is lame of gout, & has been wheeled up to the table on a red wheeled chair. his foot rests on a cushion. broad rimmed spectacles, with a round hole at end of the temples. Snuffers in tray – Soldier in blue coat, gilt epaulettes, black stock white shirt frill beneath it – white waistcoat – red facings to coat –
Ladies in full dress ∧ (opera) ∧ – Caps – hair in innumerable curls. Tall feather in each cap.
– Two young ladies with hair built up high, but no cap.

1802. Ladies at cards – dresses cling to them. & show their forms – |one| both ⟨81⟩ naked armed – & naked necked, as in evening dress at present. One of them: white muslin? dress – watch at her side – red coral necklace red coral armlet, |just above| between elbow & edge of sleeve. Hair over her forehead, & built up on crown, kept in place by a string of $\{^{\text{beads}}_{\text{pearls}}$ (?) wound round it several times – earrings. no cap.

The other girl has her hair dressed the same way, but bound round by a red band

The old lady has bead necklace & bracelets – a huge lace cap with blue ribbon. & a notched stomacher. Bell pull a ring attached to cord. Grate like Aunt Sp——s's.[661] High brass fender – 9 in. high. & perforated – Hearth rug with a broad fringe (yellow.) Table 3 legged pillar like |our| old one – green top –

⟨82⟩

1802 – Eveng dress – no cap – high feather –
1802 – ladies at a lecture – long tight sleeves, puffed at shoulders – huge feathers in head dresses.
1803 – Middle aged man – blue cut-away coat, buttoned at point of meeting – stockings – shoes.
1804 – A Ball room – muslin dresses ∧ gathered up ∧ [662] – at the tip of shoulders |bears a pink| with a knot of pink ribbon
one young lady with turban & pheasant's feathers – another ostrich feather – each has her fan – pink slippers peep out from beneath muslin dress. Gentn. dancing in blue, brown & lilac coats – all wearing queues – which are ∧ curling & ∧ flying about in difft. directions as they dance Older ladies have pink dresses – & muslin neckerchiefs over their necks: Lights chairs, rush bottomed – gentn. in shoes & breeches – flesh cold. stockings – A mantel clock – candles in branches & fixed to wells

---

661 Maria Sparks, one of Hardy's mother's sisters, wife of James Sparks and mother of Hardy's cousin Tryphena.
662 Added in a bubble above the line.

⟨83⟩

1804 – Blue coats the genl. colour. cut like
   this – but also like an ordinary
   frock coat

1804. Old maid out walking. A green double breasted dress or robe –
bonnet with cap under – fan – sunshade – boots with red tufts on
instep & red heels –
1804. Company at |tea| breakfast – same tall fender as above – &
high grate – red cord & tassel to blind – candle branches on mantelpiece. white table cloth – brown tall urn – egg-cup – eggs in plate –
gentn. all in shoes & buckles stockings & knee breeches – & cold.
square-tailed (not like |dress| present dress coats.) – Dr J. coats.
waistcoats button high up.

—

1800–5
Only cocked hats & low hats – the Dr. J. coats most prevalent in
common wear.
1806. The dress shaped coats, with rounded inner corners, have
now got among the common people but old men wear the others –
low crowned hats ⟨84⟩ universal – neckcloths (white) wound round
& round.
1809. Ladies caps with ribbon tied round them –
1806. Morning promenade – Brighton – Girls on donkeys – they
wear plum cold. brown, & yellow gowns – muslin neckerchiefs –
∧ yellow & blue ∧ hats with brims bending in to side of face or ∧ blk
& red ∧ bonnets

In B.M. is The <u>West Briton</u>, since 1811 (Truro).

M. Chronicle 1804.
Sat. June 9.
     ″   Defence of the Country.

The C. of the Ex. moved that the order of the day for the second reading of the Bill for the ∧ General ∧ Defence of the Empire be then read

. . . . . .

Mr Calcraft (in favour), Mr Yorke (cd. not support it), Mr Windham (opposes it), C.Ex. Then "Mr Fox |"| rose |of| about ½ past 12, & spoke with the greatest animation & effect till past two . . . . The House then divided

For the 2d. reading	221
Against it	181
Majority only	40!!

⟨85⟩

Leader – "We congratulate the country on what may be considered the decisive defeat of another inefficient Administrn. Mr Pitt, in his first Ministerial Measure had last night only a majority of 40 . . . . We cannot doubt that his plan will be abandoned & that some new ministerial arrangemts will speedily take place. |The Minority.|

Paris papers of the 30th. have been received. The trial of Moreau commenced on the 29th. & excites much interest.

A letter of Gen. Moreau to the 1st. Consul

Mr Fox and Mr Grey visit Mr Pitt

Monday June 11.
Advt. Two Fch. ladies, whose morals & manners will bear the strictest investigation, & who can give the highest & most respectable references &c – Duelling – this day is pubd. price. 3/6
Advt. The Trial at Large of Willm. Sparling Esq. late a lieut in the Xth regt. of Dragoons . . . & Saml. Colquitt. Esq. Capt. of H.M.S. Princess for murder of E. Grayson. Liverpool. W. Jones. (Duel fought Feb.26.1804) Tried at Lancaster Assizes. Apl 4.04

⟨86⟩

Dinner at "Carleton" House
H.R.H. the Duke of Clarence
Lord Foley
Hon Chas Dundas –
Hon George Walpole
Mr Fox
Mr Sheridan

Kings Theatre – a serious opera
T. Royal. D. Lane.
The Way to Keep him.
T. Royal   Covent Garden.
           Hamlet.

Bow Street.

Mrs Siddons[663] has for nearly 2 months been annoyed by |a young man| the personal addresses of a young gentn. He began by writing letters to her, informing her of the strong affection & love he had for her person, to which, of course, she paid no attention. Incessantly coming to her house, insisting upon waiting to see her – servants had great diffy. in forcing him away. Taken into custody . . . liberated on promising not to be troublesome any more to Mrs S.

⟨87⟩

N.B. The M. Chronicle is a Whig paper – opposed to the Govt. of Pitt – & in division list the minority against Pitt includes Fox Chas James – Windham, Wm. &c

---

March 1. ib. Hear on good authority that the amount of French gun boats at Boulogne is 1,050.

State Lottery.

D.C. Chronicle.[664] Thursday, March 19. 1829
    Trial of Kennedy for shooting at Rev H. Willoughby.

---

[663] Sarah Siddons (1755–1831), the leading tragic actress of her time.

[664] The *Dorset County Chronicle* of this date carries a full account of the trial of Private William Kennedy, aged 19, for the attempted murder of the Rev. H. Willoughby. Kennedy, of the 5th Dragoon Guards, was stationed in Dorchester Barracks; he was convicted on mainly circumstantial evidence and sentenced to death.

B.M. June 27.79[665]
Standing Orders – First Royal Dragoons.
(G.B. & Ireland – Army –) 288 b 23[666]
Form for Review

In two squadrons, & in two ranks, in order of parade, to receive a Reviewing general; ranks at open order, squadrons at proper distances files half open. – The first squadron to consist of the Colonel's Lieutenant-Colonel's ⟨88⟩ & second Captain's troops. – The second squadron of the Major's, first & third Captain's troops, – Commanding Officers of Squadrons are to be advanced one horse's length before the standards: line of officers, one horse's length before the first rank of the troops to which they belong, dividing the ground; the standards in a line with the officers; the Adjutant on the right of the front rank, between the serjeants & trumpeters. Chaplain & surgeon on the right of the Adjutant. – Serjeants Trumpeters & farriers divided on the flanks of squadrons, trumpeters in front, farriers covering them in the rear, two on each of the outward flanks, & one on each of the inward flanks, where they are to remain during the squadrons passing by the General (the trumpeters are to sound, & the farriers advance their hatchets, on the word of command being given for drawing swords) The Quarter Masters in the rear of their respective troops four horses length. dividing the ground. The whole perfectly ⟨89⟩ steady, & dressing by the right. – The squadrons are to draw swords by word of command from their respective Commanding Officers, & successively as the General approaches: the Officers to salute separately as he passes, each Officer endeavouring to time his beginning in such manner as just to have finished the last motion when the Reviewing General comes opposite him. – The Major takes post in the front of the Regiment as soon as he has saluted, & the next eldest officer advances to his post. – As the General is turning the left flank of the front rank of the left squadron, the Officer commanding it gives the word.

By the left dress;

Military Tracts. 534.d.34. contains directions to Yeomanry. Fencibles. &c[667]

---

[665] The entry from here to 'By the left dress;' on p. 89 appears to be in Emma Hardy's hand.
[666] *Standing Orders in his Majesty's First, or Royal, Regiment of Dragoons*, etc. (London, [1790?]) [288.b.23].
[667] Entry in pencil.

⟨90⟩

Gt. B. & Ireland – Army –
Standing Orders Queen's Dragoon Gds.
288, e, 22.

      6 troops –
A troop contains:- 1 Capt. 1 Lieut. 1 Cornet.

Total	Capt. M.'s	Capt. G.'s	Capt. C.'s	Major G.'s	Lieut C. L. H's	Col. T.'s			Troops
—	—	—	—	—	—	—	Colonel	Commissioned	Officers
—	—	—	—	—	1	—	Lieut C.		
—	—	—	—	—	—	—	Major		
4	1	1	1	—	—	1	Capts.		
5	1	1	1	1	1	—	Lieuts.		
4	1	—	1	—	1	1	Cornets		
—	—	—	—	—	—	—	Chaplain	Staff	Staff
1	—	—	—	—	—	1	Adjutant		
1	—	—	—	—	—	1	Surgeon		
6	1	1	1	1	1	1	Q. Masters	Non. C.	Effectn.
12	2	2	2	2	2	2	Sergeants		
6	1	1	1	1	1	1	Trumpeters		
								Men	

(91)

Trumpeters[668]

The Trumprs. must pay implicit obedience to the T.M. &
observe with the utmost exactness his directions in every respect.
They must arrive at as much perfection as possible in playing upon
the trumpet, & the instruments on which they are taught, following
in the most minute particulars to TM's directions.

They must be regular, obedient & well behaved; & they must
consider everything that is said respecting the Dragoons as equally
applying to them.

They must be extremely neat in their appearance, & they
must never fail to repair to the practise room at the hour fixed by the
T.M.

They inflict the corporal punishments of the regiment.

They must look after their own horses excepting when the
band is going out to play by permission; in which case they must
(92) pay two pence to the man who dresses their horse that night; &
they must take care that their being musicians does not spoil them as
Dragoons.

The TMs must be exact in all their sounding, they must never
vary a note on any account nor ever be a minute too soon or too late.

It is absolutely necessary that they should be very sober
people, for if they are the least in liquor. it is discovered in a moment
by their sounding, & they never know when they may be called
upon to sound the alarm.

They must be very clever horsemen & ride active light horses;
for in the field it is a matter of indispensable necessity that they
should sound their signals quite clearly at any pace.

Trumpet Major.
. . . . .

He must attend the S. Major for orders at Orderly time, &
warn his trumpeters for sounding.

(93)

"Volunteers to be clothed in <u>red</u> –"
    Soldiers Compann. 1803.

---

[668] This entry, to 'at any pace.' on p. 92, appears to be in Emma Hardy's hand.

1805. Gentleman's dress of the period (in which a clerk was hung).

Black coat & waistcoat, white plush breeches & boots – muslin handkerchief. Ann. Register

May 24 "Mr Russell the great Exeter carrier was brought up to receive judgment for suffering his hard[669] wheeled waggons to remain for whole days in the public streets of Exeter . . . . . .

25th. Aug. Dk of Gloucester died.

Morning Post 1805

May 2.   The Brest armament [fleet] appears waiting to put to sea on the first favourable opportunity. It is suspected by Govt. that the enemy meditates some serious design upon Ireland. Women |on horseback| in Row. May. Celestial blue silk cloaks, trimmed with a profusion of French lace. Straw & Leghorn bonnets & hats much worn; & white India muslin ⟨94⟩ dresses, made very short in waist & trimmed with lace.

—

Weymouth July 28, 1805. (Sunday)

Yesterday afternoon The Ryl. Fam. came on shore about six o'clock from their cruize; at 7 the Ryl. Fam. went to the theatre in their carriages drawn by beautiful Hanoverian white horses, with their usual attendants, with the addn. of the Earl of Chesterfield. The performances were "The Soldier's daughter, & No song no supper. The Widow Cheerly was extremely well supported by Mrs Grant from the Edinburgh Theatre; as was Endless by Nr Neylor, & Margaretta, by Miss Wentworth, in the Farce.

The house was tolerably well filled, considering the thinness of the town

This morning abt. 10 their Ryl. Hs the Dukes of Cumbd. & Cambridge went to the Camps to attend divine service, which was performed at the drum head of each regt.

Their Majesties & Pcesses went to Ch. about 11.

⟨95⟩

Papers for 1805 also contain a chronicle of the Prince of Wales's doings at Brighton. (In July he has a touch of gout)

———

(The R. Family at Weymouth also go to see The Heir at Law: Dr Pangloss, Mr Sandford, Lady Daberley, Mrs Neylor)

---

[669] Difficult reading: 'hard' seems closest approximation.

Dressed in a light frock coat & jockey waistcoat – (a clergyman jockey)

"God Save the King was sung as usual by the whole company" (when the King was at the theatre, Weymouth.
Among the company (at Theatre) are noticed the Marquis of Hertford, Earls Wilton & Chesterfield, Genls Cartwright & Fitzroy. ――
Ladies Ilchester Thynne & Bulkeley.

Gents. Magazine 1805 – p 1214[670]
(Royal Progress). Aug 2 – His Majesty was on horseback a quarter before 7 accom= ⟨96⟩ panied by the Duke of York & rode to the Camp when the 15 regiment of Light Dragoons & the German Legion had a grand field-day The latter regiment practised our discipline with the Dragoons with great satisfaction to his Majesty & the Duke of York who returned to the Lodge to breakfast. The King with Princesses Augusta & Sophia took a ride on horseback. The Duke of York went with his brothers to the Camp. Her Majesty with Princesses Elizabeth, Mary & Amelia took an airing on the Dorchester road. Between 5 & 6 the Royal Family went in grand cavalcade in five coaches to drink tea with the Duke of Cumberland in his marquee on Rodney Pool & hill & returned between 8 & 9.

[Radipole?]

Morning Chron. 1805.
Weymouth Aug 24. (Saturday)
          This evening the R.F. are to honour the Theatre with their presence to see the comedy of the Rivals Sir A. Abs. Mr S. Kemble, who will, after the farce, deliver a cento, selected by himself from the works of Shakesp. & addressed to the Army

⟨97⟩   1805[671]

& Navy on the threatened invasion.
          Mr Bannister, who arrived yesterday will make his first appearance in Lingo, in The Agreeable Surprise.
          Arrivals at Luce's hotel – . . . . . Mr S. Kemble . . .

---

[670] This entry, to '8 & 9.' on p. 96, appears to be in Emma Hardy's hand.
[671] In pencil.

Sept.3. (Tuesday)

The Prince [of Wales] arrived in time yesterday to dine with the R. Fam. & spent the evening with them. Early this morning his Maj. accom. by the Dks of York, Cumberland, & Cambridge rode on horseback & returned soon after 9 o'c.

Capt. Hardy, Lord Nelson's capt. was waiting the return of His Maj. & had a long convn. with him.

. . . . . 4. Arrivals at Luce's Hotel. Prince of Wales, Dk of Sussex . . . . Col. Mitchel.

5. All the troops encamped are having a grand field day at Bincombe down., for the purpose of being inspected by the Prince of Wales, whose presence has attracted nearly the whole town. Every carriage is engaged . . . The troops are under as strict discipline as if in an enemy's country. The ships & batteries ⟨98⟩ have hoisted their colours again in conseq. of the D. of Gloucester being buried. (from Aug 24 to Sept 3. Weyth. was very dull – nobody on esplanade &c – in conseq. of death of D. of G.)

6. The presence of the Prince attracts much company. Numbers are coming daily, for miles round the country to see HRH.

Yesterday after the Prince's return from the general inspection of troops encamped here, H.R.H. was entertained by the Dk. of Cumberld with a sumptuous dinner. Every assistance was given from the King's kitchen. The Ds of York & Cambridge, & all the Field Officers were of the party . . . A very elegant esplande. Theatre opened again.

9. Grandest Esplade. of the Season. His. Maj. All the Pcesses & Royal Dukes were present. The Pce. dined with their Maj's & remained at the lodge with her Maj. At dusk the Ryl. party retired to the promenade rooms – upwards of 300 nobility & persons of distinction present.

Sept 10. P. of W. left. (cf.I.7)[672]

⟨99⟩[673]

Sep 10. The Royal Family did not land from their cruise till past six o'clock last evening. Their return to shore was announced by the ships in the Harbour firing a Royal Salute. They went to the Theatre to see the Comedy of <u>The Poor Gentleman</u> & the Farce of <u>Peeping</u>

---

[672] Bracketed note in pencil.
[673] This entry, to 'Dutch property.' on p. 100, appears to be in Emma Hardy's hand.

Tom for the benefit of Mr. S. Kemble who supported the character of Sir Robert Bramble in the Play; Doctor Ollapod by Mr. Bannister. The rest of the characters were extremely well supported.

At the conclusion of the Farce Mr. Kemble delivered a Cento selected by himself from the Works of Shakespeare & addressed to the Army & Navy on the threatened Invasion of the country. Mr. Kemble concluded his engagements this evening. The Royal box was graced with their Majesties the Prince of Wales the Dukes of York, Cumberland and Cambridge Princesses |Agu| Augusta Elizabeth Mary Sophia & Amelia The house was filled in every part.

This morning the Prince breakfasted ⟨100⟩ with their Majesties & took leave previous to his leaving this town In the afternoon his Royal Highness will set off for London. To-morrow the Duke of York is expected to leave us. On Sunday the East India Fleet got up the Channel. A number of the passengers with their baggage landed here. Sunday afternoon the Unity Privateer of this port brought in a very rich prize, bound to France. She is an American bottom & is laden with West India produce & has a great quantity of dollars on board. It is supposed to be Dutch property.

Poetry – &c – moves with the general march of the human mind – Art is only the transformn into ideal & imaginative shapes of a predominant system & philosophy of life – Morley F.R.[674]

⟨101⟩

Gents. Mag. 1806.
  Royal Progress to Weyth. 1805.
    pp.40, & 165
1805
Aug 6 In the evening the Royal Fam. went in their carriages to the barracks on the Dorchester Rd. where after inspecting the buildings &c they partook of tea & other refreshments prepared by the officers – returned about 8.
Sep 25.[675] This day his Majesty took his usual amusement of a ride & an excursion to sea. Her Majesty & the Princess Elizabeth took

---

[674] John Morley in the *Fortnightly Review*.
[675] This entry, from 'Sep 25.' to 'of the officers' on p. 103, appears to be in Emma Hardy's hand. The two interpolations, 'Fullest . . . benefit' and 'Royal . . . amused-', are added by Hardy in pencil.

an airing by Upway. The Royal Family saw the Beaux Stratagem; ∧ Fullest House of any except Mr Bannister's benefit ∧ the part of Scrub by Master Dawson 6 years old. His performance was received with great applause. The ∧ Royal Fam. appd. highly amused – ∧ King sent for the boy & asked him several questions.

Aug 22. At 7, his Majesty rode to the Dorchester Barracks. On his return he gave an audience to Sir W. Curtis; & conversed a considerable time with the worthy baronet. About 11 the

⟨102⟩

Royal Family went on board the Yacht In the evening all were in the greatest anxiety for their safety till 10 o'clock. Their Majesties had commanded the Rivals At 7 the Theatre was filled; & by half past 7 the audience began to express considerable anxiety to know the cause of their non arrival; when Mr. Hughes informed them that the Royal Family had not returned from their cruise; & as the Yacht did not appear in sight he offered to proceed with the play; but this was opposed by the audience. The Manager repeated his offer but the audience would wait. It being 10 when they landed their Majesties sent to inform the Manager they should not attend. This being communicated the play began & it was midnight before the curtain dropped. The Pier was crowded with nobility &c waiting the return of the Royal Family. On their stepping on shore, they were received with three ⟨103⟩ cheers which was continued as they passed to the Lodge. The cause of their being so late was the Yacht having fallen in with the homeward-bound West India fleet which being a novel & grand sight engaged the attention of the Royal Family for three hours. On their coming in view a Royal Salute was fired which was answered by the frigate attending their Majesties. The same ceremony was observed on parting. His Majesty conversed with several of the officers

---

Fourier begins by establishing 3 abstract principles in universal nature from which he derives all things natural & spiritual.

1st.   The passive principle or matter – <u>Nature</u>
2d.   The Active principle or spirit – <u>God.</u>
3d.   The neutral principle or mathematics – <u>Justice</u>

In human nature he finds the passive principle represented by the 5 senses – the active prin by the 4 Affections, the ⟨104⟩ neuter prin. by the 3 distributive passions of the soul.[676]

In train. Young woman. married. 19. Not even the angle at juncts of brow & nose which 3.7′s bring there – perfect sweep. Eye one sweep from corner to corner. no severe curve –

B.M. Nov.25.
A. Register[677] 1805.
J.C. (death) – There were found in his house about 500 guineas in specie, tied up in small parcels of 5 gs each.
– A grocer, who made a vow never to step out of his house & kept it for 30 years till death.
– . . . They had been privately married, for some time, against her fathers consent, but they had lately obtained that & were able to be publicly joined on Thursday the 7th. When searched (he was found with his throat cut) after he died his ⟨105⟩ watch, a small box with a wedding ring|,| & some small trinkets, & a marriage licence were found on him. He had been a sea faring man, &c
– Lewis Gwynne, Co. Cardigan. He lived very private, though possessed of an extensive estate & accumulated an immense fortune. He had in his house when he died such a quantity of gold that a horse cd. not carry the weight. Amt. 100,000£ besides 50,000 in the stocks.
Morning Chronicle 1805
Torbay – reached on the evening of Sept 16th. (Monday) sailed from St Helens on the 15th. (Sunday). Ld. N. went on board at St Helens on the 14th. at six in morning. much cheered, a number of people following him, notwithstanding that he embarked at an unusual place & amid pressure of crowd . . .
. . The Victory reached close into Torbay, in order to avoid the flood tide, as the wind was to the S.W. & she bound down (Channel). but

---

[676] This and the next entry, to 'no severe curve–' on p. 104, are in pencil. Hardy has copied this from Hugh Doherty's introduction to F. C. M. Fourier, *The Passions of the Human Soul*, trans. J. R. Morell (London, 1851) p. xxxvii (section entitled 'Fourier's Analysis of Human Nature'). The influence of the French Utopian Socialist François Fourier (1772–1837) on Hardy's thought is valuably discussed by Lennart A. Björk in his *The Literary Notes of Thomas Hardy*, Vol. I (Göteborg, 1974), pp. 200–1; see also pp. xxiii–xxiv. Fourier's book is noted on the final page of the present notebook.
[677] *Annual Register.*

as soon as the ebb made his Ldp. move sail ⟨106⟩ to the Westward, in company with the frigate
1805
Sept 29. Weyth. The whole of the German Leg'n. marched from here yesterday, with their artillery.
Oct 4. King. Q. & Prcesses leave Weymouth, escorted by a party of the 14th. Lt. Dragoons.

——

Commodore Robin sends early news of it in empty boat from Bou[ne]

[Papers in Oct. brought Anne – They contain not a word of ∧ news from ∧ Nelson & his fleet – jokes about B. the march of his armies through Germany.
|Into Austria|
21st. Oct. Monday.
It is evident that some important conflict must have t. place between the Fch. & Austrian armies.
Nov.1. Friday. News of the total destruction of the Austrian army in Suabia – Gen. Mack having capitulated with 20,000 men. (at Ulm)
Nov 2. &c. Gen depression – we shall have to encounter this man fresh from the field of victory – fears of invasion renewed.

⟨107⟩

The reception of Ld. Nelson by the fleet was marked by the expressions of love attacht & devotion wh. his popularity in the service never fails to inspire.
Nov 5. Speech of Buon. to his army.
7. News of Trafalgar. ∧ (Thursday) ∧ Excitement – first announcement in the Bulletin of the Admiralty – ∧ London Gazette – reprinted in M.C. ∧ "multitudes surrounded our office at an early hour yesterday – "A blow is struck at the combined naval force of F. & S. on the very day when Mack's Army was piling their arms at the feet of their |emperor| conqueror."
Illuminations,
Nov.8. Further details expected with much anxiety, as there is yet no return of the killed & wounded.
|Portsmouth| Plymouth Nov 6. Lieut. Lapenot|ouere|iere of the Pickle schooner landed |here| with the despatches from Admiral Collingwood at Falmouth on Monday (the 4th.)[678] at 11 a.m. & came on here. (how these despatches flew |through| along the W. road!)

[678] In pencil.

⟨108⟩

Nov 11: ∧ (Monday) ∧ news of the danger of |the| our losing many of our prizes by their being driven ashore also that the man who killed Ld. N was observed in the act of firing by a midsn. on the poop of the Victory who fired & killed him.

Sir Sidney Smith returns the |cop| compt. by sending a copy of the L.G. Extra'[679] – in an empty cutter to B.

Nov.16. ∧ Additional ∧ Despatches received from Ld. Coll. (so anxiously waited for.)

Nov. 18 Published news of officer killd. – &c – but very incomplete. the names of those lost on board the Vic. being among the omitted. "The want of these returns keeps the pub. mind in suspense, particy the relatives & friends of the officers & men"

27. Another despatch from Ld. C. relieving the anxiety lest the ships most engaged should have been wrecked by the gale. & stating that the body of Ld. N. is coming ⟨109⟩ home on board the V. |Next|

Next day a complete list of the killed & wounded officers, |showing| & the number of seamen & marines, showing that the number k. on the V. is very great in proportion

Dec 3. Several more of the Victorious fleet of the 21st. have come into port. The Vict. is not arrived, but she is stated to have passed up Channel.

5. Letters from officers published.

4. Victy. arrived at Portsmouth [Letter from Bob]

Dec 10. The Victory is repairing at Portsth. & every exertion &c. = "No sight wd. be more gratifying to a Bsh. Pub. |than to see those| or be more worthy of a B. Hero's funeral honours than to see those gallant men, the crew of the Vict. accomp. their beloved commr. to the grave. The feelings of attachment which those noble fellows displayed in refusing to part with the body of their great leader deserves applause & commendation"

Dec 10 – (Vic sails for Cham.)

⟨110⟩

Mr C. of the Vict. is promoted to the rank of lieut. & appointed to the Belle Isle. Dec 12 All the first Lieuts of the ships engaged off Trafalgar are to be promoted to commanders.

[679] *London Gazette.*

Dec 19. "Capt. Hardy & Capt Blackmond are to be created Baronets"
Dec 27.   Weymouth Dec 19. The officers of the 15th (or Kings)
Light dragoons gave an entertainment in their barracks at Radipole
on Tuesday last. &c

See at B.M.[680] – "Hoyle[681] (on Games"?) for R. et Noir, &c –
Seymour Harcourts Gaming Calendar.[682]
Lucas's Memoirs of Gamesters & Sharpers[683] –
Sala's Make your Game[684]

Panvinius, Omphrius,[685] a learned Scholar of the 16 century of
Verona – De Antiquo Ritu Baptizandi Catechumenos – & De Infan-
tium B.

⟨111⟩

Baptism – of Infants a reasonable Service
– 4325.aaa.[686]
Argument from Apostc. Tradition.[687] 1765[688]

The baptism of infants was the undoubted practice of the Xn. Ch. in

---

[680] In pencil to bottom of p. 110.
[681] Edmond Hoyle (1672–1769) was a prolific writer on whist and other card games.
His famous Short Treatise on the Game of Whist was first published in 1742 and his name
later became representative of any book on games.
[682] Seymour Harcourt, The Gaming Calendar, to which is added, Annals of Gaming
(London, 1820) [7913.bbb.37].
[683] Theophilus Lucas, Authentic Memoirs . . . of . . . Gamesters and Sharpers, from the
Restoration of King Charles, 3rd ed. (London, 1744) [G.13675.(1)].
[684] George Sala, Make your Game ('or, the Adventures of the Stout Gentleman, the
Slim Gentleman, and the Man with the Iron Chest: a narrative of the Rhine or
thereabouts') (London, 1860) [12355.b.29]; not quite what Hardy was looking for!
Presumably copied on the mistaken assumption that like the three previous books its
subject was games or gaming.
[685] Omphrius Panvinius (b. Verona 1529, d. Sicily 1568).
[686] Micaiah Towgood, The Baptism of Infants: a Reasonable Service (London, 1750)
[4325.aaa.1.(2.)].
[687] John Gill, The Argument from Apostolic Tradition, in favour of Infant Baptism, with
others, advanced in a late pamphlet, called the Baptism of Infants a Reasonable Service, . . .
considered (London, 1751) [4325.aaa.33.].
[688] From '1765' to 'Apc.age.' on p. 113 in pencil, except Greek letters at bottom of
p. 112.

its purest & first ages – the ages immedy. succeeding The apostles; who could not but know what the Aposc. doctrine & practice was as to this matter. This I apprehend to be an argument of great weight. For the enquiry being about a fact, which could not but be publicly & perfectly known & not possible to be mistaken, in the ages immedly succeeding the Ap. the sense of those ages concerning this fact must needs be of gt. moment in deciding the point – Whether the apostles & Evangelists formed the first Churches throughout the whole world ⟨112⟩ upon the plan of Inf. Bap. or not; that is to say, whether they admitted <u>infants</u> togeth with their believing parents into the church by Baptism, or did <u>not</u> so admit them, was a fact of such nature as could not but be evident, & indubitably known, to all the Christians of the first age. Nor was it, humanly speaking, possible that the apostolic practice in this front should be universally departed from, disused, & thrown out in so short a space of time, as we shall presently see the B. of I. to have universally prevailed. | To prepare the way to join this proof I beg leave to promise these two things. | [He goes on to say that he appeals to the testimony of the ancient writers as reasoners

ΣΜΛΘΗ

⟨113⟩

or interpreters, but only as historians or witnesses to a public stand-ing fact – Then he proceeds to the testimonies] The first shall be from Justin Martyr, who wrote about 40 yrs after the Apc. age. He says "Several persons among us, both men & women, of 60 or 70 years old, who were proselyted or made disciples ∧ to Xt. ∧ in or from their infancy, do continue uncorrupt. Now, they cd. not be prose-lyted to Christ from their infancy without being from their infancy baptized – |<u>that is</u>| – For whosoever

EMATHET|C| EUTHESAN TO [689]

---

[689] Greek letters in pencil. Those in ink at the bottom of p. 112 = 'learned' or 'learn!' On this page, EMATHET EUTHESAN TO CHRISTO = 'he learned virtue by Christ'.

Χρ ιστω
CHRISTO

were disciplined or proselyted to Christ were by his
express order (Matt XXVIII.19) to be baptized. Note, 70 yrs. from
Justin carries us back ⟨114⟩ almost into the middle of the Apostc. age
      Iraeneus, who wrote about 67 yrs after the Aps. says concer-
ing Xt – Omnes enim venit per semetipsum salvare; omnes inquam,
qui |pre| per eum renascuntur in Deum, Infantes et paroulos et
pueros et juvenes – that he came to save all persons by himself; all I
mean, who by him are regenerated, i.e. baptized into God, Infants
& little ones, & youths & elder persons. – That word renascor,
regenerated, in the writings of these ancients, particularly of
Irenaeus, is most familiarly used to signify baptized, see from a vast
variety of instances proved, beyond all doubt, ⟨115⟩ in Wall's history
of Infant Baptism. And that by infants are here meant children,
before they come to the use of reason is evident, not only as these
must necessarily be included in the all whom he came to save, but
also because after he had mentioned infants & others regenerated,
he runs over the several ranks of age again, but with this remarkable
difference, that whereas he mentions the benefit of Xt's example as
what was to be taken by each of the other ranks viz. the parvuli, the
juvenes, & the seniores, he says no such thing concerning the
Infantes, infants, for this reason no doubt, that these only of all the
mentioned ranks were incapable of this benefit. ⟨116⟩ Tertullian,
who flourished about 100 years after the Aps. is the only person
among the antients who advises to defer the baptism of Infants
except in cases of necessity. But his advising to defer it, except in
cases of necessity is an incontestible proof that the baptising of
infants was the practice of those times. And he appears to be quite
singular in this advice; so that he was extremely whimsical & absurd
in his opinions on this as well as several other points of religion all
who have read his works very well know.

———

The M. Tertullian says they who understand the weight of baptism
will rather dread the receiving of it than the delaying of it.
S. We have nothing to do with that – all we cite him for is a voucher
to our ancient fact to prove then in his days Infants were baptized.

⟨117⟩

      Origen. also says – Adde his etram – Besides this also let it be considered; What is the reason that whereas the baptism of | infants | the church is given for forgiveness, Infants also by the usage of the Ch. are baptised; | when | There are other passages of Origen full to this point . . proving abundantly the baptism of infants to be the standing custom of his days. [I might if my memory served me, cite Cyprian who wrote 150 yrs. after the apostles. the Clementine Constitutions, Clemens Alexandrimus, Nazian ∧ zen ∧ , Basil, Ambrose, Chrysostom & Jerome

This then is the evidence on wh. we rest the antiquity of this fact. Now if all the Churches throughout the world were really established by the Apostles upon the plan of only Adult baptism, & they everywhere rejected infants | if | it will appear absy. ⟨118⟩ inconceivable, & even a moral impossibility, that the b. of i. shd. so early, so wisely, so universally prevail.

| For if the B. of I. was not an apostolic institution | Jacobi, Dr Lange[690]

⟨119⟩

G.B. & Ireland. Army. Volunteers.

189.d.1   Loyal Volunteers in their respective Uniforms – T. Rowlandson. Lond. 1798 4o

1140.a.29.   The Soldiers Companion – [Plates of Infantry in all attitudes &c] containing Instructions for the Volunteers. London 1803. 8o

534.d. 34   Memorandums of Field Exercise for the
    6   Yeomanry Cavalry.
                        Lond. 1795 8o
                (containing description of their dress.)[691]

534.d.34   Fencible Infantry.[692]
    4

---

[690] There follow ten blank, unused pages on which the right-hand pagination of alternate pages continues in Hardy's hand from 43 to 61. One sheet is then excised. Page 65 (in Hardy's pagination) of this gathering is used upside down and contains the continuation of matter from Hardy's p. 66. To preserve continuity of matter these pages are reversed in the transcription; thus Hardy's p. 66 of the gathering here becomes p. 119 and Hardy's p. 65 here becomes p. 120.

[691] *Memorandums of Field Exercise for the troops of Gentlemen and Yeomen Cavalry* By an Officer of Light Dragoons (Canterbury, 1795) [534.d.34.(6.)].

[692] *Certain Rules and Orders to be observed by the Corps of Fencible Infantry* (London: War Office, 1794) [534.d.34.(4)].

"Whereas it is necessary . . . our corps of fencible men .
. . .

Muster twice in every year, 24th. June & 24th. Dec.
Musters to be taken – to the 24th. June on the 10th.
Aug – to the 24th. Dec – on 10th. March. . . . Men effective
during the whole muster [which seems to extend over
those intervals].

⟨120⟩

. . . Captain of a company – . . .
. . Every effective N.C.Officer & Private man, whether in
Bks. or in Quarters, shall be allowed bread at the public
charge, to the amount of 10½ pr. wk or 1½ per day.
N.C. Officers . . . . Watch coats, Brushes, Pickers,
Turnscrews, Worms, Brick dust Emery & Oil.
[From this it seems they are not pikemen]

———————— // ————————

"Pikes to any extent for accepted men not otherwise armed."
        8824.b. List of Volunteer Corps.[693] (Puddletown t. 60 rank
& file. – Commandant Alex. Cunningham. Dorchester – 86 – Comt.
G. Strickland)

⟨121⟩[694]

Four & twenty hours of pure unalloyed health together are as
unknown to me as the 400,000 characters in the Chinese vocabulary.
West to Gray.[695]

All diversions here may be reduced to two articles, gaming & going
to church. Gray.

The Tiber, a river that ancient Rome makes more considerable than
any merit of its own could have done. id.

---

[693] *List of the Volunteer and Yeomanry Corps of the United Kingdom* (London, 1804)
[8824.b.26].
[694] This page is written upside down, as pp. 119–20; it is the penultimate side of the
last page in the notebook.
[695] Presumably the painter Benjamin West (1738–1820) to the poet Thomas Gray
(1716–71).

Miss Ferriers Novels – <u>Marriage</u>, <u>Inheritance</u>, & <u>Destiny</u> – among
the best in the language –

Forsyth.[696]

<u>Edgeworth</u>, <u>Ferrier</u>, & <u>Austen</u> have all given portraits of real society
far superior to anything man – vain man – has produced of like
nature.

A. Cunningham.[697]

The late Sir George Lewis[698] coupled the names of De Foe & Miss
Austen as writers of fiction "which observes all the canons of proba-
bility.

Forsyth.

(122)

3

Paragraphs, 1804, for Anne to read.[699] | Tattoo.[700]
Descripn. of Minden – & Valenciennes.
Politics of the papers.

| Wrights Caricature Hist. of the Georges. |[701]
A readable Chaucer – (C. Clarke's | ? |)[702] Yes.
Hist of English Literature

Encyclo. Brit.[703]
Smolletts Works. esp. Hy. Clinker[704]

After a barrister is called to the bar of his Inn he must be admitted to

---

[696] Entries from here to 'Hy. Clinker' on p. 122 in pencil. Susan Ferrier (1782–1854),
Edinburgh novelist, authoress of *Marriage* (1818), *The Inheritance* (1824) and *Destiny*
(1831). This is probably the evaluation of William Forsyth (1812–89), man of letters;
source unidentified.

[697] Probably Allan Cunningham (1784–1842), miscellaneous writer; refers to Maria
Edgeworth, Susan Ferrier and Jane Austen; source unidentified.

[698] Lewis (1806–63), barrister, cabinet minister and author.

[699] Anne reads from the newspaper to Squire Derriman in *The Trumpet-Major*, ch. 6.

[700] The vertical line preceding this word is Hardy's.

[701] Cf. n. 640.

[702] Charles Cowden Clarke, ed *The Canterbury Tales of Chaucer* (London, 1860)
[11603.g.5–7].

[703] *Encyclopaedia Britannica*.

[704] Tobias Smollett (1721–71), whose last and best novel was *The Expedition of
Humphry Clinker* (1771).

the bar of the courts at | or of | Westmr. or his <u>status</u> is not complete
In practice this is done by his signing the roll of the Ct. of Q's bench.
—————————————————————╲ Notes & Queries.

Dumas. B. Quarterly. 1848.[705]
–Fouriers Passions of the Human Soul. transld. by Jno R. Morell[706]
–News of Bat. of Trafalgar – Streeter on Gems.[707]
P.P.6019.c./&457. Family Herald 1844 etc 4o[708]

---

[705] Entries from here to the bottom of the page in pencil. Alexandre Dumas
(1803–70), novelist, writing in the *British Quarterly*.

[706] F. C. M. Fourier, *The Passions of the Human Soul*, trans. The Revd. John Reynell
Morell (London, 1851) [1248.c.7]. Cf. also n. 676.

[707] Edwin William Streeter, *Precious Stones and Gems, their history and distinguishing
characteristics* (London, 1877) [7106.b.4].

[708] *The Family Herald, or useful information and amusement for the million*, new series
(London, 1843–1940) [P.P.6019.c].

Appendix
Typescript Passages
omitted from *The Life of
Thomas Hardy*

Introduction

Many passages in the original typescripts of *The Life of Thomas Hardy** were suppressed either by Hardy before his death or by his widow Florence afterwards, and until now they have never been published in full. They are transcribed in the pages that follow so that for the first time we now have a complete account of Hardy's disguised autobiography as he wrote it. Florence Hardy's *Life* is one of the more curious literary deceptions of modern literary history since Hardy himself wrote, in the third person, all but the last two chapters, leaving instructions for the work to be completed and published after his death. Great pains were taken to conceal his authorship and for many years the work was accepted as genuinely having been written by his widow, an assumption not entirely preposterous since, as Florence Dugdale, she had earlier published a number of children's stories. But the situation is odd. It is common enough for an inexpert writer's autobiography to be 'ghosted' but Hardy is unique among major literary figures in reversing the process; he is, in effect, 'ghost writer' of his own biography, and this unusual work shows Hardy in flight from the attentions of unauthorised biographers. He willed the *Life* posterity as the authorised version, seeking to disguise its inevitable lack of objectivity through its third person narration and to pre-empt other biographers by the authoritative 'authorship' of his wife. The manuscript was destroyed as soon as it was typed and subsequent revisions were made by Hardy in a disguised calligraphic hand. But posterity has caught up with Hardy and discovered him doing a dance of the seven veils, wafting remnants before the reader's eyes, yet the dance is often more intriguing than what is revealed; the 'performance' is all.

The *Life* is nevertheless indispensable. What it records is largely accurate and makes full use of Hardy's copious memoranda (many

---

* Florence Emily Hardy, *The Life of Thomas Hardy* (London: Macmillan, 1962) combines the two volumes originally published separately as *The Early Life of Thomas Hardy, 1840–1891* (1928) and *The Later Years of Thomas Hardy, 1892–1928* (1930). For the standard bibliographical account of their publication see R. L. Purdy, *Thomas Hardy, A Bibliographical Study* (London, 1954), pp. 262–7, 268–73.

of which were destroyed as the *Life* was written) and it remains a workmanlike and full account of one view of Hardy's life. It is fascinating too in so far as it implies Hardy's estimate of himself and his work and the self that he wanted to be remembered. But the very process of concealment is revealing and inevitably the work evades many issues and episodes. The original typescript does not repair all these omissions since concealment was Hardy's game from the beginning, but it is rather more telling. It has benefited structurally but suffered as autobiography from the revisions of Florence Hardy and J. M. Barrie, who advised her. To cite just one example, Hardy is shown to be even more extremely sensitive to critics and reviewers than we already know, and in view of this the impulse to produce the disguised autobiography itself may be more clearly understood. Barrie advised excision of many passages of sardonic invective against critics since he thought that the book 'leaves too much an impression that any silly unimportant reviewer could disturb and make him angry' (letter, 3 Feb 1928), yet this is a true impression and their omission falsifies the record further.

Hardy's reluctance to write an autobiography is well established. In 1910 H. M. Alden, editor of *Harper's Magazine*, asked if he could serialise Hardy's memoirs. When Hardy replied that 'it is absolutely unlikely that I shall ever change my present intention not to produce my reminiscences to the world' (*Life*, 350), there is every reason to believe that he meant it. But when circumstances forced his hand, Hardy 'having observed many erroneous and grotesque statements advanced as his experiences' (*Life*, vii), the production of the work must have been a chore. This raises the teasing problem of Florence Hardy's precise role. Her secretarial abilities must have been invaluable yet she was surely more than an amanuensis. But although the venture was probably more co-operative than the standard account suggests, her function must have been mainly editorial; internal and stylistic evidence precludes any real doubt about Hardy's basic authorship to the end of ch. 36. He makes consistent and detailed emendations to the typescripts up to this point (the end of 1920) and then adds a note saying that material for continuing the work is to be found in the notebook 'Memoranda, II'. In the remaining two chapters the work is uniquely that of Florence: the style is distinctly even more perfunctory, the typescripts have new pagination, there are no amendments by Hardy, and some of the manuscript in Florence Hardy's hand survives. 'Memoranda, II' is the notebook with entries from January, 1921, but it has the date 'Feb.1923.' written inside the front cover. That Hardy presumably wrote up this notebook, from which entries were (as he directed above) taken and reproduced in the *Life*, in 1923 suggests that by this time the *Life* chapters up to 1920 may have been completed, at least in draft form. Since Hardy's letters to Sir George Douglas (see introduction to notebooks) obliquely suggest that the work was begun about 1919, the bulk of the *Life* was probably drafted within these four years. But evidence will be adduced to show that Hardy was still involved with details of the work as late as November 1927, just two months before he died.

Hardy and Florence must at least have worked in close consultation: if Hardy was as stealthy as he appears to have been, Florence must have been his only critical arbiter. Since they were virtually partners in intrigue we may well wonder how much their friends were allowed to know of what was going on. Even here a fascinating ambiguity informs the extant materials from which we might seek an answer. An oblique clue to the real authorship of the *Early Life* appears as early as 1929 in Lascelles Abercrombie's article on Hardy for the *Encyclopaedia Britannica*: 'In 1928 appeared his *Memoirs*, written in the third person.'* C. J. Weber deduces from this that Hardy had reposed his confidence in Abercrombie,† yet this 'revelation' might simply have been a reasonable inference from the title page statement that the *Early Life* (the only volume to have appeared before Abercrombie's entry on Hardy) is 'compiled largely from contemporary notes, letters, diaries, and biographical memoranda, as well as from oral information in conversations extending over many years.'*

It has similarly been assumed that both J. M. Barrie and T. E. Lawrence (of Arabia) were let into the secret but the epistolary evidence is inconclusive. After Hardy's death Barrie kept up a close and frequent correspondence with Florence Hardy, advising her on deletions and revisions as the *Early Life* typescript was prepared for the printers, but the tone of these letters is ambivalent and does not

---

* *Encyclopaedia Britannica*, 14th ed. (London, 1929), Vol. XI, p. 193.
† C. J. Weber, *Hardy of Wessex* (London, 1940; rev. ed., 1965), p. 285.
* Cyril Clemens, in *My Chat with Thomas Hardy* (Webster Groves, Missouri, 1944), claimed that Hardy had 'in confidence' told him that 'each day I slant my memoirs as though my wife were writing them herself' and had described how Florence made 'invaluable suggestions . . . almost always incorporated into the text' (p. 26). The authenticity of this 'chat' is highly dubious (see R. L. Purdy's letter, *TLS* (30 Dec 1960), 845), since it is largely an unscrupulous pastiche from other sources, so that its value as evidence is neglible.

tell us how much he knew. As early as 18 March 1926 Barrie was wanting to read 'the first part of the book in type-writing', but evidently he was denied this until after Hardy's death: on 23 January 1928 he wrote to Florence that 'the book of him is what I want to see more than anything.'† On 3 February Barrie could tell Mrs Hardy that 'the book is a remarkable achievement, and if I thought of you mighty well before I think even more of you now.' The impression that this praise reveals Barrie's belief in her sole authorship may be modified by his further remark on 7 March: 'I can see what feelings must overcome you when you open the Biography and attempt to work on pages every one of which must have poignant memories to you of the actual moments when you and he discussed them' (though again the inference may have been drawn from the title page). And on 25 May Barrie says: 'I suppose you have not yet come to any decision about whether you will do the whole second volume yourself or hand it on to another.' But nowhere is it made clear, either by implication or direct statement, that whatever he may have privately believed Barrie had been told that Hardy was the true author. It seems unlikely that Barrie, who was shrewd and perceptive enough and whose advice reveals balanced literary judgement, could have failed to recognise the idiosyncratic style that pervades the *Life*, or that he could have been entirely deceived by the calligraphic hand with which Hardy took care to disguise his emendations. It would seem virtually impossible that the truth should be kept from Barrie (a frequent visitor to Max Gate) both by Hardy before his death and by Florence afterwards, especially since she must (despite her loyalty) have been concerned about passing off the biography as her own work, if it were not for the unusual secrecy in which the whole project was carried out.

Conclusive empirical evidence is notably lacking. The operative word in Barrie's letter of 25 May is in his speculation whether Florence Hardy will 'do' the whole second volume herself; unfortunately for us he does not say 'write' and he does not say 'edit', though I would suggest that he means the latter, whether or not it might be so understood by Florence. (It is of course possible that their relationship contained a rather comic situation of deceit and counter-deceit, Florence concealing the full truth from Barrie who in turn was by no means misled but outwardly kept up the pretence.) It was the editing of Hardy's diary (i.e., the *Life*) that was apparently

---

† Typescript copies of Barrie's letters (DCM).

offered to T. E. Lawrence in 1925, as Lawrence indirectly revealed in a letter to Jonathan Cape on 21 April: 'a very distinguished person's wife once asked me if I would care to edit or 'ghost', her husband's diary, written quite intimately before he became famous, but showing, very wonderfully, the growth of his mind and the slow accumulation of his knowledge.'* Lawrence goes on to enjoin Cape to secrecy: 'Please keep this entirely to yourself. The existence of the materials is not known, even to Macmillan's . . . indeed only five people do know of it.' This too has been taken to mean that Lawrence was fully aware of what Hardy was doing, and in referring to 'materials' he does use Hardy's own evasive term for the work in progress. But if he had been told, his letters are circumspect, as in his comments to Florence six days earlier: 'Of course: I'll read it very gladly, and tell you anything I can . . . About reading the M.S. If you would like it soon I will come over on Saturday . . . My mind is a very slow machine: so please do not ask me to pontificate quickly: the jury are allowed to retire before bringing in their verdict' (15 April 1925; DCM). His letter of 26 August – 'You said to me that I might see that work of yours again, some time' (DCM) – credits Florence with the work and reveals that by now Lawrence had actually seen it. By 20 January 1926 he is wanting to keep the book by him for some weeks: 'I don't promise to do any good to it, at all. Only I'll try my best. It's a great honour to be allowed to try' (DCM). But by the time he next writes on 13 February, a month before Barrie's unsuccessful request to read it, he has returned the typescript:

> Yes, I was sorry to send the book back. I had been reading it deliberately, tasting it all over: and I swear that it's a very good thing. There is a strange *individual* taste about the story of those early days. It's very beautiful. Rarely so. If T.H. injures it, a very great harm will be done. He is no judge (in this subject alone!) indeed he should be disqualified from sitting on the bench. Also you have done it.
>
> I was seeing, every page I read, little things which might be done to polish the jewel more excellently. I do hope you will send it me back. I'll tackle it more humbly and honestly. (DCM)

His next two letters indicate, again with teasing ambivalence,

---

* David Garnett, ed., *The Letters of T. E. Lawrence* (London, 1938), pp. 474–5. Letters from Lawrence to Florence Hardy are in the Dorset County Museum; those not published are indicated by DCM in brackets in the text. For an account of Lawrence's friendship with Hardy, see n. 336.

Hardy's involvement. On 20 May: 'The more T.H. puts into the material of the book the better. You will have the delicate job of editing him! Great fun.' (DCM). And what he writes on 21 June confirms Hardy's attitude to the manuscript:

> I'm very sorry about that MS. Always I feared that something of the sort might happen to it. Of course Mr. Hardy can't see it as outsiders will. His life matters so much to him & he is 80: and he resents other people fussing over something of his own which he cannot himself keep. Especially as he has been so reticent always. However, you still have the other copies, and they are so good. The early, formative, life is so beautifully done.*

But, after lamenting that Mrs Hardy could hardly detach herself 'cruelly enough' to write 'a documented, intimate study of [Hardy's] old age', he goes on to give the credit for what he has read entirely to her: 'You have done a most excellent thing.' He may simply have believed that Florence herself carried out what he called in his 1925 letter to Cape the 'scissors and paste job' of 'ghosting' which she had offered to him. He need not have known the full story of Hardy's more active involvement.†

Some diffuse light is shed in a 'Private Memorandum' (so headed) entitled 'Information for Mrs Hardy in the preparation of a biography', and this is published for the first time, under 'Ancillary Documents', in the present volume (p. 288). It appears to be the draft of a formal statement (or even a directive of a legal nature) which will give the work the status of an official biography and confirm Hardy's approval. The first page is in Hardy's hand and subsequent pages are typescript copies amended by him. The first paragraph, similar in tone to the Prefatory Note printed over Mrs Hardy's initials in the Early Life, defines the necessity that 'an authentic volume should at any rate be contemplated by [Mrs Hardy], & materials gathered by her while there is time.' The memorandum is undated but is prob-

---

* Letters, ibid., p. 498. Presumably this refers to the destruction of (part of?) the original manuscript.
† There may have been another candidate for the task, at least with regard to the Later Years. On 21 July 1932, Virginia Woolf wrote to Florence Hardy in appreciation of the two biographical volumes: 'the simplicity and the understanding were precisely what suited him . . . Naturally it is a great pleasure to me to think that it ever crossed your mind to suggest my doing it. But once more I feel sure– and I have just been reading it again–that nobody could have given the book the atmosphere and the unity that you did' (DCM). The irony of such high praise may have discomfited Florence but shows the success of Hardy's scheme.

ably less of a prospectus than a formal endorsement of a project already in progress. Since Hardy must have been nearly 80 when he began work on the *Life* it is not surprising that he should feel the need to leave written instructions in case he did not live to finish the work or to revise those parts already written. This would account for the flexibility remaining within the firm guidelines laid down:

> The facts to which she has access will form a chronicle more or less complete of my life. They are not enjoined to be included every one in the volume, if any should seem to be indiscreet, belittling, monotonous, trivial, provocative, or in other ways inadvisable; neither are they enjoined to be exclusive of other details that may be deemed necessary.

The next paragraph reveals some confusion between the first and third person: a reference to 'Mr. Hardy's letters' is amended to read 'my letters', and the rest of the memorandum is altered to the first person. Perhaps the first page was rewritten in Hardy's hand after he realised that to leave a set of instructions in the third person might both reduce the statement's authority and be too revealing about the mode of composition of the 'biography' itself. Hardy's confusion of tense is consistent with this possibility: in a reference to the potential publication of Hardy's letters, 'though this was not desired by him' becomes 'though this is not desired by me.' An alternative implication of the original use of the third person may be that Hardy first intended the memorandum to be the basis of a prefatory note.

The final paragraph shows more anxiety about the fate of the manuscript after Hardy's death:

> The whole book before printing should be put into correct literary form, by an experienced writer and scholar. Should Mrs Hardy wish that her name alone should stand on the title page, such a one might possibly be found who would do what was required if paid a reasonable fee.

This would account for the role tentatively assigned to T. E. Lawrence, who said in his letter to Cape that 'its anonymity appeals to me', and later fulfilled on an honorary basis by Barrie. The latter's 25 May 1928 letter to Florence makes it clear that there was at least one other nominee (perhaps E. M. Forster, who became a friend of Hardy in the twenties?) for this responsibility:

I suppose you don't want at present to come to any decision [whether or not to "do" the whole second volume], and that may be the soundest course. But if you had now decided to pass it on to Mr. Forster or other person, I feel that there is now in the second volume a considerable amount of matter . . . which has more significance coming from you than from any one else.

The letter also contains the strongest hint that Barrie may either have recognised or else have been informed of a division of labour between Hardy's authorship and Florence's secretarial-editorial 'work on it':

To talk as if the second volume was not already largely done is all wrong – I am assuming that the chief work of any other hand would be in "summing up", literary criticism and so on. All I am after is that nothing suitable to Vol. 1 should be left for Vol. 2 if you don't do the latter nominally. As you know I have a mighty opinion of it as it stands and a pride in your work on it and so I go on badgering in case anything is left undone that might be done.

Yet there is nothing in the extant correspondence of Barrie or Lawrence to suggest that, whatever they may have inferred or guessed, they *knew* any more than the terms of Hardy's *'Private Memorandum'*. Florence, meticulous in her loyalty, may have formally upheld the fiction to the end.

Barrie's function after Hardy's death was almost avuncular. He was protective of Hardy's reputation and Florence's feelings, and both were more cautious than Hardy. They excised many passages either on grounds of propriety or, more often, because of Hardy's outspokenness in response to reviewers. The original typescripts show the *Life* as an even more defensive, and lively, document than it remains, in its often caustic hostility to adverse critics. T. E. Lawrence recognised this function of the *Life* as, paradoxically, both a defensive and offensive *apologia* when he wrote from Karachi to Florence Hardy on 16 April 1928:

The biography is a very difficult thing. They will trouble you very much about that. Do no let these troubles go in too far. What he told you, on November 28, that he's done all he meant to do, absolves you from infinite toil. He will defend himself, very very completely, when people listen to him again.*

---

* *Letters of T. E. Lawrence, op. cit.*, p. 592.

This complete defence implies above all the *force majeure* of Hardy's works but its details as embodied in the *Life* preoccupied Hardy to the end. However much he may have regarded its composition as drudgery and delegated details to Florence, we can at least say with certitude that he continued to be emotionally involved. The notes headed *'Insert in Materials.'* (see p. 290) are for transposition into the *Life*. They are written on the back of three sheets pasted together, one of which is an invitation to the Olympia Show in October 1926, thus showing that Hardy was still occupied with the details of the work some time after this late date.

A more pointed paragraph is also published under 'Ancillary Documents' (see p. 291). Apparently meant for inclusion in the *Life*, this note is written in Hardy's hand on the back of an envelope date-stamped 14 November 1927, and must have been one of the last things Hardy ever wrote. The illness which was to prove fatal began on 11 December. It must also have been approximately coincidental with his virtually valedictory statement to his wife on 28 November, alluded to by Lawrence above and quoted in full in the *Life*, 444. This wry note on 'H[ardy]'s altruism' was never included in the *Life*, but it is signal evidence that less than two months before his death Hardy was still concerned with undermining misrepresentations about himself and completing the self-portrait he intended for posterity.

The omitted passages do not radically alter that self-portrait but they do point up details of the canvas. Some, for example, throw into greater relief Hardy's self-consciousness about his humble origins, as when a reference to 'the little dwelling' of his childhood is misleadingly altered to 'the rambling dwelling', and even the status of his first architect employer is enhanced: in the course of revision, Hicks is promoted from being 'fairly' to 'exceptionally' well-educated. And when Hardy records his courtship of Emma, in which he met with hostile opposition from her family, he is disingenuous in claiming that it was a case of 'any want of smoothness lying on his own side.'

The interest of passages transcribed here is inevitably variable since my purpose is to enable readers to have a full account of the *Life* as originally written, and this has meant including some passages of lesser interest. But the aim has not been to record every single variant between the typescripts and the *Life* as published since many of them are trivial, often confined to syntactical polishing or recasting of single words, and contribute nothing new.

Though I have exercised editorial discretion in this respect, I have erred on the side of completeness. Short passages and phrases (sometimes a single word) are included in all cases where the meaning, emphasis or tone of what Hardy writes is changed or modified by seeing the original form; or where a fact is made more specific, an attitude or opinion hinted at, or where the later version shows Hardy apparently clouding over an issue. All omitted passages of a sentence or longer are included. Locating quotations from the *Life* (as explained in *'Identification of the context of omitted passages'*, p. 210) are given summarily when they are simply needed as a means of showing where the omitted passage would occur in the *Life*, but at greater length when they may enlighten the meaning of the omitted passage.

Some of the omitted passages declare their purpose with distinct clarity, especially the largest generic group amongst them: Hardy's sharp rejoinders to his critics. More than thirty such passages are suppressed, from early reaction to the 'cuckoo-cries' and 'fooleries' of critics of *Far from the Madding Crowd*, through a reasonable assertion that *The Hand of Ethelberta* is 'a very clever satire' and through his pained fury over the reception of *Tess* and *Jude*, to his response to the criticism that perhaps distressed him as much as any, the reception given to his poetry. He was justifiably angry that many critics arrived at antecedent judgements because their 'obsession of the idea that novel-writing was Hardy's trade, and no other' generated conclusions that his poetry 'must perforce be harsh and clumsy in form, for how can a writer of prose have any inner acquaintance with the music of verse?' He felt that he was persecuted too because he was not imitative, not least on publication of *The Dynasts*. Hardy's castigation of critics for their 'incompetence' and 'absolute want of principle' is moved by mordant passion. When Mrs Grundy discovered sexual obscenity in his novel of Platonic Idealism, *The Well-Beloved*, his reaction was unusually severe but, in the circumstances, not unreasonable: 'What foul cess-pits some men's minds must be, and what a Night-cart would be required to empty them!' It is good to see Hardy letting off steam. Despite his ultimately capacious resilience, we can see that critical strictures have gone in very deep and his response is usually born of an intellectually and emotionally anguished stoicism such as we find poignantly articulated in the dog-days when *Jude the Obscure* was most crushingly under attack:

It is curious to conjecture what must be the sensations of critics like the writers of these personalities in their times of loneliness, sickness, affliction, and old age, when equally with the criticized they have to pause and ask themselves: What have I been trying to do for so many years? Surely they must say, 'I withered the buds before they were blown, and turned back the feet of the morning.' Pheu, pheu! So it is and will be!

Many passages of a less serious cast were left out by Florence Hardy, such as Caddell Holder's humorous reminiscences and Hardy's wry record of a letter sent him in 1920 by a man saying: 'I am driven to wonder why the devil you don't answer letters that are written to you!' And, being less broad-minded than Hardy, she clearly thought better of his description of Lady Duff-Gordon as being 'emphatically in the family way'. But a more pernicious, if understandable, strain is implicit in her treatment of Hardy's first wife. Several references to Emma are stricken from the record for no apparent reason, from a celebration of her corn-coloured hair ('A lock still in existence shows . . . that there was no exaggeration in his friends' admiring memories of it') to an interesting account of Emma's 'courage' in chasing off three thieves who threatened to rob Hardy in Italy in 1887. It may have been reasonable for Florence not to wish the scenes of Hardy's first courtship, which she dutifully visited with him in 1914, to be described as 'interesting to her', but it is a pity that she should choose not to record that, contrary to the traditional account of his first wife's aversion to Hardy's later work, Emma was interested enough to make a suggestion about Tess's wearing of jewels. There are several other instances, extending also to references to Emma's family. Emma's memory is unfairly dulled by these omissions.

There is no doubt, however, that such deletions were made through very human impulses, and elsewhere Florence emerges as a loyal guardian of Hardy's reputation. Maybe his own instruction that anything 'indiscreet' should be omitted persuaded her to ignore Hardy's apt mockery of Henry James for leaving in the middle of a dinner they both attended in 1886 because he was piqued to be placed low down the table. Perhaps a more subjective criterion was invoked when she decided to omit a fairly long paragraph about the lady by whom Hardy was so impassioned in his middle years, the 'rare fair woman' Florence Henniker, with its admission that 'some of his best poems were inspired by her'. And since Florence felt a distinct animosity towards Gertrude Bugler, the young Dorset girl who played Tess and Eustacia in local productions and caught the old author's eye (see n.155), it is not surprising that she omits this reference to her, along with Hardy's later telling additions as italicised: 'and Gertrude Bugler as Eustacia looked the part *to a T*, enacting *the hand-kissing scene with Charley* also some phases excellently.' Elsewhere it seems to have been Hardy himself who had second thoughts about elaborating details of old passions. The *Life*'s account of his feeling for Louisa Harding in his early twenties eschews mention that his 'wildly beating heart' was exercised by her for a year or longer, and that her memory was perpetuated by Hardy the romantic: 'a nameless green mound in the corner of Mellstock Churchyard was visited more than once by one to whom a boyish dream had never lost its radiance.' Even more poignant and passionate are his heavily crossed-out thoughts about Julia Augusta Martin, the lady of the manor for whom he experienced 'lover-like' feelings in his youth. Here the reticent Hardy must have felt that he had been much too explicit: 'though their eyes never met again after his call on her in London, nor their lips from the time when she had held him in her arms, who can say that both occurrences might not have been in the order of things, if he had developed their reacquaintance *earlier*, now that she was in her widowhood, with nothing to hinder her mind from rolling back upon her past.' Passion of a different kind directs his spirited defence of his late friend Swinburne against 'contemptible' reporters, and his equally spirited dismissal of G. K. Chesterton as a 'phrasemongering literary contortionist', both of which flourishes are omitted from the *Life*.

If Hardy is sometimes unconsciously Pooteresque in the precision with which he records minor experiences, he is never more so than in his record of the social round in London. Our spirits tend to sink when he announces in the *Life* that 'During —————— they were again in London' since this is usually prelusive of a list of social notables encountered at crushes and dinners. Barrie's advised excision of many such passages (see n.724) is aesthetically right; the *Life* flows better without them. But his belief that they 'get an importance . . . in his life in false proportion' is less sure: Hardy enjoyed being lionised and circulating among Dukes, Duchesses, Princesses and Cabinet Ministers. His reason for including such accounts – 'to illustrate what contrasting planes of existence he moved in – vibrating at a swing between the artificial gaieties of a London season and the quaintnesses of a primitive rustic life' (*Life*, 245) – is biographically speaking at least as good a reason for keeping them in as

Barrie's for keeping them out, and all the suppressed social passages are resurrected here. Hardy delights in having what he calls in one passage 'a charming hob-and-nob time' in high society, and in teasing us with reportage worthy of a superior Hedda Hopper ('Lady Camilla her cousin asked me in a roguish whisper if I did not think Winifred looked gloomy. *Talked to Lady Rosamund C——. She tells me she is in trouble about the colour of her hair; but it is certainly not red as she says. Lady* ———, *whose eyes had a wild look, declares she has not slept for TWO MONTHS*'). One of his favourite roles is that of 'father-confessor' (his term), as when a typically unidentified Lady C reveals to him 'a "wicked, *wanton*" flirtation she had once indulged in'. Some of the social chronicles are dull because they consist entirely of lists of names (though even here it is interesting to know who Hardy met) but they are often enlivened by his connoisseurship of the beauty of young women. He appreciates Miss Amélie Rives at a gathering in 1889 as 'the pretty woman of the party – a fair, pink, golden-haired creature, but not quite ethereal enough, suggesting a flesh-surface too palpably. A girlish, almost childish, laugh, showing beautiful young teeth', reflects that a lady with 'quite a "Tess" mouth and eyes . . . can afford to be indifferent about the remainder of her face', and on meeting the novelist Lucas Malet he is first struck by her '*full, slightly voluptuous* mouth, red lips, black hair and eyes'. It is interesting to discover that some of the omitted passages have been quarried as a novelist's raw material: Lady Marge W----- (who 'looked pretty in gauzy muslin') and the 'round luminous enquiring eyes' of Lady Katherine Milnes-Gaskell, for example, are transposed into *The Well-Beloved* in the incarnations of, respectively, Lady Mabella Buttermead and Nichola Pine-Avon.

The restoration of these passages from Hardy's original draft of the *Life*, fragmentary as they are, yields some additional lights and shades to Hardy's self-portrait. Beside the creative work of a supreme poet-novelist they are minor writings, though not fugitive; the details of life-experiences are never done down by Hardy, for 'he was a man who used to notice such things' ('Afterwards'), and everything that he ever wrote is idiosyncratic in the noticing. These passages conjoin with the *Life* itself to constitute Hardy's autobiography exactly as he wrote it. At the end of this volume, to round out our knowledge of his final days, a few extracts from a makeshift diary used by Florence Hardy from September to December 1927 are printed, including a rather tragi-comical description of the visit of a little Chinese man to Max Gate, and 'sad-coloured' references to

Hardy and Florence's habitual 'melancholy little walk' and his wearing of a shabby old black felt hat on the fifteenth anniversary of Emma's death.

There is, though, a final piquant disclosure in the typescripts themselves, in a passage written and then deleted by his second wife in describing his death. As if in affirmation of a universal principle in Hardy's work that '"Life offers – to deny!"' ('Yell'ham-Wood's Story'), we discover that some minutes before Hardy died, 'a few broken sentences, one of them heartrending in its poignancy, showed that his mind had reverted to a sorrow of the past.' It is fitting that we can impose no exegesis upon this moving incident, and that the intensely resilient, reticent, 'time-torn' Hardy should be able to keep his final sorrows to himself.

Textual Introduction

(1) INVENTORY OF TYPESCRIPTS AND MANUSCRIPTS

The original typescripts in the Dorset County Museum are contained in a series of envelopes. An inventory of the contents of each envelope is given here: it is from these materials that I have been able to collect and collate those passages in Hardy's original drafts which are omitted from the published version. The numbering of the envelopes is mine.

1. *Early Life*, carbon, complete.
2. *Later Years*, two carbons: (a) ch.XX-XXIV with synopsis of last four chapters; (b) ch.XX-XXXII with a fragment of XXXIII.
3. *Later Years*, one top copy and one carbon: ch.XXXV-XXXVI, and fragment of another typing of these chapters.
4. *Later Years*, top copy, ch.XXXVII; two top copies (separate typings), ch.XXXVIII.
5. *Later Years*, top copy, ch.XXXVII; manuscript, ch. XXXVIII; manuscripts, Appendices I and II.
6. *Early Life* and *Later Years*, top copy fragments from *Early Life*, typescript pp. 58–61, 74, 80, 82, 92–3, 96–7, 105, 105a, 106, 128–31, 140–2, 149–52, 162–3, 191, 198–9, 212, 266, 307–12, 314–27, and *Later Years*, 512–39 (ch.XXXII–XXXIII).
7. *Early Life*, carbon, 'Notes of Thomas Hardy's Life by Florence Hardy' (1840–1862); *Later Years*, manuscript by Godfrey Elton [cf. *Life*, 420–22]; Appendix II, carbon, letters to Dr Saleeby.
8. Manuscript and carbon, 'Private Memorandum' to Mrs Hardy; manuscript, notes for insertion into *Early Life* and *Later Years*; manuscript, note on 'Hardy's Altruism. [These items are reproduced under 'Ancillary Documents', after the *Life* passages, below.]
9. *Early Life*, typescript, extract from Emma Hardy's 'Some Recollections'.

Variant readings from all of these documents are recorded in my transcription in correspondence with the relevant page in the *Life*. The synopsis of ch.XXXV–XXXVIII in envelope 2, and the 'Notes of

Thomas Hardy's Life' in envelope 7, are not however included since they contribute nothing new.

For the same reason I have not included the minor textual variants between Godfrey Elton's written account (envelope 7) and the published version. The only revision which is not simply of punctuation is the omission of this sentence [cf. *Life*, 422: 'he contemplated another visit.* This too']:

*As well as many generous things, there are one or two hard things said, deservedly enough, of Oxford in *Jude the Obscure*, but it was clear that it was a great pleasure to Hardy to be a member of one of its Colleges.

Also from envelope 7 we see that the final paragraph of Hardy's 2 February 1915 letter to Dr Saleeby is omitted [cf. *Life*, 451]:

By the way, as a kindred matter can you explain the meaning of the paragraph I enclose? To me it seems nonsense – Please return it when writing, in case I should want to ask the author when I am at Cambridge.

And the omitted second paragraph of Hardy's letter of 16 March 1915 concerns Dr Saleeby's invitation to speak at a Temperance meeting in Dorchester; if he comes, Hardy offers to put him up.

The typescript of the published extract from Emma Hardy's 'Some Recollections' (envelope 9) shows some revisions in Hardy's hand, all of a minor order. Hardy deletes Emma's recollection that her sister 'had had a jealous feeling' towards her, and tones down the self-referential element in two places where Emma gives herself undue prominence while describing the affairs of others. He modifies a potentially snobbish description of the working class ('mostly ill-natured' becomes 'often ill-natured'), and decides against a reference to his own youthful beard as 'yellowish[?]'. The only piquant amendment is his removal of Emma's underlining of the phrase 'unhappy happenings' at the end of her recollections: 'As one watches *happenings* (and even if should occur unhappy happenings), outward circumstances are of less importance if Christ is our highest ideal' (*Life*, 73). A fuller account of Emma's manuscript itself is found in Emma Hardy, *Some Recollections*, ed. Robert Gittings and Evelyn Hardy (London, 1961).

All other variant readings, from envelopes 1 to 6, are recorded.

(2) PHYSICAL DESCRIPTION OF THE TYPESCRIPTS

THE EARLY LIFE

Typescript carbon copy, $8\frac{1}{4}$" × $10\frac{1}{2}$", bound in soft brown card covers and stapled through. The outside cover is blank. Pages are numbered but the pagination of most has been altered at least once, often twice. The final pagination runs to 332 pages. Additions and corrections are made in Hardy's calligraphic hand; sometimes Florence Hardy ('copying his alterations as made on a duplicate typescript', Purdy, p. 226) uses a different calligraphic hand.

The first verso is blank. The first recto has 'Mrs. Hardy. / (Personal Copy)' in top right. Below this, to left, there appears in a large hand: 'T.H./Vol.I./1840 to 1891./Birth to Middle-age.' To lower right there appears a printed slip, with lettering in red, pasted onto the page: 'From A. P. WATT & SON, Hastings House, Norfolk Street, Strand, London, W.C.2, to whom please address all communications about the MS. to which this slip is attached. *Folio No. . . . . . .' (A. P. Watt was a literary agent.) In the bottom right hand corner: '[2nd. Copy]' The writing throughout is in ink.

The final typescript entry is on page 332 (corresponding to *Life*, 240), and is followed by: '(Query) End of Vol.I./(November 1891.)' There follow brown cardboard covers after this last typed sheet, two blank rectos and two blank versos.

THE LATER YEARS

Chapters XX to XXIV

Two typescript carbon copies, same size and similar bindings to that of Vol.I, but tied with string rather than stapled.

(1) Soft light brown card cover front and back, 543 + 3 pp. This is marked '[2nd. Copy]' and contains chapters XX–XXXIV, with a 'SYNOPSIS OF REMAINDER OF BOOK/(probably about 100 more pages of typescript ⟨sic⟩.' (thus headed, and describing in brief ch.XXXV–XXXVIII, to 1926).

(2) Soft dark brown front cover only, back cover missing, 520 pp. This is marked '3rd.—/[(Rough) Copy.]' and contains chapters XX–XXXII, with a fragment of XXXIII.

Pagination in both copies has been altered at least once, usually twice. Additions and corrections are made in Hardy's calligraphic hand in both copies; Florence Hardy's intervention is more evident in (1), the later version. (The page reproduced in Purdy, opposite p. 273, is from (2).) The process of revision appears to follow the pattern (2) to (1) to final text.

The cover of (1) has 'Mrs. Hardy./(Personal Copy.)' in top right. Below this, to left, there appears in a large hand: 'T.H./Vol.II/1892 to [end] . . . /Middle-age to . . . . . .' In the bottom right hand corner: '[2nd. Copy]'. All writing is in ink.

The cover of (2) has in a large hand: 'T.H./Vol.II./[1892 to end.]/Middle-age to . . .' (the last line in pencil – all writing otherwise in ink). In the bottom right hand corner: '3rd. – / [(Rough) Copy.]'

At the head of each typescript this appears:
'Mem:

> Vol II. might begin here — if 2 vols.

[Number of typoscript pages in the whole, probably about 650, or under, when finished, which at 230 words each page makes 150,000. (a fair length for a biography.)]'

A separate envelope contains top copy typescript pages of ch.XXXII–XXXIII, with numerous calligraphic amendments (recorded in this transcription). These chapters in bound typescript (1) are re-typed on slightly smaller pages and include the extensive alterations.

Chapters XXXV and XXXVI

Top copy and carbon copy, pagination following from the two previous typescript copies. Pages are the same size as earlier ones.

(1) Top copy. Slightly stiff darker front cover and back cover, the sheets being bound with string. The writing on the front cover is in red crayon and written in a large hand: 'T.H./Memoranda & Notes for completing/the Remainder of Vol.II. (to end of book).' In the bottom right hand corner: '[original]'.

(2) Carbon copy. No stiff covers, the sheets being bound with string. The writing on the front cover is in ink and written in a large hand: 'T.H./Memoranda & Notes towards completing/the remainder of Vol.II, (which will/be the end of book).' In the bottom right hand corner: '[3rd. (Rough) Copy.]'

On the last page of (2) a fragment of a page is pasted in, on which is written in green crayon:

"Last words of book:-

Hardy often said that a poet's writings could not be judged till the last line had been written, which was the death of the author. The opinion was particularly true of his own poetry, and indeed of all his productions.' Beneath this, in pencil: 'p.428. Jan.1899.' Hardy had included this meditation, differently phrased, on p.428 of the typescript of Vol. II (*Life*, 302), under the date January, 1899.

Both (1) and (2) have a piece of blue writing paper pasted onto the first sheet, with the following written in ink (1) or pencil (2): 'From this point (Part VIII, Chap.XXXV, p. 546) to the end, the compilation is mostly in the form of undigested memoranda, requiring critical consideration as to what biographical particulars shall be retained, differently expressed, or omitted.' In (2) the initials 'F.E.H.' follow.

There are some printers' marks on (2). In addition to (1) and (2) there are in a separate envelope numerous loose sheets corresponding to ch.XXXV and XXXVI, some of which contain printers' marks. These sheets, some top copies and some carbons, have no textual value but do show that there was another typescript of these chapters. They do not tally page for page with (1) and (2) and the pagination is different. (Consecutive pagination in (1) and (2) – originally discretely paginated 1 to 41 – was presumably added during the process of revision.)

Chapter XXXVII
From here on the pagination no longer follows consecutively from the series culminating at p.586 at the end of ch.XXXVI. The final two chapters are each numbered separately. There are two separate top copy typescripts of ch.XXXVII and though the content of each is almost identical, the pagination is different in each. One is apparently a first draft, the other a corrected copy. Alterations from here are in Florence Hardy's hand.

Chapter XXXVIII
One manuscript version in Florence Hardy's hand on lined paper. There are two typescript copies, one top copy, the other mainly a carbon copy of a different typing. (There was at some stage yet another typing since in Florence Hardy's ms. at the page corresponding to *Life*, 439, there is a fragmentary top copy page corresponding in layout and pagination to neither of the other two extant copies.)

Appendices
I: Manuscript. II: Manuscript copy of Hardy's letters to Dr. Saleeby

(in an unidentified hand), and carbon typescript of typed version. III: not in manuscript or typescript.

(3)   A NOTE ON DELETIONS

Many of the passages recorded here were silently deleted: i.e., they appear intact in the typescript and must have been deleted at a late editorial stage prior to the books's publication. Such deletions are almost certainly the work of Florence Hardy, sometimes acting on the advice of J. M. Barrie. Other passages have been crossed through in the typescript, sometimes as a result of Hardy's second thoughts and elsewhere at a later stage by Florence. No consistent empirical criteria, alas, can be applied to discover who deleted what. But internal evidence is sometimes persuasive, and where there are reasonable grounds for presumption that an explicit deletion was the work of Florence, this attribution is indicated in footnotes.

Readers may find it useful to have the passages that were silently deleted (all of them probably by Florence Hardy) identified in the following list, the passages being indicated by corresponding page and paragraph in the *Life* (as explained in 'Editorial Conventions', below). Two principles of excision were consistently applied by Hardy's widow. On Barrie's advice she severely limited Hardy's diatribes against critics (and she is clearly responsible too for many of the explicit deletions of such passages). More personally revealing is the number of references to Hardy's first wife, and even to her family, that Florence decided to suppress.

Silent deletions:
16.4, 21.1, 48.9, 62.1, 73.3, 74.1, 88 (last para.), 100.5, 101.2, 101.5, 102.3, 108.6, 110.1, 135.5, 137.2, 137.4, 156.1, 160.1, 167.2, 168.3, 171.7, 171.8, 172.1, 180.4, 180.5, 181.1, 182.6, 185.5, 189.4, 200.4, 201.6, 212.1, 216.2, 220.3, 220.5, 221.1, 224.5, 235.5, 237.2, 237.3, 239.1, 251.3, 256.2 (second passage), 264.3, 280.4, 292.2 (second passage), 293.1, 295.1, 300.4, 305.4, 319.1, 319.2, 323.2, 326 (last para.), 345 (last para.), 357.3, 359.5, 377.6, 385.1, 385.4, 387.1 (first passage), 387.4, 388.1, 391.5, 392.3, 392.5, 394.4, 394.7, 395.4, 395.5, 397.1, 397.3, 398.4, 404.1, 406.2, 407.1, 407.7, 408.3, 410.3, 410.6, 411.3, 412.2, 412.4, 413.1, 413.4, 426.4 (new paragraph), 428.4, 433.3, 439.6, 444.2, 444.5, 446.2, 446.6.

(4) ORIGINAL CHAPTER TITLES

Some chapter titles in the published version differ from the original typescript versions; the original forms of those which vary in particulars other than minor details of punctuation are given below.

V   *A Journal, a Supplement, and Literary Vicissitudes* 1870: Aet.29–30
VI   *A Plot: an Idyll, and a Romance.* 1870–1873: Aet.30–33
X   *London Life, France, and Cambridge.* 1879–1880: Aet.39–40
XI   *Writing under difficulties; and a change.* 1880–1881: Aet.40–41
XII   *Wimborne and the Astronomical Romance.* 1882–1883: Aet.41–43
XIV   *The New Home and "The Woodlanders".* 1885–1887: Aet.45–46
XV   *Italy* 1887: Aet.46
XXXIII War Efforts, and two volumes. 1915–1917: Aet.74–77
XXXV   Letters, Visits, and Mellstock Club-Room 1918–1919: Aet.78–79

(5) EDITORIAL CONVENTIONS

Word(s) enclosed within pointed brackets ⟨word(s)⟩ = editorial insertion.

Word(s) or punctuation enclosed within vertical lines |word(s)| , words or punctuation typed, or written (if a calligraphic addition), and then deleted.

Oblique stroke / = end of a typescript page.

Word(s) in italics = word(s) added to the original form of the sentence. (Such amendments are usually in Hardy's calligraphic hand. Sometimes these words are enclosed within vertical lines: this indicates that the additional words have subsequently been crossed through.)

N.B. Italics are also used when, according to normal bibliographical practice, they are used in the typescripts to indicate a periodical or book title, or a foreign word. When Hardy otherwise uses italics this is indicated in an editorial note.

[Example: in this passage Hardy has made numerous revisions to the original sentence before arriving at its final form –

  "But | he comforted himself with | |*he held that those* | this *weighed little* |*beside*| *with Hardy beside* the thought that not to be attacked by papers like *The Quarterly* was not to show any literary *esprit* whatever.''|

IDENTIFICATION OF THE CONTEXT OF OMITTED PASSAGES

I have given the date to which each omitted passage refers. Beneath this I have indicated where each passage would have appeared in the published version, and since the one-volume *Life of Thomas Hardy* is now the most widely available edition I have used this as the referential text.

A major editorial problem has been how to present these discon- nected passages, deleted or omitted from the *Early Life* and *Later Years* for one reason or another, in such a manner that their original point or purpose is not lost in isolation, now that they are taken from their original context. Some of them are discrete sense-units, others are not. I have, I hope, overcome this by means of contextual quotations and (where necessary) footnotes which combine to make the context and meaning of each passage clear.

In doing this I have not been able to assume that every reader will have a copy of the *Life* available for cross-reference and have pro- vided supportive annotation with this in mind. At the same time it will undeniably be helpful for readers to have a copy of the *Life* so that they can see the wider context of Hardy's revisions.

The following example shows how the exact original context of an omitted passage is established in my transcription:

JUNE–JULY, 1886
181.1 (and *also talked to George Meredith)

who left suddenly in the midst of the meal because he was placed low down the table, as I was. Rather comical in Henry.' Hardy

This reflection on the peevish behaviour of Henry James at a Rabelais Club dinner was first added by Hardy to the original typescript, and at a later stage deleted silently by Florence (it is among the list of silent deletions given earlier). Its context in the *Life* is established first by page and paragraph reference (181.1 = para- graph 1 on p. 181). In brackets, by means of an asterisk, its exact placing in the printed sentence is shown. A footnote identifies

'Henry' as Henry James, and cross-references are given to other mentions of James which are similarly belittling in tone.

Two observations about the identifying quotations from the *Life*:

(*a*) Where words are italicised this shows the amendment Hardy has made to his original sentence as a result of the deletion of the passage reproduced here. Example:

JUNE, 1894

265.2 (being afraid of the censure from * *conventional critics*)

a conventional public

Hardy has crossed through the first phrase and substituted the second. It is necessary to indicate the revised phrase if we wish to see how the omitted phrase or passage was originally set in the sentence.

(*b*) Word(s) contained within oblique strokes/word(s)/ = word(s) subsequently added (probably by Florence Hardy) but not in extant typescript, i.e. word(s) appearing for the first time in the *Life* itself. Where short passages have been silently deleted, phrases to amend the sense of the sentence have sometimes had to be silently added.

The Omitted Passages

1840

3.1 (The Hardy homestead, too, is * / weather-worn/)

much demeaned

1840

6.1 (The Talbothays farm * *was* a small outlying property)

had been sold to his father owing to its being, as it always had been

1840

6.1 (detached in a ring fence, * its possessors)

awkwardly situated for its then owner,

1840–1885

9.3 (the latter as the local builder * had constructed)

or master-mason

1840–1855

12.3 (feeling * *'no more than malkins'*)

"mops and brooms"

1840–1855

13.1 (And thus ended his *devoted* musical services to Stinsford Church, in which he had occupied the middle seat of the gallery with his bass-viol on Sundays for a period of thirty-five years – to no worldly profit * ; *far the reverse, indeed*.)

since his receipts from the Christmas collections for the choir were much more than expended in entertaining the other members at his house on practice-nights.

1840–1855

13.3 (till warned by his wife that this fast perishing style might tend * *to teach them what it was not quite necessary they should be familiar with, the more genteel 'country-dance' having superseded the former*.)

to vulgarize the children in their admiration for it.

1840–1855

14.2 (*The children had* * a quaint old piano *for their practice*)

She bought herself

1840–1855
14.4 (in his cradle, * *she found a large snake*)

a snake was found

1840–1855
15.5/16.1 (the *ᴬ *lining* having disappeared *ᴮ.)

A brim
B catching butterflies

1840–1855
16.4 (It may be added here that this sensitiveness to melody, though he was no skilled musician, remained with him through life.*)

, was remarkable as being a characteristic of one whose critics in after years were never tired of repeating of his verses that they revealed an ear deaf to music.

1849–1850
19.2 (But as the * *rambling* dwelling, field, *and sandpits*)

little[709]

1849–1850
21.1 (But Thomas Hardy the Second * *had not the tradesman's soul.*)

was in nature the furthest removed from a tradesman that could be conceived.

1849–1850
21.1 (lying on a bank of thyme or camomile with the grasshoppers leaping over him. * Among his)

Furthermore the dwelling, with garden, and field attached, was the place of his birth|.|, *having, as stated,* |It had| been built by his grandfather John for his (*Thomas the Second's*) father on the latter's marriage, as the beginning of a house which was meant to be enlarged but never was. So he remained there even through after-years, when he owned several small freeholds elsewhere. His wife, seeing what his feeling was, acquiesced at last with the cheerfulness natural to her, and made the best of it she could. Before his death he |made| *entered on* some |attempts| *negotiations* to purchase also the freehold of this Bockhampton spot of which

---

[709] Hardy's substitution of a misleadingly expansive adjective reflects his consciousness in later years of his relatively humble origins.

he had the lifehold; but, as has been | stated | *explained*, by this time he owned *other* freeholds |elsewhere|, and the place though picturesque, was cramped and inconvenient. The landlord, too, *who owned the reversion* was obdurate, though it lay on the outside edge of his estate; so T.H. 2 finally gave up the idea of retaining the Higher Bockhampton house in his family after his death.

To return to their son. Among his other

1853–1854

26.1 (They all appear, however, to have been quite fugitive, except perhaps the one for Louisa. *)

which may have lasted a year or longer, since he used to meet her down to his 23rd. or 24th. year on his visits to Dorset from London.[710]

1853–1854

26.4 (That the vision remained may be gathered from a poem 'Louisa in the Lane' written not many months before his death *. *Louisa lies*)

, and a nameless green mound in the corner of Mellstock Churchyard was visited more than once by one to whom a boyish dream had never lost its radiance

JULY, 1856

27.2 (Hicks, too, was *[A]*exceptionally* well educated *[B]*for an* ordinary country architect.)

A fairly
B and somewhat above the level of the

JULY, 1856

28.1 (in the morning * *before breakfast*.)

between 4 and 7

AUGUST, 1856

31.1 (learning a new dialect – and * Homer)

ultimately a new Greek text was obtained instead of the old ones which contented them at first.

---

[710] Louisa Harding (1841–1913), daughter of a gentleman-farmer at Stinsford. The phrase 'and a wildly beating heart on his part', which would have occurred at the end of para. 3, is also omitted from the published version, where the account of Hardy's feelings is more circumspect. See also the poems 'The Passer-By' (in ms. the subtitle is 'In Memoriam L— H—. (She speaks).') and 'Louie'.

1860–1861
32.1 (the Hardys still being traditionally * *string-bandsmen*)

fiddlers

1860–1861
33.2 (a fragmentary way * *only. Nevertheless his*)

and his substantial knowledge of them – for this was not small –
was by having translations at his elbow when looking into the
originals.

JULY 2, 1865
48.9 (there is no first link to his excellent chain of reasoning, and down you
come headlong. *)

Poor Newman! *His gentle childish faith in revelation and tradition
must have made him a very charming character.*[711]

SUMMER, 1867
53.3 (Blomfield, who must have been inconvenienced by it, * suggested)

through his plans and elevations not getting finished as promptly
as before

SUMMER, 1867
53.4/54.1 (would go himself, and * *at the latter part of July (1867) went down to
Dorchester*)

on July 20th (1867) left Paddington for

1869
62.1 (degeneracy of the age. *)

*There is no doubt that this scene, if printed, would have brought down
upon his head the cudgels of all the orthodox reviews.*[712]

---

[711] The date of Hardy's reading is confirmed in his commonplace book, 'Literary
Notes, I' (DCM), where more than a dozen extracts are copied under it from J. H.
Newman's *Apologia Pro Vita Sua* (1864). Though Hardy thought better of including
this mild depreciation, he continued to admire Newman's style rather than his logic:
cf. *Life*, 105 ('Read again . . . Newman . . . in a study of style'), 233 ('[Newman's] was a
feminine nature, which first decides and then finds reasons for having decided'), and
Percy Lubbock, ed., *The Diary of A. C. Benson* (London, n.d.), p. 82 (in 1904 Hardy told
Benson 'very firmly that N. was no logician; that the *Apologia* was simply a poet's
work, with a kind of lattice-work of logic in places to screen the poetry').

[712] A scene in *The Poor Man and the Lady*, Hardy's unpublished first novel, describing the narrator's meeting with an architect's mistress, a music-hall dancer who
designed church furnishings to supplement her lover's income.

1869

63.2 (finish the churches *. Probably)

since Hardy had already had a hand in them while Hicks was living

1870

73.3 (her corn-coloured hair abundant in its coils. *)

A lock still in existence shows, even after the fading and deterioration of *more than* |fifty years|*half a century*, that there was no exaggeration in his friends' admiring memories of it.[713]

1870

74.1 (*from beginning to end,* * *and with encouragement from all parties concerned.*)

any want of smoothness lying on his own side as to the question of ways and means to marriage.[714]

1872

87.2 (from time to time. * Hardy)

The proverbial new broom was sweeping large spaces clear in the city for the purpose of these erections.[715]

1872–1873

87.2 (but Hardy * *seems to have* declared)

promptly

APRIL, 1872

88. last para. (which Hardy accepted * . It)

, caring nothing about the book[716]

---

[713] Silently deleted, presumably by Florence Hardy, after Hardy's death. His second wife believed his recollections of Emma to be idealised: 'all the poems about her are a fiction,' she wrote to Sydney Cockerell, 'but a fiction in which their author has now come to believe' (Wilfred Blunt, *Cockerell* (London, 1964), p. 233). But the excision of this detail seems ungenerous.

[714] The whole sentence, from 'His own wooing' to this omitted passage, was added by Hardy to the original typescript; since in reality Hardy met with considerable opposition from Emma's family his statements are disingenuous, especially this passage, which he was wise to omit.

[715] New schools for the London School Board.

[716] *Under the Greenwood Tree.*

1874

100.5 (the poet. * The)

> *She was an interesting and well-known woman, daughter of Basil Montagu, and grand-daughter of the fourth Earl of Sandwich by Miss Martha Ray, who was shot by a jealous lover in 1778.*[717]

SEPTEMBER, 1874

101.2 (Archdeacon of London *. In the)

> , a relation *relative* for whom the bride had great affection. *Dr Gifford*[718] *himself had | the year before | married as his second wife a sister of Sir Francis Jeune, afterwards Lord St Helier, and the family connection thus formed was a source of much social intercourse to the Hardys in after years.*

NOVEMBER, 1874

101.5 (Mudie's label on the covers. *)

> Its author's unawareness of the extent of its popularity may have been partly owing to the reviews which, in spite of a general approval, were for the most part leavened with minor belittlements in the manner beloved of so many Victorian critics, and possibly later ones, though there were a few generous exceptions.[719]

1875

102.1 (He replied, but, as it appears, did not go to see her. *)

> Thus though their eyes never met again after his call on her in London, nor their lips from the time when she had held him in her arms, who can say that both occurrences might not have been in the order of things, if he had developed their reacquaintance *earlier*, now that she was in her widowhood, with nothing to hinder her mind from rolling back upon her past.[720]

---

[717] Mrs Anne Benson Procter, wife and soon widow of Bryan Waller Procter (1787–1874), who wrote poetry under the pseudonym 'Barry Cornwall'.

[718] Dr Edwin Hamilton Gifford, Emma's uncle.

[719] *Far from the Madding Crowd*, which had been published on 23 Nov 1874.

[720] Hardy's friendship with Julia Augusta Martin (1810–93), the lady of the manor at Kingston Maurward (1845–53) for whom the young Hardy had entertained 'lover-like' feelings, her kindness to him in his youth, their subsequent correspondence and meeting in 1862 (reputedly the inspiration for the poignant poem 'Amabel'), are described in *Life*, 18–20, 41, 101–2. The letter Hardy mentions here was written on 16 July 1875. Hardy appears to have had second thoughts about the emotional fervour of this speculation, which is heavily crossed through in the typescript.

1875
102.3 (a house-decorator (!) * Criticism like this)

  also with cuckoo-cries on his limitations, which were really the
  irritation of dullards at his freshness.[721] So, forgetting the wise
  counsel of Mr Macmillan's reader, to take no notice of "the
  fooleries of critics", the latter cry *(influenced him to put aside a
  woodland story he had thought of (which later took shape in The Woodlanders))*

1876
108.6 (without any sense of improbability. *)

  Had this very clever satire[722] been discovered to come from the
  hands of a man about town, its author would have been pro-
  claimed as worthy of a place beside Congreve and Sheridan |.| ;
  indeed such had been hinted before its authorship was well known. But
  rumours that he had passed all his life in a hermitage smote like an
  east wind upon all appreciation of the tale. That the stories of his
  seclusion were untrue, that Hardy had been living in London for
  many years in the best of all situations for observing manners,
  was of course unknown.

MAY, 1876
110.1 (Strassburg, * and)

  where Mrs Hardy was laid up, probably by excessive walking). A
  thick brown mysterious fluid which her husband obtained at an
  Italian apothecary's and could never afterwards identify, set her
  right in a day or two,

APRIL 22, 1878
121.1 (it is to see the beauty in * ugliness.')

  so-called

---

[721] This reflection that demands for more of his writing coincided with 'quizzing personal gossip' which claimed that the author of *Far from the Madding Crowd* was a house-decorator, as well as the criticisms mentioned here, is the first of several bitter reactions against critics which Florence Hardy later suppressed (on the advice of J. M. Barrie, who wrote to her on 3 Feb 1928 that 'the book leaves too much an impression that any silly unimportant reviewer could disturb and make him angry'). 'Mr Macmillan's reader' was John Morley (1838–1923) and this advice had been offered in Sep 1871, in his criticism of the ms. of *Under the Greenwood Tree*.
[722] Hardy's 'Comedy in Chapters', *The Hand of Ethelberta*, published 3 Apr 1876.

SEPTEMBER, 1878
122.6 (the map was made. *)

It was afterwards adopted by R. L. Stevenson in *Treasure Island*.[723]

1878
123.2 (*in the music itself. * *)

It may, however, please the serious reader, if there should be one, to have a fragment of the air as Hardy recalled it.

FEBRUARY 7, 1879
125. last para. (the Rector of *A W———, became a miller at *B O——— Mill)

*A   Woodsford-and-Tincleton
*B   Owre-Moigne

MARCH, 1880
135.5 (she showed a great liking for Hardy and his wife, and * she always)

especially for Mrs Hardy, which she did not show for every woman |.| : *far from it!*

MARCH 24, 1880
137.2 (Mrs. Proctor was born in 1800. *)

During the first half of 1880 Hardy also became friendly, / in one way and another, with Colonel Chesney, author of "The Battle of Dorking", *with* Lord Houghton, a fellow-member of the Rabelais Club, Professor Huxley (met before), Thomas Woolner the sculptor, George du Maurier, and several more.[724]

MARCH, 1880
137.4 (sportfully cast out-of-doors.' *)

Through the long years after, when only the bad lines were quoted from his verses by certain critics, and only the careless

---

[723] The practice of including in a novel a sketch-map of the scene of its action; Hardy had drawn one for *The Return of the Native*.

[724] The first of a number of lists of people Hardy met socially in London, sensibly limited by Florence Hardy in the published version on J. M. Barrie's advice (letter, 3 Feb 1928): 'To my mind they are an excrescence on the book and get an importance in it and so in his life in false proportion. I believe it was a very fortunate thing for him, that he had these holidays away from himself so to speak, they probably freshened his brain and spirits as nothing else could have done. But given so elaborately they don't belong, they would be misunderstood.' They are included here for completeness.

sentences and doubtful opinions from his prose, he would speak on this point and say, "These people are hopeless! *Why* don't they see that the same treatment of any poet great or small who ever lived would produce the same results, and therefore that they prove nothing by their probings except their own incompetence for their business."

NOVEMBER, 1880

146.7 (as the case might be: * *This*)

John the Baptist, Paul, and others might also have been introduced, to the exclusion of greater men.[725]

AUTUMN, 1882

156.1 (by the obvious inference. *)

All the rector's[726] reminiscences, however, were not of this tragic cast. When curate-in-charge of a populous parish in Gloucestershire he had preached the afternoon sermon, and was about to doff his surplice in the vestry when he was called by the clerk. He was tired, but readjusted his robes, and going into the chancel saw that all the congregation had left except a young woman sitting in the front pew. Thinking she had come to be churched, as was often the case, he quickly opened his book and began with some little impatience at the hindrance: "Forasmuch as it hath pleased God to give you safe deliverance, and hath preserved you in the great danger of childbirth." The young woman thereon sprang up and cried, "O no, Sir, no: I haven't had a baby – I wouldn't do such an undecent thing! I've come to be christened!" He apologized, and they went to the font, where he began the form for adult baptism.

JUNE 24, 1883

160.1 (comparatively nothing. *Presently*)

Presently Lady Duff-Gordon and another lady arrived – the former emphatically in the family way.

---

[725] Hardy's argument is that if Comte had diplomatically introduced these men among his calendar of worthies, Positivism would have been acceptable to thousands who otherwise rejected a philosophical system that they instinctively felt was true.

[726] The Revd. Caddell Holder, Emma Hardy's brother-in-law and rector of St. Juliot, Cornwall, who had just died.

JUNE-JULY, 1884
167.2 (a great actress.' *)

During this summer they became acquainted with Lord and Lady Portsmouth and their daughters. Lady Portsmouth (Eveline, daughter of the 3rd. Earl of Caernarvon) a woman of large *social* experience/who afterwards proved to be the kindest and firmest of friends till her death, told Hardy that Ethelberta in his novel, who had been pronounced an impossible person by the reviewers, *and the social manners unreal*, had attracted her immensely because of her reality and naturalness, acting precisely as such women did or would act in such circumstances; and that the society scenes were just as society was, which was not the case with other novels.

AUGUST 16, 1884
168.3 (attached to the word. *)

On October 18th. he dined at the Mansion House with a number of other writers at a banquet given by the Lord Mayor to the Society of Authors. The ex-Lord Mayor, who was Hardy's neighbour at table, told him that during the year of office nothing but the duties of the Mayoralty could be attended to. This was probably Hardy's first dinner there, though he often dined there afterwards.

OCTOBER 20, 1884
168.5 (courses reasoned out * from the circumstances)

by those who take them

OCTOBER 20, 1884
165.5 (But are they not in the main *the outcome of passivity* (Hardy's italics) – acted upon by * *unconscious propensity*?')

such and such a disposed person or persons, who happens to be here at such a time, – even he, not voluntarily but from simple propensity, taking it into his head to move himself and the rest in such a way?"[727]

---

[727] Hardy's alteration of a note presented as a *literatim* transcription from an old notebook shows how the editorial process is not quite straightforward and honest: the opportunity is taken to 'improve' the wording and we cannot know how many other 'notes' in the *Life* have been similarly polished.

MAY 28, 1885
17.7 (while Em called a little way further on * . . . .)

to enquire after -----'s children . . . .

MAY 28, 1885
171.7 (part of the tragedy.' *)

. . . . . At last E. returned,[728] telling me the children were ill – that little L---- looked quite different, and when asked 'Don't you know me?' said, 'Not now; but I used to know you once.' How pathetic it all is!

MAY 31, 1885
171.8 (of her death. * Browning also present.)

Madame M---- and Baroness ----- came in while I was there.

MAY 31, 1885
172.1 (attach to wreaths'. *)

"In the evening met Frederic Harrison, Beesly, and Dr. J. H. Bridges (a Dorset man).

During the latter half of May and through June, Hardy was reading philosophy at the British Museum, and going with his wife to some parties and dinners in the evenings – among others frequently to Mrs Jeune's, where they always met a good many people they knew, including Mrs Hardy's relations; and once or twice to Lord Houghton's and his sister Lady Galway's combina-/tion crushes, where they scarcely knew a single soul except the host and hostess.

JUNE 29, 1885
175.1 (during the * *four or five* months in each year)

three or four

NOVEMBER 25, 1885
176.4 (one from Leslie Stephen, |who| *with* remarks on |a| books he had read)

'any vacuum in my occupations is very soon filled up (not that my nature abhors it' '

---

[728] From the errand indicated in the previous omitted note.

MARCH 4, 1886

177.7 (Home Rule Bill for Ireland. * *The first* that Hardy says about it)

but all

APRIL 8–11, 1886

178.4 (Saw the dandy * *party* enter in evening-dress,)

section of the Tories

JUNE-JULY, 1886

180.4 (' * M—— W—— is still as childlike as when I first met her)

Lady

JUNE-JULY, 1886

180.5 (*Hardy met * Walter Pater*)

the Humphry Wards, both amiable people, and

JUNE-JULY, 1886

180.5 (*without spilling them.' * Also*)

At Mrs Jeune's *at different times about now* they met Lord Lytton, Mrs Butler, (Miss Elizabeth Thompson) *J. A. Froude, Lady Pembroke, Sir John and Lady Lubbock,* and J. R. Lowell.

JUNE-JULY, 1886

181.1 (and * also talked to George Meredith)

who left suddenly in the midst of the meal because he was placed low down the table, as I was. Rather comical in Henry.' [729] Hardy

JUNE-JULY, 1886

181.1 (he met Whistler and Charles Keene, * *Bret Harte*)

also H. Reeve, Editor of the Edinburgh,

JULY, 1886

182.6 (*Oscar Wilde, etc. * *)

Also met on the 16th at Mrs Robinson's (Mary R's mother) my very remote consanguinean Iza Duffus Hardy, [730] *with some others with whom we had*

---

[729] Another example of Hardy's amused belittlement of Henry James after he had discovered the latter's condescending remarks about him in letters to R. L. Stevenson; see 'Memoranda, I' and nn. 118, 119; and n. 748 below.

[730] Iza Duffus Hardy (d. 1922), minor novelist, daughter of the distinguished palaeographer Sir Thomas Duffus Hardy (1804–78).

OCTOBER, 1886

183. last para. (It was not till many years after that he made and edited a selection of Barnes's poems. *)

At the beginning of December he attended a meeting in Dorchester for considering a memorial to the poet.[731] Various ideas were broached – a middle-Gothic cross, a Runic cross, to stand at the |cross-|*branching* roads near his residence – / but ultimately other counsel prevailed, and a bronze statue was selected, and executed by Mr Roscoe Mullins.

JANUARY, 1887

185.5 ('After looking at the landscape / ascribed to / Bonington in our drawing-room * I feel)

[given to Mrs Hardy by T. Woolner. R.A. the sculptor]

SPRING, 1887

189.4 (*Emperors: Faustinas.'* *)

Two or three slightly unpleasant occurrences chequered their stay in Rome, but were not of serious moment. One was that when Hardy was descending the Via di Aracoeli, carrying a small old painting he had just bought in a slum at the back of the Capitoline Hill, three men prepared to close on him as if to rob him, apparently mistaking him for a wealthy man owing to his wearing a fur-edged coat. They could see that both his hands/were occupied in holding the picture, but what they seemed not to be perceiving was that he was not alone, Mrs Hardy being on the opposite of the narrow way. She cried out to her husband to be aware, and with her usual courage rushed across to the back of the men, who disappeared as if by magic.

Another risk, of which however they were not conscious at the moment, was one incurred by herself, who in her eagerness for exploration lingered for rather a long time in the underground dens of the Coliseum. An attack of malaria in a mild form followed, which went off in a few days; but with, to them, the singular result that at the same date in spring for three or four years afterwards the same feverishness returned, in decreasing strength, till it finally left off appearing.

The third was nothing more than amusing, it being that the

---

[731] William Barnes (1800–86), who died on 7 Oct. The statue is situated by the Dorset County Museum in High West Street, Dorchester.

priest who conducted them through the Catacombs of S. Callistus, and had seemed puzzled about the way, was a new man who had himself got lost in them for some hours the day before.

SPRING, 1887
190.2 (the Basilica of Constantine. *)

It was with a sense of having grasped very little of its history that he left the city.

APRIL, 1887
199.3 (which he * *often* thought one of the finest of Browning's)

always[732]

MAY 16, 1887
200.3 (Met Lowell at Lady Caernarvon's.' *)

Also Lady Winifred Byng for the first time since her marriage. Lady Camilla her cousin asked me in a roguish whisper if I did not think Winifred looked gloomy. *Talked to Lady Rosamund C——. She tells me she is in trouble about the colour of her hair; but it is certainly not red as she says. Lady ——, whose eyes had a wild look, declares she has not slept for two months, / since she met with an accident out hunting.* Lady Marge W---- looked pretty in gauzy muslin – going to a ball, she told me.[733]

MAY, 1887
200.4 (THOMSON.' *)

"End of May. Read Drummond's 'Natural Law in the Spiritual World' -- worthless. Also some of Calderon's plays -- Fitzgerald's translation.

JUNE 14, 1887
200.9 (– (Characteristic.)' *)

"14th. To Lady Caernarvon's with E. The dullest and stupidest of all her parties this season. A Rajah there. Talked to Lady Winifred, Lady Camilla Wallop, &c. Introduced to her sister Lady Kath: Milnes-Gaskell. The latter the prettiest of all Lady Ports-

---

[732] Refers to Browning's poem 'The Statue and the Bust'.
[733] Cf. *The Well-Beloved* (Pt. II, ch. 1): 'the Lady Mabella Buttermead, who appeared in a cloud of muslin and was going on to a ball'; and see Michael Millgate, *Thomas Hardy: His Career as a Novelist* (London, 1971), pp. 300–3.

mouth's daughters. Round luminous enquiring eyes.[734] Lady
Winifred puts on the married woman already.

JUNE 18, 1887
200.10 (he was going to say.' * On the 21st)

"18. To dinner at Mansion House."

JUNE, 1887
201.4 (passed by the Hardys gaily enough. * *At some houses* the scene)

At dinners, crushes, luncheons and other functions, where they
encountered a great many people of every sort, title, and fame. At
one dinner Lord Lytton's, he entered the adjoining house by
mistake, the door standing open and the hall being brilliantly
lighted, and did not discover his error till he got upstairs. At
some houses such as Lady Halifax's, and the Hon. Meynell
Ingram's,

JUNE 26, 1887
201.4 ((who seems to have been the * /Raja/of Kapurthala))

Anniwalia

JULY 1, 1887
201.6 (Thornycrofts, Mrs. Jeune, etc. *)

"July 1. Dined at the House of Commons with Justin McCarthy.
Met T. P. O'Connor, Dillon, &c. Sat on terrace after dinner."

APRIL 26, 1888
207.9 (It affects even Arnold's judgement * .')

a little

JULY 8, 1888
210.5 (like the District Railway-trains under*ground just by)

the gardens by the Thames

JULY 9, 1888
211.3 (James's subjects are those one could be interested in at moments
where there is nothing * *larger* to think of.')

better

---

[734] Nichola Pine-Avon's eyes, in *The Well-Beloved*, are 'round, inquiring, luminous'
(Pt. II, ch. 2); and cf. Millgate, op. cit., p. 302.

JULY 13, 1888
212.1 (*with any rubbish at hand.' *)

"Lord Portsmouth says that it was his direct ancestor who went down to Devon in the reign of Queen Elizabeth, raised a levy, sailed to Ireland, conquered Desmond King of Munster (?), cut off his head, and sent it to the Queen.

SEPTEMBER 10, 1888
214.4 (' * O richest City in the world! "She knew the rules."')

Think of that,

JANUARY, 1889
216.2 (in front of the great Titian.' *)

"Business seems very dull just now in some shops. Em |. | being unwell, I went to a druggist's for a simple remedy. The master-druggist went and poured out the liquid, while the assistant got the bottle, and the shop-boy stood waiting with string and sealing-wax."

JUNE 29, 1889
220.3 (a future to please them.' *)

"June 29. Em had an afternoon party. The same evening we dined at Mrs Jeune's, [*Lady St Helier*] meeting the Lord Chief Justice and Lady Coleridge, [*Hon.*] Evelyn Ashley, Sir George Russell, and Lady Russell, Mr Long (painter), Mr Nelson Page (American), and others. Lady Coleridge could honestly claim to be a beauty. Responsive and open in manner. Really fine eyes. She told me about going on circuit, and sitting in court half-an-hour to please her husband, who, if she does not, says that she takes no interest in his duties. When Lord Coleridge and she had left the ladies discussed her age. Mr and Mrs Jeune went on to the Duchess of Abercorn's. |" |

JULY 17–23, 1889
220.5 (Very impressive.' *)

"July 17–23. We lunched here and there this week and earlier, meeting a dozen people at Lady Catherine Gaskell's; Mrs Fawcett and Lord Greenock at Lord Portsmouth's; and Lady Metcalf at Mrs Reeve's, Rutland Gate, (Reeve has a humorous face, as if copied from a print by Rowlandson). Also met Lady Rothschild at Mrs Jeune's; an amply-membered, pleasant woman, un-fashionalby dressed in brown silk. She and I talked a good deal – about wit, and the nude in art (of all things). H---- |s| with his underground voice was also there. Also |W.M.| Mallock[735] in a painfully fashionable frock coat, who would keep talking to Lady ----/about 'the Duchess's ball last night'. Miss Amélie Rives was the pretty woman of the party – a fair, pink, golden-haired creature, but not quite ethereal enough, suggesting a flesh-surface too palpably. A girlish, almost childish laugh, showing beautiful young teeth.

"In the afternoon at Macmillan's I talked to Mr Craik,[736] who spoke very justly of what he called 'sane criticism' – instancing John Morley's and Leslie Stephen's.

JULY 24, 1889
220.7 (Cf. Tennyson: "a deeper deep").' *)

There does not appear to be any possible personal reason for his quoting this[737] *at the moment.*

JULY, 1889
221.1 (situations were approximately of the kind afterwards introduced to English playgoers by translations from Ibsen. *)

In fact Hardy foreseeing this difficulty, had taken *as in other cases* but little interest in the dramatization, *though it is believed to have been a good one.*[738]

MARCH 15, 1890
224.5 (With E. to a crush at the Jeunes' * .)

to meet the Duke and Duchess of Teck. Young Princess Mary also there. Duchess in black velvet with long black sleeves and a few diamonds. She bears a likeness to the Queen. The daughter is a pretty young woman in skim-milk-blue muslin. [*afterwards Queen*

---

[735] William Hurrell Mallock (1849–1923), author of the satire on English society, *The New Republic* (1877).

[736] George L. Craik, a partner in the Macmillan publishing house and nephew of George Lillie Craik, author of *The Pursuit of Knowledge under Difficulties* (1831). His wife was authoress of *John Halifax, Gentleman* (1857).

[737] 'And if there be a woe surpassing woes, it hath become the portion of Oedipus' from Sophocles' *Oedipus Tyrannus*.

[738] J. T. Grein's dramatic adaptation of *The Woodlanders*, which, Hardy believed, aroused no theatre manager's interest because the novel was morally too advanced.

Mary.]⁷³⁹ Lady Burdett Coutts was in a head-dress that was a castellated façade of diamonds; she has strongly marked features.

MARCH 16, 1890
224.5 (where would their beauty be?' *)

At lunch at |Mrs|*Mary* Jeune's next day I found she had a cough and feverish flush, though she was as bright as ever. She told me that at the end of her reception it seemed as if she had a red-hot ball in her throat."

MARCH-APRIL, 1890
225.1 (Tories will *often* do by way of *ᴬ exception to their *ᴮ principles more extreme acts of democratism or broad-mindedness than Radicals * ᶜ do by * ᴰ rule –)

A   impulsive
B   *supposed*
C   will
D   way of

JUNE, 1890
226.4 (relation to existence. *)

In a note *to Hardy* on other matters at this time Mr Gosse remarks:
"Such a ridiculous thing has happened with the poem dedicated to you as 'T.H.' in my new book. An absurd poetaster, whom I scarcely know, has written me a profuse letter of thanks!! His name is T---- H---- and he thinks I must mean him"

JUNE 30, 1890
228.1 (kindly natured, winning woman with really a heart. * I fear)

Em is quite in love with her,⁷⁴⁰

JULY, 1890
228.2 (on account of the illness and death of her father * .)

at Plymouth

---

⁷³⁹ Queen Mary (1867–1953) was known as Princess May of Teck in her youth. She married the Duke of York in 1893, and he acceded to the throne as George V in 1910, reigning until 1936.
⁷⁴⁰ The actress Ada Rehan.

JULY, 1890
228.3 (scarcely able to follow the lines.' *)

After meeting a few more people, including Sir Henry Thompson, Lord Pembroke, Lady Waterlow, and Mr Nelson Page, he returned to Dorset, having the day before been to a military exhibition where he mused over Colonel Champion's sword, which had never been unsheathed since the Battle of Inkerman when, wounded, he sheathed it and it had stuck to the scabbard immoveable afterwards.

DECEMBER 18, 1890
230.7 (that of the poet.)' *)

"Was reminded yesterday of Thackeray's 'How these women love one another!' when going through the hall at W---- House |between| *at the same time as* the X---s waiting there for their carriage, Em being in front of me and rather well-dressed. I beheld Mrs X---- looking up with green gimlet eyes at Em as she passed by unconscious."

MARCH, 1891
233.5 (In March they were again in London * . A deep snow)

, and attended a party at Mrs Jeune's to meet the Prince and Princess Christian and their two daughters, but do not seem to have done anything beyond this.

APRIL, 1891
235.5 (among all the wily crew * , there was)

of harlots

JULY, 1891
237.2 (*brown locks are getting iron-grey.*' * On the 13th)

: and the day after they had a surprise visit at their flat from Lady Camilla Gurdon and Sir Brampton, whom they thought in the country. "She came bounding in, in her old spontaneous way. She is still Raffaelesque, but paler."

JULY, 1891
237.3 (at the Milnes–Gaskells', * Lady Catherine)

in Hereford Gardens Hardy judged that Lady Catherine had at this date "less of Raffaele, and more of Rubens than her sister

Camilla, with a dash of coquetry and pride added; also quite a 'Tess' mouth and eyes: with these two beauties she can afford to be indifferent about the remainder of her face.

JULY, 1891
237.3 (superstitious as any woman. *)

At Max Gate there are still growing violets sent by her[741] years ago from Wenlock.

AUGUST, 1891
239.1 (original * MS. that had been omitted from the serial publication.)

That Tess should put on the jewels was Mrs Hardy's suggestion.[742]

DECEMBER, 1891
240.3 (much about the matter.' *)

The end of the year was saddened for Hardy and his wife by the deaths of two or three relations in quick succession, one of them being Mrs Hardy's mother.[743]

1892
243.3 (quite inexplicable to * the writer himself.)

any fair judge, and |*its just judges and*|

1892
243.3 (quite inexplicable to the writer himself. *)

The sub-title of the book,[744] *added as a casual afterthought, seemed to be especially exasperating.* |It| All this would have been amusing if it had not revealed such antagonism at the back of/it, |such distortions of the truth| bearing evidence, as Hardy used to say, "Of that absolute want of principle in the reviewer which gives one a start of fear as to a possible crime he may commit against one's person, such as a stab or a shot in a dark lane for righteousness'

---

[741] Lady Catherine Milnes-Gaskell.
[742] After Hardy's death Florence omitted this interesting detail which he had added. It shows that in 1888–90 Emma took sufficient interest in her husband's work to make such suggestions.
[743] Another example of Florence's apparent tendency to delete personal references to the first Mrs Hardy. (The deletion is in red ink and later internal evidence suggests that such deletions are by Florence's hand.)
[744] 'A PURE WOMAN / FAITHFULLY PRESENTED BY / THOMAS HARDY', the sub-title of *Tess of the d'Urbervilles*.

sake." Such critics, however, "who, differing from an author of a work purely artistic, in sociological views, politics, or theology, cunningly disguise that illegitimate reason for antagonism by attacking his work on a point of art itself", were not numerous or effectual in this case. And, as has been implied, they were overpowered by the dumb current of opinion.

1892
245.4 (They ought all to have been hanged!' *)

"Called on 'Lucas Malet'.[745] A striking woman: |rather large| *full, slightly voluptuous* mouth, red lips, black hair and eyes; and most likeable. Met her sister Miss Rose Kingsley there.

"At Lady Dorothy Nevill's. She told me about her recent visit to Dorsetshire, *and that the only family relic she could find in her girlhood's house [at 'Weatherbury'] was an old door-trig with her father's coronet upon it.* Also an extraordinarily tangled scandal about a Princess – now long deceased.

SPRING, 1892
246.1 (Some of the best women don't marry – perhaps wisely.' *)

"Mrs. Joseph Chamberlain[746] seems quite a girl in talking to her. Did not care so much for the appearance and manner of her husband *at first*, but that may have been superficial only. Lady Hilda |Broderick| is also charming in her girlish naivete. Also talked to Arthur Balfour and Sir Charles Russell.

APRIL 11, 1892
246.2 (before the baby was born.' *)

"11. In the afternoon called on Lady Hilda Broderick and had a long and pleasant tête-à-tête with her. She had wept bitterly over "Tess", she told me, *and made me feel a criminal.*

APRIL 15, 1892
246.4 (it is easy to be smart and amusing if a man will forego veracity and sincerity . . . . * How strange)

---

[745] Pseudonym of Mrs Mary St. Leger Harrison (1852–1931), daughter of Charles Kingsley; she wrote powerful novels, including *Colonel Enderby's Wife* (1885) and *The Wages of Sin* (1890).
[746] Joseph Chamberlain (1836–1914), Radical politician, leader of the Liberal Unionists from 1891 and later Secretary for the Colonies.

You can see in every line that the reviewer[747] has his tongue in his cheek. The article is, in fact, full of unblushing misstatements: 'e.g., 'This clumsy sordid tale of boorish brutality and lust.'

"In one place Bludyer says the story is told in a coarse manner; in another that it is not. So you may go on.

APRIL 15, 1892
246.4 (no more novel-writing for me. A man must be a fool to deliberately stand up to be shot at.' *)

"Such reviews as *The Quarterly* are a dilemma for the literary |man| *worker*. There is the self reproach on the one hand of being/conventional enough to be praised by them, and the possible pecuniary loss of being abused by them on the other.

But |he comforted himself with| |he held that those| *this weighed little* |beside| *with Hardy beside* the thought that not to be attacked by papers like *The Quarterly* was not to show any literary *esprit* whatever.

APRIL, 1892
246.5 (Hardy's * good-natured friends Henry James and R. L. Stevenson)

dear

APRIL, 1892
246.5 ((*Letters of Henry James.*) *)

When Hardy read this[748] after James's death he said, "How indecent of those two virtuous females to expose their |prudish| mental nakedness in such a manner."

APRIL 22, 1892
247.2 (What became of the baby?' *)

"April 22nd. The tune of many critics of my book:-
"'First edition. Poor fellow: it is a fair piece of work. We'll give him a little encouragement.
"'Second edition. H'm. He's making some noise.

---

[747] Mowbray Morris, editor of *Macmillan's Magazine* (1885–1907), had rejected *Tess* for serial publication on 25 Nov 1889; over five years earlier he had mildly bowdlerised *The Woodlanders* when it was printed in his magazine. 'Culture and Anarchy', *Quarterly Review*, CLXXIV (Apr 1892), 319–26, is a condescending review which ironically summarizes the story and condemns it as immoral and unwholesome: Hardy 'has gratuitously chosen to tell a coarse and disagreeable story in a coarse and disagreeable manner.'
[748] Cf. 'Memoranda, I' and nn. 118, 119; and omitted typescript passage relating to June-July 1886, and n. 729, above.

"'Third edition. Why should he be thought more of than we?
"'Fourth edition. Miserable impostor! We must slaughter a
rascal who is lording it over all of us like this!'"

At the beginning of June in reply to an invitation from the South
Dorset Liberal Association to nominate their candidate in the forthcoming election Hardy wrote:

"I am and always have been compelled to forego all participation
in active politics, by reason of the neutrality of my own pursuits,
which would be stultified to a great extent if I could not approach
all classes of thinkers from an absolutely unpledged point – the
point of 'men, not measures', – exactly the converse of a true
politician's".

*May 2. Wasted time in the B. Museum in hunting up a book that
contains a tragedy, according to Lang in the New Review,*[749] *of which
"Tess" is a plagiarism. Discovered there was no resemblance, it being
about an idiot. Why should one's club-acquaintance bring such charges?*

During May they were again in London, going out a deal deal.
"Took in to dinner my friend Lady N----, who does not know who
her mother was." Among others Hardy met at dinners at this date
were Lady Salisbury, who was "at first stiff, but grew very
friendly", Lord and Lady Wimborne again, with whom he
dined,/and the Prince and Princess Christian, "who were by this
time most affable".

SEPTEMBER [3], 1892
249.3 (at so much a year.' *)

"Sept. Mr Shorter,[750] Editor of the *"Illustrated News"*, called for
a story or article. Stayed to lunch.

SEPTEMBER 11, 1892
249.6 (are a Dorset family.' *)

"Sept.11. Article on 'An Ancient Earthwork',[751] originally

---

[749] Andrew Lang, *New Review*, VI (Feb 1892), 247–9. Lang does not exactly say that
Tess is a plagiarism but that 'Mr. Hardy's story, though probably he does not know it,
is a rural tragedy of the last century – reversed.' The story is that of 'Poor Jack
Walford' in W. L. Nichols, *The Quantocks* (London, 1891).

[750] Clement K. Shorter (1858–1926) edited the *Illustrated London News* and the
English Illustrated Magazine at this time.

[751] The short story now entitled 'A Tryst at an Ancient Earthwork' had been
published in the *Detroit Post* in 1885 and now appeared with some revisions as
'Ancient Earthworks at Casterbridge' in the *English Illustrated Magazine* (Dec 1893).

printed in an American paper, revised and sent to Mr Shorter, for him to consider if he will reprint it in the I.L.N., as I have nothing else.

OCTOBER 12, 1892
251.3 (and William Watson.' *)

"The *Daily News* of yesterday coins the word 'Tessimism' in the following sentence:- 'At this hour the world is pessimistic, and pessimism (we had almost said Tessimism) is popular and fashionable.'[752] I think I discern in this bit of smart journalism the fine Roman hand of A. Lang.

DECEMBER 18, 1892
251. last para. (*old rummaged-up candlesticks.*' *)

"Dec.18. Met at lunch or dinner Col. Mackenzie, Lady Shrewsbury, Hon. Mrs Barrington, Henry Irving, Arnold Morley, Mrs Adair, Hamilton Aidé, Terriss, and Grossmith. Talked a good deal to Lady Sh., Mrs A., and H. Aidé.

SPRING, 1893
253.2 (found themselves much more comfortable under this arrangement than they had been before. *)

|Before entering| *While getting into* the house, however, Hardy stayed with their friends the Jeunes, and met there among many others, "the Bancrofts, Miss Mary Moore, Mr Goschen, Lord and Lady Wimborne, Miss Julia Peel, Lady Louisa Loder, Lady Hilda Brodrick and her husband, Sir Spencer Ponsonby Fane, Lord Sudely, and Mr Peel." |After a| *During a* large party one evening, "M.J. remembered she had promised friends to be at theirs early; but three of her |people| men about town guests stayed and stayed as if they would never go. At length the last one did leave, and we rushed off to Lord Stanhope's in Grosvenor Place, arrived about half-past twelve, had a charming hob-and-nob time, everybody but four being gone, and reaching bed about two o'clock."

---

[752] *The Daily News*, Tuesday, 11 Oct 1892, p. 4. A column headed 'Literature of the Future' attacks Flaubert, Zola and their Naturalistic followers for denying 'human sunshine' and remarks: 'At this hour the world is pessimistic, and pessimism (we had almost said *Tessimism*) is popular and fashionable. But when society settles down, and runs clear after the flood . . . Pessimism and gloom and Naturalism will not reflect the spirit of the time.'

SPRING, 1893
253.3 (known you spiritually".' *)

I sat opposite Princess May at table: she is not a bad-looking girl, and a man might marry a worse. She has nice eyes, as have so many of the Royal family. The Duke was vexed that he had been put next to the Countess of ----. Lady Dorothy Nevill, Sir H. James, and Mr Justice Hawkins also present.

APRIL 14–15, 1893
253.4 (importance to the world.' *)

"14. Dined with Charles Whibley at Millbank Street, a quaint place: I wonder how he found it out. Met there W.E. Henley, Bob Stevenson, and Pennell. An enjoyable evening.

"15. Dined with Roy Lankester at the Savile, and met James Knowles, Sir H. Thompson, Dr Lauder Brunton, and others."

MAY 22, 1893
255.1 (because it was Whitsuntide. *)

Afterwards drove with Em to the Castle, which we had a good look over, returning afterwards to Phoenix Park.

⟨MAY 24, 1893
255.5 (the discovery *of a roll of bloody clothes*[753]))

MAY 24, 1893
255.6 (*Very funny altogether, this little Court.*' *)

Talked to Captain Jekyll. As some people wanted to leave, Lord Charlemont hinted to the Viceroy to that effect, and 'The Queen' was played. We joined him afterwards in the smoking-room.

MAY, 1893
256.2 (took the boat to Holyhead. * Reached London)

Found on board General Milman and Miss Milman, Sir Eyre Shaw, Mrs Henniker and others.

---

[753] A cutting from the *Sunday Times* is here attached to the typescript, p. 355. It records the 80th birthday of Sir George Otto Trevelyan (1918), nephew and biographer of Macaulay and for 30 years an M.P., and recalls that after the murder of Lord Frederick Cavendish in Phoenix Park, Sir George gallantly volunteered to go to Ireland in the dead Secretary's stead, knowing of the risk to his life. On his first visit to the Secretary's Lodge in Phoenix Park he pushed aside a curtain and beneath its folds found Lord Frederick's blood-stained coat.

MAY, 1893

256.2 (the same evening. *)

The chief significance of Hardy's visit to Dublin was his meeting there with Mrs Arthur Henniker (Florence Henniker)[754] *who became afterwards one of his closest and most valued friends, remaining so until her death many years after. As befitted the daughter of Monkton Milnes (Lord Houghton) she had a love of the best in literature, and was herself a writer of novels and short stories, none of which, unfortunately, ever received the recognition which, in Hardy's opinion, they undoubtedly deserved. Some of his best short poems were inspired by her, and the only time he ever wrote in collaboration was with her in a short story, 'The Spectre of the Real'.*

JULY, 1893

257.3 (of the usual sort. * A memorial service)

A little dinner at Lady Shrewsbury's, a public one at the Mansion House.

JULY, 1893

257.last para. (performance by Irving. * His)

At Mrs Arthur Kennard's he met Lady Harcourt and the widowed Lady Mayo, and at Lady Shrewsbury's her bright brisk-thoughted daughter Lady Gwendolen Little – elsewhere becoming acquainted with Lady Powis, *Mrs Patrick Campbell, Lady Charles Beresford, Lord Rowton*, and renewing acquaintance with Mr J. Chamberlain.

AUGUST 4, 1893

258.3 (on June the 1st.' *)

"August 4. I feel very guilty this morning. A lady I much respect writes that she wept so much over the last volume of "Tess" that her husband or brother said with vexation he would leave her to read it by herself. When finished she said to him/that a man (meaning me) ought not to give readers so much pain. I have apologized. Truly, whatever romance-writers feel about being *greater*, they may feel that they are *crueller* than they know.

AUGUST, 1893

253.last para. (shade of the ruins, * and)

Hardy discussed social problems with Lady C, and was *her*

---

[754] See 'Memoranda, II', n. 221.

father-confessor on a/"wicked, *wanton*" flirtation she had once indulged in, which had pricked her conscience ever since;

SEPTEMBER 14, 1893
259.5 (May [afterwards Lady Stracey] looked remarkably well * .')

, and Sophy [afterwards |Mrs Hall Walker| Lady Wavertree] middling pretty."

MARCH, 1894
262.2 (their father's tombstone. *)

   Hardy passed the first half of march in |Town| *London*, again seeing a good many people, some of whom were old and some new friends, among them being Lady Pembroke, Sir Edward Lawson, who told Hardy interesting points in his history, Princess Christian and/her daughter Victoria, |Princess Mary and| the Duke *and Duchess* of Teck, Mrs Lyttleton, Lord Rowton, and Lord Herschell the Lord Chancellor, who told Hardy some of his *odd* legal experiences.

MARCH, 1894
262.4 (Lord Lansdowne. *)

Elsewhere he met at this time Lord Randolph Churchill and the humorous Lord Morris.

MAY, 1894
264.3 (was surprised to find himself in a group of fashionably dressed youngish ladies * , the Princess Christian)

instead of struggling dowdy females,

MAY, 1894
264. last para. ('My entertainer's sister, Lady * P——, was the *most beautiful* woman there.)

   Lady Powis

JUNE, 1894
265.2 (being afraid of the censure from * *conventional critics*)

a conventional public

JUNE 25, 1895
268.2 (met many Members there. *)

   In the same year at the flat the Hardys themselves entertained more than usual, one of which gatherings, noted in an old diary of Mrs Hardy's, is enough to mention:

"June 25. Had a large lunch-party, including Lord Houghton [Crewe], Lady Jeune and Madeline [*later Countess of Midleton*], Lady Lewis, Mr and Lady Margaret Watney, the Hon. Mrs Henniker, General Milman and his daughter Lena, Mrs Craigie and Mr Richards, Mr McIlvaine, Mr and Mrs Maurice Macmillan, Hon. F. Wallop, Mr Forbes Robertson, Mr Julian Sturgis. Several stayed till five o'clock"

JUNE 29,.1895

268.3 (for he had no leanings to Roman Catholicism * . However)

, while his wife was an old-fashioned Evangelical like her mother.

NOVEMBER 8, 1895

269. last para. (on the 8th, * *he sets down*)

He enters a note: "The Reviews begin to howl at Jude". But other subjects drew off his attention from the book, for on the same day he notes:

NOVEMBER, 1895

270.1 (writing with a quill. *)

However, the booings at "Jude the Obscure" drew him back again to the subject of that volume, and his notes during the two or three ensuing months have more or less bearing upon it, though in after years he destroyed the great bulk of them, which at first he had intended to embody in an article of reply to the strictures. The | discussion | *clamour* is not worth reviving *in detail* at this distance of time; nevertheless he was called by the most opprobrious names, | and there were several points in | the criticisms*being* | that were | outrageously personal, unfair, and untrue; for/instance, the charge in *Blackwood* brought by a fellow-novelist[755] that | he | *Hardy* had published the story in a magazine

---

[755] The prolific writer Mrs Margaret Oliphant (1828–97), in 'The Anti-Marriage League', *Blackwood's Magazine*, CLIX (Jan 1896), 135–49. Hardy had met Mrs Oliphant in 1885, when he wrote to his wife Emma: 'I don't care a bit for her – and you lose nothing by not knowing her. She is propriety and primness incarnate' (C. J. Weber, ed *'Dearest Emmie'* (London, 1963), pp. 2–3). These qualities directed much of Mrs Oliphant's violent diatribe against *Jude*, in which she remarked that 'there may be books more disgusting, more impious as regards human nature, more foul in detail, in those dark corners where the amateurs of filth find garbage to their taste; but not, we repeat, from any Master's hand.' Admitting in a letter to Sir George Douglas (5 Jan

version to make a "shameless" double profit out of it; when the truth was that, having entered into an arrangement with the editor of the magazine before he had written the story, and having found on thoroughly going into |it| *the plot* that it might not suit a family magazine, he had asked to be allowed to withdraw from the contract; as is proved by the following extract from his letter to the editor[756] some months before the story began in Harper's Magazine:

"I have some misgivings as to whether my story will suit the magazine . . . . Unfortunately novels will take shapes of their own as the work goes on, almost independently of the writer's wish."

And the following to the publishers:

"I am quite unable to assure myself that the novel will be suited to the pages of your magazine. I therefore, to avoid any awkward contingency in respect of the magazine, will ask you to release me from the agreement entered into concerning it."

To which they replied that such a step would seriously embarrass them because there was no time to get a substitute, the serial fiction in the magazine being arranged for *long* in advance. Hence he had decided to make laborious changes and fulfil his engagement.

NOVEMBER 15, 1895
271.1 ('A.C. Swinburne.' *)

Hardy's letter to the editor of *The Animals' Friend* in the middle of this month shows that his mind had been running on quite other subjects than the "obscenity" asserted of him by the reviewers:

"Sir,
"During the writing of a recent novel of mine it occurred to me that one of the scenes might be made useful in teaching mercy in the slaughtering of animals for the meat-market – the cruelties involved in that business having been a great grief to me for years.

1896; National Library of Scotland) that he has been 'much upset' by such reviews, Hardy remarks that 'a rival novelist in *Blackwood* sneers at my letting *Jude* appear in Harper's.' His bitterness over the review inspired a reference to 'the screaming of a poor lady in *Blackwood*' in a 'Postscript' to the preface, written for the 1912 Wessex Edition of *Jude*, and this extract shows that the episode was still troubling him over twenty years after the original article.
[756] 7 Apr 1894, to the editor, H. M. Alden.

The story is now published, and I send herewith a proof of the scene[757] alluded to – which I offer you gratuitously the right of publishing in *The Animals' Friend* or elsewhere.

> "I am, sir,
> "Yours faithfully
> "Thomas Hardy."

DECEMBER, 1895

274.1 (In London in December they * went to see)

met some interesting people – Sir Donald M. Wallace, Lady Wynford, ˙

DECEMBER, 1895

274.4 (non-necessity of either . . . .' *)

"The dear old marionettes that critics love, and the dear old waxen hero, and the heroine with the glued-on hair! This cowardly time can stand no other." . . .

"It is curious to conjecture what must be the sensations of critics like the writers of these personalities in their times of loneliness, sickness, affliction, and old age, when equally with the criticized they have to pause and ask themselves: What have I been trying to do for so many years? Surely they must say, 'I withered the buds before they were blown, and turned back the feet of the morning.' Pheu, pheu! So it is and will be!"

SPRING, 1896

276.1 (flirted with by the woman in consequence. *)

: meeting at dinner here and there Mr and Mrs J. Chamberlain, Mr and Mrs Goschen, the Speaker and Mrs Gully, the Russian Ambassador and Mme de Stael, Mr and Mrs Barrie, Lady Henry Somerset, Mr Astor, the Poet-Laureate, and others; being guests, too, at a literary lunch at Mrs Arthur Henniker's, where there gathered William Watson, Mrs Craigie, "Lucas Malet", Rhoda Broughton,[758] Anstey/Guthrie, Mr and Mrs Labouchere, Lord Crewe, Sir Wemyss Reid, and possibly more.

But though the comments on "Jude" had not much effect on "Society", they had an unfortunate result of a practical nature on the dependents of Society – Theatre-managers. The popularity of "Tess" had led, as has been mentioned, to Hardy's receiving

---

[757] The pig-sticking scene (*Jude the Obscure*, Pt. I, ch. 10).
[758] Rhoda Broughton (1840–1920), novelist, whom Hardy had first met in 1883.

numerous requests from leading actresses to turn the novel into a play, as they saw great possibilities for themselves in the character. These included, in addition to English tragediennes, Bernhardt, and Duse,[759] who had probably read the French and Italian translations of the story. There had also been surreptitious dramatizations; and at last Hardy was led to try his hand on a stage version. He had offered it to Mr Frederick Harrison & Mr Forbes Robertson for the Haymarket Theatre. They now finally refused it, the clamour against "Jude" possibly intimidating them. Hardy was not greatly concerned, and took the play no further, for though he sometimes considered the dramatization of the novels to be not much more than "an exercise in ingenious carpentry", he would admit that once in a while a novel might make a good play, just as history might, even if it could not be enough to reckon upon. So the play remained in a drawer till about thirty years later, when at the request of the Dorchester amateurs Hardy hunted it up for them, as will be seen.[760]

SPRING, 1896

278.2 (a man whose personal conduct, views of morality, and of the vital facts of religion, hardly differed from his own * .)

– that is, to be sure, if he were sincere, which was by no means proven.

The unkindest cut of all, however, seemed to him at the time to come from his acquaintance and fellow-novelist Mrs Oliphant, who after abusing him shamelessly in *Blackwood* as aforesaid, wrote to the bishop[761] commending his action. And yet shortly before this, on hearing that she was ill, Hardy had wasted an afternoon at Windsor in finding her house and seeing her. Now he, no doubt, thought how these novelists love one another!

JUNE, 1896

278.4 (Lord Rosebery took occasion in a conversation * to inquire)

on the *amusing* subject of the bishop's doings

JULY 17, 1896

280.4 (Hardy's sense of the comicality of it had saved his feelings from being much hurt by the outrageous slurs. *)

---

[759] Sarah Bernhardt (1844–1923); Eleanora Duse (1859–1924).

[760] Cf. 'Memoranda, II', entry of autumn 1924, and n. 383.

[761] William Walsham How (1823–97), Bishop of Wakefield, who announced to the press that he had thrown *Jude* on the fire.

She evidently had not perceived the sarcasm that lurked in his letter.[762]

AUGUST, 1896
282.1 (went to Dover * , where Hardy)

; where Mrs Hardy, having brought her bicycle with her, was knocked off it by a young man learning to ride, and was laid up for some days by the accident.

SEPTEMBER 8, 1896
282.4 (existence of a God, etc.' *)

The meaning of this does not seem quite clear.

SEPTEMBER 16, 1896
282.5 (Having remained at Dover about a fortnight * they crossed)

and recovered, Mrs Hardy from her accident, and |Hardy| *her husband* from a bad cold,

OCTOBER 17, 1896
285.1 (*as if I were a clamorous* atheist, *which* in their crass |ignorance| *illiteracy* they seem to think is the same thing * . . . . If Galileo)

as that harmless person an agnostic

MARCH, 1897
286.1 (/Certain critics affected to find unmentionable moral atrocities in its pages but/ * Hardy did not answer)

The amazing consequence of the publication of the book[763] was that certain papers affected to find unmentionable moral atrocities in its pages – quite bewildering to the author as to what could be meant by such statements about so fanciful a story, till it was explained to him that some oblique meaning had been ingeniously foisted into the novel as a peg whereon to hang a predetermined attack, which was a purely personal one |, and| . *It* made him say, naturally enough, "What foul cess-pits some men's

---

[762] This honest revelation of the true mode of Hardy's letter to the censorious Jeannette L. Gilder has been diplomatically and silently deleted, apparently after his death. Sarcasm is at odds with his 'sense of the comicality' of her review, claimed in the previous sentence.
[763] *The Well-Beloved*.

minds must be, and what a Night-cart would be required to empty them!''[764]

Altogether it was a remarkable instance of what intolerance can do when it loses all sense of truth and honour. But being |case-hardened| *review-proof* by this time, and feeling the person |attacked| *deserving "two years hard" (as some print put it)* to be a lay figure not himself, *also remembering the epithet "swine-borne" which Swinburne endured from the press*, he was almost if not quite/indifferent to these things,[765] and

MARCH, 1897
286.5 (this form of imaginative work, which had ever been secondary to his interest in verse. *)

as was natural when he had been |so| often compelled ? ? ? ? ? nobody knows how much in his novels ? ? ? ? ? ? ? explicitly as it was.[766]

MARCH, 1897
287.2 (Those few words present, I think, the finest *drama* (Hardy's italics) of Death and Oblivion, so to speak, in our tongue. *)

Having rediscovered this phrase[767] it carried me back to the buoyant time of 30 years ago, when I used to read your early works walking along the crowded London streets, to my imminent risk of being knocked down.

SPRING, 1897
291.3 (he felt that he might leave off further chronicles of that sort. * But)

; and it will be found that from this point the writer of these pages has very little material of the kind available.[768]

---

[764] 'That a fanciful, tragi-comic half allegorical tale of a poor visionary pursuing a vision should be stigmatized as sexual and disgusting', wrote Hardy to Sir George Douglas on 25 Mar 1897, 'is I think a piece of mendacity hard to beat in the annals of the press' (National Library of Scotland).

[765] An astonishing statement in view of the preceding (and subsequent published) comments.

[766] Hardy's calligraphic amendment is illegible where indicated.

[767] Swinburne's translation ('Thee, too, the years shall cover' in 'Anactoria') of a fragment of seventh century Greek lyric poetess Sappho, whose lines are intermittently invoked in *The Well-Beloved*. (Hardy's translation of Sappho's poem is entitled 'Sapphic Fragment'.) For an account of Hardy's youthful admiration for Swinburne, cf. 'Memoranda, I', entry of [April] 1909, and n. 88.

[768] Another judicious omission: the remainder of the *Life* is by no means devoid of social chronicles and there is certainly more 'material of the kind available' in the notebooks.

SPRING, 1897
292.2 (After two or three weeks' stay * they)

, during which, according to Mrs Hardy's diary, they went to a large dance at Londonderry House, given for Lady Helen Stewart.

SPRING, 1897
292.2 (people like them who had no residence of their own in London. *)

, and no invitation to any Jubilee function.

JUNE, 1897
293.1 (in the *snowy* presence of * the maiden-monarch that dominated the *whole* place)

a greater Queen,

JUNE, 1897
295.1 (on account of the heat. * It was)

He used to say that he had a curious sense of impending tragedy during these days of illness. [769]

JUNE, 1897
295.3 (in July he * expressed)

went with Lady Jeune to the jubilee dinner of women, and "talked to Mrs Flora Steel, Elizabeth Robins, Lady Battersea, and numerous others." He also

AUGUST 10, 1897
296.2 (King's House still.' *)

After taking Mrs Hardy to Stonehenge, which she had never seen:-

AUGUST 21–26, 1897
296.6 (and fill the pocket!' *)

On August 21 they went to Arlington Manor, Berks, where a lively house-party gathered, including Lord Beauchamp (who walked about hatless) Lady Arthur Butler, Lady Henry Somerset's son and his wife Lady Catherine, Mr and Mrs Henry Allhusen and their baby, Sir Evelyn Wood, and the genial Colonel John Hay the American Ambassador, who appeared in the lightest of

---

[769] Hardy suffered heat exhaustion after climbing mountain paths near Zermatt.

summer suits at dinner, his luggage having gone astray, and who reminded Hardy that they were not strangers as he seemed to suppose, but had met at the Rabelais Club years ago.

On August 26. Hardy went to Salisbury again, to meet Mlle. Madeleine Rolland[770] of Paris, the charming and accomplished translator of some of his novels, and sister of M. Romain Rolland; she wished to consult him, and with her mother was passing through the city to Oxford. Hardy used to say | drily | that Mdlle Rolland was the only lady, foreign or British, he ever remembered corresponding with whose letters were written in perfectly correct and graceful English. She afterwards visited at Max Gate.

SEPTEMBER, 1897
296.7 (Kipling abandoned the idea. *)

, though Hardy heard afterwards that the house was uitimately sold for the price Mr Kipling had offered.

OCTOBER, 1897
297.3 *(in better company!"' *)*

It may not be inappropriate to mention here that but for/this estimable woman's commonsense T.H. might never have walked the earth. At his birth he was thrown aside as dead till rescued by her as she exclaimed to the surgeon, "Dead! Stop a minute: he's alive enough, sure!"[771]

SPRING, 1898
298.2 (by Luzzi.' *)

At a dinner at Sir Henry Thompson's he continued his past conversation with Sir W. Russell on his war experiences, and next morning learnt that Mr Gladstone had just died.

SPRING, 1899
299.2 (prose for so many years. *)

That his reviewers[772] should choose not only the subjects but also the methods in which he should exercise his pen; not that he should choose them, their own business being limited to pro-

---

[770] Madeleine Rolland was a frequent correspondent between 1896 and 1923, and appears to have visited Hardy at least three times (1899, 1907 and 1923).
[771] The incident had already been recounted (*Life*, 14).
[772] Of *Wessex Poems*, Hardy's first volume of poetry, which had been published during the week of 11 Dec 1898.

nouncing if or not he had achieved what he aimed at; was to these, as it still is to such, a canon of criticism. There were, however, many worthy exceptions.

SPRING, 1899

299.3 (a long time intermediately. *)

But there was really a |good| *valid* excuse for the short-sighted belittlement of Hardy's art by these minor men whenever it occurred, even had his art been of the best, which perhaps he did not perceive so quickly as he might have perceived. |The right and proper plan| *By no fault of their own the power* of looking clearly and responsively into *his* poetry *as* form and *as* content, – meeting the mood of the poet half-way, as it were, – was denied to critics in |his| *Hardy's* case (except those of distinctly acute vision, few of whom would have been set by editors to waste their powers on a poet's first volume.) They *could not* look clearly into it, by reason of the aforesaid obsession of the idea that novel-writing was Hardy's trade, and no other. There were those prose works standing in a row in front, catching the eye at every attempt to see the poetry, and forming an almost/impenetrable screen.[773]

Had the criticasters who were baffled into an antecedent conclusion by this screen been minds of any *great* power in judgment, they would have perceived that there might be an obvious trap for their intelligence in his order of publication. Theirs was so cheap a criticism that they |would| *might* have guarded against it, and have been more inclined to exaggerate the other way, to show their insight.

SPRING, 1899

299.4 (author *dreamt of* novels, * *the critics'* view)

and many more *verses* thought of *before then*,

SPRING, 1899

300.1 (*A *It may be observed that in the* art-history *B of the century)

A Had they been acquainted with
B – even if only that of the moment –

---

[773] Typical of the criticism which angered Hardy is this, from the *Saturday Review*, LXXXVII (7 Jan 1899), 19: 'as we read this curious and wearisome volume, these many slovenly, slipshod, uncouth verses, stilted in sentiment, poorly conceived and worse wrought, our respect lessens to vanishing-point, and we lay it down with the feeling strong upon us that Mr. Hardy has, by his own deliberate act, discredited that judgment and presentation of life on which his reputation rested.'

SPRING, 1899
300.3 (I and my sisters are one.' *)

He amused himself by conjecturing that what had probably passed through the adverse section of the Fleet Street mind – and perhaps did in many cases, not inexcusably, |for| owing to the baffling obstacle mentioned – was reasoning of this sort, which he more than once expressed:-

"It must perforce be prosy, for has he not long been a writer of prose?

"It must perforce be harsh and clumsy in form, for how can a writer of prose have any inner acquaintance with the music of verse?" /

He would *drily* to on to trace the logic of those who reasoned thus:

"To prove the truth of my conclusion above stated – that a writer who publishes prose a long while before he publishes verse cannot be a true poet – I will pick out the prosy lines that can be found in his volume, and pillory them in my review, and convince readers by the following syllogism:

"This book of verse contains the above expressions.

"These expressions are not poetry.

"Therefore this book is not poetry."

That this syllogism, |he| *Hardy* would add, exhibited – designedly or not – the familiar fallacy known as the Undistributed Middle, did not prevent it being employed – usually merrily employed – in dozens of reviews of his poems at this time and for many years later, almost indeed down to the end of his writing. The fact that all the poets of all the ages could be rejected by the same argument did not apparently strike its advancers at all.

Some famous bygone exemplars of this notorious fallacy were of course Gifford, Lockhart, and Macaulay. Looked at dispassionately it seems strange that it still lives on in reviewing practice. "If a valuer should pick out all the blasted and mildewed grains from a sack of a farmer's corn, put them together, and exhibit them as a sample of such corn, we should call him a rascal; but when a reviewer picks out the bad lines from a whole volume and quotes them alone as samples of the poet's work, he is/considered a critic of honest insight." Such treatment was dealt out to Hardy by some smart hands – happily not nearly by all.

SPRING, 1899
300.4 (*never published them.*] *)

A point he realized more fully somewhat later was that he had flown in the face of his chances of a welcome by not being imitative. The only absolutely safe method of winning a hearty reception is that of shadowing and developing the philosophy, manner, and theology of some eminent poet who has lived shortly before *the writer's date.* There were Wordsworth, Tennyson, Browning: he had only to copy one of them to win commendation – or at any rate toleration, since the fact of having once written prose might prevent more. But no, he did not adopt that royal road.[774]

SPRING, 1899
300.6 (*acquired by art.'* *)

One smart paragraphist said that he was nearly deluded into a belief in Hardy's verses after reading them one night; but he saved his critical credit by getting up on a cold wet morning and reading them again on an empty stomach. It happily cured his weakness. It was an apt illustration of the vicious practice of those who, in Henry James's words, prepare beforehand to limit their surrender to the book under review.

SPRING, 1899
301.1 (some particular line of a poem exemplifying this principle was greeted * with)

by one of those terrible persons, the funny man of the critical press,

SPRING, 1899
301.2 (the metre was intended to be onomatopoeic, * plainly)

resembling the flapping of liquid;[775]

SPRING, 1899
302.1 (aid of a 'Gradus'. *)

He could not discern, he said, in reviewers of the rank and file, that they had any sense of comparative values in literature,

---

[774] Cf. n.802 and the omitted passage to which it refers, where Hardy gives similar advice in a 1919 letter to 'an unnamed young poet'.

[775] 'On Sturminster Foot-Bridge'. An example of the poem's onomatopoeic metre is: 'The current clucks smartly into each hollow place/That years of flood have scrabbled in the pier's sodden base;/The floating-lily leaves rot fast.'

though this was of the essence of a good judgment. If a new poet were to arise in the future, to whose personality they had some objection in the role of a poet, they might as above stated devote a whole article to a few awkward phrases or imperfect rhymes picked out here and there from his volume, though it should contain the greatest idea or strongest emotions of the century, on which endowment – the thing that would chiefly matter – they might say nothing.

Another obvious remark of these judges was: This man was a writer of novels and stories; therefore many of these poems are novels and stories in verse, which sufficiently condemns them. But when some of Browning's best poems, and Wordsworth's, and Chaucer's, and the immortal old balladists', are stories – not to mention all metrical plays – criticism is not helped by the remark.

SPRING, 1899
302.3 (he had written his poems . . . because he wanted to say the things they contained and would contain. * He)

– *mainly the philosophy of life afterwards developed in "The Dynasts".* ; and so little did he expect from the press after his bitter experience of its caprices, so much less did he expect than he got, that

JANUARY, 1899
303.3 (strong expressions of agreement * .)

from those who saw eye to eye with him.

SUMMER, 1899
304.2 (through the Deanery. *)

The last week or two of their stay in London this year was spent in seeing other friends, *amongst them Hamilton Aidé. the earliest of his London acquaintance except Blomfield*, and in attending the marriage of Mr (afterwards Lord) Harcourt.

JULY, 1899
305.1 (*His wife, though * an indifferent walker*,)

|*a feeble* |

APRIL, 1900
305.4 (stayed on at the West Central Hotel in Southampton Row. * He)

whose proprietor, Mr Frederick Smith, Hardy had known

almost from the time when Mr Smith was the esteemed secretary
to the Band of Hope Temperance Society. Taking no great interest
in fashion and rank as such, of which they had both seen a good
deal during the previous twenty years, (though he much valued
the friendships it sometimes brought). |Hardy| *he*

NOVEMBER-DECEMBER, 1900
307.2 (baptism of its validity.' *)

During the latter weeks of the year his wife was called from
home to be with her sister,[776] the widow of the Rev. Caddell/Hol-
der, the former incumbent of St. Juliot, who was in her last illness,
her death occurring in December.

MAY 22, 1901
308.3 (idealized prize-fighter."' *)

On May 22. Hardy dined with Sir Henry Thompson[777] at one of
his "octaves" in Wimpole Street, and at the end of the month,
while staying at Aldeburgh, visited with others there the grave of
Fitzgerald the translator of Omar Khayyam,[778] in Boulge Churchyard, whereon was growing the rose-bush that had been raised
from hips brought from Omar's grave in Persia.

JANUARY, 1902
311.3 (inexorable and masterful.' *)

In London the same month he attended a meeting at the rooms
of the Society of Authors, and *with his wife* was a guest at the
wedding of Lady Helen Stewart and Lord Stavordale, afterwards
Lord Ilchester.

JANUARY, 1903
317.3 (have got the volume. *)

In January (1903) he and his wife were at the wedding of Miss
Madeleine Stanley and the Hon. St. John Brodrick, *afterwards the*

---

[776] Emma's sister Helen.

[777] Sir Henry Thompson (1820–1904), an eminent surgeon whose many talents also
included painting (a frequent exhibitor at the R.A.) and writing (author of two novels
and many articles). His famed 'octaves' were dinners of eight courses for eight people
at 8 o'clock, attended by the most distinguished artists, authors, scientists, politicians
and diplomats of the age, from 1872 until his death.

[778] Edward Fitzgerald (1809–83), whose poetic translation of *The Rubáiyát of Omar
Khayyám* was published in 1859.

Earl of Midleton, at St George's Hanover Square, and through May and June in London continuously.

JANUARY, 1904

319.1 (As *The Dynasts* contained ideas of some freshness, and was not a copy of something else, * a large)

the course of a large number of critics was clear to them – not to consider it on its merits as a *dramatic* poem, but to save all trouble by treating it facetiously. This *facetiousness* was, to be sure, one form of censure, and presupposed the application of literary tests; though as a fact these were not applied as they should have been, primarily.

JANUARY, 1904

319.2 ('On what ground do you arrogate to yourself a right to express in poetry a philosophy which has never been expressed in poetry before?' *)

This, of course, was not said directly, but veiled behind objections to other features of the production, in which the old game was played of describing the worst, and saying no word about the best.

MAY, 1904

322.2 (before and after. *)

The only large party they attended this summer seems to have been at Stafford House, St. James's; but at teas on the Terrace of the House of Lords *and at small parties at Lady Londonderry's, Lady Windsor's, & Mrs Macmillan's* they renewed acquaintance with other friends.

JANUARY, 1905

323.2 (those of Velazquez. *)

, which were just then so much lauded.

APRIL, 1905

324.3 (the previous August * . Hardy)

, and whose sister was Mrs Hardy's aunt by marriage

MAY 6–10, 1905

325.1 (with Sir F. Pollock.' *)

"May 6. On opening *the Times* this morning we found that Emma's uncle [Dr. E.H. Gifford, sometime Archdeacon of London, Hon. Canon of Worcester], who married us 30 years ago, died yesterday under an operation." It was just a month after the death of his brother-in-law *Lord St Helier* related above, and the two events threw a shadow over the Hardys' London sojourn this year.

"May 10. Lunched at the House of Lords with Gosse. Dined with the Omar Khayyam Club and met Lord Windsor, S. Solomons, Aston Webb, Lord Aberdeen, Sir Brampton Gurden, &c."

SEPTEMBER, 1905
326. last para. (to Hardy to get his opinions for * *a popular morning paper*)

The Daily Mail

FEBRUARY, 1906
329.1 ('Who knows that this work ⟨*The Dynasts*, Pt.II⟩ may not turn out to be a masterpiece?' *)

Hardy makes no remark, however, upon its reception, unless the following may be considered one:-

"Critics. – The business of *knowing* is mostly carried on in the papers by those who don't know – and for the matter of that, everywhere."

SPRING, 1906
329.4 (they entertained *many* friends at the flat as usual, * and went out)

— *among them, according to Mrs Hardy's diary, being Lady Queensberry, Count and Countess Lützow, Mr and Mrs Crackanthorpe, Lady Burghclere, Mr Owen Wister, Lady Grove, M. and Mme. Jacques Blanche, Miss Tobin of San Francisco, and others whom they were accustomed to see at these times —*

MAY, 1907
334.3 (Mr. *Richard* Whiteing, * and others.)

Lady Strachey and daughters, Colonel and Mrs Mount-Batten, Sir Walter and Lady Grove

JUNE 2, 1907
335.1 (that which I had * *denoted* in my previous volumes of verse)

shared out

AUGUST 13, 1907
336.1 ('who were not at ease'. *)

> To a Japanese correspondent
> "Mr K. Minoura, Vice-President, House of Representatives, Tokio.
>
> "August 13. 1907
> "Dear Sir:
> "I am unable to express well-defined opinions on Japan, and her people. I can only express a hope, which is that your nation may not become absorbed in material ambitions masked by threadbare conventions, like the European nations and America, but that it may develop to an enlightened spirituality that shall become a shining example."

AUTUMN, 1907
336.4 (By the last three lines of the quoted epitaph:
"If a madness 'tis to weepe
For a man that's fall'n asleepe,
How much more for that we call
Death – the sweetest sleepe of all!"
The following is written in light pencil and almost erased:)

> ?
> Surely griefe shd. be but small
> At

MAY-JUNE, 1908
342.4 (many of the house-party * went into the wood)

> , which included Lady Elcho, Mr and Mrs Charteris, Sir J. and Lady Poynder, Lord Robert Cecil, Mr Haldane, Alfred and Mrs Alfred Lyttleton, Mr and Mrs Rochfort Maguire, Lord and Lady Cromer, Arthur Balfour, and Professor Walter Raleigh.

JULY, 1908
342.5 (to his after regret. *)

> This month he lunched at the House of Commons with Sir Benjamin Stone, renewing acquaintance with Arthur Balfour, T.P. O'Connor, Sir E. Poynter, Sir E. Maunde Thompson, and the Japanese Ambassador, afterwards going over to Westminster School with Dr Gow.

JULY, 1908
342.6 (The remainder of the month was spent in Dorset, * *where* he met)

where he took his wife *as usual* to local garden-parties, at one of which

MAY, 1909
345. last para. (saw on a poster the announcement of the death of Meredith. * He)

|, and after| After the shock *he* was reminded of the odd verdict of the *Spectator* many years before – "Mr George Meredith is a clever man, without literary genius, taste, or judgment."

JULY, 1909
347.3 (her appearance less so. *)

But the fact that d'Erlanger the composer was also a Director of the Company went rather against his Opera:[779] *critics wished to show their independence.*

MARCH, 1910
349.1 (Hardy visited Swinburne's grave at Barchurch, and |wrote|*composed* the poem entitled 'A Singer Asleep'. * It)

He must have seen some paragraph about the poet's life and ways to make him write the following either now or a little later:-
    "What a wretched spectacle |is that of| the scribblers *present* who cringed for admission to Swinburne's house, and then went off to write satirical details about his appearance, manners, dinner, and beer-bottle! Surely the most contemptible of all trades is that of the common informer who eats a meal at a man's table, and then betrays |him| *his weaknesses* to the highest bidder."

MARCH, 1910
349.1 (*little churchyard.* * Hardy gathered a spray of ivy and laid it on the grave)

With a touching simplicity

AUTUMN, 1910
350. last para. (at Max Gate * . A brief visit)

during the autumn, among others, Mrs Hardy's cousin Charles Gifford, Paymaster-in-Chief to the Royal Navy, Mr Stephen Col-

---

[779] *Tess*, presented at Covent Garden.

eridge, Mr William Strang R.A., and Miss Dugdale,[780] a literary friend of Mrs Hardy's at the Lyceum Club, whose paternal ancestors were Dorset people dwelling near the Hardys, and had intermarried with them some 130 years earlier.

DECEMBER, 1910
354.last para. (supposing the meaning of his poem would be clear enough to readers. *)

However what happened was that nobody seemed to read more of the poem[781] than the title, the result of this and kindred |poems| *lines* of his being that |for ten years after Hardy was quaintly denounced here and there as a blaspheming atheist, for turning into poetry| *the poet was grotesquely denounced as a blaspheming atheist by a "phrasemongering literary contortionist" (as Hardy used to call him),[782] and rebuked by dogmatists, because he had turned into verse* the views of the age.

APRIL, 1911
355.1 (both here and in America. *)

, and the curiously blundering reception of the verses[783] here was an amusing instance of English criticism. Unhappily for himself, Hardy was, in fact, *like the "stretch-mouth'd rascal" in The Winter's Tale,[784]* always supposed to "mean mischief" *against Church, State, or morals* when he was not understood. |They| *The verses* were imitated in *Punch* for two weeks in/succession by its accomplished editor, and people supposed that these *mere* imitations were

---

[780] The first mention of Florence Dugdale, later to become Hardy's second wife, is heavily crossed through, perhaps because Hardy realised that this third-person reference to the supposed author of the *Early Life* and *Later Years* might give a clue to the fiction of her authorship.

[781] 'God's Funeral', in fact published in the *Fortnightly Review* not at the end of 1910 but in Mar 1912. The poem was *completed* in 1910.

[782] G. K. Chesterton (1874–1936), who attacked Hardy in *The Victorian Age in Literature* (1913), calling him 'a sort of village atheist brooding and blaspheming over the village idiot'; the phrase was widely quoted. Hardy took his revenge in an 'Epitaph' for Chesterton, dictated on his own deathbed in Jan 1928: 'Here lies nipped in this narrow cyst/The literary contortionist/Who prove and never turn a hair/That Darwin's theories were a snare/He'd hold as true with tongue in jowl/That Nature's geocentric rule/ . . . . true and right/And if one with him could not see/He'd shout his choice word "Blasphemy".' (DCM).

[783] Under the heading 'Satires of Circumstance' 15 poems appeared in the *Fortnightly Review*, Apr 1911.

[784] *The Winter's Tale*, IV. iv: 'and where some stretch-mouthed rascal would, as it were, mean mischief and break a foul gap into the matter.'

clever satires of the poems; not perceiving, even with the title before their eyes, that the originals themselves were satires, which indeed the writer of the imitations had apparently not perceived himself.

APRIL, 1911
355.2 (and Hereford. *)

; he also looked at London flats, but did not take one; though he was in town at the dinner of the Royal Academy.

APRIL, 1911
355.3 ('View the matrices rather than the moulds' * .)

, which is not very intelligible.

JULY, 1911
356.2 (In July * Hardy)

Mrs Hardy accompanied by her friend Miss Florence Dugdale went to stay at Worthing, and on her return

JULY, 1911
356.2 (they returned home. *)

A garden-party at Max Gate the first week in September wound up the summer weather, and about this time he became a life-member of the Council of Justice to Animals and later one of the Vice-Presidents.

1911
357.3 (included in a volume with *A *other poems.* *B)

A "Satires of Circumstance, Lyrics and Reveries."

B *He was unaware at this time that the new style*[785] *arose at Gloucester partly in consequence of the money that poured in at the shrine of Edward II.*

MARCH, 1912
357.5 (the death of his friend General Henniker, * and)

in March that of his neighbour Mrs Caledon Egerton, whom he had known since girlhood;

---

[785] The fifteenth-century Perpendicular style of Gothic architecture.

JUNE, 1912
358.4 (*strings* with her. * An)

and Prince Albert of Schleswig-Holstein, meeting the heroine, Miss Moffat, at dinner next day; also his old friend Mrs Stuart Wortley (afterwards Lady Stuart).

SUMMER, 1912
358.4 (had not gone at all. *)

He was occasionally in Town during the remainder of the summer season, meeting Mr Gosse, Sir Edward Poynter, Sir J. Crichton Browne, Professor Herkomer, Sir George Frampton, and general friends; and coming to arrangements with his American publishers.

NOVEMBER 25, 1912
359.5 (he suggested that she should not in her weak state, she did go down. * *The* strain)

Unfortunately they stayed a *very* long time, and the

DECEMBER, 1912
360. last para. (*presentiment * must have crossed her mind*)

– perhaps dictated by the heart-pains to wh. she[786] *was so subject*

MARCH, 1913
361.3 (returning by way of Plymouth *ᴬ *arranged* for a memorial tablet to *ᴮ Mrs. Hardy*)

A went to a stonemason and selected materials
B his wife

MARCH, 1913
361.3 (*in the preparation of which memorials he had to revive* * a species of work)

reviving for this sadly unforeseen occasion

JUNE, 1913
361.4/362.1 (to go up himself for a pass-degree, which was *ᴬ *abandoned mainly owing to his* discovery that he could not conscientiously carry out his idea of *ᴮ *taking orders*.)

A only frustrated by an accident, added to the
B entering the church; and by his frequent visits to the place.

---

[786] Emma Hardy, who had died unexpectedly on 27 Nov.

JULY, 1913
362.2 (was begun * *as a serial in Germany* at this time)

in a Zurich evening paper

AUGUST, 1913
362.4 (Blandford, 1825'. *)

A few motor drives about the country, and a picnic on "Egdon
Heath" succeeded, and in the latter part of August the copy for
the collected stories called "A Changed Man" was sent to the
publishers.

AUTUMN, 1913
362.last para. (Frederic Harrison; * and)

; there was a cinema production of "Tess of the d'Urbervilles" by
"The Famous Players Film Company";[787]

AUTUMN, 1913
363.2 (*but Hardy was not present on the occasion* * .)

, though he witnessed the representation at the Weymouth Pavil-
lion Theatre for weeks later

FEBRUARY, 1914
363.5 (the subject of this memoir married the present writer * .)

, who had been for several years the friend of the first Mrs Hardy,
and had accompanied her on the little excursions she had liked to
make *when her husband could not go*. As previously stated there had
been a marriage between the Hardy and Dugdale families in 177–,
and very possibly earlier, seeing that for centuries they had lived
within a few miles of each other in Dorset.

The wedding[788] was of the quietest kind, at Enfield, the then
residence of this branch of the Dugdales, taking place at eight
o'clock in the old parish church; and though the morning was

---

[787] The first of several early film versions of Hardy's novels: others included *Far
from the Madding Crowd* (1915, see 'Memoranda, I', entry of June 1915, and n. 98); *The
Mayor of Casterbridge* (1921, see 'Memoranda, II', entry of 2 July 1921, and n. 154); *Tess*
again (1924); and *Under the Greenwood Tree* (1929). Hardy attended the press review of
the film mentioned here on 21 Oct 1913, at Pykes' Cinematograph Theatre, 105
Charing Cross Road, London.

[788] This account of Hardy's second marriage is shortened to the briefest statement
in the *Later Years*, presumably by his widow on J. M. Barrie's advice (letter, 4 Apr
1928): 'I think you should just keep your own marriage as a sacred thing to yourself
and merely mention that the marriage took place at Enfield at that time.'

exceptionally bright and sunny for February, and the church-door stood wide open |, | *to the street* not a soul among the passers-by entered the building.

In April died at Stoke, Plymouth, his late wife's cousin Florence Yolland, daughter of Lieutenant Yolland, R.N.

SUMMER, 1914
364.2 (and back across Dartmoor. *)

– all of them scenes familiar to him, and interesting to her, as having been so often mentioned to her by her late friend |. |[789] *and* himself

JUNE, 1914
364.3 (*ᴬ *After serving* as a Grand Juror at the Assizes *ᴮ he)

A On his ensuing birthday he served
B and later in the month

JUNE, 1914
364.3 (had passed away. *)

|Dinners| *His wife and he put up in London* at Lady St Helier's and *were often at* Lady Macmillan's, *and elsewhere,* | and| / |friendships renewed| renewing friendships with Mr and Mrs Humphry Ward, Mr and Mrs Winston Churchill, Mr and Mrs Stuart-Wortley, Lady Lewis, and others |brought this| *before the war cloud burst & brought pleasure-* visits to an end. |& the|

AUGUST, 1914
366.1 (led him to despair of * *the world's history thenceforward.*)

human nature

NOVEMBER, 1914
367.3 (the latter filling but fifteen pages in a volume of 230 pages. * *These*)

But the reviewers, perhaps because the satires were named first in the title,[790] went for them/almost entirely, and with a few excep-

---

[789] Emma Hardy; Florence Hardy may have found the journey around places evocatively associated with Hardy's first wife (especially the 1913 expedition to scenes of his first courtship) less congenial than Hardy supposed.

[790] *Satires of Circumstance, Lyrics and Reveries* was published on 17 Nov 1914. The title, which led to the imbalance of which Hardy complains, was chosen by Macmillan and not by the author. In fact the 107 poems are divided in the volume as follows: Miscellaneous Pieces, 39 poems; Lyrics and Reveries, 34; Poems of 1912–13, 18; Satires of Circumstance, 15; Postscript, 1.

tions passed over the bulk of the book. Through a lack of apprehension, or wilful guile *in these judges, the pieces though they had been imitated all the world over* were solemnly pronounced to be "mistakes" – just as they had been when they were printed in *The Fortnightly* years earlier |, | – the |reviewers| *critics* apparently not perceiving that they

NOVEMBER, 1914
367.3 *(These were caustically humorous productions which had been issued with a light heart before the war.* * *So much shadow)*

Nevertheless, even though only of this character – or perhaps in consequence of being so – they had somewhat embarrassed their author, though not for the reasons on which the |reviewers'| critical head-shakes were founded.

NOVEMBER, 1914
367.3 *(he would readily have suppressed them if they had not already gained such currency from magazine publication that he could not do it.* * *The)*

So, by their being put into the book, and by their receiving almost exclusive notice, they were made to give a false tone to the whole volume, and stifled the ⟨'Lyrics and Reveries'⟩

NOVEMBER, 1914
367.3 *(contained some of the tenderest and least satirical verse that ever came from his pen.* *)

The effect of this misrepresentation upon the poems he most cared for grieved him *much*; but it could not be helped.[791] It was another instance of the inability of *so* many critics to catch any but |the| shrill notes, remaining oblivious to |the| deeper tones.

NOVEMBER 25, 1914
368.1 (the production was artistically successful. *)

The critics, as is always the case when art takes a step onward, were bewildered, and, as Hardy said, looked at the performance[792] much as a bull looks at a land surveyor's flag in the middle of a meadow, not knowing whether to toss the strange

---

[791] That the volume thus ill-received included the magnificent elegiac 'Poems of 1912–13' must surely have engendered some of Hardy's distress.

[792] Harley Granville-Barker's production of scenes from *The Dynasts* at the Kingsway Theatre.

object or walk respectfully around it. One trembles to think what would have occurred had the whole philosophy of the play had been put in; but Mr Barker, remembering what happened to Ibsen in this country, was too wise to represent the thought of the age in an English theatre at the beginning of the twentieth century |.| *and during a war*.

DECEMBER, 1914
368.3 (*that* /the/ * *war*)

so mad and |most| *brutal a*

AUTUMN, 1915
371.3 (short as his career has been.' *)

   Their neighbour Mrs Brinsley Sheridan's son Wilfrid was killed a little later.

SEPTEMBER, 1916
372.4 (breaking the journey at Launceston * . Thence)

to visit Miss Kate Gifford and her sister, relatives of the first Mrs Hardy

OCTOBER, 1916
374.5 (*Selected Poems of Thomas Hardy* . . . received some very good * reviews)

conventional

OCTOBER, 1916
374.5 (reviews; * *and* in December)

though of course containing such well-worn *clichés* as "infelicities", "no magical images", "prose is Mr Hardy's métier", and so on – all matters of opinion advanced as if they were fact, – repeated mechanically by those who did not know a good line from a bad, who had never heard that *de gustibus non est disputandum*, but had/to say something *in ten minutes*; and knew those were safe things to say because they had been said before.

OCTOBER, 1916
374.5 (The performances were for Red Cross Societies * .)

, and he had suggested introducing speeches to that effect, which were delivered by Mrs Cecil Hanbury and Lady Mary Fox-Strangways.

JANUARY 6, 1917
374.7 (" * *Art* is concerned with seemings only")

Imaginative work

MARCH, 1917
376.2 ('Much confusion has arisen and much nonsense has been talked lately in connection with the word "atheist". *)

One writer's almost whole stock-in-trade consists of that word and 'blaspheme'.[793] I believe I have been called one by a journalist who has never read a line of my writings.

JULY, 1917
377.4 (*too bright lighting.* *)

On that occasion beside the host there were present Mr Arnold Bennett, Mr G.B. Shaw, Mr and Mrs H.G. Wells and the Hardys.

OCTOBER, 1917
377.6 (stay there and came home. *)

"Last week in October. – The trees are undressing, flinging down their brilliant robes and laces on the grass, road, roof, and window-sill. One leaf waltzes down across the panes every second almost. One gets caught in a spider's web, and dangles in the breeze like an executed criminal in raiment of gold."[794]

NOVEMBER 13, 1917
378.7 (This * *unassertive air, unconsciously worn,*)

unaffected manner

DECEMBER 31, 1917
379.3 (*New Year's Eve. Went to bed* * *at eleven.*)

ill

JANUARY 2, 1918
383.1 (On January 2 *A Hardy *B attended a performance)

A Mrs
B and himself

---

[793] Another reference to G. K. Chesterton; cf. n. 782.

[794] Presumably omitted since the note forms the basis of the poem 'Last Week in October', which appeared in *Human Shows* (1925). The poem seems to have been directly inspired by the note and makes use of all these images, as in: 'The trees are undressing, and fling in many places – /On the gray road, the roof, the window-sill.'

JANUARY, 1918
383.2 (at Max Gate, * and she)

and was warmly attached to both Emma and Florence."[795]

JANUARY, 1918
384.1 (Why does he (the critic) not think of the art of concealing art? There is a good reason why.' *)

Probably the reviews of his last book set him thinking of these things. But he does not comment on the reviews themselves though there were some comicalities in them, like those of the reviewer who supposed that because Browning invented the name "Dramatic Lyrics" he also invented the thing, or those of the *fair* critic who pretended to be a man, but alas, betrayed her sex at the last moment *by* condemning a poem because its heroine was/dressed in a tasteless Victorian skirt!

JANUARY 31, 1918
384.4 (* *Arranged* for the admission of the present "Mellstock" Quire)

Paid

MARCH, 1918
385.1 (whither it led.' *)

It may be added that the same kind of thing[796] had been written about "The Dynasts". The author, they announced, determined to write the biggest drama in existence. The facts were, as he often said, that he was absorbed by the subject, and sat down to write it in the *smallest* possible compass, compressing as he went on till he could get it no smaller at all./Pitfalls surround those who attribute motives.

APRIL, 1918
385.4 (In April there * was)

appeared in the *Edinburgh Review* an excellent article on Hardy's lyrics from the experienced pen of Mr Edmund Gosse;[797] and in the same month

---

[795] Their neighbour Mrs A. Brinsley Sheridan of Frampton Court, who died this month.

[796] Hardy has quoted an American journal: 'Thomas Hardy is a realistic novelist who . . . has a grim determination to go down to posterity wearing the laurels of a poet.'

[797] 'Mr. Hardy's Lyrical Poems', *Edinburgh Review*, CCVII (Apr 1918), 272.

MAY 10, 1918

386. 4 (Hardy was seized with a violent cough and cold which confined him for a week * . However)

, and was followed by a bilious attack

MAY, 1918

386.last para. (the thought of his own.' *)

(From hereabout the writing is mostly in the form of Memoranda only. F.E.H.)[798]

The MS: is in approximately printable condition to here (p.545)[799]

MAY 20, 1918

387.1 (* *Sunday, June 2.*)

To Rendel Harris Esq. Manchester.

May 20.1918

"Your letter on the proposals you are bringing forward, in conjunction with Lord Bryce and Professor Gilbert Murray, for an Anglo-American University at Plymouth, is of much interest to me, both for general reasons and from my having had a domestic connection with the town for many years.

"It appears to me that if the scheme as outlined could be carried into effect the results would be far-reaching and admirable. And as to situation, the large population of Plymouth, the close relation of that port with American history, and the beauty of the town and neighbourhood, point to it as an ideal site for such a University. Curiously enough I was quite lately standing on the stone at the Barbican that marks the spot where the Pilgrim Fathers embarked.

"I quite understand that it would offer no rivalry to the proposed English University at Exeter and the Southampton University College.

"The idea being but in embryo as I gather, I am unable to offer any criticisms as you suggest, which would depend largely on details. However, if any remarks upon the proposal should occur

---

[798] This signals the end of the first stage of composition, though not the end of Hardy's authorship (see introduction).

[799] This is written on a piece of stiff brown paper inserted between typescript pp. 544 and 545.

to me I will send them. Meanwhile I can only express my hope that the idea may mature."

JUNE 10, 1918
387.1 (Weymouth Bay. *)

"June 10.1918

To W.M. Stone. Esq. Blind Asylum. Edinburgh.

"You have my permission to print "The Woodlanders" and "The Return of the Native" in Braille type for the use of the blind, and I hope the books may be of interest to them."

In the same summer Mrs Champ Clark of Washington, who had sometimes visited him and his wife in London, wrote to tell him of her husband's political adventures. He had been elected Speaker of the House, and would have been elected President of the United States, she said, if the majority had/ruled in the Democratic National Convention as it did in the Republican. However, Mr Champ Clark died within about two years.

AUTUMN, 1918
387.4 (I think better of the world. *)

Hardy also heard from the Chief Rabbi, who sent him his book of "Jewish Thought"; and towards the end of the year received from Athens a poem in modern Greek on Tess of the d'Urbervilles, and Mr Charles A. Speyer's music to the lyric "When I set out for Lyonesse".

SPRING, 1919
388.1 (back to their own country. *)

She[800] wrote to him again a few months later, explaining her "polyphonic prose", which had appeared in the volume she had sent him:

"I do not think that polyphonic prose is a very good name for it. It is not intended to be prose at all, but poetry. . . . . Of course the way to read it is just to take it the way it comes without accentuating either the rhythm or the rhyme, since they are only used to enrich the form, and are not supposed to produce the same effects

---

[800] Amy Lowell (1874–1925), American imagist poet.

that they produce in metrical verse . . . . Perhaps it is an impossible form, but when I read it aloud to my audiences (for I have been acting the part of John the Baptist, going all over the country and giving readings and talks to stimulate interest in poetry) I have no difficulty making them apprehend it."

AUGUST 23, 1919
391.5 (when you come this way again.' *)

To Mr W.J. Malden – Chairman of the Wessex Saddleback Pig Society.

"August 23.1919.

"I must thank you for your attention in sending me particulars of the Wessex Saddleback Pig Society and the Herd Book. "I do not know much about breeding such stock, and am more bent on humane methods of slaughtering that on anything else in relation to it. So that in accepting with appreciation Honorary Membership of the Society I add a suggestion that the question/of slaughtering, and transit before slaughtering, should be among the matters that the Society takes up, with a view to causing as little suffering as possible to an animal so intelligent. This worthy object would, I think, add distinction to the Society.

"I am not aware if the stupid custom still prevails of having pork "well bled". This impoverishment of the meat for the sake of a temporary appearance should, I feel, be discouraged by the Society."

It is satisfactory to know that Hardy's suggestions were acted upon by the Society.

OCTOBER 30, 1919
392.3 (* /On October 30 the following was written at his request:/)

To Mr ---- Exeter College, Oxford.   October 30th. 1919

OCTOBER 30, 1919
392.4 (The rumour, if it still persists, was * started some years ago.)

stated by idle pressmen[801]

OCTOBER 31, 1919
392.5 (*impossibility of anything of the sort.* *)

On the last day of October he assisted *the Bishop of Salisbury* at

---

[801] Hardy refers to theories that *Jude* was autobiographical.

the opening of a children's hospital in Swanage. *The wind was very cold and the Bishop looked so ill that Hardy, who had known him some while, expressed regret that he had been dragged there such a day. "Oh, never mind," said Dr Ridgway drily: "if it hadn't been here it would have been somewhere else!" He was genuinely sorry when he heard of the overworked and worthy Bishop's death shortly after.*

DECEMBER 2, 1919
394.4 ('Mr. Robert Penny's'. *)

The |following| *short* speech made by Hardy at |the| *this opening,* |of the Bockhampton Reading-room and Club on the 2nd. December 1919| *being amongst the very few he ever made in his life, is here given, as it* was not reported in any newspaper.

DECEMBER 2, 1919
394.7 (But we will let that pass. * . . .)

"Before I proceed to the formal function of starting the pendulum of the Club, so to speak, I may be allowed to say a word or two about the bygone times of this Parish and Village, and the changes which led on to the present happy stage in the history of |this| *the* place. There would be many things to interest us in the past of Bockhampton if we could only know them, but we know only a few.

DECEMBER 2, 1919
395.3 (the tradition on the spot. *)

But though Bockhampton has had all these interesting features in the past it has never till now had a War Memorial – never had a Club-room for social intercourse and reading. That had to wait till your kind-hearted friend and President Mr Hanbury, and no less kind-hearted Mrs Hanbury, came along, and in consultation with your valued friend Mr Cowley, set it going; and here the thing is.

DECEMBER 26, 1919
395.4 (reading-room to be open.' *)

December 26.1919.

Dear Professor Phelps:
I am much honoured by the request of the Governing Body of Yale University and yourself that I should deliver the first of the lectures instituted as a memorial to Francis Bergen. It is, however,

quite out of my power to entertain the notion of such an undertaking; and this for more than one reason. I have never practised lecturing, or had any inclination to do so, and the time of life is now come to me at which, even if I had practised it, I should be compelled to leave off for physical reasons. All the same I thank the University for sending the suggestion to me, and including my wife in the welcome that is offered."

DECEMBER 30, 1919

395.5 (* /To a correspondent, on December 30, Hardy writes:/)

To Mrs Ambrose Dudley.
                        December 30.1919

DECEMBER, 1919

396.1 (to give him the opportunity.' *)

To an unnamed young poet –
                        (about December 1919.)
"The only practical advice I can give, and I give that with great diffidence, is to begin with *imitative* poetry, adopting the manner and views of any recent poet – say Wordsworth or Tennyson – You will thus attract the praises of the critical papers, and escape the satire and censure which they are sure to bestow on anything that strikes them as unfamiliar. Having won them by good imitations you can introduce your originalities by degrees. For if you want to sell it is fatal to begin/with any original vein you may be blest with – |to hear| *the hearing of* "some new thing", which so fascinated the Athenians, being |a red rag| to the English reviewer *as a red rag to a bull.*

"Be also very careful about the mechanical part of your verse – rhythms, rhymes, &c. They do not know that dissonances, and other irregularities can be produced advisedly, as art, and worked as to give more charm than strict conformities, to the mind and ear of those trained and steeped in poetry; but they assume that a poet who commits one of these irregularities does so because of his ignorance, and the inferiority of his ear to that of the critic himself. *Ars est celare artem* they have never heard of or forget it.[802]

---

[802] Cf. the earlier omitted passage, dated Spring 1899; corresponding to *Life*, 300.4. Also cf. Hardy's earlier thoughts on the aphorism *ars est celare artem* in 1875; *Life*, 105.

JANUARY 24, 1920

397.1 (in a pool of water under an oak.' *)

> To the Secretary of the Navy League.
>
> Jan. 24. 1920.
>
> "I am sorry to say that I do not belong to a Naval family, though I have many friends both in the English and American navies. All that I can state with certainty is that both Admiral Sir Thomas Hardy's family and my own have been Dorset for centuries, dwelling within a few miles of each other, and that they are reputed to come from the same ancestry, as is antecedently probable for several reasons. But they branched apart long before the Admiral's time.
>
> "He had no direct descendant in the male line, having left two daughters only."

FEBRUARY 3, 1920

397.3 (After lunching with * /friends/)

> the Giffords at Arlington House – *Hardy's cousins by his first marriage —*

FEBRUARY 3, 1920

398.4 (the whole day having been of a most romantic kind. *)

> *, and the performance of "The Dynasts" by the O.U.D.S. everything that could be desired. It was said that the bookings applied for would have filled the theatre for three weeks, had it been available.*

MARCH 7, 1920

404.1 (* '/. . ./ As to your question)

> "It is very curious that yesterday at lunch I said apropos of nothing: 'I never hear or see anything of John Slater nowadays.' And lo, here is a letter from you!

MARCH 7, 1920

404.1 (So, shall I leave the decision to your judgment? * ')

> But if you think there would be any doubt in the mind of any member of the Council, please don't propose it.
>
> "Your letter recalls those times we had in Bedford Street together. Are there any such amiable architects now as Roger Smith was? Not many. Also, what became of Conder? – the one who had such a keen sense of humour."
>
> (Conder, strangely enough, died in Japan that very year.)

JUNE 2, 1920
405.1 (The occasion was a pleasant one, and the * lunch lively.)

*affection shown by his visitors gave Hardy |unqualified pleasure| much
gratification*

JUNE 2, 1920
406.2 (it behoves young poets and other writers to endeavour to stave off
such a catastrophe.' *)

The aforesaid somewhat unexpected celebration of his eigh-
tieth birthday seems to have set Hardy's mind running on his
ancestry and connections: for later in June he made inquiries as to
the descendants of the Revd. C. Holder his deceased brother-in-
law, formerly rector of St. Juliot, and about the same time he
inquired of a Cornish friend as to the welfare of the newspaper
"The West Briton", which had been founded by his great-great
uncle on the maternal side in M..., and the reply was: "How
interesting, your family connection with the birth of 'The West
Briton' – which still lives. It has circulated mainly in the mining
districts, and is now the property of a Company at Truro, where it
is published."

JULY 28, 1920
406.5 (a South-western University at Exeter. *)

July 28. Hardy sent the poem on Keats at Hampstead as a
contribution to the book proposed to be published on the Centenary of Keats's death, saying "I wish I could have let you have
something more worthy of the occasion and the man; but worthy
writing does not come at call at my age."

AUGUST, 1920
407.1 (which will be often and often.' *)

> From Mr A---- M---- of Letchworth.
> August 1920.

Dear Sir:
I am driven to wonder why the devil you don't answer letters
that are written to you!
> Very Truly,
> A---- M----"

NOVEMBER 13, 1920

407.6 (' *A *More interested* than I expected *to be*. The dancing was just as *it used to be* at Higher Bockhampton in my childhood *B)

A   A much better play

B   and Gertrude Bugler as Eustacia looked the part *to a T*, enacting *the hand-kissing scene with Charley* also some phases excellently."

The dramatic company were entertained at Max Gate later in the month.[803]

DECEMBER 8, 1920

407.7 (/Hardy/ writes: *)

"December 8: 1920.

To Howard Ruff Esq.

"I have to acknowledge the receipt of your letter of the 4th. informing me of the gratifying suggestion of your Committee that I should become an Honorary Vice-President of your now well-known and popular Society.

"I am sorry to answer that I have been compelled of late, for reasons I need not trouble you with, to forgo such distinctions ...
. . . . . All the same

DECEMBER 13, 1920

408.3 (which was probably Hardy's reason for * antagonism in his letter)

writing to him, who would be aware there was no personal

DECEMBER 19, 1920

410.1 (The * *writer* comments: "Truly this pessimism is insupportable.)

|reviewer| *pennyaliner who writes it*[804]

DECEMBER 19, 1920

410.3 (Knowledge might be terrible.' *)

It may be added that, as has been stated before, the above mentioned view that the Cause of things, so far from being malignant, was indifferent and unconscious had long been Hardy's. Mr Noyes conception that a Cause *which, as Hardy somewhere says, "is*

---

[803] The passage referring to Gertrude Bugler has apparently been deleted by Florence Hardy's hand; Hardy's elaboration of his account of her performance bears witness to his regard for her. For an account of his friendship with Miss Bugler, and Florence's animosity towards her, see n. 155.

[804] Hardy quotes a hostile review which 'marvels that Hardy is not in a madhouse' as a result of his pessimism.

but the Invariable Antecedent," in philosophy, could not be less than the thing caused required no refutation, *the opposite* being evidenced everywhere.

DECEMBER, 1920

410.6 (This apparent possibility to him, and to so many, * is very likely owing to his running his head against a *Single* ⟨Hardy's italics⟩ Cause)

has been long ago proved non-existent by philosophers,

411.3 ('At the Entering of the New Year' appeared in the *Athenaeum*. *)

⟨Variant readings in the two typescripts:⟩
[*The rest is in small Notebooks of Memoranda beginning 1921*]
[*Refer to Note Book of Memoranda beginning 1921, for continuation.*]

JANUARY, 1921

412.2 (Early in January he was searching through registers of Stinsford for records of a family named Knight, connected with his own. *)[805]

He found several interesting entries that repaid his search.

MAY 27, 1921

412.4 (the last of "the seven brethren".' *)

May 27. Was going to London this week but did not, on account of the death of Barrie's adopted son.[806]

JUNE 2, 1921

413.1 (in submitting to it. * . . . In all that)

When Mr. Justice Shallow sought to instruct Sir John Falstaff in the choice of soldiers, the knight said: "Care I for the limb, the thewes, the stature, bulk and big assemblage of a man? Give me the spirit, Master Shallow." So would you have answered him, for

JUNE 2, 1921

413.4 ('We thank you, Sir, for all that you have written * . . .)

, especially for The Return of the Native, The Mayor of Casterbridge, Tess of the d'Urbervilles, Jude the Obscure, Far from the Madding Crowd, Under the Greenwood Tree and the Wessex Poems,

---

[805] From the beginning of ch. XXXVII the typescript pages are no longer consecutively numbered to follow the series concluding at the end of the previous chapter; even the separate typings of each of the two last chapters are paginated differently.
[806] Cf. n. 140.

JUNE 2, 1921
413.5 (also our grateful homage. * ')

We are, dear Mr. Hardy,
Your faithful comrades.

JUNE 16, 1921
414.1 (The others mentioned in this poem were known to him by name and repute. *)

He had discovered the story of Eve Greensleeves, of the poem, during his researches in the copy of Stinsford Register in January of this year. She was Eve Trevelyan.[807]

JANUARY, 1922
415.5 (When the new Prayer Book appeared, however, his hopes were doomed to disappointment, and he found that the revision had not been in a rationalistic direction *)

but in a retrograde direction

JANUARY, 1922
415.5 (and from that time he lost all expectation of seeing the Church representative of modern thinking minds. *)

The point is dwelt upon at some length in the preface, called an "apology", to "Late Lyrics and Earlier".

AUGUST 11, 1922
417.4 (he writes in his notebook: ' * Motored)

In Newman Flower's car with him and his wife and boy and F. to Sturminster Newton, and back by Bishop's Caundell, Glanville's Woolton, Middlemarsh, and Dogberry Gate, where we lunched.

JUNE 3, 1923
419.8 (Mr. and Mrs. Max Beerbohm. * 'June 10.)

On June 3rd the following tributes from Mr Edmund Gosse and Mr Alfred Noyes appeared in the "The Sunday Times".

TO THOMAS HARDY
ON HIS EIGHTY-THIRD BIRTHDAY.

---

[807] Cf. n. 130.

According to the laws of the Brahminical religion, the man who reaches his 84th year becomes, by that occurrence, a Saint.

Yesterday was the birthday of St Thomas of Max Gate. On behalf of the readers of the "Sunday Times" I greet with benediction the poet who is, without dispute, the head of the literary profession in England, as (I believe) the first of living men of letters in the world.

On my own behalf I greet with emotion the friend of five and forty years. Happy is the country which can boast of such a presence in this mellow length of years. "Venerable" he is: but I prefer to call him "veteran", our commander-in-chief in the war against ignorance and dullness.

May he be with us through future birthdays as he is now, with powers unimpaired and sympathies unblunted.

Edmund Gosse.[808]

A breath of hope, for those who have known despair;
    Of victory, for those who have drunk defeat;
Of harvest, when the wounded fields lie bare,
    Or but a mist of green foreruns the wheat;

A breath of love, when all we loved lies dead;
    Of beauty, too remote for tongue to tell;
Of joy, when sorrow veiled and bowed the head;
    Of Heaven, for those that daily walked in Hell; –

His music breathes it, for his wrestling soul
    Through agonies of denial postulates
All that young eyes affirm. He proves his goal
    Divine, because he mourns the fast barred gates;
And by his grief for love and hope brought low;
    Proves that the Highest ne'er would have it so.

Alfred Noyes.

----

[808] J. M. Barrie confirmed Florence Hardy in her intention to omit this. He writes (10 Aug 1929): 'You are right I feel to omit the Gosse tribute of the 83rd birthday. It is a capital example of Gosse at his charming best, but this is not the book for it.'

JUNE 27, 1923
422.3 (* *The Hardys* motored back to Max Gate)

On the next morning, June 27th, the Hardys bade farewell to Oxford and to their friend Mr Elton, who had done so much to make their visit pleasant. They

JULY 20, 1923
422.5 (On July 20 the Prince of Wales paid a visit to Dorchester, *)

being part of an extended tour through the Duchy of Cornwall, which included parts of Dorset. The Prince was

JULY 20, 1923
422.5 (owing to the thoughtfulness of the Prince and his simple and friendly manner, * all passed off pleasantly.)

in essentials so like Hardy's own,

JULY 20, 1923
422.5 (all passed off pleasantly. *)

The Prince and Hardy passed through dense and cheering throngs, a triumphal progress all the way.

DECEMBER 30, 1923
424.1 (Mr. and Mrs. G. Bernard Shaw and Colonel T.E. Lawrence lunched with the Hardys and spent several hours with them. *)

to Hardy's great pleasure

DECEMBER 31, 1923
424.2 (*New Year's Eve.* * Did not sit up.)

To Weymouth to lunch with Mr and Mrs St John Ervine at the Royal Hotel.

JULY 1, 1924
425.7 (While having tea after the play they gathered round Hardy, who talked to them with * *a sincerity* and simplicity that few but he could have shown.)

an affection

AUGUST 6, 1924
426.4 (he received a visit from Siegfried Sassoon and Colonel T.E. Lawrence. *)

Hardy was devoted to this world-famous soldier, and their not infrequent meetings during the last few years of Hardy's life were a source of great interest to both.[809]

On the 9th August Mr Sassoon, Colonel T.E. Lawrence, and Mr Edmund Blunden were again at Max Gate, this time with Mr H.M. Tomlinson. All the members of the party were staying in the neighbourhood.

APRIL 22, 1925

48.1 (his nose between his paws. *)

Four days after, on April 22nd, Hardy attended the funeral of Mr. Watkins at Dorchester Cemetery where he had fifteen months before attended the burial of the ashes of Sir Frederick Treves in a grave adjoining.

AUGUST 12, 1925

428.4 (worse corruption of language was never perpetrated.' *)

On August 12. his friends Mr and Mrs Eden Phillpotts, came to see him, having motored all the way from Torquay in a downpour of rain.

DECEMBER 6, 1925

429.2 (The following description of this incident is taken from a letter written by one of the company to a correspondent in America who had particularly desired her impression of the visit: *)

> 31 Lancelot Place,
> Knightsbridge,
> London.

19 July 1926.

Dear Sir:

. . . We went down to Dorchester on the Sunday morning, putting up at the Hotel and returning on Monday morning so I had not the chance of seeing very much of Mr Hardy – but I did get a very firm impression of his dislike to publicity of any description and as I was in a sense his guest I am taking it that you do mean exactly what you say in your letter that your request for impressions is in no way intended for publication.[810]

---

[809] Cf. n. 336.

[810] A separate typed copy of the quoted letter also includes the date, the sender's address and identity, and the name of the 'correspondent in America' (R. L. Purdy), and the opening paragraph to here. Its content makes this paragraph inappropriate for publication and it is therefore omitted from the draft: all the other passages quoted from the letter do appear there and are crossed through in the typescript.

"The chief impression I got from the atmosphere of Mr Hardy's comfortable secluded house was that of a simple, kindly and most hospitable domesticity. We might have been any cheerful band of amateurs playing on any Sunday evening for the amusement of any kindly parent. At least that is how I felt. Exactly as I felt when as a child I dressed up and took part in charades.

DECEMBER 6, 1925
429.4 (Mr. Hardy made a point of chatting with everyone. *)

He was very interested in the fact that my ancestors were actually inhabitants of the "Tess" country a certain Mrs J--- C---[811] living only a few miles from the home of the d'Urbervilles. After tea we were conducted to a bedroom and dressed by the light of candles.

DECEMBER 6, 1925
429.6 ('Mr. and Mrs. Hardy, * , a friend of the Hardys,)

a press representative (more or less) smuggled in as a "critic"

DECEMBER 6, 1925
429.8 (It was beautiful. * Mr. Hardy insisted on talking to us until the last minute.)

We all felt it must be a tiring and exciting evening for Mr Hardy and arrangements had been made for us to leave by car as soon as the play was over. We changed and packed as quickly as possible but

DECEMBER 6, 1925
430.2 ('The gossip of the * country has it that his house was designed and the garden laid out with the idea of being entirely excluded from the gaze of the curious.)

village

DECEMBER 6, 1925
430.2 (personally I should say he had succeeded. * ')

I feel that this is a most inadequate impression of a meeting with such a writer, but I think one often finds it the case – when one is confronted with a great artist. In the one direction that of his

---

[811] Identified as Jean Carter in the copy mentioned in n. 810.

intense and immense imagination the outsider can only reach him through his work – in other respects he is disconcertingly normal.
I am, Yours very sincerely, ---- ------[812]

DECEMBER 20, 1925
430.4 (Siegfried Sassoon, a nephew of Sir Hamo's, happened to be paying Hardy a visit at the time * .)

, with his friend Glen Byam Shaw

AUTUMN, 1926
432.9 ((*Ombre*, ii.158, 159.) *)

In the early autumn he received from Weymouth Massachussetts the following reply to his message:

Honorable Sir:
It is with sincere gratitude that the Rotary Club of Weymouth Massachussetts accepts your very appropriate gift.
The splendid expressions of friendship coming from Weymouth England to the daughter town in America on this occasion of the celebration of our Sesquicentennial of Independence are but an indication of the ties of a common origin, language, race and idealism. Moreover we believe that this exchange of felicitations is a prophesy ⟨*sic*⟩ of the time when the world shall dwell in peace under the leadership of the great English speaking peoples.
The contributions to international good-will flowing from your pen are along the lines of the ideals of "Rotary International" that teaches world wide service."
. . . .
This message was brought to Max Gate by the Mayor of Weymouth Dorset, and a deputation with whom Hardy spent a friendly hour.

SEPTEMBER 20, 1926
433.2 (Performance of *Mayor of Casterbridge* at Weymouth by London Company, a "flying matinée". *A Beautiful afternoon, scene outside the theatre finer than within. *B ')

---

[812] The separately typed copy identifies the writer as Margaret Carter (name crossed through), and in the lower left corner identifies the recipient as 'Richard L. Purday Esq.' ⟨*sic*⟩.

A Motored down with F. Mr Ridgeway & Drinkwater, who called
   before we started.
B Snapshotters for newspaper illustration very pestering.

SEPTEMBER, 1926
433.3 (Writing to a friend about a proposed dramatization of *Jude the Obscure*, he observes: *)

9th. September 1926.

Dear Mr Ervine:
|I think the best plan would be to see what happens to the
Mayor of Casterbridge, now just produced, before you spend any
time on Jude the Obscure, for though the latter is, as I have said,
much the more modern and up-to-date novel, its success as a play
might be influenced by the fate of the other. I will send you the
authorization you ask for as soon as I feel it will be worth your
while to set about the job. |
   I am happy to send you the authorization you ask for — that is, that you
have the sole right to dramatize "Jude" for twelve months from the
beginning of November next. [813]

SEPTEMBER, 1926
433.5 (I thought the one I called (I think) "4th Scheme" most feasible. *)

If you wanted to begin further back than the First Act of this, you
could split the act up into 2 or 3 scenes. [814]

NOVEMBER, 1926
434.1 (Hardy was grieved that he had not seen the actual departure, and
said that he had particularly wished to see Lawrence go. *)

During Lawrence's absence Hardy often said that he thought
Lawrence would return before the time usually allotted to troops
sent to India. This indeed actually happened, but not in time for
another meeting.

---

[813] There is an additional typed copy of the letter (to St. John Ervine) in the
envelope and on Max Gate notepaper. The first paragraph, drafted twice, is omitted
from the chapter typescript. This copy was clearly the original copy of the letter
before Hardy decided to amend it and grant Ervine the authorization sought. The
first version of the para. is crossed through in pencil and the revised version is in
Hardy's hand and written in pencil.
[814] This sentence appears only in the letter described in n. 813 and not in the
chapter typescript.

DECEMBER 29, 1926
436.1 (perhaps hundreds of years. * ')

We have had a sad aftering to our Christmas. Our devoted (and masterful) dog Wessex died on the 27th, and last night had his bed outside the house under the trees for the first time in 13 years. We miss him greatly, but he was in such misery with swelling and paralysis that it was a relief when a kind breath of chloroform administered in his sleep by 2 good-natured Doctors (not vets) made his sleep an endless one – A dog of such strong character required human doctors![815]

Best wishes for the coming year that the scheme, or no scheme, of the universe will permit from both and with many thanks believe me

Very sincerely yours
Thomas Hardy.

P.S. Sight bad: accounting for this scrawl of a letter. T.H.

JULY 6, 1927
437.5 (after their performance on the lawn of *Iphigenia in Aulis* he talked with them freely, appreciating their boyish ardour and their modesty. *)

The leader, Mr Philip Mason, spent the night at Max Gate, and in the morning he was joined by one or two of the other players and after another talk with Hardy in the garden they said 'goodbye' and went off to give 'Iphigenia' at Corfe Castle. One of these, writing seven months later, said that he would never forget the sight of their host waving vigorously and boyishly from the gate as they departed.

The three visits of the Balliol Players to Max Gate were pleasant episodes in Hardy's quiet life.

AUGUST 8, 1927
439.6 ('I am not at all a * critic,)

good

AUGUST 8, 1927
439.6 (the tragedy that always underlies Comedy if you only scratch it deeply enough. * ')

---

[815] Cf. n. 460.

I was going to tell you some passages I particularly liked in your book, but must leave off, and with renewed thanks I am

Sincerely yours,
(signed) Thomas Hardy.

AUGUST, 1927
440.1 (But now a curious sadness brooded over them * ;)

like a cloud

AUGUST, 1927
440.2 (In Bath Hardy walked about and looked long and silently at various places that seemed to have an interest for him. *)

No doubt they brought back memories of a much earlier visit when he stayed there at the same time as | Miss Gifford, whom he afterwards married | *his first wife, before their marriage.*

SEPTEMBER 6, 1927
440.5 (better, in fact, than they had ever seen him. *)

During the visit another friend of the Hardys, Miss Winifred Ashton (Clemence Dane)[816] called, having motored from Axminster in the pouring rain.

OCTOBER 30, 1927
442.2 ('October 30. * At lunch T.H. talked)

|Monday.| J. Middleton Murry to lunch.

OCTOBER 31, 1927
442.3 (Henry Williamson, the author of *Tarka the Otter*, called. * ')

, and afterwards Lady Ilchester brought Captain Cazalet to tea. Speaking of Kipling, (Captain Cazalet being a friend of Kipling's) T.H. said that Kipling had given to party what was meant for mankind. Captain Cazalet did not know this quotation from Dryden and asked T.H. to repeat it. He seemed impressed.

NOVEMBER 4, 1927
442.8 (Stinsford * /was a favourite haunt/until the last few months)

he visited regularly

---

[816] Novelist and playwright.

NOVEMBER 4, 1927
443.2 (He reminded me of what he said yesterday.' *)

A beautiful autumnal day but rather too warm for the time of year.

NOVEMBER 27, 1927
444.2 ('T.H. has been writing almost all the day, revising poems. When he came down to tea he brought one to show me, about a desolate spring morning, and a shepherd counting his sheep and not noticing the weather. * ')

A fine poem but it had such a gloom. However I did not care to tell him that.
Since writing the above I have been up to T.H.'s study and read the poem again and told him how much I liked it. The title is "An Unkindly May. 1877."[817]

NOVEMBER 29, 1927
444.5 (the memory had always haunted him. *)

On November 29 he was told of the serious illness of a friend[818] and of sad circumstances connected with that illness. The look of tender compassion in his eyes as he listened and the effort he immediately made to help the sufferer was very noticeable.

DECEMBER 26, 1927
445.3 (He remarked that there was not a * grain of evidence that the gospel story was true in any detail.)

single

DECEMBER, 1927
445.6 (But the weakness increased daily * .)

, and there was slight bladder trouble, from which Hardy had suffered more or less ever since his serious illness in 1880

---

[817] The date 1877 was omitted when the poem was published. It is not clear why Hardy associated the poem with that year, though he records some country observations made in May 1877 in *Life*, 113–14.
[818] The second wife of Middleton Murry. Florence Hardy notes in her diary: 'Nov. 29th Drove to Abbotsbury to see poor Mrs Middleton Murry, dying of consumption. She said pathetically that Dr Smerdon was very pleased with her and thought she was much better. There was death in her face. She looked so pretty. T. H. was much touched by my account of the visit. The little girl, my god-daughter, is a darling.'

JANUARY 11, 1928
446.2 (had confident hopes of his recovery, * /and/an atmosphere of joy
prevailed in the sick-room.)

so much so that

JANUARY 11, 1928
446.4 (The doctor was summoned and * /came quickly, joining Mrs. Hardy
at the bedside./)

was swiftly at his bedside and his wife was with him.

JANUARY 11, 1928
446.4 (Hardy remained unconscious until a few minutes before the end * .
Shortly after nine he died.)

,when a few broken sentences, one of them heartrending in its
poignancy, showed that his mind had reverted to a sorrow of the
past.

JANUARY 12, 1928
446.6 (The dawn of the following day * /rose in almost unparalleled splen-
dour/.)

, beheld from the garden of Max Gate, was awe-inspiring

JANUARY 12, 1928
446.6 (Flaming and magnificent the sky stretched its banners over the dark
pines that * /stood/sentinel around.)

the hand of the master had placed to stand

Ancillary Documents

⟨This undated memorandum and the two documents following are discussed in the introduction to the *Life* extracts. The memorandum is written in Hardy's hand to the end of p. 1. The remainder is a typescript carbon copy but the amendments and additions are all in Hardy's hand.⟩

⟨p.1⟩   Private Memorandum

Information for Mrs Hardy in the preparation of a biography.
As there seems to be no doubt that so-called biographies of myself will be published which are unauthorized & erroneous, one having already appeared,[819] it becomes necessary that an authentic volume should at any rate be contemplated by her, & materials gathered by her while there is time.

The facts to which she has access will form a chronicle more or less complete of my life. They are not enjoined to be included every one

⟨p.2⟩ in the volume, if any should seem to be indiscreet, belittling, monotonous, trivial, provocative, or in other ways unadvisable; neither are they enjoined to be exclusive of other details that may be deemed necessary. This statement does not apply to the extract from Mrs Emma Hardy's "Recollections", which being past revision by the writer are to be printed intact.

The facts here given can be supplemented by the insertion of some more of |Mr. Hardy's| *my* letters of an interpretative kind at their several dates, if wished; or not, if otherwise, (as they might be printed separately, though this |was| *is* not desired by |him| *me*). Also by references to newspapers, reviews, and other publications if thought expedient.

⟨p.3⟩   It must, however, be remembered, in consulting newspaper "Interviews" with, and other personal sketches, |of him,| or reports

---

[819] This suggests F. A. Hedgcock's *Thomas Hardy, Penseur et Ariste* (Paris, 1911): Hardy's sharp reaction to the book is shown in terse annotations in his own copy (e.g. 'This is not literary criticism, but impertinent personality & untrue'); and in his refusal to allow an English translation.

of what |he| I may have said, that they were not revised by |him| myself, and that some were surreptitiously obtained or imagined; they must therefore be accepted with considerable reserve. Also that, in respect of other letters than |his| my, permission to print such (if any are required) must be obtained from such writers' representatives, except in the case of extracts that are too brief to be of consequence.

The whole book before printing should be put into correct literary form, by an experienced writer and scholar. Should Mrs Hardy wish that her name alone should stand on the title page, such a one

⟨p.4⟩ might possibly be found for her who would do what was required if paid a reasonable fee.

Memorandum:-

Portraits etc. recommended for the book:-

Plan of Gallery in Stinsford Church (annexed to MS.)
T.H.'s mother and father.
Wife Emma – from the photograph now hanging in the study. (in a low dress when a young woman) – which was enlarged by Griffin from the miniature in green case containing hair.
Wife Florence – From Mr Lea's photograph, enlarged: side face, hanging in drawing room; or from coloured photo. by Swaine, showing her seated writing.

———————

⟨p.5⟩

Optional.
Any others of the above, or other relatives.
Also any of T.H. himself. (Perhaps the one at 21 would be interesting.)

Illustrations of houses &c, could be inserted if desirable. But this is optional. (There is a selection of such among the photographs. &c.)

*   *   *

⟨The following notes are written in pencil in Hardy's hand on the back of three sheets pasted together to form a single sheet measuring 14½″ × 6″. The sheets are subscription forms for the Royal Society of Arts and an Austin Motor Co. invitation to the Olympia Show, 22–30 Oct 1926. Hardy was clearly still concerned with the details of his disguised autobiography towards the end of 1926 or in 1927. "Materials" was Hardy's term for the work.⟩

Insert in Materials.   (pages unknown – find them)

The page where it is mentioned that H. occasionally had to alter his novels in their serial form to suit public taste: state that in a footnote to the "R. of the N.", & in another to the "Distracted P." he shows how he would have ended those stories.

At one time he thought of re-writing some of his early hurried & immature novels, nobody knowing their faults better than he did. But being convinced that no really live & creative minds ever condescended to such tinkering, it being the mark rather of | the | uninventive & plodding temperaments, he left the faulty novels alone, taking the track of showing his enlarged perceptions by creating entirely new works.

? page. Wherever it is said that H. decides to invent his own philosophy, adapting nobody's, add "like Descartes." in all copies.

More about Laurence Hope & her poetry (she gave me 2 vols) That |most| impassioned & beautiful woman.[820]

Insert in the page about Lady Wimborne's party. Sat with her [Dss of Marlbh.] in a quiet corner away from the rest of the guests [when she told about Randolph] Such an unlikely friendship: & yet there was a friendship.[821]

---

[820] Laurence Hope was the pseudonym of Adela Nicolson (1865–1904), authoress of luxuriant verses, two volumes of which (*The Garden of Kama* and *Stars of the Desert*) she presented to Hardy. She committed suicide after the death of her husband and Hardy wrote a brief notice about her (*The Athenaeum* (29 Oct 1904), p. 591), saying that she 'was still in the early noon of her life, vigour, and beauty, and the tragic circumstances of her death seem but the impassioned closing notes of her impassioned effusions.' Cf. *Life*, 322, which remains the only mention of her.

[821] 'She is a nice warm-feeling woman, and expressed her grief at what had happened to her son, though her hostess had told her flatly it was his own doing. She deplores that young men like —— should stand in the fore-front of the Tory party, and her son should be nowhere' (Dec 1890; *Life*, 230). Randolph Churchill was the Duchess of Marlborough's son. This additional detail does not appear.

Insert where McTaggarts principle of a limited God is mentioned that it was also an idea of J.S. Mill's that the universe | was | might be governed by a Deity of limited powers.[822]

---

p. |Insert at interview with Lady Yarborough [Marcia]. "a beautiful 369 woman, though not so beautiful as her sister Lady Powis" (That she was the lady of the "pretty pink frock" may now be mentioned, stating that the deceased was not her husband, only her uncle). [Also insert that Mrs H. was the heroine of the accordion *dress*?][823] |

Insert at mention of the poem on the Wessex dialect,[824] & our relationship to Germans: "Fussy Jingoes, who were hoping for knighthoods, |denied| attacked H.'s *for his* assumption|s| . & asserted that we had no sort of blood relationship with Germany: But the Germans themselves, with far more commonsense, translated the poem, & |remarked| approved of it, & remarked that when relations *did* f|e|all out they fought more bitterly than any."

*   *   *

(The following note is written in pencil in Hardy's hand on the back of the front cover of an envelope addressed to him and date-stamped "Philadelphia, Pa./Nov.14/2– A.M./ – /1927." Though apparently designed for inclusion in the disguised autobiography this reflection does not appear, probably because the short illness which was to prove fatal began on 11 Dec. This wry note, almost an epitaph to Hardy's literary career, must have been one of the very last things he wrote (see introduction to the *Life* extracts).)

H's altruism
It must not be forgotten that H's own life & experiences had been smoother & happier than many – perhaps than the majority. It was

---

[822] 'This idea of a limited God of goodness, often dwelt on by Hardy, was expounded ably and at length in MacTaggart's *Some Dogmas of Religion* several years later' (5 Feb 1898; *Life*, 297). Mill's analogous idea is not added.

[823] Cf. *Life*, 264. The second of these three amendments is inserted; the others are omitted, though Hardy had already remarked below that Lady Powis (disguised as 'Lady P—') 'was the most beautiful woman there'. The 'accordion' allusion occurs in stanza 3 of 'The Pink Frock' ('Puff-sleeved and accordion-pleated!'); but since it is a feature of the same dress, the meaning of Hardy's note is not clear. This note is textually interesting since here a typescript revision of 1926 can be directly attributed to Hardy's hand.

[824] 'The Pity of It' (*Complete Poems*, p. 542), written in 1915, argues that the English and German peoples are 'kin folk tongued' and instances various Germanic words surviving in ordinary Wessex dialect: 'Thu bist', 'Er war', 'Ich woll', 'Er sholl'. Some of the many protests that this wartime poem provoked are preserved in a scrapbook in the DCM. The poem is not, however, mentioned in the *Life*.

his habit, or *strange* power of putting himself in the place of those who endured sufferings from which he himself had been in the main free, or subject to but at brief times. This altruism was so constant with him as to cause a complaint among his readers that he did not say "all's well with the world" because all was well with him. It should really have caused commendation.

*   *   *

⟨The following extracts are taken from a stiff-backed exercise book used by Florence Hardy as a personal diary for the period 6 Sep–26 Dec 1927. Florence used this to make notes for the writing of the last part of the *Life*; Hardy's own notes in 'Memoranda, II' conclude in the same month in which Florence's makeshift diary commences. Most of the entries went straight into the *Life*. I have taken from the diary only passages which add a few details of Hardy's last months to the account we already have in the *Life* and the omitted passages.⟩

<u>October 8th</u>. A strange visit from a little Chinese man – Yu Shan Kuo. He had written asking if he might call, but had been refused. Then he wrote again, a letter arriving on the morning of the 8th – a Saturday – saying that he would be at our door at 3 o'clock. He said that he <u>must</u> see T.H. as he had a tragic story to tell him. The little man arrived punctually. I saw him first and warned him that T.H. could not give any autographs. He was a melancholy little fellow, large round Chinese face, but the profile was in some strange way exceedingly beautiful.

T.H. came down & saw him. The China-man said he was haunted by the terribly tragic memories of his life that he carried about with him, and that he thought it would relieve his mind if he wrote them down in the form of an autobiography or a novel. He wanted T.H. to advise him as to which.

The story was that he had lost both his parents when young. His elder brother became head of the family, & he married. There was a sister who did not get on with the brother's wife (human nature is apparently the same in China as in England). The sister was betrothed to a man for whom she did not care, one who was a stranger to her. The sister was found to be in "the same condition as 'Tess'" – these were the words of the Chinaman. He, a boy of 13, was deputed to murder the infant when born: he sat upon it. Then, to save the honour of the family, the sister was invited to commit suicide. Her brothers gave her opium in wine, which she drank, & then died.

While relating this story the little Chinese student (he told us that he had studied at the Sorbonne) was overcome with emotion. I heard the tears in his voice first, & wondered at the emotional quality of a Chinese voice. Then he broke down & sobbed aloud.

T.H. said afterwards that he felt so touched when the Chinaman produced a clean pocket handkerchief, neatly folded, & proceeded to dry his eyes with it, without unfolding it. He really was a pathetic figure as he stood before T.H. bending slightly forward, reciting his story in an emotional, heart-breaking voice.

But was he a very clever actor? He said, as nearly as I can remember his words:

'When people ask me if I have a sister I say 'No, I have no sister.' If I told them that I had a sister they would ask, "Then where is she?" How can I tell them that I have murdered my sister?

Then he sobbed aloud. T.H. spoke to him very quietly and very kindly and I could see that he was touched.

The Chinaman said that when he read 'Tess' he realized that instead of condemning his sister he ought to have reverenced her.

But he spoke English so badly that it was difficult to follow exactly what he said. My faith in his truthfulness was a little shaken when he wanted T.H.'s autograph, & suggested that he should help him to write this tragic history. And I saw a volume of T.H.'s poems, newly bought, left in the hall with the visitor's hat & coat, obviously brought to be autographed.

It is difficult to believe in the bona-fides of anyone who comes and asks for an autograph. One's respect for the applicant vanishes immediately.

The visitor went away sad & very disappointed I thought.

.   .   .

October 24th. . . . He cannot bear untidiness out of doors, or indoors either for the matter of that. I wish that I were more tidy . . . .

He tells me that although he seems so very well he feels terribly weak at times. He appears to be working hard all day.

.   .   .

November 11th. . . . In the afternoon we took our melancholy little walk round "the triangle".[825]

November 27th. 1927.

Anniversary of the death of Emma Lavinia Hardy, T.H.'s first

---

[825] *Life*, 443, has 'one of our usual little walks'.

wife. Thursday was the anniversary of the death of Mary, his elder sister. For two or three days – & this morning – he has worn a very shabby little black felt hat that he must have had for twenty years – as a token of mourning. It is very pathetic – all the more so when one remembers what their married life was like.[826]

December. 26th. Boxing day.

T. has been ill in bed since Dec. 11th. – a chill, so he says, & neuritis or acute rheumatism in his shoulder. He seems very weak, but I think he will get better. . . .

T. has been talking about his will. He wishes to make some alteration – an annuity to Kate & Henry instead of capital paid down – which is, of course, much to be preferred. Also he says he will leave Sydney Cockerell £500 instead of the percentage on his royalties. However he may never make this alteration. I shall not attempt to influence him.

He said that young Mr Stephen Tennant reminded him, in his walk of Swinburne – that he had never seen anyone else walk like Swinburne.

I think, & Sir Henry Head agrees, that the visit of Mr Wells, the American publisher, on Dec. 10th – with Mrs Wells & Mr and Mrs H.M. Tomlinson was the cause of this illness. The strain was too great. Yesterday (Christmas day) T. said he felt he would never sit again in the drawing-room at a tea-party. He certainly will not if I can help it.

It was a quiet Christmas day. I sat by myself most of the time, & thought of many Christmas days especially one in 1910.[827]

---

[826] The details of Florence's original diary note on the 15th anniversary of Emma Hardy's death are more piquant than those in the published version – cf. *Life*, 443–4.

[827] Hardy did not make the planned alterations to his will. Sir Henry Head was an eminent neurologist and a personal friend (see n. 380). Hardy did not come downstairs again after Christmas Day and he died 16 days after his wife made this final note.

Index

Notes: References to Hardy's works are indexed under 'Hardy, Thomas'. In three areas I have deliberately limited index entries: the painters listed summarily in the 'Schools of Painting notebook' are omitted, the details of Hardy's researches in the 'Trumpet-Major notebook' are not usually listed, and I have exercised editorial discretion in severely limiting the number of names of dinner party and 'crush' guests who are listed extensively and sometimes repetitively in the omitted passages from the *Life*.